Anna

with

Jara Happy Birthday

from

Granpa & Grannie

February 99

FIREFLY•POCKET•GUIDES

ENCY
CLO
PEDIA

COMPOSITION
OF THE EARTH

PICKLE MILK
CAP FUNGUS

PERSONAL
COMPUTER

CHEMICAL
REACTION

TENOR
SAXOPHONE

INDIAN
TIGER

FIREFLY · POCKET · GUIDES

ENCYCLOPEDIA

Written by
JOHN FARNDON

TORNADO FIGHTER PLANE

VENUS FIGURINE

OSCAR AWARD

FIREFLY BOOKS

A DORLING KINDERSLEY BOOK

Project directors Bob Gordon, Helen Parker
Editor Neil Kelly
Designer Matthew Cook
DTP Designer Chris Clark

DK team Anna Kruger, Peter Bailey,
Alastair Dougall, Sarah Crouch, Cynthia Hole,
Caroline Potts, Ruth Cobb
US Editors Constance M. Robinson, Laaren Brown

First American Edition, 1997
2 4 6 8 10 9 7 5 3

First published in Canada in 1997
by Firefly Books Ltd.,
3680 Victoria Park Avenue,
Willowdale, Ontario, M2H 3K1

Copyright © 1997 Dorling Kindersley Ltd., London

Canadian Cataloguing in Publication Data

Farndon, John
 Encyclopedia

(Firefly pocket guides)
Includes index.
ISBN 1-55209-041-8

1. Encyclopedias and dictionaries. I. Title. II. Series.

AE5.F37 1997   031   C97-930037-1

Color reproduction by Colourscan, Singapore
Printed and bound in Italy by L.E.G.O.

CONTENTS

Manned
Maneuvering
Unit

Formation
of an
Iceberg

HUMAN
HEART

BACTERIUM

HOT-AIR
BALLOON AND
BASKET

CHEMICAL
SOLUTION

PATAGONIAN PUDU

ICE-HOCKEY
PLAYER

HOW TO USE THIS BOOK

These pages show you how to use the *DK Pockets Encyclopedia*. The book is divided into nine sections of photographs, cutaway artworks, fact boxes, and illustrated timelines. At the beginning of each section there is a picture page with a list of contents.

INTRODUCTION
This provides a clear overview of the subject. After reading this, you should have an idea what the pages are about.

CORNER CODING
The corners of the pages in each section are color-coded to remind you which section you are in.

■ SPACE

■ PLANET EARTH

■ THE LIVING WORLD

■ THE HUMAN BODY

■ SCIENCE AND TECHNOLOGY

□ TRANSPORTATION

■ THE WORLD

□ PEOPLE AND SOCIETY

HISTORY

HEADING
This describes the subject of the page. This page is about crustaceans.

LABELS
For extra clarity, some pictures have labels. They may give extra information, or identify a picture when it is not obvious from the text what it is.

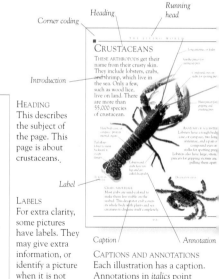

Corner coding

Heading

Running head

THE LIVING WORLD

CRUSTACEANS

THESE ARTHROPODS get their name from their crusty skin. They include lobsters, crabs, and shrimp, which live in the sea. Only a few, such as wood lice, live on land. There are more than 55,000 species of crustacean.

Introduction

Long antennae, or feeler

Senslike pincers for rooting out prey

Compound eyes on stalks for spotting prey

Have pincer for gripping and crushing prey

Hard body case or carapace, protects internal organs

Tail allows lobster to swim backward to evade danger

Lobsters and crabs have ten legs and are called decapods

*ANATOMY OF A LOBSTER
Lobsters have a tough body case, or carapace, two long antennae, and a pair of compound eyes on stalks for spotting prey. Lobsters also have large, strong pincers for gripping victims and pulling them apart*

Label

*CRAB CAMOUFLAGE
Most crabs are sand-colored to make them less visible on the seabed. This decorator crab covers its whole body with plants and sea creatures to disguise itself completely.*

Decorator crab

Caption

Annotation

CAPTIONS AND ANNOTATIONS
Each illustration has a caption. Annotations in *italics* point out features of an illustration and usually have leader lines.

1 0

RUNNING HEADS
These remind you
which section you are
in. The top of the
left-hand page gives
the section name.
The right-hand page
gives the subject.

*Country
fact page*

*World
atlas page*

WORLD SECTION
The book includes
a countries section
with full-color maps
of all the countries of
the world as well as
country fact pages
with essential
statistics.

VISUAL TIMELINES
Timelines on history,
space, music, art –
and many more
topics – show what
happened when.

*History
timeline has a
different band for
each continent*

Fact box

LIFE CYCLE
Crustaceans begin
life as eggs, which are
usually laid in water.
After the eggs hatch,
they pass through
several larval stages
before taking on
their adult form.
As adults, they grow
bigger by molting,
or shedding their
outer layer.

FACT BOXES
Many pages have a fact
box containing at-a-glance
information about the subject.
This fact box gives interesting
information on crustaceans.

TWO INDEXES
There are two indexes at the back
of the book – a gazetteer index, which
lists major towns, cities, rivers, mountain
ranges, and lakes that appear on the map
pages, and an extensive subject index.

SPACE

THE UNIVERSE

FROM THE EARTH under our
feet to the farthest stars,
everything that exists is
part of the universe.
The universe is so large
that it contains countless
billions of stars, and it is
still expanding rapidly.
However, most of it consists
of nothing but empty space.

LIGHT FROM A STATIONARY STAR

LIGHT FROM A MOVING STAR

LIGHT AND MOTION
If a star is moving away from
Earth, its light waves stretch out in
comparison with those from other
stars. The star's light becomes redder,
moving toward the red end of the
spectrum. This phenomenon is
known as red shift.

UNIVERSE FACT

• There are an
estimated 100
billion galaxies
spread throughout
the universe; each
of these contains
approximately
1 billion stars.

THE SCALE OF THE UNIVERSE
The universe is so vast that measurements
such as miles and kilometers eventually
become meaningless. A special unit called
a light-year is used to calculate the distances
between stars and galaxies. A light-year is
equivalent to 5.9 trillion miles (9.4 trillion
km), the distance that light travels in one
year. The known universe spans more than
20 billion light-years.

GROUND LEVEL

FLYING AT LOW
ALTITUDE
0.6 MILES
(1 KM)

ORBITING AT HIGH
ALTITUDE
620 MILES
(1,000 KM)

EARTH
FROM SPACE
62,000 MILES
(100,000 KM)

EARTH
AND MOON
620,000 MILES
(1 MILLION KM)

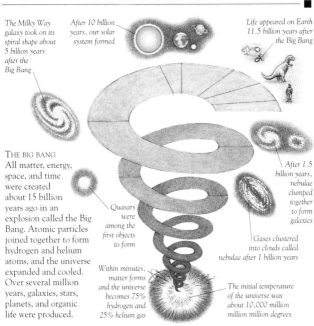

The Milky Way galaxy took on its spiral shape about 5 billion years after the Big Bang

After 10 billion years, our solar system formed

Life appeared on Earth 11.5 billion years after the Big Bang

THE BIG BANG
All matter, energy, space, and time were created about 15 billion years ago in an explosion called the Big Bang. Atomic particles joined together to form hydrogen and helium atoms, and the universe expanded and cooled. Over several million years, galaxies, stars, planets, and organic life were produced.

Quasars were among the first objects to form

After 1.5 billion years, nebulae clumped together to form galaxies

Gases clustered into clouds called nebulae after 1 billion years

Within minutes, matter forms and the universe becomes 75% hydrogen and 25% helium gas

The initial temperature of the universe was about 10,000 million million million degrees

| THE SOLAR SYSTEM 6.2 BILLION MILES (10 BILLION KM) | INTERSTELLAR SPACE 620 BILLION MILES (1,000 BILLION KM) | NEAREST STARS 100 LIGHT-YEARS | MILKY WAY GALAXY 100,000 LIGHT-YEARS | LOCAL GROUP OF GALAXIES 10 MILLION LIGHT-YEARS | EXTENT OF THE KNOWN UNIVERSE 20 BILLION LIGHT-YEARS |

GALAXIES

STARS ARE clustered together in enormous groups called galaxies, which were created when stars forming from spinning clouds of condensing gas were pulled toward each other by gravity. Some galaxies still rotate rapidly, maintaining a spiral shape, while others slow down and form ellipses (ovals) or less regular shapes. Large galaxies may have 1 trillion stars, but even the smallest contains a few hundred thousand.

DISTANT NEIGHBOR
The Andromeda galaxy is one of the nearest to the Milky Way, but its light still takes 2.2 million years to reach Earth. We see the galaxy not as it is now, but as it was 2.2 million years ago.

FOUR TYPES OF GALAXIES

ELLIPTICAL
The most common type of galaxy, ellipticals contain mostly old stars and vary in shape from ball- to egg-like.

SPIRAL
These disk-shaped galaxies are flat, with a central nucleus of old stars. New stars form from clouds of gas in the spiral arms.

BARRED SPIRAL
One-third of spiral galaxies have a nucleus that is elongated into a bar. The vast spiral arms extend from the end of the bar.

THE MILKY WAY

The Sun is just one of 500 billion stars in our own galaxy, the Milky Way. Ours is a spiral galaxy, with a nucleus of old stars surrounded by a halo of even older stars. All the young stars, such as the Sun, are located in the spiral arms. The galaxy is called the Milky Way because it looks like a bright, creamy band of stars stretching through space when viewed from Earth.

GALAXY FACTS

• The brightest, oldest, and most distant of galaxies are "quasi-stellar objects," or quasars, some of which are 14 billion light-years away.

• Some astronomers think that the Milky Way is a barred spiral galaxy.

MILKY WAY GALAXY:
EXTERNAL SIDE VIEW

Nucleus is the brightest region of the galaxy

Galactic halo contains the oldest stars

From the side the spiral arms look like a flattened disk

MILKY WAY GALAXY:
EXTERNAL OVERHEAD VIEW

Crux–Centaurus arm

Galactic nucleus

Sagittarius arm

Location of the solar system

Orion arm (Local arm)

IRREGULAR

The rarest galaxies are those that do not fit any known pattern. Some have a hint of a spiral or elliptical structure.

STARS

A STAR is an immense globe of fiery hydrogen gas powered by nuclear reactions at its core. Stars range in size from massive supergiants to small dwarf stars. The Sun is one of billions of stars scattered throughout the universe. It is a yellow star, a typical star of average size and temperature.

THE EVOLUTION OF A STAR

1 GAS CLOUD
A star begins life as material within a nebula, an enormous cloud of gas and dust. Parts of the cloud are pulled together under their own gravity, spinning balls of gas known as protostars.

2 STARBIRTH
The protostar shrinks, and its core becomes denser. Nuclear reactions begin, creating heat and light. As the star begins to shine, the leftover dust is blown away by stellar wind or forms planets around the star.

3 MAIN SEQUENCE
The major period of a star's lifespan is called its main sequence. During this period, the star shines steadily, radiating energy. The bigger and brighter the star, the quicker it burns hydrogen, which reduces its lifespan.

STAR FACTS

• The biggest stars collapse to form black holes, which are so dense and have such a powerful gravitational pull that even light cannot escape.

6 SUPERNOVA
Heat from the star's core leads to a massive explosion, called a supernova. The star is as bright as a billion suns as it blows apart. The core collapses in a single second.

5 RED SUPERGIANT
The star continues to swell, swallowing up its surrounding planets. Its core fuses carbon atoms into iron but lacks energy for further contraction.

INSIDE A STAR
A star shines because of the amount of light and heat produced by the nuclear reactions taking place within it. The fusion of hydrogen atoms, creating helium, produces so much energy that the core of a star reaches millions of degrees, making the surface glow.

Temperature and pressure increase toward core

Energy released at surface as light and heat

Nuclear reactions in core produce energy

4 GROWING OLD
When its supply of hydrogen is exhausted, the star's core contracts, fusing helium atoms to make carbon. The star's surface gases burn, and the outer layers swell and glow red. The star is now called a red giant.

THE NORTHERN SKY

PEOPLE LIVING IN the Northern Hemisphere see a completely different range of stars than do people in the Southern Hemisphere. The star pattern turns steadily through the sky as Earth rotates, so the stars visible on any given night depend on the latitude, time of year, and time of night.

Arcturus

CONSTELLATIONS
Stars viewed from Earth seem to form patterns in the sky. These patterns are known as constellations. Ancient astronomers divided Earth's skies into 88 different constellations, each of which, such as Orion, is supposed to represent a mythological person, creature, or object.

ORION

PROJECTED SPHERE
This sky map is a projection of the northern half of the celestial sphere onto a flat surface. Earth's North Pole is situated directly below the center of the map. The stars near the center of the sky map are called circumpolar and can be seen throughout the year. The North Star, also known as Polaris, appears to remain directly above the North Pole.

The Big Dipper

North celestial pole
(North Pole projected out into space)

Celestial equator

The edge of the map marks the celestial equator – stars here can be seen by Southern Hemisphere observers

Polaris

The stars around the edge come into view month by month during the year.

Betelgeuse

2 1

THE SOUTHERN SKY

THE SOUTHERN HEMISPHERE presents a very different picture than the northern one, due to the rotation of Earth and the galaxies. The range of stars that people can see is dependent on factors such as climatic conditions, the latitude, the time of year, and the time of night.

THE CELESTIAL SPHERE

The stars viewed from Earth seem to be set on the inside of a giant sphere in the sky, called the celestial sphere. As Earth rotates on its axis and orbits around the Sun, different sections of the sphere are revealed. The motion of the planets can be plotted against the sphere.

PROJECTED SPHERE

This sky map is a projection of the southern half of the celestial sphere onto a flat surface. Earth's South Pole is situated directly below the center of the map. Alpha Centauri, one of the nearest stars to the Sun, is a Southern Hemisphere star. The celestial equator is a projection of Earth's equator out into space.

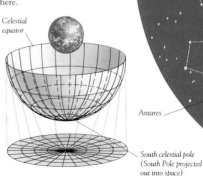

Alpha Centauri

Celestial equator

Antares

South celestial pole (South Pole projected out into space)

The edge of the map marks the celestial equator – stars here can also be see by Northern Hemisphere observers

Sirius

Canopus

The stars near the edge become visible month by month through the year.

2 3

THE SUN AND SOLAR SYSTEM

OUR SOLAR SYSTEM consists of the Sun and the many objects that orbit around it – nine planets, over 60 moons, and countless asteroids and comets. The system occupies a disk-shaped volume of space more than 745 billion miles (1 billion km) across. The Sun contains more than 99 percent of the system's mass.

PLUTO

Pluto has the most eccentric orbit

NEPTUNE   URANUS   SATURN

JUPITER

The inner system (Mercury, Venus, Earth, Mars) is separated from the rest by the asteroid belt

MARS

VENUS   MERCURY

EARTH

Enlargement of the inner solar system

SPINNING IN SPACE
The whole solar system moves through space. Within the system, individual planets orbit around the rotating Sun. The planets follow elliptical paths, all moving in the same direction but at different speeds. The time taken to complete one orbit varies greatly, depending on the planet's distance from the Sun. In addition, each planet also spins on its axis.

STRUCTURE OF THE SUN
The Sun is a vast, fiery ball of spinning hydrogen and helium gases. Heat produced by nuclear reactions at the Sun's core erupts from its surface as millions of upsurges of gas, called granules. Sunspots are dark surface patches of cooler gas caused by disturbances in the Sun's magnetic field.

Convective zone

Supergranule – a convection cell

Radiative zone

Chromosphere

Photosphere

Corona

Sunspot

THE SUN: INTERNAL AND EXTERNAL FEATURES

Core temperature 27 million°F (15 million°C)

Photosphere temperature about 9,900°F (5,500°C)

Orbits are elliptical (oval) rather than circular

The time taken for a planet to make one orbit of the Sun is called the orbital period

SOLAR PROMINENCES
Enormous jets of hot hydrogen gas shoot out from the Sun's surface at intervals, and can stretch for many thousands of miles. The largest jets, called solar prominences, may last for several months. Some prominences are held in loops by the Sun's magnetic field.

THE INNER PLANETS

THE FOUR PLANETS closest to the Sun – Mercury, Venus, Earth, and Mars – are known as the inner planets. Each planet has a core of hot iron and a rocky crust, but surface conditions vary greatly.

Iron core contains 80% of the planet's mass

Silicate rock mantle

NO MOONS

MERCURY DATA

- Distance from Sun: 36 million miles (57.9 million km)

- Time taken to orbit Sun: 88 Earth days

- Diameter at equator: 3,031 miles (4,878 km)

MERCURY
A small rock world with a large, dense core, Mercury is the planet closest to the Sun. It is marked with craters, has no real atmosphere, and experiences extreme variations in surface temperature.

Daytime temperature about 806°F (430°C)

Thin rocky crust

Night temperature about –292°F (–180°C)

Semisolid iron-nickel core

Rocky mantle

VENUS
The planet Venus is about the same size as Earth. Its surface is very different, however, with intense heat, crushing pressure, and unbreathable acid air. Overhead are thick clouds of sulfuric acid droplets.

Silicate crust

NO MOONS

VENUS DATA

- Distance from Sun: 67.2 million miles (108.2 million km)

- Time taken to orbit Sun: 224.7 Earth days

- Diameter at equator: 7,520 miles (12,102 km)

IMPACT CRATER FORMATION ON ROCK PLANETS

A meteorite impact blasts out a circular crater, ejecting debris.

Rock compressed by the impact forms a conical central peak.

Crater gradually filled as debris slips from walls and peak.

EARTH DATA

- Distance from Sun: 93 million miles (149.6 million km)
- Time taken to orbit Sun: 365 Earth days
- Diameter at equator: 7,926 miles (12,756 km)

EARTH

1 MOON

The third planet from the Sun, Earth, is the only planet in the solar system with liquid water and an oxygen-rich atmosphere. These two factors make it the only known planet capable of supporting life.

Solid rock core

Mostly solid silicate mantle

Crust of silicate rock

2 MOONS

Silicate rock mantle

Rock crust with under ice permafrost

MARS

A cold, barren planet with a thin atmosphere, Mars has polar ice caps, water-carved valleys, chasms, and giant volcanoes. Its red color is caused by iron oxide dust spread across its surface.

MARS DATA

- Distance from Sun: 141.6 million miles (227.9 million km)
- Time taken to orbit Sun: 687 Earth days
- Diameter at equator: 4,217 miles (6,786 km)

THE OUTER PLANETS

BEYOND THE ORBIT of Mars lie four giant planets formed from liquefied gas – Jupiter, Saturn, Uranus, and Neptune. Farther out still is Pluto, a small, icy rock planet.

Liquid hydrogen and helium outer mantle

Rock core about twice the size of Earth

JUPITER DATA

- Distance from Sun: 484 million miles (778.3 million km)
- Time taken to orbit Sun: 12 Earth years
- Diameter at equator: 88,849 miles (142,984 km)

16 MOONS

Great Red Spot

Metallic hydrogen inner mantle

JUPITER

The largest, fastest-spinning planet, Jupiter could contain 1,300 Earths. Composed mainly of swirling gases, its most prominent feature is the Great Red Spot, a rotating storm bigger than the Earth.

Metallic hydrogen inner mantle

18 MOONS

Liquid hydrogen outer mantle

Rock and ice core

SATURN

The second largest planet is Saturn, its famed ring system made up of tiny ice-coated rock fragments and dust particles. The planet's mass is so thinly spread that on average it is less dense than water.

SATURN DATA

- Distance from Sun: 887 million miles (1,427 million km)
- Time taken to orbit Sun: 29.5 Earth years
- Diameter at equator: 74,900 miles (20,536 km)

Rings of rock fragments about 39 in (1 m) across

15 MOONS

URANUS
The frozen methane atmosphere of Uranus gives it a blue-green appearance. The planet, and its rings and moons, are all tilted by more than 90°, traveling around the Sun on their side.

Mantle of water-ice, ammonia and methane

Solid rock core

URANUS DATA
- Distance from Sun: 1.8 billion miles (2.9 billion km)
- Time taken to orbit Sun: 84 Earth years
- Diameter at equator: 31,764 miles (51,118 km)

NEPTUNE DATA
- Distance from Sun: 2.8 billion miles (4.5 billion km)
- Time taken to orbit Sun: 165 Earth years
- Diameter at equator: 30,776 miles (49,528 km)

NEPTUNE
The outermost gas giant, Neptune's atmosphere is very similar to Uranus, but thinner methane in its outer layer gives it a deeper blue color. Huge, cyclonic storms form the planet's Great Dark Spot.

Silicate rock core

Methane, ammonia, and water-ice mantle

Great Dark Spot

8 MOONS

Dark, low clouds of hydrogen sulfide

Icy surface of water and methane

Thin atmosphere of methane and nitrogen

Ice mantle

1 MOON

PLUTO
The smallest and most distant of all the planets, Pluto is made of ice, rock, and frozen gases. Its orbit around the Sun is uniquely tilted at 17°, and for about ten percent of its journey it is closer to the Sun than Neptune is.

Large rock core

PLUTO DATA
- Distance from Sun: 3.7 billion miles (5.9 billion km)
- Time taken to orbit Sun: 248 Earth years
- Diameter at equator: 1,419 miles (2,284 km)

EARTH'S MOON

THE MOON, Earth's only natural satellite, is
a ball of rock held in place by our planet's gravity.
A quarter of the size of Earth, the Moon is dead,
waterless, and airless. As Earth orbits the Sun,
the Moon in turn rotates around Earth.
Each rotation, or lunar cycle, takes
about a month.

Waning

New Moon

SUNLIGHT

Full Moon

Waxing

PHASES OF THE MOON
The Moon shines when
light from the Sun is reflected off the
lunar surface. As it travels around Earth, the sunlit area
we see changes. A monthly cycle of lunar phases is
produced as it waxes (grows) from New Moon to
Full Moon and wanes (shrinks) back to New Moon.

Asteroid collides with Earth

LUNAR ORIGINS
Most astronomers
believe that a huge
asteroid collided with
Earth 4.6 billion years
ago. Vast amounts of
rock fragments thrown into
space by the impact came
together, forming the Moon.

MOON DATA
- Distance from
  Earth: 238,860 miles
  (384,400 km)
- Time to rotate on
  axis: 27.3 Earth days
- Diameter: 2,160
  miles (3,476 km)
- Lunar temperature:
  −247°F to +105°C
  (−155°C to +221°F)

BATTERED SURFACE

Meteorite impacts scar the lunar surface with craters.

The lunar seas form from volcanic lava.

Rays of rock fan out from the rim of new craters.

3,800 million years ago
The Moon's surface receives a heavy meteorite bombardment.

2,800 million years ago
Volcanic eruptions fill the largest craters with dark lava.

Today
The surface has hardly changed apart from a few recent ray craters.

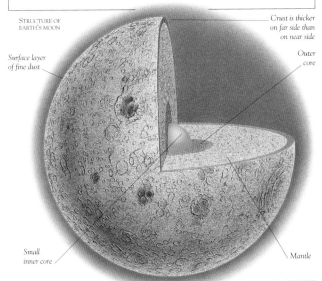

STRUCTURE OF EARTH'S MOON

Crust is thicker on far side than on near side

Surface layer of fine dust

Outer core

Small inner core

Mantle

ASTRONOMY

VISIBLE STARLIGHT magnified by optical telescopes is only a small part of the electromagnetic spectrum, which includes all forms of radiation. Astronomers learn about the visible and invisible parts of the universe by looking at other types of radiation, such as radio waves and X-rays. Space telescopes provide the best view, collecting information from wavelengths usually absorbed by the atmosphere.

HIGH AND DRY
The domes of the Cerro Tololo International American Observatory are sited in the Andes foothills of Chile. A dry climate with cloud-free nights and a steady atmosphere makes this an ideal location for clear viewing through an optical telescope.

DIFFERENT IMAGES OF THE CRAB NEBULA

VISIBLE LIGHT
This visible light image of the nebula has been computer-enhanced to show hydrogen (red) and sulfur (blue) gas filaments still streaming out from the explosion.

UV LIGHT
The Crab Nebula is the remnant of a supernova explosion. Viewing the ultraviolet light (UV) produced by the explosion reveals glowing, energetic particles interacting with the surrounding space.

X-RAY
The X-rays emitted by the Crab Nebula explosion show a bright object at the center of the nebula. This pulsating star, or pulsar, is the remains of the presupernova star.

RADIO VISION
A radio telescope, like an ordinary radio, can be tuned to pick up a particular wavelength. After measuring the intensity of the radio energy, computers are used to produce a "radio map" of the sky. Radio astronomy was responsible for the discovery of quasar galaxies and pulsar stars.

Radio waves

The VLA dishes are arranged in a Y-shape

Radio signals from space collected by 27 linked dishes

Each dish is 82 ft (25 m) across

VERY LARGE ARRAY (VLA)
RADIO TELESCOPE,
NEW MEXICO

ASTRONOMY FACTS
• The world's largest radio telescope is at Arecibo, Puerto Rico, with a dish 1,000 ft (305 m) across.
• The largest optical telescope is the Keck Telescope, situated at Mauna Kea, Hawaii.
• The oldest existing observatory was built in South Korea in A.D. 72.

HUBBLE SPACE TELESCOPE
Operating outside the Earth's atmosphere, the orbiting Hubble Space Telescope (HST) can see much farther than Earth-based telescopes. Its large mirror detects very faint light, which is then directed by a secondary mirror into an onboard scientific instrument package or high-resolution camera.

Large solar panels power the equipment aboard the HST

Cameras and instruments located inside

Protective hinged cover

Antenna transmits information to Earth via a communication satellite

NASA

esa

3 3

ROCKETS AND SPACECRAFT

THE FIRST ARTIFICIAL satellite, Sputnik 1, was launched into space in 1957. Since then, hundreds of spacecraft have been launched, including manned missions for exploration, orbiting space laboratories, and probes to other planets. Powerful rocket engines enable spacecraft to escape the pull of Earth's gravity.

STAGE FLIGHT
Rockets are designed in separate stages, so that when all the fuel from a stage has been used up, that stage drops away and the next takes over. The giant three-stage Saturn V rocket carried astronauts to the Moon.

SATURN
V

Solid fuel boosters jettisoned 2 mins 5 secs after lift-off, at an altitude of 28 miles (45 km). Shuttle now travelling at 4.5 times the speed of sound (Mach 4.5)

Shuttle reaches altitude of 81 miles (130 km) at Mach 15. External tank released, burning up in Earth's atmosphere

Shuttle engines put orbiter into circular orbit

Solid fuel burns for two minutes. Each solid fuel rocket produces the thrust of 11 Boeing 747 airliners at take-off

Main engines on orbiter take fuel from external tank. Two solid-fuel rocket boosters fire for lift-off

External tank
Orbiter
Solid-fuel boosters

THE SPACE SHUTTLE
The US space shuttle is the world's first reusable spacecraft. Typical shuttle missions include launching, retrieving, or repairing satellites, and performing scientific experiments. The shuttle is launched by reusable solid fuel rockets, and protected from the heat of reentry by 32,000 carbon or silica insulating tiles.

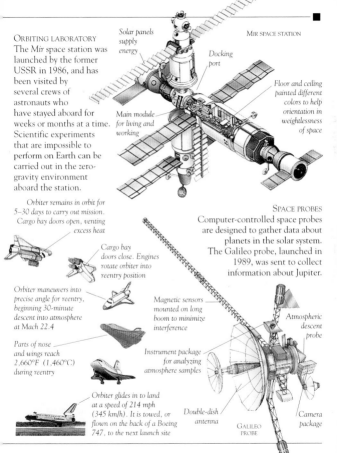

ORBITING LABORATORY

The *Mir* space station was launched by the former USSR in 1986, and has been visited by several crews of astronauts who have stayed aboard for weeks or months at a time. Scientific experiments that are impossible to perform on Earth can be carried out in the zero-gravity environment aboard the station.

Solar panels supply energy

MIR SPACE STATION

Docking port

Floor and ceiling painted different colors to help orientation in weightlessness of space

Main module for living and working

Orbiter remains in orbit for 5–30 days to carry out mission. Cargo bay doors open, venting excess heat

Cargo bay doors close. Engines rotate orbiter into reentry position

Orbiter maneuvers into precise angle for reentry, beginning 30-minute descent into atmosphere at Mach 22.4

Parts of nose and wings reach 2,660°F (1,460°C) during reentry

Orbiter glides in to land at a speed of 214 mph (345 km/h). It is towed, or flown on the back of a Boeing 747, to the next launch site

SPACE PROBES

Computer-controlled space probes are designed to gather data about planets in the solar system. The Galileo probe, launched in 1989, was sent to collect information about Jupiter.

Magnetic sensors mounted on long boom to minimize interference

Atmospheric descent probe

Instrument package for analyzing atmosphere samples

Double-dish antenna

Camera package

GALILEO PROBE

1926–1968

1926 US engineer Robert Goddard designs and launches first liquid fuel rocket.

1942 Wernher von Braun, later to play a major role in the postwar US space program, develops Nazi Germany's rocket-powered *V2* flying bomb.

1957 Launch of USSR's *Sputnik 1*, the world's first artificial satellite.

1957 Russian dog Laika becomes first living creature in space aboard *Sputnik 2*.

1961 The first manned spacecraft, *Vostok 1*, carries Soviet cosmonaut Yuri Gagarin into Earth orbit.

Yuri Gagarin

1962 US probe *Mariner 2* flies past Venus, becoming first human-made object to "flyby" another planet.

1963 First woman in space is USSR's Valentina Tereshkova, orbiting Earth 48 times in two days in *Vostok 6*.

1965 Russian cosmonaut Alexei Leonov takes the first walk in space. US probe *Mariner 4* finds no sign of water or life on Mars.

1966 Unmanned Soviet probe *Lunar 9* lands on Moon.

1968 US astronauts enter lunar orbit in *Apollo 8*.

1969–1976

1969 US astronauts Neil Armstrong and Edwin M. Aldrin are the first humans to walk on the Moon.

Edwin M. Aldrin steps onto the lunar surface

1970 USSR's *Venera 7* lands on Venus. It is the first probe to touch down on another planet.

1970 Soviet robot *Lunokhods*, the first extraterrestrial land vehicles, are driven across the Moon's surface.

1971 The first orbiting space station, the USSR's *Salyut 1*, is launched.

1972 *Apollo 17* is sixth and last US manned mission to the moon.

1973 Launch of *Skylab*, the first US space station. Close-up images of Jupiter taken by US *Pioneer 10*.

1974 US *Mariner 10* transmits first pictures of Mercury.

1975 First images of the surface of Venus sent by USSR's *Venera 9*.

1976 Surface tests carried out by US probe *Viking 1* confirm no life on planet Mars.

Martian surface

1977–1983

1977 US *Voyagers 1* and *2* launched on their long journey to the outer planets and beyond.
1979 US *Pioneer 11* reaches Saturn after a six-year voyage, finding a new ring and new moons.
Voyagers 1 and *2* pass Jupiter, observing active volcanoes on the moon, Io, and discovering three new moons.
1980 *Voyager 1* takes the first detailed close-up photographs of Saturn's ring systems and discovers an additional six moons.

Saturn, photographed by Voyager 1

1981 Launch of US space shuttle *Columbia*, the world's first reusable spacecraft. *Voyager 2* finds four more moons around Saturn, bringing the total to 18.
1982 USSR's *Venera 13* probe approaches Venus, sending back color photographs of the planet's surface. US astronauts Mark Lee and Judy Davis become the first married couple in space aboard the shuttle *Endeavor*.

1984–1996

1984 Manned Maneuvering Unit (MMU) used by US astronaut Bruce McCandless to maneuver independently alongside space shuttle *Challenger*.

Bruce McCandless in MMU

1986 Shuttle program halted after *Challenger* explosion kills the crew of seven. *Voyager 2* reaches Uranus and finds a ring system and 15 moons.
1988 Launch of *Columbia* resumes the US space shuttle program.
1989 *Voyager 2* reaches Neptune and discovers six new moons.
1990 Hubble space telescope launched (with faulty mirror).
1992 US COBE (Cosmic Background Explorer) finds hotspots in "microwave background" radio energy, providing evidence for the Big Bang theory.

COBE image of microwave background

1994 Hubble telescope repaired.
1996 US scientists find fossil evidence in meteor fragments that microbes may once have existed on Mars.

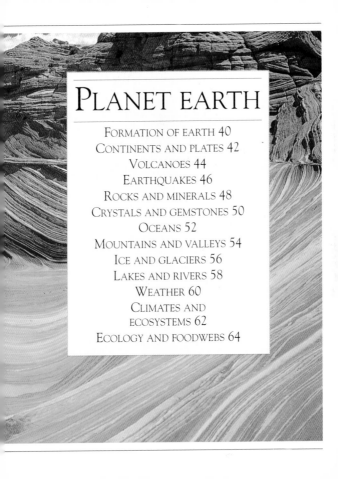

PLANET EARTH

FORMATION OF EARTH

ABOUT 4.6 BILLION years ago, the
planets of the solar system were just
a vast cloud of gas swirling around
the newly formed Sun. Earth and
the other planets formed when
parts of this cloud began to
cluster together.

3 EARTH'S CRUST
About 4 billion years
ago, Earth's crust began to
form. Blocks of cooling,
solid rock floated on a
molten rock layer.
The rock sometimes sank
and remelted before
rising again.

**1 FORMING
THE SUN**
A spinning cloud
of dust and gas
contracted to form
the Sun. Cooler
matter from this
dust cloud combined
to shape the planets.

*Dense cosmic
gases surrounded
Earth as it formed*

**2 FORMING
EARTH**
Radioactivity in
Earth's rocks caused
the planet's surface to
melt. Lighter minerals
floated to the surface,
and heavier elements,
such as iron and
nickel, sank to form
Earth's core.

**4 MAKING THE
ATMOSPHERE**
Over millions of years
Earth's crust thickened,
while gases from erupting
volcanoes began to
form the atmosphere.
Water vapor condensed
to make oceans.

Sea 70.8%

Land 29.2%
PROPORTION OF LAND AND SEA

EARTH DATA

- Distance from Sun: 93 million miles (150 million km)

- Time to rotate on axis: 23 hours, 56 minutes

- Time to orbit Sun: 365 days, 6 hours

- Speed of Earth's orbits of Sun: 18.5 miles/sec (29.8 km/sec)

Crust composed of rocks similar to those on surface – 4–43 miles (6–70 km) deep

Atmosphere – about 400 miles (640 km) deep

Mantle of mostly solid rock – 1,800 miles (2,900 km) deep

COMPOSITION OF EARTH

Our planet is composed of several layers of rock around a core of iron and nickel. The deeper the layer, the higher the temperature.

Outer core of liquid iron, nickel, and oxygen – 1,240 miles (2,000 km) deep

Inner core of solid iron and nickel – 1,700 miles (2,740 km) deep

5 LAND FORMS
Large landmasses, or protocontinents, began to form on the planet's crust about 3,500 million years ago. Today's continents look very different.

6 EARTH TODAY
The planet is still changing – the huge tectonic plates (see pp. 42–43) that make up Earth's crust are constantly moving, pulling some continents nearer and pushing others apart.

CONTINENTS AND PLATES

THE SEVEN HUGE landmasses that make
up most of Earth's surface are called
continents. They are always slowly
moving, shifted around by
forces deep inside Earth.
This movement is known
as continental drift.

The crack
or boundary
between two plates
sliding past each
other is called a
transform fault

TECTONIC PLATES
Earth's crust, or
lithosphere,
is made up of
vast pieces
of rock, called
tectonic plates.

Earth's tectonic plates
fit together like jigsaw
puzzle pieces

PLATE BOUNDARIES
Where they meet, tectonic plates
may be sliding past each other,
pulling apart, or colliding.
These different types of motion
cause earthquakes and volcanoes,
create steep-sided valleys, form deep-
sea trenches, and build mountains.

CONTINENTAL DRIFT

N. America — Europe
— Asia
PANGAEA
— India
Africa — Australia
S. America — Antarctica

N. America — Asia
LAURASIA — Europe
Africa — India
GONDWANALAND — Australia
S. America — Antarctica

1 Some 220 million years ago (mya)
the continents were joined together
in the giant supercontinent of Pangaea
(a Greek word meaning "all lands").

2 By 200 mya, Pangaea had split into
two landmasses, Gondwanaland
and Laurasia. Around 135 mya, these
landmasses also began to divide.

Midocean ridge

Where two plates pull apart, molten rock bubbles up from the mantle and fills the gap, creating new crust

When two plates collide, one may ride over the other and force it down into the mantle – this is called a subduction zone

PLATE MOVEMENT
In the "push" theory, heat makes the mantle rise and erupt, pushing the plates apart.

PUSH THEORY

The "pull" theory says they are dragged down and apart under the weight of erupting magma (molten rock) as it cools near midocean ridges.

PULL THEORY

Magma forced down into mantle

N. America   Europe
Africa   Asia
   India
S. America   Australia
   Antarctica

3 Over the next 120 million years, the products of this division became the continents, drifting closer or farther apart to take up their current positions.

N. America   Europe
   Africa
   Asia
S. America   Australia
   Antarctica

4 The continents are still moving at a slow but steady rate. This is how Earth may look in 150 million years.

VOLCANOES

A VOLCANIC ERUPTION takes place when hot, molten rock called magma rises up from deep inside Earth and forces its way to the surface. The magma may erupt as a flow of red-hot lava, or explode into clouds of ash, rock, and dust.

Ring of Fire continues through volcanic islands of Japan

The chain of volcanoes around the edge of the Pacific Ocean is known as the Ring of Fire

Crack in Earth's crust

Side vent

Lava

Vent

VOLCANO SITES
In general, volcanoes occur near plate boundaries or under the ocean at plate edges. Hotspot volcanoes, however, burst through the middle of a plate; they are not related to plate margins.

ERUPTION SIZES
The amount of ash thrown out during an eruption is a good indicator of the size of an eruption.

| MT. ST. HELENS US 1980 | MT. VESUVIUS ITALY A.D. 79 | MT. KATMAI ALASKA 1912 | MT. KRAKATOA INDONESIA 1883 | MT. TAMBORA INDONESIA 1815 |

FISSURE VOLCANO
This type of volcano is a long crack in the crust. Liquid lava seeps out along its length and forms a plateau.

VOLCANO FACTS
• The worst volcanic eruption was Mount Tambora, Indonesia, which killed 92,000 people in 1815.
• Kilauea, Hawaii, is the most frequently active volcano.

COMPOSITE VOLCANO
Cone-shaped volcanoes build up from hardening sticky lava. Inside are layers of thick lava and ash from previous eruptions. Gas builds up pressure inside the volcano until it erupts violently.

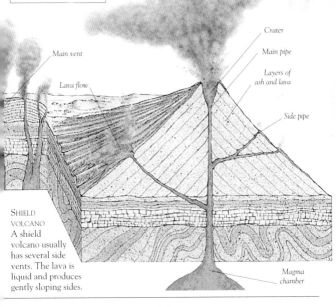

Clouds of ash, rock, and dust

Main vent

Lava flow

Crater

Main pipe

Layers of ash and lava

Side pipe

SHIELD VOLCANO
A shield volcano usually has several side vents. The lava is liquid and produces gently sloping sides.

Magma chamber

EARTHQUAKES

A MAJOR EARTHQUAKE occurs when the massive tectonic plates that make up Earth's crust suddenly move. A mild earthquake can feel like a truck passing; a severe one can destroy roads and buildings and cause huge tidal waves in the ocean.

The focus is usually deep inside Earth

The earthquake is strongest at its epicenter

Shock waves can travel right through Earth to the other side

FOCUS
AND EPICENTER
The point at which an earthquake begins is the focus. The point on Earth's surface directly above the focus is the epicenter.

CLOSE-UP OF AN EARTHQUAKE
At transform faults, where two plates are moving in opposite directions, the jagged edges of the plates may lock together. Stress builds up within the plates, until suddenly they slip, making the ground shake violently as they jolt into a new position.

BEFORE AN EARTHQUAKE

AFTER AN EARTHQUAKE

The plates slip and lurch past each other, causing an earthquake.

This fault line marks the boundary of two plates

EARTHQUAKE FAULT ZONES

Most earthquakes occur on or near the edges of Earth's tectonic plates (see pp. 42–43) at cracks in the crust called faults. Deep earthquakes take place where one plate is sliding under another.

EARTHQUAKE-PROOF BUILDINGS

In earthquake-prone areas, specially designed buildings can lessen the effects of an earthquake.

Earthquake belts usually follow the edges of Earth's tectonic plates

Many earthquakes occur on the northeast coast of Asia. This is at the boundary of two of Earth's plates

Pyramid-shaped buildings are built to withstand stress

The central column of the pagoda absorbs the shaking

TRANSAMERICA
BUILDING, SAN
FRANCISCO

ANCIENT BUDDHIST
PAGODA, JAPAN

EARTHQUAKE FACTS

• The strongest known earthquake occurred in Colombia in 1906, with a magnitude of 8.9 on the Richter scale.

• The highest recorded number of deaths from an earthquake is 830,000, occurring in Shansi, China, in 1556.

• The worst earthquake damage on record took place in Kwanto, Japan, in 1923, destroying 375,000 homes and killing 144,000 people.

ROCKS AND MINERALS

THERE ARE MANY different types of
rock, all of which are composed of
one or more minerals. Rocks are
the building blocks from which
Earth's crust is formed.

Earth's surface

Extrusive igneous rock *Intrusive igneous rock*

TYPES OF ROCKS

The study of rocks is called
geology. All types of rocks fall into
one of three categories: igneous,
sedimentary, or metamorphic.

EXTRUSIVE AND INTRUSIVE ROCKS
Igneous rock either settles within
Earth's crust (intrusive igneous rock)
or erupts from volcanoes onto the
surface (extrusive igneous rock).

METAMORPHIC ROCK
When igneous or
sedimentary rock is changed
by heat and/or pressure, it is
called metamorphic rock.

Gneiss is a metamorphic rock.

Basalt is an igneous rock.

IGNEOUS ROCK
When molten magma
rising from deep within
Earth begins to cool
and solidify, it forms
igneous rock.

Sandstone is a sedimentary rock.

SEDIMENTARY ROCK
Wind and rainwater
deposit rock fragments as
sediments in lakes, rivers, sand
dunes, and on the sea floor. They
are compressed over millions of years
into layers of sedimentary rock.

MINERAL HARDNESS
The hardness of a mineral is
graded on a scale of 1 to 10,
devised by German mineralogist
Friedrich Mohs (1773–1839).

MOHS' SCALE

1: TALC   2: GYPSUM   3: CALCITE   4: FLUORITE

MINERALS

A mineral is a non-living substance occurring naturally in Earth's crust. Most minerals are formed from silicates (compounds of oxygen and silicon).

Granite is composed of the minerals quartz, feldspar, and mica.

ROCK-FORMING MINERALS

Different combinations of minerals form different types of rock.

Chalcopyrite (copper ore); copper is a good conductor, widely used in the electricity industry.

ORE MINERALS

About 80 types of pure metal are extracted from ore minerals.

THE ROCK CYCLE

All rocks are constantly passing through a recycling process.

Igneous rocks are weathered away and washed into the ocean

Mineral particles sink to the sea floor where they are compacted into sedimentary rock

Rock may melt and rise to the surface where it cools to form igneous rock

Heat from molten rock changes surrounding sedimentary and igneous rock into meta-morphic rock

| 5: APATITE | 6: ORTHOCLASE | 7: QUARTZ | 8: TOPAZ | 9: CORUNDUM | 10: DIAMOND |

CRYSTALS AND GEMSTONES

A CRYSTAL IS a solid material in which atoms are arranged in a regular pattern. Crystals form, or crystallize, either from molten minerals or from minerals that are dissolved in liquids.

CRYSTAL HABIT

The characteristic general shape of a crystal is called its habit.

PRISMATIC; UNIFORM CROSS SECTION (BERYL)

DENDRITIC; TREELIKE SHAPE (COPPER)

MASSIVE; UNDEFINED SHAPE (LIMONITE)

ACICULAR; NEEDLELIKE (SCOLECITE)

RENIFORM; SHAPED LIKE KIDNEYS (HEMATITE)

CRYSTAL SYSTEMS

The geometrical shape in which a mineral crystallizes is called its crystal system.

CUBIC SYSTEM
All 90° angles. All edges equal in length.

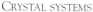

TETRAGONAL SYSTEM
All 90° angles. Two edges equal in length.

ORTHORHOMBIC SYSTEM
All 90° angles. No edges equal in length.

MONOCLINIC SYSTEM
Two edges meet at 90°.
No edges equal in length.

HEXAGONAL SYSTEM
Edges form angles of 90° and 120°. Two equal-length edges.

TRIGONAL SYSTEM
No angles meet at 90°.
All edges of equal length.

TRICLINIC SYSTEM
No edges meet at 90°.
No edges equal in length.

GEMSTONES

Minerals valued for their beauty, rarity, and durability are called gemstones. There are about 100 types; the most valued include diamonds and rubies.

EMERALD
HARDNESS:
7–7.8
SYSTEM: TRIGONAL/
HEXAGONAL

RUBY
HARDNESS: 9
SYSTEM: TRIGONAL/
HEXAGONAL

DIAMOND
HARDNESS: 10
SYSTEM: CUBIC

LARGEST GEMS

- Cullinan diamond, found in South Africa, 1905. Gemstone weight: 3,106 karats (1.37 lb/0.62 kg)

- Pearl of Lao-tze, Philippines, 1934. Gemstone weight: 31,850 karats (14 lb 1 oz/6.37 kg)

ORGANIC GEMS

A gemstone that has a plant or animal origin is called an organic gem.

Spider trapped in amber, the fossilized resin of trees

AMBER

PEARL IN OYSTER

The most highly valued pearls come from oysters and mussels

Mother-of-pearl

CAROB SEED

1 KARAT RUBY

23.5 KARAT GOLD BAR

The purity of gold is also measured in karats

KARATS AND BEANS

A gemstone's weight is measured in karats: one karat = 0.007 oz (0.2 g). The term karat is the Greek word for carob seed; these were once used as weights.

OCEANS

MORE THAN TWO-THIRDS of Earth's surface lies under its oceans. The water in these oceans is never still; it is constant motion from currents, tides, and waves.

1 Volcanic gases form Earth's early atmosphere.

2 Atmospheric water vapor falls as rain and collects in vast hollows.

3 Earth cools, eruptions reduce, and sea level stabilizes.

Warm current (red arrow) Cold current (blue arrow)

OCEAN CURRENTS
Major currents circulate the oceans in a clockwise direction in the northern hemisphere and counterclockwise in the southern hemisphere. Currents may be warm or cold, flowing across the surface of the ocean or deep beneath it.

FEATURES OF THE OCEAN FLOOR

Island arc

Deep-sea trenches are about 60 miles (100 km) wide and may be thousands of miles long

Guyot (flat-topped seamount)

Escaping magma forms midocean ridge

ISLAND ARC
Molten rock from a melting, subducted oceanic plate rises through the upper plate, forming volcanic islands.

TRENCH
Where the ocean floor sinks into the mantle, long, deep trenches occur.

WAVES

Wind blowing over the surface of the ocean causes waves. The height and power of waves depend on the strength of the wind.

Particles near the surface turn over and over

The top part of the wave, the crest, continues up the beach

The beach slows down the base of the wave

TIDES

High and low tides occur daily or twice daily. Twice each month tides are greater (spring tides) or smaller (neap tides). The tidal cycle is based on the relative positions of the Moon, Sun, and Earth.

Earth's rotation balances the Moon's gravitational pull.

Earth spinning on its axis affects the tides.

The Moon's gravity pulls the oceans.

A seamount is an underwater volcano that rises over 3,280 ft (1,000 m)

A sediment-covered plain lying at a depth of 13,000 ft (4,000 m) is called an abyssal plain

Rivers flowing into the sea can erode submarine (underwater) canyons

Tectonic plates move apart

Magma rises to fill gap between plates

The steep incline descending from the continental shelf is called the continental slope

A continental shelf is a vast ledge of land under the sea. It can be up to 43 miles (70 km) wide

53

MOUNTAINS AND VALLEYS

WHEN EARTH'S rocky tectonic plates collide, the crust may buckle and fold, forcing up lofty mountain peaks. Volcanoes also erupt at plate boundaries and sometimes build into mountains. All are slowly weathered away, as erosion wears down peaks, carves out valleys, and opens up underground caves.

LIFE OF A MOUNTAIN

1 YOUNG
High-peaked mountains that formed in the last few million years.

2 MATURE
Eroded mountains created several hundred million years ago.

3 ANCIENT
Mountains so old and worn down that only a few hills remain.

TYPES OF MOUNTAINS

FOLD MOUNTAIN
Where two of Earth's plates collide, the rock layers buckle and bend, forcing the rocky crust up into a mountain range.

VOLCANO
Layers of volcanic lava, ash, and rock ejected from Earth's interior build up into a mountain.

FAULT-BLOCK MOUNTAIN
When Earth's plates push together, faults or cracks appear in the crust, forcing up huge blocks of rock.

DOME MOUNTAIN
Rising magma makes the rock above bulge upward, creating a dome-shaped mountain.

HOW A RIVER VALLEY FORMS

High up in the mountains, fast-flowing streams create steep-sided, V-shaped gullies. In the middle part of the valley, the water meanders (winds) across a broad valley. Near the sea, the river flows across a flat plain or fans out into a delta.

Rainfall runs down gullies

V-shape of a river valley's upper course

River curves back and forth in a series of meanders

Cut-off meander forms oxbow lake

Flat land slows water flow

MOUNTAIN FACTS
• The world's highest mountain is Mount Everest in the Himalayas, Nepal, reaching a height of 29,028 ft (8,848 m) at its peak.

Fan-shaped delta at river mouth

River sheds sediments on flat floodplain

Broad shape of valley at river mouth

HOW CAVES FORM

Limestone caves are formed when carbonic acid in rainwater seeps into cracks in limestone and dissolves the rock. Sea caves are created by the pressure of waves or the corrosive effect of salt on the foot of cliffs. Ice caves are carved out by a stream of meltwater running beneath a glacier (see pp. 56–57).

Stream plunging undergound at a sinkhole

Stalactites hang down from roof

Water seeps into cracks in rocks

Stalagmites grow upward from the cave floor

CROSS SECTION OF A LIMESTONE CAVE

Columns form where stalactites and stalagmites join

ICE AND GLACIERS

MORE THAN ONE-TENTH of Earth's surface is permanently covered with ice. At the Poles and in high mountain regions, vast areas are covered by ice sheets and rivers of ice called glaciers.

Ridge, or arête, between two glaciers

Cirque, or corrie, a hollow where glacier begins

Compacted "firn" ice

When ice moves over a sharp incline, it cracks to form crevasses

Snout or front of glacier

Melting ice flows from the snout

Pile of rocks and boulders called terminal moraine

FEATURES OF A GLACIER
Snow collects in a high mountain hollow called a cirque and compacts into "firn" ice. The firn flows slowly downhill, its hard ice and sediment scouring the surrounding rock along the way.

ICE MOVEMENT
Warm-based glaciers move mainly by basal slip, where the melting base causes the whole glacier to move. Cold-based glaciers move mainly by internal deformation, where a glacier slips and its surface flows faster than its base.

Warm base (about 32°F, 0°C)

Direction of movement

Cold base (below 32°F, 0°C)

Basal ice melts

Layers of ice slide over each other

BASAL SLIP

INTERNAL DEFORMATION

ICEBERGS
Fragments of ice that float out to sea after breaking off ice sheets, ice caps, and glaciers are called icebergs. This process is called calving. Only 12 percent of an iceberg is visible above the sea's surface.

FORMATION OF AN ICEBERG

ICE FACTS
• About 75 percent of the world's fresh water is stored in ice caps and glaciers.
• The world's fastest moving glacier is the Quarayaq in Greenland, which can flow 65–80 ft (20–24 m) per day.

Tidal movement and buffeting by waves breaks off iceberg

An iceberg's movement is controlled by ocean currents and the wind

PLEISTOCENE EPOCH – THE LAST ICE AGE

EXTENT OF ICE IN THE WORLD TODAY

ICE AGES
In Earth's history, there have been many ice ages interspersed with warmer periods called interglacials. During the most recent ice age, about 30,000 years ago, ice covered much of North America and Europe.

GLACIAL DEPOSITION
The ice in a glacier is choked with rocky debris. When the ice melts, it leaves behind piles of debris (moraine), which form small mounds or hummocks.

Horn peak

Cirque with tarn

Arête

Hanging valley

Striations

U-shaped valley

Lake chains jammed with moraine

LAKES AND RIVERS

WHEN RAINWATER falls on the land, it may seep into the ground, collect in lakes, or form rivers running down to the ocean. Rivers gradually mold the land, as they wear down material in some places, and re-deposit it in others.

Water vapor from plants released into atmosphere

Rain and snow fall on high ground

Wind

Water evaporates from oceans and lakes to clouds of vapor

Water seeps underground and flows to sea

River flows into ocean

THE WATER CYCLE
The Sun's heat causes water to evaporate from oceans, lakes, and rivers. As it rises into the atmosphere, the water vapor cools and condenses into clouds. Eventually the droplets fall back to Earth as rain.

TYPES OF LAKES

Water fills depressions or hollows

Hollow eroded by glacier forms lake

Rainwater collects in crater

KETTLE LAKE
Melting ice blocks from glaciers fill depressions in rocky glacial debris to form kettle lakes.

TARN
Circular mountain lake that forms in hollows worn by glacial erosion or blocked by ice debris.

VOLCANIC LAKE
Ancient volcanic craters fill with water, producing lakes such as Crater Lake, Oregon.

SOURCES OF RIVER WATER

All rivers receive their water, either directly or indirectly, from precipitation (rainfall).

Melting glacier

MELTWATER

Many rivers begin as melting snow and ice from a glacier.

SPRING

Spring

Aquifer rock layer

Rainwater stored in the aquifer rock layer may reemerge at a spring.

Rainfall runs off mountain slopes into river system

Tributary streams feed the main river

OVERLAND FLOW

Clouds

Rain running downhill gathers into streams.

Streams

Waterfall wears rock and cuts a steep gorge

River plunges over hard shelf of rock, forming waterfall

FEATURES OF A RIVER

A river is a body of water that flows downhill in a channel, winding through the landscape and carving out deep valleys in solid rock. Rivers carry huge amounts of silt that are eventually laid down to form broad floodplains.

River flows over steep slope of hard rock, forming swirling rapids

Meander cut off after flooding forms an oxbow lake

River cuts into bank, widening meander (loop)

Wide, flat floodplain is submerged when the river floods

Fresh river water meets salty seawater at estuary

Sediment deposits cause river to split into separate streams, which fan out to form a delta

RIVER FACTS

• The world's longest river is the Nile, Africa, at 4,160 miles (6,695 km) long.

• The world's highest waterfall is Angel Falls, Venezuela, at a height of 3,212 ft (979 m).

WEATHER

THE CONSTANT motion of the lower layers of the atmosphere means that air conditions are always changing, creating weather variations such as wind and rain, snow, frost, fog, and sunshine.

Trade winds

Polar easterly

Westerlies

Cold polar air

Cells of air circulate above the planet

Warm air rises, spreading over cold air

FORMATION OF CLOUDS
Clouds form when water vapor in warm air rises, cools, and condenses.

Warm air containing water vapor rises.

Water vapor cools and condenses, forming clouds.

Cloud continues to form as long as warm, moist air rises.

THE WORLD'S WINDS
Wind is simply air moving from areas of high pressure to areas of low pressure. Three bands of prevailing (persistent) winds are found around the world – dry trade winds, warm westerlies, and cold polar easterlies.

AIR MASSES AND FRONTS
Huge bodies of air that form over continents and oceans are called air masses. They can be warm, cold, moist, or dry depending on where they form. A front is the boundary between two air masses.

Warm, moist air mass rises above cold air mass

Thin cloud

Dense, high clouds

Thick rain clouds

Rain at base of front

Shallow gradient

WARM FRONT

Steep gradient

COLD FRONT

Cold air moves over warmer air along Earth's surface

Heavy rain

TYPES OF CLOUDS

Clouds are classified according to their shape and their height above the ground.

Freezing level

Cumulonimbus – giant, dark, anvil-headed thundercloud – forms at 49,000 ft (15,000 m)

Stratocumulus – white or gray lumpy cloud at top of cumulus – forms at 0–6,500 ft (0–2,000 m)

Nimbostratus – thick, gray rain cloud – forms at 0–6,500 ft (0–2,000 m)

Stratus – low-level, flat, gray sheet of misty cloud – forms at 0–6,500 ft (0–2,000 m)

Cirrus – wisps of cloud made of ice crystals – forms at 16,000–42,000 ft (5,000–13,000 m)

Cirrocumulus – rippled ice crystal cloud like fish scales – forms at 16,000–42,000 ft (5,000–13,000 m)

Altocumulus – fluffy cloud – forms at 6,500–23,000 ft (2,000–7,000 m)

Altostratus – gray or white sheet of cloud – forms at 6,500–23,000 ft (2,000–7,000 m)

Cumulus – large, white, fluffy cloud – forms at 0–6,500 ft (0–2,000 m)

TYPES OF RAIN

Most of the world's rain comes from water droplets freezing into icy particles high in a cloud. The particles grow into snowflakes, turning to raindrops as they fall. In the tropics, small raindrops join up to make bigger drops heavy enough to fall as rain.

Drops smaller than 0.2 in (5 mm) fall as drizzle

Larger raindrops

Rising air

Water droplets freeze into ice crystals

Snowflakes melt inside cloud or on their way to ground

Some rain falls without freezing

Sleet

TROPICAL RAIN

MELTED SNOW

CLIMATES AND ECOSYSTEMS

THE TYPICAL LONG-TERM weather conditions of an area are referred to as its climate. A region's climate varies according to its distance from the Equator and the ocean, and its height above sea level. The interacting range of plants and animals within a climate is called an ecosystem.

MAP OF WORLD CLIMATE ZONES

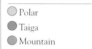

TYPES OF CLIMATE
The world's climates are split into three broad zones: tropical, temperate, and polar. The farther from the Equator and above sea level a zone lies, the colder the climate. The greater distance from an ocean, the more extreme its winters and summers.

KEY TO CLIMATE ZONES

- Polar
- Taiga
- Mountain
- Temperate
- Tropical rain forest
- Hot desert

HOT DESERT
Few species can survive in desert climates. Temperatures can exceed 100°F (38°C) and it may not rain for several years.

TROPICAL RAIN FOREST
Heavy rain and high temperatures all year round make rain forests the world's richest plant and animal habitats.

POLAR AND TUNDRA

In the polar regions, temperatures rarely rise above freezing for more than a few months of the year. Fresh water is permanently frozen, and plants cannot grow. The cold, dry land bordering the ice caps is known as the tundra.

CLIMATES AND ECOSYSTEMS FACTS

• The highest recorded temperature, taken at al'Aziziyah, Libya, measured 136°F (58°C).

• The coldest inhabited place is Oymyakon, Siberia, with a temperature of –90°F (–68°C).

TAIGA (COLD TEMPERATE)

The vast coniferous forest called the Taiga stretches across Canada, Scandinavia, and the former Soviet Union. Four to six months of the year are dark, with the temperature falling well below 32°F (0°C).

TEMPERATE

Winters are cool and summers warm in temperate climates, with many plants and trees becoming dormant in winter.

MOUNTAIN REGIONS

Low temperatures prevent vegetation growing on mountain peaks; trees and plants thrive on the lower slopes.

ECOLOGY AND FOOD WEBS

THE LIVING WORLD is built on complex relationships between plants, animals, and the places they inhabit. Ecology is the study of these relationships and how communities of living things interact with their habitats.

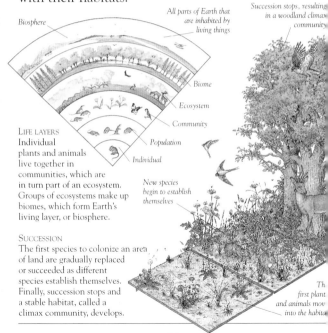

Biosphere

All parts of Earth that are inhabited by living things

Biome

Ecosystem

Community

Population

Individual

LIFE LAYERS
Individual plants and animals live together in communities, which are in turn part of an ecosystem. Groups of ecosystems make up biomes, which form Earth's living layer, or biosphere.

SUCCESSION
The first species to colonize an area of land are gradually replaced or succeeded as different species establish themselves. Finally, succession stops and a stable habitat, called a climax community, develops.

Succession stops, resulting in a woodland climax community

New species begin to establish themselves

Th first plant and animals mov into the habita

FOOD WEBS

Some organisms within an ecosystem may feed off
each other. In a salt marsh, for example, shrews feed
on snails and marsh hawks feed on shrews. This series
of feeding links is called a food chain. Each species is
involved in a number of chains, and these chains link
up to form interconnecting food webs.

FOOD WEBS LINKING ANIMALS
LIVING IN OPEN WOODLAND

*Frogs link the
two webs*

*Arrows link
food source to
consumer*

POND FOOD WEB   MEADOW FOOD WEB

FEEDING LEVELS

In most food chains there are various stages or trophic levels.

SUN

CABBAGE   CATERPILLAR

THRUSH

FUNGI

Producers
Green plants use
sunlight to make
their own food.

Primary consumer
Herbivores such as
caterpillars eat
producers.

Secondary consumer
Carnivores eat
herbivores and
other carnivores.

Decomposer
Fungi and bacteria
decompose dead
organisms.

THE LIVING WORLD

EVOLUTION

SINCE LIFE appeared 3.8 billion years ago, millions of different creatures have come and gone. As habitats changed, some species survived by adapting, while others died out quickly. This gradual turnover of species is called evolution.

PORPOISE'S FRONT FLIPPER

"Finger" bones form a powerful flipper for swimming

Two sets of short "arm" bones

Two sets of long bones make up the arm

Five sets of finger bones make up hand

HUMAN ARM

ADAPTATION
Evolution works by slowly adapting existing features to suit different purposes. Although they look very different, humans and porpoises both have two "arm" bones and five "finger" bones.

LIFE-FORMS THROUGH THE AGES
By working out when certain rocks formed, and then studying the fossils found in them, paleontologists – who study the life-forms of the past – have built up a remarkable picture of the way species have changed since the dawn of the Cambrian period 590 million years ago. Little is known of Precambrian life forms because very few fossils remain.

PRECAMBRIAN	PALEOZOIC	
	Cambrian	Ordovician

4600–590 mya
Single-celled life-forms such as bacteria and algae appear, then soft multi-celled life-forms, like worms and jellyfish.

590–505 mya
No life on land. Invertebrates flourish in the seas. First mollusks and trilobites.

505–438 mya
First crustaceans and early jawless fish appear. Coral reefs form. Sahara glaciated.

How evolution works
According to Darwin's theory of
evolution, animals and plants
developed over millions of
years, surviving according to
their ability to adapt to a
changing environment.
Until the mid-19th-century,
people believed that life-forms
did not change since their
creation by an omnipotent deity.

Charles Darwin (1809–1882)
The theory of evolution was
developed by English naturalist
Charles Darwin after studying
the animals of the Galápagos
Islands. He published his
findings in 1859 in his book
On the Origin of Species.

EVOLUTION OF THE HORSE

Eohippus
*This hare-sized
creature
browsed in
woodlands.*

Mesohippus
*Over millions of
years, Eohippus
evolved into a larger
grazing animal.*

Merychippus
*As early horses adapted
to the grasslands, they
developed longer limbs to
escape from predators.*

Modern horse
*The horses of today are
highly developed grazers;
they have long legs for
running and sharp senses.*

Silurian	Devonian	Carboniferous	Permian

438–408 mya
*First jawed fish.
Huge sea scorpions
hunt in the sea.
Small land plants
colonize the shore.*

408–355 mya
*Age of sharks and
fish. Insects and
amphibians appear
on land. Giant
ferns form forests.*

355–290 mya
*Warm swampy
forests leave
remains that will
turn to coal.
First reptiles.*

290–250 mya
*Reptiles diversify,
conifers replace
tree ferns. Mass
extinction as Earth
turns cold.*

FOSSILS

THE REMAINS of living things preserved naturally, often for many millions of years, are called fossils. Most fossils are formed in rocks; however, remains can also be preserved in ice, tar, peat, and amber. Fossils tell us nearly all we know about the history of life on Earth.

Spider trapped inside resin

SPIDER IN AMBER
Amber is fossilized tree resin that may also preserve trapped insects.

AMMONITES BECAME EXTINCT 65 MYA

KINDS OF FOSSILS
Most fossils form on the seabed, so shells and sea creatures are the most common. Fossils of land animals and plants are rarer. Footprints, burrows, or droppings may also be preserved.

Fossilized shell

MESOZOIC			CENOZOIC	
Triassic	Jurassic	Cretaceous	Tertiary	
			Palaeocene	Eocene

250–205 mya Mammals and dinosaurs appear. The climate warms and seed-bearing plants dominate.	205–135 mya The age of the dinosaurs. The first known bird, Archaeopteryx, appears.	135–66 mya First flowering plants. Period ends with a mass extinction that wipes out dinosaurs.	66–53 mya Warm, humid climate. Mammals, insects, and flowering plants flourish.	53–36 mya Mammals grow larger and diversify. Primates evolve.

1 ANIMAL DIES
The body of a dead animal lies decaying on the surface of the land.

2 REMAINS SINK
Gradually, the body becomes covered with sand or mud.

FOSSILIZATION AT SEA
Dead organisms sink to the seabed and are buried. As the sediment turns to rock, their remains are either chemically altered or dissolve to leave a cavity, which may fill with minerals to form a cast.

3 BONES ALTER
Over time, the bones are altered, and the sand and mud turn to rock.

4 FOSSIL IS EXPOSED
Eventually, weather and erosion expose the fossil at the surface.

Oligocene	Miocene	Pliocene	Quaternary	
			Pleistocene	Holocene

36–23 mya
First humanlike creatures appear. Hunting birds thrive. Some mammals die out.

23–6.3 mya
Climate cools, and forests shrink. Deerlike hoofed mammals flourish. First hominids.

6.3–1.6 mya
Cold and dry. Mammals reach maximum diversity. Many modern mammals appear.

1.6m–10,000 ya
Ice Ages. Homo sapiens evolves. Mammoths and saber-toothed tigers die out.

10,000 ya to present
Humans develop agriculture and technology. Human activity threatens many species.

DINOSAURS

FOR 150 MILLION YEARS,
Earth was dominated by giant
reptiles called dinosaurs, including
Seismosaurus, the largest creature
ever to walk on land. Then,
65 million years ago, all the
dinosaurs mysteriously died out.

Light bones
for flying

Wings
of skin

Furry
body

PTEROSAUR
While dinosaurs ruled the
land, giant reptiles, like
Pterosaur, flew
in the air.

DINOSAUR GROUPS
Scientists divide dinosaurs into two orders according
to the arrangement of their hipbones. Saurischians
have lizardlike hips and include both plant and
meateaters. Ornithischians have
bird-like hips and are all plant
eaters. The two orders are
divided into five subgroups.

Muscular
tail balanced
the front of
the body

Long neck
for browsing
in treetops

Ruff

SALTASAURUS

Horn

STYRACOSAURUS

*Sauropods (Saurischians) were huge,
long-necked four-legged planteaters.*

*Marginocephalians (Saurischians) had
a bony ruff and horns for self-defense.*

TYRANNOSAURUS

STEGOSAURUS

CORYTHOSAURUS

*Thyreophorans (Ornithischians)
were spiny-backed planteaters.*

*Theropods (Saurischians) were
two-legged meateaters.*

*Ornithopods (Ornithischians)
had a horny beak and birdlike feet.*

One lower hip bone points
forward and the other points
backward

Skull

Backbone

Ribs

TYRANNOSAURUS REX
(SAURISCHIAN, OR LIZARD-HIPPED)

Both lower
hip bones point
backwards

IGUANODON
(ORNITHISCHIAN,
OR BIRD-HIPPED)

DINOSAUR SKELETONS

By studying the fossils of dinosaur bones,
scientists can learn more about the lives and
habits of these giant reptiles that lived millions
of years ago. The way the hips are arranged
helps them to group the dinosaurs.

Tough,
waterproof skin
was covered
with scales

TYRANNOSAURUS
REX

Strong neck
muscles for
holding prey

Powerful jaws
for crushing
bones

Serrated teeth up to
7 in (18 cm) long
for slicing through
flesh and bones

GIANT REPTILE?

Dinosaurs may look
like reptiles, but
some walked
with their limbs
directly under
their body,
like birds and
mammals,
and may
have been
warm-
blooded.

Clawed hands
for gripping prey

Thick, heavy
legs to support
weight

Huge claws
for holding
prey on the
ground

DINOSAUR FACTS

• Over 350 dinosaur
species have so far
been identified.

• Some dinosaurs may
have lived 200 years.

• Dinosaur means
"terrible lizard."

CLASSIFICATION OF LIFE

THE NATURAL WORLD contains
millions of living things, which
can be classified according to the
features they have in common.
The largest groups are the five
kingdoms: animals, plants, fungi,
protists, and monerans.

ALGAE

PROTOZOA

MONERANS
These simple
single-celled organisms,
such as bacteria, are
visible only under a
microscope. They were
the first life forms and
there are now around
4,000 species.

BACTERIA

PROTISTS
Complex single-celled
organisms, such as protozoa
and amoebas, are called
protists. Protozoa are like
animals. Algae are like
plants. There are over
50,000 protist species.

THE PANTHER

COMMON OYSTER MUSHROOM

MEADOW
CORAL
FUNGUS

CURLY-HAIRED ELF CUP

FUNGI
Fungi often look like plants
but have no leaves and
absorb food from other living
or dead matter. There are
about 100,000 species.

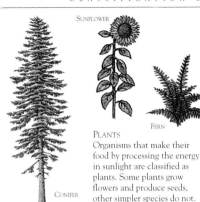

SUNFLOWER

FERN

CONIFER

PLANTS
Organisms that make their food by processing the energy in sunlight are classified as plants. Some plants grow flowers and produce seeds, other simpler species do not. There are over 400,000 species.

CLASSIFICATION
Each kingdom is divided into smaller and smaller groups according to its characteristics. This is how a serval (*Felis serval*) would be classified.

Kingdom
Animal (Animalia)
Many-celled, must find food

Phylum
Chordate (Chordata)
Single nerve cord during life

Class
Mammal (Mammalia)
Suckles young

Order
Carnivores (Carnivora)
Adapted to hunting

Family
Cats (Felidae)
Sharp, retractable claws

Genus
(*Felis*)
Short tail, tufted ears

Species
serval
(*Felis serval*)

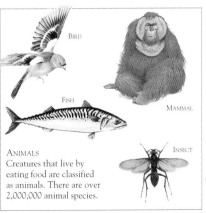

BIRD

FISH

MAMMAL

INSECT

ANIMALS
Creatures that live by eating food are classified as animals. There are over 2,000,000 animal species.

FELIS SERVAL

CELLS

ALL LIVING THINGS are made up
of tiny, self-contained units called
cells, usually so small that they are
visible only under a microscope.
A cell takes in energy and uses
it to grow and reproduce. Some
organisms consist of just a single
cell, others have billions.

EGG CELL
Cells vary in size from
minute fractions of an
inch to eggs, which are
the largest cells of all.

ANIMAL CELL
An animal cell is a tiny jelly-filled
sac with a soft and flexible
skin or membrane.
Different kinds
of cells, such as
blood cells and
skin cells, perform
different tasks in
the body. Inside
each, there are
organelles that
control and
run the cell.

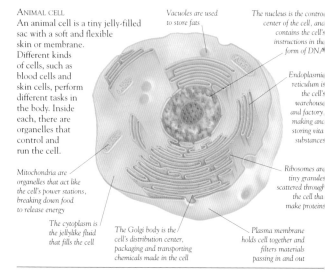

Vacuoles are used
to store fats

The nucleus is the control
center of the cell, and
contains the cell's
instructions in the
form of DNA

Endoplasmic
reticulum is
the cell's
warehouse
and factory,
making and
storing vital
substances

Ribosomes are
tiny granules
scattered through
the cell that
make proteins

Mitochondria are
organelles that act like
the cell's power stations,
breaking down food
to release energy

The cytoplasm is
the jellylike fluid
that fills the cell

The Golgi body is the
cell's distribution center,
packaging and transporting
chemicals made in the cell

Plasma membrane
holds cell together and
filters materials
passing in and out

PLANT CELL

The features of a plant cell are very similar to those of an animal cell, but plant cells are enclosed in a rigid shell of cellulose. They also have organelles called chloroplasts, made bright green by a pigment called chlorophyll. Chloroplasts are like solar batteries, enabling plants to trap energy from the sun in a process called photosynthesis.

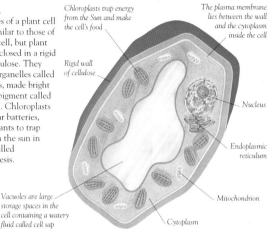

Chloroplasts trap energy from the Sun and make the cell's food

The plasma membrane lies between the wall and the cytoplasm inside the cell

Rigid wall of cellulose

Nucleus

Endoplasmic reticulum

Mitochondrion

Vacuoles are large storage spaces in the cell containing a watery fluid called cell sap

Cytoplasm

CELL DIVISION

Living cells multiply by splitting in two again and again. This is how worn-out cells are replaced and plants and animals grow. To ensure that the chromosomes (the cell's life-plan) are passed on to each new cell equally, most cells divide by a complex process called mitosis.

Chromosomes unwind into chromatids

Nucleus

Nucleus

Two genetically identical cells prepare to divide.

Chromatids prepare to split

Spindle begins to form

The old nucleus disintegrates and the spindle pulls equal numbers of chromatids to opposite ends of the cell to form two new nuclei. The cytoplasm then divides to form two new, identical cells.

MICROORGANISMS

THE MOST NUMEROUS living things
in the world are usually too small
to see except under a microscope.
These microorganisms, including
bacteria and protozoa, are
everywhere – there are 100 trillion
in your body alone. All are made
of just a single cell.

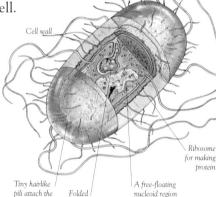

*Long, hairlike
flagella on some
bacteria whip
from side to
side to move
the cell along*

*A tough,
slimy capsule
protects the
cell wall*

Cell wall

*Ribosome
for making
protein*

*Tiny hairlike
pili attach the
cell to food or
other cells*

*Folded
plasma
membrane*

*A free-floating
nucleoid region
contains the
bacteria's instructions*

BACTERIA
The most abundant
living things on Earth,
and among the most
ancient, bacteria live
everywhere from the
upper atmosphere
to the ocean depths.
Many feed on dead
matter and help to
recycle nutrients.
Others, called germs,
feed on living things and
cause disease. Bacteria
cells are prokaryotic,
which means they have
no nucleus.

COCCUS

BACILLUS

SPIRILLUM

BACTERIA SHAPES
Bacteria may be classified
by shape – coccus (round),
bacillus (rod-shaped), or
spirillum (coiled).

PROTOZOA

Like bacteria, protozoa are single-celled organisms, but they have a nucleus and grow much bigger. They live in damp habitats, like soil, ponds, and oceans. Amoebas are protozoans with no fixed shape. They move by changing shape, and feed by engulfing food. Some live in water and soil. Others are parasites living inside plants and animals.

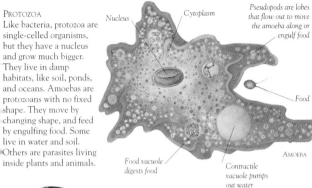

Pseudopods are lobes that flow out to move the amoeba along or engulf food

Nucleus

Cytoplasm

Food

Food vacuole digests food

Contractile vacuole pumps out water

AMOEBA

VIRUSES

A virus is a tiny package of chemicals coated with protein. It is not a living organism – it relies on invading living hosts to reproduce itself.

INFLUENZA VIRUSES SEEN THROUGH AN ELECTRON MICROSCOPE

USEFUL BACTERIA

Bacteria play a vital role in breaking down dead matter and recycling nutrients, helping us digest food. Bacteria are important in the production of many foods such as cheese, yogurt, vinegar, and beer.

YOGURT

CHEESE

VINEGAR

MICROORGANISM FACTS

• One gram of soil may contain 150,000 protozoa.

• There may be 2000 bacteria per square inch of human armpit.

• The largest protozoa (now extinct) grew to 7.9 in (20 cm) across.

• Viruses are visible only under an electron microscope.

FUNGI AND LICHENS

MUSHROOMS, toadstools, mildew, and mold are all kinds of fungi. Like plants, fungi often grow in soil, but they cannot make food from sunlight. Instead they absorb chemicals from living and dead plants and animals, manure, and other organic material.

FUNGUS VARIETY
There are fungi of all shapes and sizes. Some are good to eat, but many are so poisonous they can kill

FUNGUS STRUCTURE
The stalk and head of the toadstool are the fungi's "fruiting body," which releases tiny, seed-like spores. Wherever these spores land, they send out new hyphae (threads).

Cap

Cap releases spores

Mature sporophore produces spores

Sporophore grows above ground

Spore germinates; mycelium develops

Sporophore forms

Cap

Spores form in gills

Stem ring

Stalk holds cap high enough for the spores to be released into the air

Hyphae form mycelium (main body), which absorbs nutrients and anchors sporophore (fruiting body)

FRUITING BODY AND MYCELIUM OF FLY AGARIC

FUNGAL BONDING
Fungi begin to reproduce when one mass of underground threads meets another of the same species. They bond and produce a fruiting body (sporophore) that usually grows above ground and makes spores.

BRACKET FUNGI
Instead of growing in soil, some fungi grow in tiers on dead or dying trees and logs. Knowing which types of wood attract which types of fungus makes it easier to identify different fungus species.

Fruiting bodies grow in tiers on dead wood

LICHENS

STRUCTURE

Lichens are a partnership between fungi and algae, a little like a sandwich, with fungal bread and algal filling. The green algae trap sunlight to make food to feed the fungi, which in turn protect the algae and retain water.

FOLIOSE
(Hypogymnia physodes)

Lichens attach themselves to stones or wood. They eventually break down rocks and help to form soil.

SQUAMULOSE
(Cladonia floerkeana)

The many species of lichens grow in five distinct ways. Three are shown here.

FRUTICOSE (Cladonia portentosa)

PLANTS

PLANTS make their own food
out of water, air, and sunlight.
This makes them the starting
point of most food chains, and
most other living organisms
depend on them for food.
Plants have adapted to the
most extreme habitats, from hot
desert to icy tundra.

Seeds ripen

Seed germinates: leaves and roots grow

Seed

Plant grows

Ova is pollinated

SEXUAL REPRODUCTION
Many plants reproduce by
ova being fertilized by pollen,
whether from the same flower
or plant or a different one.
This is sexual reproduction.

ASEXUAL REPRODUCTION
Many plants can
reproduce without
pollination or
fertilization taking
place. This is called
asexual reproduction.

Parent plant

Runner

New plants develop from tip of underground runners

STRAWBERRY PLANT

TYPES OF PLANTS
The earliest plants
on Earth did not have
flowers or produce seeds.
Simple plants like this
still exist, but now they
share Earth with their
flowering relatives.
Plants come in all
shapes and sizes, from
tiny algae to grasses
and giant trees.

NON-FLOWERING PLANTS

ALGAE

SEAWEED

MOSSES AND LIVERWORTS

FERNS

FLOWERING PLANTS

GRASSES

SHRUBS

HERBS

TREES

CO₂ enters via tiny holes called stomata

Sunlight is absorbed

Flowers carry reproductive parts

Flower bud

Sepal

Water enters leaf via stalk

Oxygen is given off

Leaf

Petal

PHOTOSYNTHESIS

A green pigment in the leaves called chlorophyll uses energy from the Sun to combine carbon dioxide (CO_2) from the air with water from the soil. This produces food in the form of sugars and starches, and oxygen is released.

New leaves growing from axil

PLANT STRUCTURE

During its life, a typical flowering plant, such as this hibiscus, grows a stem, roots, shoots, leaves, flowers, and fruits containing seeds.

Midrib

Vein

AMARYLLIS BULB CROSS SECTION

New plant grows from tip

Fleshy scales store food

Roots anchor plant in soil

Stem supports plant and carries water and minerals from roots to leaves

TUBERS, RHIZOMES, AND BULBS

During the growing season, many plants produce swollen underground tubers, rhizomes, and bulbs to store food in the form of starch for the following growing season.

Root hairs absorb water and minerals from soil

FLOWERS AND FRUITS

FLOWERS help ensure that a
plant is pollinated so that it can
produce seeds and fruit. A fruit is
anything that contains a seed or
seeds, from a coconut to a tomato.

Tough, bumpy surface

POLLEN GRAIN
Microscopic pollen grains,
which look like orange
dust, are produced by a
flower's anthers. A plant
is fertilized when a single
grain lands on the stigma
of the same type of flower.

FLOWER PARTS
The reproductive organs of a flowering
plant are found within the flower.
The flower heads of some plants
have a stamen (male parts) and a pistil
(female), while in others they are
separate.

Filament

*Anther – pollen is made in
pollen sacs inside anther, which
split open when ripe to release
the pollen*

*Stigma – sticky
head for trapping
pollen*

*Stamens – the
male parts of the
flower that consist
of an anther and
a filament*

*Style carries
pollen from the
stigma to the
ovary*

*Pistil – female
parts of the flower
consisting of an
ovary, stigma,
and style*

*Ovary – where
the ova (eggs)
are made.
Once the
ova are
fertilized
the ovary
swells to
become
a fruit*

*Sepal – protects
flower when it
is in bud*

*Petal –
guides insects
to anthers
and stigma*

Pollen sticks to bee's back as insect looks for nectar

Bright, scented petals attract pollinating insects

Stigma

Style

Ovary

Embryo

Micropyle

Pollen grain

Pollen tube

Ovule

Male nucleus

FERTILIZATION OF THE OVA BY POLLEN

POLLINATION AND FERTILIZATION
When pollen lands on a stigma, probably carried there on the back of an insect, it grows a tube that probes into the style and penetrates the ovule (the egg container) via a hole called the micropyle. Two male sex cells from the pollen ease their way through the tube to fertilize the egg.

FRUIT
Once fertilized, the ovary forms seeds then swells to become fruit. If the seeds are spread by animals, the fruit is soft and juicy. If they are spread by the wind, they are hard and dry.

Each segment forms from a single ovary

Seed

Oranges are compound fruits – developed from several ovaries.

Prickly case protects nuts

Nut is seed

Horse chestnuts are nuts – single seeds in a hard, dry case.

A pea pod is a legume – formed from a single ovary.

Fruit wall

A pea is a seed

PEA POD

Pits are seeds

Core is true fruit

Apples are false fruits – the apple is the swollen base of the flower.

Hard pit is seed

Nectarines are drupes – fleshy fruits containing a hard seed.

TREES

TREES ARE WOODY PLANTS, which means they have hard stems and grow for years – often to immense sizes. Leaves can be broad, like oaks and beeches, or narrow, such as pine needles, or palm fronds.

TALLEST TREE
The tallest living tree is a coast redwood in Redwood National Park, California. It soars 365 ft (111.25 m) high, as tall as an Apollo space rocket.

Leaves range from long "needles" like these to short, flat scales.

CONIFERS
Most conifers are evergreen with leaves that last three to four years and often have a dark, waxy skin to help save water.

Most conifers bear their seeds under the scales of hard cones.

Palm trees get their name because leaves are sometimes shaped like a hand

Palm trees are flowering plants

PALM TREES
Palm trees grow mainly in the tropics. They have no branches; instead giant multiple leaves grow from a single point, called the apical bud.

BROAD-LEAVED TREES

Most broad-leaved trees are deciduous, which means they shed their leaves seasonally to save water.

Heartwood

Sapwood

One year's growth

Cambium

Waterproof bark

Many broad-leaved trees can be identified by the shape of their leaves.

Crown

Leaves absorb sunlight and convert it to food

THE TRUNK

The series of rings that can be seen on a sawn log mark each year's growth. The dark center of the tree is dead "heartwood." Around this is paler, living, sapwood with a thin rim, or "cambium," where it grows. Protecting the sapwood is a layer of bark.

Oak trees produce nuts called "acorns" in autumn

COMMON OAK

All broad-leaved trees are flowering plants and bear flowers and fruits.

Single trunk carries nutrients from roots to leaves

TREE FACTS

- Mangroves are the only trees that can grow in salty water.
- The oldest living trees on Earth are 5,000-year-old bristlecone pines of Arizona.

INVERTEBRATES

NINE-TENTHS of all animals are invertebrates, which means they have no backbone. They include jellyfish, sponges, starfish, coral, worms, crabs, spiders, and insects.

Intestine

Body shape maintained by fluid

Dorsal blood vessel

Gizzard (part of stomach)

Ovary

Spermatheca (reproductive organ)

Ventral nerve cord

Mouth

EARTHWORM CROSS-SECTION

Hard shell to protect soft body

Soft body

Eyes on stalks

MOLLUSKS
These soft-bodied invertebrates are often protected by a hard shell. Most mollusks, such as squid and octopuses, clams, mussels, and scallops, live in water, but some, like snails and slugs, live on land.

WORMS
A worm is an animal with a long soft body and no legs. There are many different kinds, including flatworms, tapeworms, earthworms, roundworms, and leeches.

Echinoderms have a five-part body plan.

Arm

Ossicles are hard plates just under the skin that keep the body rigid

STARFISH AND URCHINS
Starfish, sea urchins, and sea cucumbers are all of echinoderms. All are predators, and most have sucker-tipped "tube feet" through which they pump water to move along and feed. The five broad arms of a starfish can wrench open a shellfish to suck out the contents.

Underside of arm is covered with fluid-filled tube feet for moving and feeding

Arm

LIFE CYCLE
Each invertebrate
has its own life
cycle, but most
species lay eggs.
Some go through
several larval
stages; others
hatch as
miniature adults.

Buds break away as free-swimming adults

Jellyfish

Fertilized larva

Polyp divides into eight-part buds

Larva grows into a polyp

SPIDER

ARTHROPODS
Insects, spiders, and lobsters
are all arthropods. They
have jointed limbs and a
tough external skeleton.

CROSS SECTION OF A JELLYFISH

Bell-shaped body

Digestive cavity

Mouth lobe

Tentacle

Mouth

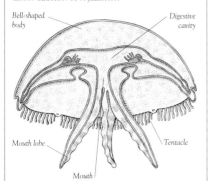

Jellyfish, anemones, and coral are all kinds
of coelenterates – sea creatures with a mouth
surrounded by tentacles. These tentacles
usually carry a stinger to stun or kill prey.
Some coelenterates, called polyps, always
attach to a solid object, such as a rock;
others, called medusas, move by contracting
their bell-shaped bodies.

SPONGES
These primitive sea
creatures feed by drawing
water into the holes
in their soft bodies
and filtering out
any food.

INVERTEBRATE FACTS

• Up to 500 million
hookworms may be
found in a single
human.

• Roundworms are
probably the most
numerous animals
on Earth.

Mollusks

After arthropods, mollusks are the largest group of animals on Earth. There are over 50,000 species, ranging from tiny snails to giant squid as big as sperm whales. Most mollusks, except slugs, squid, cuttlefish, and octopuses, have soft, moist bodies protected by hard shells.

MOLLUSK SHELLS
The shells produced by mollusks are made of layers of calcium carbonate, and form in many shapes, sizes, patterns, and colors.

WHELK

COCKLE SHELLS

ROYAL CLOAK SCALLOP

PACIFIC THORNY OYSTER

Types of Mollusk

GASTROPODS
There are 35,000 species of gastropods, including snails, slugs, and whelks.

CEPHALOPODS
There are 600 species of these complex mollusks including octopus, squid, and cuttlefish.

BIVALVES
There are 8,000 species of these double-shelled mollusks, such as oysters, clams, and cockles.

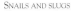

SNAILS AND SLUGS

Slugs and snails are gastropods. They move by a wave of contractions that runs from the rear of the foot to the front, sliding along on a trail of slime. They have soft bodies, but snails are protected by a hard, coiled shell.

Lung Heart Kidney

Mucus gland Mantle

Eye

Shell

Tentacle

Mouth Foot Reproductive organs

GIANT AFRICAN LAND SNAIL

LIFE CYCLE

Mollusks start life as eggs. Many marine mollusks, like this oyster, hatch first as larvae and then develop into adults. Land snails, however, hatch as miniature adults.

Oyster egg

Young adult sinks to seabed and settles in a suitable place

Larva grows larger; shell develops

Free-swimming larva

MOLLUSK FACTS

• Great gray slugs mate for 7–24 hours, hanging from a trail of mucus.

• Giant clams can live for over 200 years.

• Limpets' teeth are so strong that they leave scratch marks on rocks.

TUSK SHELLS
There are 350 species of these rare sea creatures with tusk-shaped shells.

SOLENOGASTERS
There are 5,540 species of these worm-like marine mollusks.

MONOPLACOPHORANS
There are only ten species of these limpets. They live in the depths of the ocean.

CHITONS
There are 500 species of these armor-plated shelled creatures.

INSECTS

INSECTS MAY BE TINY, but there are more of them than all other animals put together. Over five million species, from tiny flies to giant beetles, are known, and there may be over 200 million insects for every human. They have existed for over 400 million years and are found everywhere from the Arctic to the Sahara.

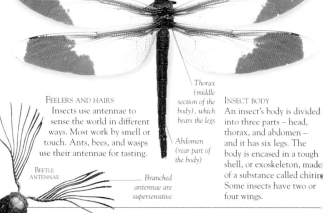

Antenna

WASP'S HEAD

Compound eye

COMPOUND EYES
The compound eyes of most insects have six or more facets. Dragonflies have 30,000 facets in each eye, which help to spot movement.

DRAGONFLY

Compound eye

Head

Veins in wing keep it rigid

Wing

Thorax (middle section of the body), which bears the legs

Abdomen (rear part of the body)

FEELERS AND HAIRS
Insects use antennae to sense the world in different ways. Most work by smell or touch. Ants, bees, and wasps use their antennae for tasting.

BEETLE ANTENNAE

Branched antennae are supersensitive

INSECT BODY
An insect's body is divided into three parts – head, thorax, and abdomen – and it has six legs. The body is encased in a tough shell, or exoskeleton, made of a substance called chitin. Some insects have two or four wings.

COMPLETE METAMORPHOSIS

Insects such as butterflies, beetles, and flies start life as larvae, which hatch from eggs. The larvae then turn into pupae, from which an adult emerges. This process is known as complete metamorphosis. The larva bears no resemblance to the adult it becomes.

Egg / *Caterpillar*

Adult butterfly / *Chrysalis*

WASPS' NEST / *Nest of chewed wood*

INSECT NESTS

Some insects, such as bees, wasps, termites, and ants, live in ordered societies and build elaborate homes.

INCOMPLETE METAMORPHOSIS

Insects such as grasshoppers or damselflies hatch into wingless "nymphs" before molting and growing into adults. This is known as incomplete metamorphosis.

Winged adult emerges from final molt

Egg

Wingless nymph

Nymph grows and molts

Final nymph resembles adult

INSECT FACTS

• A queen termite lays 440 million eggs – one per second for 14 years.

• A bee must visit more than 4,000 flowers to make one tablespoon of honey.

MOLTING

A young insect's tough exoskeleton cannot stretch. Instead it is discarded and replaced with a new one several times. This sequence shows the final molt of a damselfly as it changes from nymph to adult.

Legs grip stem

Old skin

Crinkled wings

Blood pumps into wings

Wing buds

Nymph crawls out of water up a stem

Soft-bodied adult emerges

Adult rests before flying off

Abdomen turns blue

Types of insects

Insects range from fairyfly wasps
only 0.2 mm long, to giant stick
insects, up to 17.7 in (45 cm)
long. They are divided into
32 orders, six of which are shown
here. Other insects include flies,
grasshoppers, earwigs, and fleas.

TERMITES
(ISOPTERA)
2,300 SPECIES

PRAYING MANTIDS
(MANTODEA)
1,800 SPECIES

COCKROACHES
(BLATTODEA)
3,700 SPECIES

ANTS, BEES, WASPS
(HYMENOPTERA)
110,000 SPECIES

BEETLES
(COLEOPTERA)
300,000 SPECIES

Tiny overlapping scales
cover each wing

Sensitive feelers, called antennae, detect
smells, air movement, and vibrations

Forewing

Two pairs of
wings, called
forewings and
hind wings

Hindwing

PEACOCK
BUTTERFLY

BUTTERFLIES AND MOTHS
(LEPIDOPTERA)
136,800 SPECIES

ARACHNIDS

SPIDERS, SCORPIONS, ticks, and mites belong to a group of arthropods called arachnids. There are more than 73,000 species, living in almost every habitat.

Eight jointed legs

CHILEAN RED-LEG SPIDER

Powerful jaws

SPIDERS
All spiders are meat-eaters. Some jump on prey; others trap prey in a web, paralyze it with venom, then eat it.

ARACHNID ANATOMY
Arachnids usually have eight legs and their body is divided into the cephalothorax (front and middle) and the abdomen (rear). Scorpions have six legs and two pincer-like pedipalps for gripping prey.

MITES AND TICKS
(ACARI)
30,000 SPECIES

SPIDERS
(ARANEAE)
40,000 SPECIES

Poisonous sting in the tail for paralyzing prey

Waterproof, flexible outer covering, or exoskeleton

Legs are jointed in several places for flexibility

SCORPION

Powerful claws, called pedipalps, hold on to prey

ARACHNID FACTS

• The biggest arachnid is a bird-eating spider (*Theraphosa leblondi*), with a leg span of 11 in (28 cm).

• The largest web is spun by the tropical orb spider (*Nephila*), and measures up to 10 ft (3 m) across.

CRUSTACEANS

THESE ARTHROPODS get their
name from their crusty skin.
They include lobsters, crabs,
and shrimp, which live in
the sea. Only a few,
such as wood lice,
live on land. There
are more than
55,000 species
of crustacean.

Long antenna, or feeler

Sawlike pincer for
cutting up prey

Compound eyes on
stalks for spotting prey

Blunt pincer for
gripping and
crushing prey

Hard body case, or
carapace, protects
internal organs

Tail allows
lobster to swim
backward to
escape
danger

Lobsters and
crabs have ten
legs and are
called decapods

EUROPEAN
LOBSTER

ANATOMY OF A LOBSTER
Lobsters have a tough body
case, or carapace, two long
antennae, and a pair of
compound eyes on
stalks for spotting prey.
Lobsters also have large, strong
pincers for gripping victims and
pulling them apart.

DECORATOR CRAB

CRAB CAMOUFLAGE
Most crabs are sand-colored to
make them less visible on the
seabed. This decorator crab covers
its whole body with plants and sea
creatures to disguise itself completely.

CRABS

Most crabs have a hard, shieldlike shell called a carapace for defense. The flexible abdomen is usually tucked underneath for protection. Crabs move by scuttling sideways.

Huge pincers for gripping and tearing food

Hard outer shell, called the carapace

FURROWED CRAB

Jointed legs with clawed toes

LIFE CYCLE

Crustaceans begin life as eggs, which are usually laid in water. After the eggs hatch, they pass through several larval stages before taking on their adult form. As adults, they grow bigger by molting, or shedding their outer layer.

Adult shrimp

Egg

Egg hatches into first larval stage

LIFE CYCLE OF A SHRIMP

Final post-larval stage

Second larval stage

CRUSTACEAN FACTS

• The largest crustacean is the Japanese spider crab (*Macrocheira kaempferi*), with a leg span of almost 13 ft (4 m).

• The smallest crustaceans are tiny water fleas (*Alonella*), which measure less than 0.25 mm long.

VERTEBRATES

GORILLA
SKELETON

ONLY ABOUT three percent of all
animals have backbones, and these
are called vertebrates. There are
more than 40,000 different species
of vertebrates, divided into
classes of mammals, birds, fish,
reptiles, and amphibians. Their
sense organs and nervous systems
are well developed, and they have
adapted to almost every habitat.

BACKBONE
Vertebrates have a skeleton
of bone, with a backbone,
two pairs of limbs, and a
skull that protects the brain.
Inside are the heart,
lungs, and other organs.

REPTILES
Lizards, snakes, crocodiles, and geckos
are reptiles. They all have a tough,
scaly skin. Young reptiles hatch
from eggs, and look like
tiny versions of their
parents. This chameleon
is a type of lizard.

*Spines along
backbone give
protection
from attack*

*Scaly
skin*

*Female frog lays eggs,
called frogspawn*

MADAGASCAN
CHAMELEON

*Male
fertilizes
spawn*

ANIMAL REPRODUCTION
In vertebrates, offspring are created when
males and females come together and the
male's sperm join the female's eggs.
This is called sexual reproduction,
and usually involves
mating. A few animals are
neither male nor female,
and they reproduce asexually.

*Prehensile
tail for
holding onto
branches*

SENSES

Mammals and other vertebrate animals have senses to help them find their way, locate food, and avoid enemies. For land animals, such as this caracal, sight, hearing, and smell are the most important senses. Sea creatures rely more on smell and taste to escape danger and find food.

Sharp eyesight for hunting, even at night

Long, sensitive ears pick up even the faintest sounds

Strong sense of smell

Sharp teeth

CARACAL

FISH

With streamlined bodies covered in slippery scales, these vertebrates are perfectly suited to life in the water.

TWINSPOT WRASSE

Scales covered in slimy mucus

BIRDS

The only animals that have feathers are birds, and most of them are powerful fliers. Birds have a beak, or bill, instead of teeth, and all reproduce by laying eggs.

COUNT RAGGI'S BIRD OF PARADISE

RED-EYED TREE FROG

Large eyes spot prey

AMPHIBIANS

Frogs, toads, newts, and salamanders are amphibians. These vertebrates spend part of their lives in water and part on land. They all reproduce by laying eggs.

Long legs for jumping

PORCUPINE

Spiny quills protect body

Fur helps keep body warm

MAMMAL

A mammal is usually covered by fur or hair. It gives birth to live young, which it feeds with milk.

AMPHIBIANS

THERE ARE more than 4,200
species of amphibians. They
begin life in water as fish-
like tadpoles, after hatching
from clusters of eggs called
spawn. Soon the tadpoles
grow legs and lungs for life
on land. Young amphibians
breathe using gills, and the
adults can breathe through
their skin.

TIGER SALAMANDER

Damp skin absorbs oxygen

Bright warning spots

NEWTS AND SALAMANDERS
Salamanders have long bodies,
short, thin legs, and cylindrical
tails. They usually spend their
adult life on land and breathe
by absorbing oxygen through
their damp skin. The bright color
of their skin is a warning to predators.

Large, bulging eyes for spotting prey

Round external eardrum called a tympanum

Thick, bumpy skin covered with warts

Squat body

FROGS AND TOADS
Both frogs and toads have
short, compact bodies, and
strong back legs for jumping
long distances. As they grow
up from tadpole to adult, they
lose their tails. There is no clear
distinction between frogs and toads,
but frogs tend to spend more of
their life in or near water, while
toads can survive in
damp spots on
land, returning to
water to breed.

Feet are webbed for swimming

EUROPEAN COMMON TOAD

Adult has no gills

Egg

Tadpole has gills

LIFE CYCLE OF A NEWT

Back legs appear

Front legs appear

LIFE CYCLE OF AN AMPHIBIAN
Amphibians lay their eggs in water; the eggs are not waterproof and would dry out on land. After a week or so, the eggs hatch into tadpoles, and these become strong swimmers. In newts, the front legs appear about three weeks after hatching. The back legs appear at seven to eight weeks. Finally, the gills disappear and the newt metamorphoses (changes) into an adult.

MIDWIFE TOAD
The female midwife toad lays about 50 eggs. After the male has fertilized the eggs, he carries them on his back for up to one-and-a-half months until they are ready to hatch.

Male wraps eggs around back legs

MIDWIFE TOAD (MALE)

Vivid colors act as warning signal to predators

DEADLY POISONS
Some amphibians produce powerful poisons from glands in their skin. These creatures are often brightly colored to warn predators of the danger. Poison-dart frogs are the most poisonous amphibians.

POISON-DART FROG

Patches of green complete the toad's disguise

YELLOW-BELLIED TOAD

AMPHIBIAN CAMOUFLAGE
Some amphibians manage to avoid predators by the unusual colors and patterns on their bodies. This yellow-bellied toad hardly shows up against tree bark.

REPTILES

SCALY-SKINNED crocodiles,
lizards, and snakes are all reptiles.
There are almost 6,000 species.
Reptiles are found on land and in
water, but they cannot live in cold
places because they need the sun's
warmth to give them energy.

EGGS
Most reptiles hatch from
eggs with thick, leathery
shells that stop them from
drying out. Some reptiles
are "viviparous," giving
birth to live young.

IGUANA
These large American
lizards often have a
crest on their backs

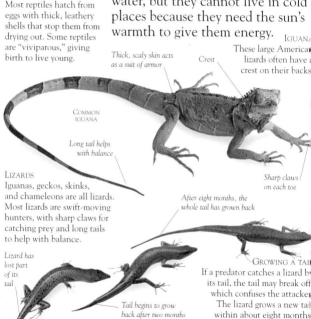

Thick, scaly skin acts
as a suit of armor

Crest

COMMON
IGUANA

Long tail helps
with balance

LIZARDS
Iguanas, geckos, skinks,
and chameleons are all lizards.
Most lizards are swift-moving
hunters, with sharp claws for
catching prey and long tails
to help with balance.

Sharp claws
on each toe

After eight months, the
whole tail has grown back

Lizard has
lost part
of its
tail

Tail begins to grow
back after two months

GROWING A TAIL
If a predator catches a lizard by
its tail, the tail may break off,
which confuses the attacker.
The lizard grows a new tail
within about eight months.

Shell made of horn

STARRED TORTOISE SHELL

TURTLES AND TORTOISES
Tortoises, turtles, and terrapins
are called chelonians. They have
a hard shell made of bony
plates. By hiding inside the
shell they can escape most
predators, so they do not need
to move quickly. Tortoises live
on land and terrapins and turtles
live in water.

RED-EARED TERRAPIN

Cobra inflates hood to make itself appear bigger

MONOCLED COBRA

Long, thin body

SNAKES
Snakes are
long, legless
reptiles. They hunt
prey by smelling the air with their
forked tongue. Constrictors such
as pythons coil around prey and
suffocate them. Venomous
snakes such as this cobra stun or
kill their prey with poison from
hollow teeth called fangs.

REPTILE FACTS

• A giant turtle found
in Mauritius in 1766
survived for another
152 years.

• The venom glands
of the Australian
taipan snake hold
enough poison to
kill 200 people.

CROCODILES AND ALLIGATORS
Alligators, crocodiles,
caimans, and gavials are
called crocodilians.
These hunters with
huge jaws and
sharp teeth live
in tropical
swamps and
rivers.

Crocodile swims by waving its flattened tail

Peglike teeth for tearing flesh apart

Female carries young in her mouth and guards them until they can fend for themselves

Short, strong legs

ESTUARINE CROCODILE

FISH

THERE ARE more than 20,000
species of fish, all of which live
in water from deep oceans to
ponds, rivers, and lakes. Most
fish have streamlined, scaly
bodies, fins for swimming,
and gills for breathing. They
reproduce by laying eggs.

Water flows into mouth

Gill rakers strain water

Water flows over gills

HOW FISH BREATHE
Fish are able to breathe underwater
using their gills. As water flows
over the gills, oxygen passes into
the bloodstream through special
thin skins called membranes.

BONY FISH
The largest group of fish includes carp
and other bony fish. These fish have
bony skeletons and an internal air bag
called the swim bladder that keeps
them afloat in the water.

Dorsal fin

Scales

Eye

Mouth

Caudal fin

Gill cover

CARP

Anal fin

Pelvic fin

Pectoral fin

HOW CARTILAGINOUS FISH SWIM
A cartilaginous fish, such as a dogfish,
swims by swinging its tail in an "S"
shape; it steers by waving its pectoral
and pelvic fins. The dorsal fin helps
keep the fish upright as it swims. Bony
fish swim by moving their fins only.

Tail

Head

First
dorsal fin

Pelvic fin

*The fish swings its head to the right, and an
S-shaped wave begins to travel along the body.*

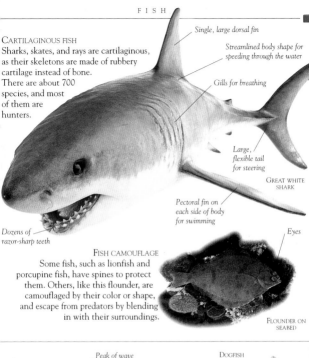

CARTILAGINOUS FISH
Sharks, skates, and rays are cartilaginous, as their skeletons are made of rubbery cartilage instead of bone. There are about 700 species, and most of them are hunters.

Single, large dorsal fin

Streamlined body shape for speeding through the water

Gills for breathing

Large, flexible tail for steering

GREAT WHITE SHARK

Pectoral fin on each side of body for swimming

Dozens of razor-sharp teeth

FISH CAMOUFLAGE
Some fish, such as lionfish and porcupine fish, have spines to protect them. Others, like this flounder, are camouflaged by their color or shape, and escape from predators by blending in with their surroundings.

Eyes

FLOUNDER ON SEABED

Peak of wave

Peak of wave

The peak of the wave reaches the area of pelvic and first dorsal fins.

The peak of the wave is now between the two dorsal fins, and the tail thrusts to the right.

DOGFISH

Peak of wave

The peak of the wave reaches the tail, and the fish's head swings for the next wave.

BIRDS

RED-TAILED MINLA

FROM THE TINY BEE hummingbird, which weighs only 0.056 oz (1.6 g), to the ostrich, which weighs up to 344 lb (156 kg) and grows up to 8.9 ft (2.7 m) tall, birds are the only animals with feathers. They also have wings and beaks, and most are expert fliers. Birds reproduce by laying eggs.

Wing size and shape depends on a bird's lifestyle

Wing feathers spread in flight to give lift

Beak made of bone covered by layer of horn

BIRDS IN FLIGHT
Birds fly by flapping their wings, or by gliding. Each bird has its own flight pattern. Small birds have a bouncing flight, and glide between flaps to save energy. Larger birds fly level and flap their wings all the time. Some birds take to the air for a few minutes at a time; others stay airborne for weeks or even months.

Tail helps bird to balance and change direction

Scaly, clawed feet for gripping branches

FROM EGG TO CHICK
As a chick develops inside an egg, the parent birds sit on the egg to keep it warm. This is called incubation. Small birds incubate their eggs for two weeks, eagles for seven weeks, and albatrosses for eleven weeks.

The chick hatches by pecking the shell with the "egg tooth" on its bill.

The chick pecks a circle around the top of the egg and pushes.

Flight feathers in wings and tail enable bird to fly

Body feathers overlap and keep bird waterproof

Down feathers trap warm air next to the skin

FEATHERS

A bird's feathers keep it warm and enable it to fly. Feathers are light yet strong because each strand is linked together with hooks called barbs and barbules.

Tail feathers are extra long for steering, balancing, and braking

NESTS AND YOUNG

Most birds build nests. A nest keeps the eggs warm and safe until they are ready to hatch, and provides a home for the newly hatched young. Each bird species has its own way of building a nest. Magpies build nests of twigs in trees; weaverbirds weave elaborate nests from grass.

NESTLINGS

CHICK EMERGING FROM EGG

The top of the shell breaks off and the chick struggles free. Its feathers are still wet.

The fluffy down soon dries out and will be replaced by feathers as the chick grows.

Types of birds

Birds have adapted to life in almost all parts of the world. Some, like birds of prey, are meateaters, while others eat only seeds and fruits. There are at least 9,000 species divided into 28 orders.

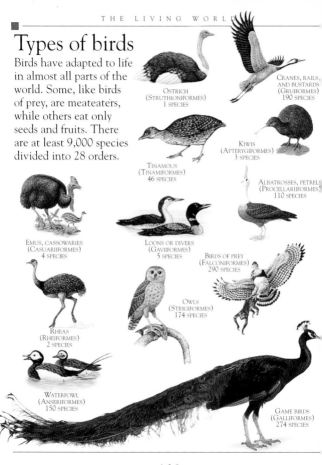

OSTRICH
(STRUTHIONIFORMES)
1 SPECIES

CRANES, RAILS
AND BUSTARDS
(GRUIFORMES)
190 SPECIES

KIWIS
(APTERYGIFORMES)
3 SPECIES

TINAMOUS
(TINAMIFORMES)
46 SPECIES

ALBATROSSES, PETREL
(PROCELLARIIFORMES)
110 SPECIES

EMUS, CASSOWARIES
(CASUARIIFORMES)
4 SPECIES

LOONS OR DIVERS
(GAVIIFORMES)
5 SPECIES

BIRDS OF PREY
(FALCONIFORMES)
290 SPECIES

OWLS
(STRIGIFORMES)
174 SPECIES

RHEAS
(RHEIFORMES)
2 SPECIES

WATERFOWL
(ANSERIFORMES)
150 SPECIES

GAME BIRDS
(GALLIFORMES)
274 SPECIES

SHOREBIRDS,
GULLS,
TERNS, AUKS
(CHARADRIIFORMES)
337 SPECIES

PELICANS, GANNETS,
CORMORANTS
(PELECANIFORMES)
55 SPECIES

PARROTS, LORIES, COCKATOOS
(PSITTACIFORMES)
342 SPECIES

MOUSEBIRDS
(COLIIFORMES)
6 SPECIES

HERONS,
STORKS, IBISES
(CICONIIFORMES)
117 SPECIES

NIGHTJARS, FROGMOUTHS
(CAPRIMULGIFORMES)
109 SPECIES

PASSERINES
(PASSERIFORMES)
5,414 SPECIES

KINGFISHERS,
E-EATERS, HOOPOES
CORACIIFORMES)
204 SPECIES

SANDGROUSE
(PTEROCLIDIFORMES)
16 SPECIES

SWIFTS,
HUMMINGBIRDS
(APODIFORMES)
429 SPECIES

CUCKOOS,
TURACOS
(CUCULIFORMES)
159 SPECIES

PIGEONS
(COLUMBIFORMES)
300 SPECIES

GREBES
ODICIPEDIFORMES)
21 SPECIES

WOODPECKERS,
TOUCANS, BARBETS
(PICIFORMES)
381 SPECIES

TROGONS
(TROGONIFORMES)
39 SPECIES

PENGUINS
(SPHENISCIFORMES)
18 SPECIES

MAMMALS

DOLPHIN

ALL MAMMALS are warm-
blooded animals, so their blood is
always at the correct temperature for
their body processes to work well.
To keep warm, mammals usually have
thick fur or a layer of fat or blubber.
Mammals are found all over the world,
on land, in water, and even in the air.

CARNIVORES
Some mammals are carnivores (meateaters), and most carnivores are hunters.
The deadliest hunters of the mammal
world are the big cats, such as lions, tigers,
cheetahs, and leopards. They have strong,
agile bodies for chasing
prey, and sharp claws
and teeth for
killing it.

SEA MAMMAL
Whales and dolphins spend their live
in the sea and come to the surface to
breathe. They are called cetaceans

Exceller
hearin

Good sens
of sight an
sme

*Striped pattern
camouflages
tiger in long
grass*

*Body covered in
fur for warmth*

INDIAN TIGER

*Powerful,
low-slung
body*

Massive pau
and sharp clau
can strike
fatal blo

110

HERBIVORES

Mammals that eat only plants are called herbivores. Some herbivores, such as giraffes, browse on the buds of bushes and trees. Others, including zebras and cattle, graze on grass. Herbivores often have special teeth for grinding plant matter.

GUERNSEY COW

Tiny newborn kangaroo crawls into pouch

MARSUPIALS

Kangaroos, koalas, and other marsupial mammals have a pouch into which their newborn baby crawls. The young animal lives in its mother's pouch until it is fully developed and able to fend for itself.

GRAY KANGAROO

MONOTREMES

Platypuses such as this Australian duck-billed platypus are the only mammals that lay eggs.

Young kangaroos are called joeys

Kittens feed on their mother's milk

MOTHER'S MILK

Mammals are the only animals to feed their young on milk, produced in the mother's body. Milk is nourishing, and it contains substances that protect the young from disease.

Types of mammals

Mammals range from Kitti's
long-nosed bat, which is
the size of a bee, to the
massive blue whale, which is
the size of a jumbo jet. There
are more than 4,600 species
of mammals, found all over
the world. Mammals
are divided into 21
orders, shown here.

TREE SHREWS
(SCANDENTIA)
19 SPECIES

APES, MONKEYS, LEMURS
(PRIMATES)
233 SPECIES

ELEPHANT SHREWS
(MACROSCELIDIA)
15 SPECIES

MONOTREMES
(MONOTREMATA)
3 SPECIES

PANGOLINS
(PHOLIDOTA)
7 SPECIES

RODENTS
(RODENTIA)
2,021 SPECIES

MARSUPIALS
(MARSUPIALIA)
272 SPECIES

SEALS, SEA LIONS, WALRUSES
(PINNIPEDIA)
34 SPECIES

SEA COWS
(SIRENIA)
5 SPECIES

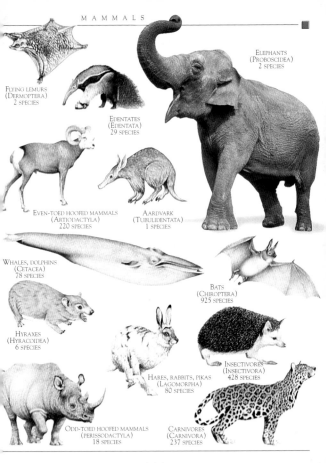

FLYING LEMURS
(DERMOPTERA)
2 SPECIES

ELEPHANTS
(PROBOSCIDEA)
2 SPECIES

EDENTATES
(EDENTATA)
29 SPECIES

EVEN-TOED HOOFED MAMMALS
(ARTIODACTYLA)
220 SPECIES

AARDVARK
(TUBULIDENTATA)
1 SPECIES

WHALES, DOLPHINS
(CETACEA)
78 SPECIES

BATS
(CHIROPTERA)
925 SPECIES

HYRAXES
(HYRACOIDEA)
6 SPECIES

HARES, RABBITS, PIKAS
(LAGOMORPHA)
80 SPECIES

INSECTIVORES
(INSECTIVORA)
428 SPECIES

ODD-TOED HOOFED MAMMALS
(PERISSODACTYLA)
18 SPECIES

CARNIVORES
(CARNIVORA)
237 SPECIES

THE HUMAN BODY

BODY SYSTEMS

THE HUMAN BODY is an amazingly complex organism made up of 50 trillion microscopic cells. There are more than 200 kinds of cell, all organized into a dozen or so body systems, each with its own function. Here are the major systems that are common to all humans

Skeleton is made of 206 bones

Skull protects brain

Skeletal (voluntary) muscles are attached to bones

Backbone supports head and limbs

Skin retains body moisture

SKELETAL SYSTEM
The skeleton is the rigid framework of bone that supports the body and protects its internal organs.

MUSCULAR SYSTEM
Every movement of the body (both involuntary and voluntary) is caused by muscles contracting.

INTEGUMENTARY SYSTEM
This system consists of the skin, hair, and nails. Skin and hair cover the body, and help to protect it.

RESPIRATORY
SYSTEM
This takes
oxygenated
air into the
lungs and
pushes out
waste gases.

DIGESTIVE
SYSTEM
The digestive
tract breaks
down and
absorbs food,
and gets rid of
solid waste.

URINARY
SYSTEM
This filters
soluble
wastes from
the blood
for disposal
as urine.

*Nerves transmit
signals to and
from brain, the
body's control
center*

*Heart constantly
pumps blood
around body*

*Endocrine
organs, such
as the
pancreas,
produce
hormones
(chemical
messengers)*

*Blood
circulates
through body
in blood
vessels*

*Blood pumped around the
body by the heart supplies*

*Lymph nodes
filter lymph
and cleanse
it of infection*

NERVES AND HORMONES
The nervous system and
hormones coordinate all
the body systems and
direct our actions.

CARDIOVASCULAR SYSTEM
Blood pumped around the
body by the heart supplies
tissues with oxygen and
removes waste products.

LYMPHATIC SYSTEM
Lymph, containing
immune cells, is
collected by a network
of lymph vessels.

BONES AND TEETH

THE INNER FRAMEWORK of the human body consists of interconnecting bones that form the skeleton. Without a skeleton we could not stand or move.

- Cranium (skull)
- Clavicle (collarbone)
- Scapula (shoulder blade)
- Humerus (upper arm bone)
- Vertebrae (spine)
- Radius (forearm bone)
- Ulna (forearm bone)
- Carpals (wrist bones)
- Coccyx (tailbone)
- Phalanges (finger bones)
- Rib
- Femur (thigh bone)
- Tibia (shinbone)
- Patella (kneecap)
- Tarsals (ankle bones)
- Fibula (calf bone)
- Metatarsals (foot bones)

- Hard, compact, outer bone
- Spongy bone
- Fatty bone marrow

BONE STRUCTURE
The hardest part of a bone is the outer layer, containing calcium and phosphorus. Inside long bones there is a soft, living tissue called marrow. Yellow marrow stores fat, and red marrow forms blood cells.

SKELETON FACTS
- The femur is the longest, strongest bone.
- A woman's pelvic bones are shallower and wider than a man's to allow childbirth.

SKELETON
The skeleton supports and protects delicate internal organs such as the brain, lungs, and heart. It also provides strong, fixed points of attachment for the muscles.

JOINTS

Where bones meet, a joint forms. In a mobile joint, the bone surface is coated with slippery cartilage and is lubricated with synovial fluid. Most joints are held together by cords called ligaments.

Interlocking bones do not move.

FIXED (SKULL)

Ball-and-socket joints move in all directions.

BALL-AND-SOCKET (SHOULDER, HIP)

Hinged joints move in only one plane.

HINGED (ELBOW, KNEE)

UPPER JAW

Canines (4)

Canines are pointed for gripping food

Incisors bite off chunks of food

Wisdom teeth are also molars

LOWER JAW

Premolars and molars grind and crush food

Molars (12)

Premolars (8)

Incisors (8)

TEETH

Humans have two sets of teeth. Children lose their first "baby" teeth when they are about six years old. These are gradually replaced by a second, permanent set of 32 teeth, each with a different job to do.

Enamel protects the surface of the tooth

Dentine is bonelike layer

Crown

Neck

Root

Pulp is soft tissue inside the tooth that contains blood vessels and nerves

Gum

Jawbone

Cementum is a hard substance that anchors the tooth to its root

Blood vessels

Nerve

TOOTH STRUCTURE

Teeth are harder than bone, and consist of several layers. The enamel is the hardest substance in the body, and forms the tough, nonliving exterior surface of the tooth. The dentine is the living tissue that gives the tooth its shape. The pulp contains vessels that bring blood to the tooth, enabling it to live and grow.

MUSCLES

ALL THE body's functions are controlled by muscles, which convert chemical energy into movement. We consciously control voluntary muscles, but involuntary muscles work automatically.

MUSCLE USE

When muscles are used, they warm up, providing the body with about one-fifth of its heat. Regular exercise increases the flow of blood to the muscles. This keeps them toned and makes them grow in size.

Frontalis raises eyebrows

Trapezius brace shoulder

Serratus anterior pulls shoulder around

Pectoralis major rotates arm

Deltoid raises and tilts upper arm

Biceps branchii bends lower arm and clenches fist

Rectus abdominis pulls in abdominal wall

Sartorius bends hip and knee and twists thigh

Quadriceps femoris bends hip and straightens knee

Tibialis anterior raises foot

Gastrocnemius bends knee and lifts heel

TENDONS

Skeletal muscles are attached to bones at either end by tough cords called tendons.

Tendon of biceps femoris muscle at back of knee

Achilles tendon

MUSCLE ACTION

A muscle can pull, not push, because it works by contracting. Muscles often work in pairs. A "flexor" muscle flexes, or bends a joint, and an "extensor" muscle straightens it again.

To raise the lower arm the biceps contracts

The contracting muscle is called the agonist.

Triceps relaxes

To lower the arm, the triceps contracts and the biceps relaxes

The relaxing muscle is called the antagonist.

MUSCLE STRUCTURE

Voluntary muscles consist of bundles of cells called myofibers. Inside are strands of myofibrils containing the proteins actin and myosin. In a contracting muscle, the myosin filaments overlap, making the muscle shorter.

Contracted myofibril *Relaxed myofibril*

Myofibril

Myofiber

Bundle of myofibers

MUSCLE FACTS

• There are more than 600 different voluntary muscles in the body.

• Muscles make up 40 percent of a person's total weight.

• The largest muscle is the gluteus maximus, in the buttock.

TYPES OF MUSCLES

The three types of muscles are skeletal, cardiac, and smooth.

Skeletal muscles enable the body to move.

Cardiac muscles are found only in the heart and cause it to contract rhythmically.

Smooth muscles perform automatic tasks such as propelling food through the stomach and gut.

Skeletal muscle attached to bone

Cardiac muscle in the heart

Smooth muscle in the stomach

SKELETAL MUSCLES

CARDIAC MUSCLES

SMOOTH MUSCLES

SKIN, NAILS, AND HAIR

THE SKIN is the body's waterproof coat, protecting it from the outside world and preventing it from drying out. It is also a sense organ, sensitive to touch, pressure, warmth, and pain. The skin produces nails, which shield the tips of fingers and toes, and hair, to provide extra warmth and protection.

SKIN STRUCTURE

The skin has two main layers. The thin, tough, outer epidermis consists mostly of dead cells that are constantly shed and replaced by new skin cells. The thick, living inner dermis layer contains nerves, blood vessels, sense receptors, glands, and hair follicles.

Each hair is coated with dead cells

Movement of hair gives sensation of touch

Outer layers of epidermis consist of dead cells made of a hard protein called keratin

Hair erector muscle makes hair stand on end in the cold to help trap warmth

BLOOD CLOTTING

When skin is cut, the damaged blood vessels bleed. White blood cells fight infection. Fibrin threads bind small, sticky blood cells (platelets) together to form a clot. This clot dries as a scab.

Damaged blood vessel

White blood cells attack germs

Scab forms a protective layer over wound

Fibrin threads bind platelets together to stop blood flow

Sebaceous glands make sebum (oil) to keep hair and skin supple

Hair follicle

Sweat glands produce sweat to help keep the skin cool

NAIL STRUCTURE
The dead tissue made from a tough protein called keratin forms our nails. Keratin is made by living cells at the base and side of each nail, which are protected by folds of skin called cuticles.

Finger bone

Cuticle

Nail

Nail root

HAIR STRUCTURE
Head and body hair consists of tubes of keratin, which grows from roots in the skin called follicles.

Epidermis is made of layers of dead and living cells

Basal layer of epidermis makes new cells

HAIR TYPES
Hair is straight, wavy, or curly, depending on the shape of the hair follicle.

Curly hair

OVAL FOLLICLE

Straight hair

Wavy hair

FLAT FOLLICLE   ROUND FOLLICLE

Dermis

Blood vessels expand to help heat loss when body is hot

Layer of subcutaneous fat insulates body

Pain, pressure, warmth, and touch receptors

SKIN FACTS
• The skin is the body's largest organ.

• In a normal lifespan, the body sheds 40 lb (18 kg) of skin.

• Household dust is mainly dead skin.

• About 80 scalp hairs fall out every day.

BRAIN AND NERVES

THE NERVOUS SYSTEM is a dense, branching network of nerve fibers. It coordinates the body's actions and sends a never-ending stream of sense data to the brain.

BRAIN STRUCTURE
The human brain is a complex network of nerve cells linked to the rest of the body via the cranial nerves and spinal cord. The brain has two halves, or hemispheres. Each controls the *opposite* side of the body.

Touch   Vision

Skilled movement

Behavior and emotion

Speech

Hearing

Taste

SENSORY AREAS
Parts of the brain are specialized. "Sensory" areas receive and interpret data from sense organs; "motor" areas control voluntary muscles.

Cerebrum is a folde mass of nerves whe conscious activit takes plac

Thalamus transmits nerve signals between brain and spinal cord

Hypothalamus controls hunger, thirst, body temperature, sleeping, and waking

Pituitary gland sends out hormones (chemical messengers) that stimulate other glands to release hormones

Brain stem, or medulla, controls basic bodily functions such as breathing and heart rate

Cerebellu works subconsciou to coordinate all o body movemen

Spinal cord

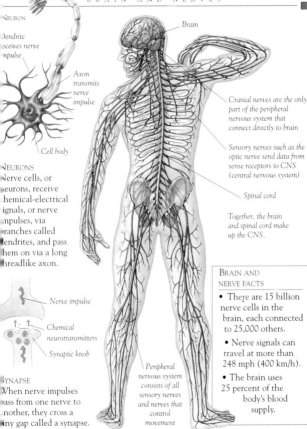

NEURON

Dendrite
receives nerve
impulse

Axon
transmits
nerve
impulse

Cell body

NEURONS
Nerve cells, or
neurons, receive
chemical-electrical
signals, or nerve
impulses, via
branches called
dendrites, and pass
them on via a long
threadlike axon.

Nerve impulse

Chemical
neurotransmitters

Synaptic knob

SYNAPSE
When nerve impulses
pass from one nerve to
another, they cross a
tiny gap called a synapse.

Brain

Cranial nerves are the only
part of the peripheral
nervous system that
connect directly to brain

Sensory nerves such as the
optic nerve send data from
sense receptors to CNS
(central nervous system)

Spinal cord

Together, the brain
and spinal cord make
up the CNS.

Peripheral
nervous system
consists of all
sensory nerves
and nerves that
control
movement

BRAIN AND
NERVE FACTS

• There are 15 billion
nerve cells in the
brain, each connected
to 25,000 others.

• Nerve signals can
travel at more than
248 mph (400 km/h).

• The brain uses
25 percent of the
body's blood
supply.

SIGHT

AT THE FRONT of each eye is a lens system that projects an image onto the lining of the eye, called the retina. Millions of light-sensitive cells in the retina, called rods and cones, respond to the image and send signals to the brain.

Tear duct

Tear gland

TEARS

The tear glands above each eye continually produce tears. Tears keep the eyes moist and clean. Excess tears are drained down into the nose via the tear ducts.

Sclera

Muscle ring controls lens

Lens focuses image

Pupil lets light in

Cornea projects image

Aqueous humor is watery

Iris controls size of pupil

Retina contains light-sensitive rods and cones

Vitreous humor is jellylike

Optic nerve leads to brain

Choroid consists of blood vessels

EYES

The eyeball is divided into two chambers on either side of the lens. One chamber is filled with aqueous humor, the other with vitreous humor. The casing consists of three layers: the sclera (the white of the eye), the choroid, and the retina.

EYE FACTS

• Rods respond to light but not color.

• Cones respond to color but not without light.

• Most people blink about 15 times a minute.

HEARING

SOUND CONSISTS of tiny vibrations in the air. We hear sound because the ear amplifies the vibrations, channeling them toward sensitive hairs in the inner ear. These hairs are stimulated by the vibrations and send signals to the brain.

EAR FACTS
- The ear canal is about 1 in (2.5 cm) in length.
- Humans can detect 1,500 different tones.
- The sensation of ears "popping" is caused by air pressure equalized in the middle ear.

EARS
The ear consists of three parts – the outer ear (including the pinna and the ear canal), the middle ear (including the eardrum and ossicles), and the inner ear (including the cochlea).

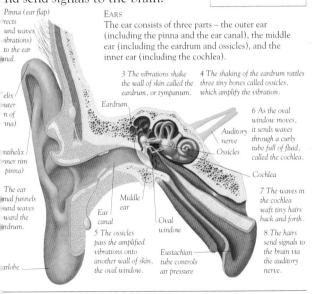

Pinna (ear flap) directs sound waves (vibrations) to the ear canal.

Helix (outer rim of pinna)

Antihelix (inner rim of pinna)

The ear canal funnels sound waves toward the eardrum.

Earlobe

3 The vibrations shake the wall of skin called the eardrum, or tympanum.

Eardrum

Middle ear

Ear canal

5 The ossicles pass the amplified vibrations onto another wall of skin, the oval window.

Oval window

Eustachian tube controls air pressure

4 The shaking of the eardrum rattles three tiny bones called ossicles, which amplify the vibration.

Auditory nerve

Ossicles

6 As the oval window moves, it sends waves through a curly tube full of fluid, called the cochlea.

Cochlea

7 The waves in the cochlea waft tiny hairs back and forth.

8 The hairs send signals to the brain via the auditory nerve.

TASTE

THE SENSES OF taste and smell are closely related, and work together to help us identify flavors. The microscopic chemical receptor cells on the tongue, called taste buds, are the main organs of taste.

TONGUE SURFACE MAGNIFIED

TONGUE
This muscular structure is used in talking, eating, and tasting. It is covered with taste buds which can detect sweet, sour, bitter, and salty flavors.

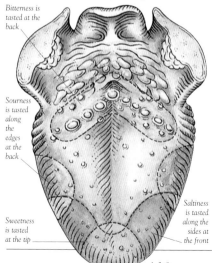

Bitterness is tasted at the back

Sourness is tasted along the edges at the back

Sweetness is tasted at the tip

Saltiness is tasted along the sides at the front

Pore   Tongue tissue

Nerve fibers   Taste bud recepto

TASTE BUDS
There are about 10,000 taste buds on the tongue surface. Each taste bud contains 10–20 receptors. Chemicals dissolved in saliva reach these taste receptors through pores.

TASTE FACTS
• Babies have taste buds all over the inside of their mouths.
• Taste bud cells last only a week before they are renewed.

128

SMELL

THE SENSE of smell detects chemicals in the air. These chemicals dissolve in the nasal mucus inside the nose and stimulate hairlike endings on the olfactory bulb. The fine hairs are so sensitive that they can detect even faint traces of chemicals.

There are five million receptors in the olfactory area

Fine hairs, or cilia, on the olfactory bulb are sensitive to the chemicals in mucus

15,000 fibers in the olfactory nerve send messages to the brain

NOSE
The septum divides the nose into two nostrils, each lined with hairs and membranes that secrete sticky mucus. Smell relies on the olfactory area at the top of the nose.

Nose warms and moistens air before it reaches the lungs

Nasal hairs filter out large particles as they are breathed in

Chemicals from the air dissolve in mucus before they reach smell receptors

Age 20
82%

SMELL CAPABILITY

Age 60
38%

Age 80
28%

LOSS OF SENSITIVITY
Babies are very sensitive to smells, which may help them to identify their mother. But as we grow older, our sensitivity to smell diminishes, as this chart shows.

SMELL FACTS

• Humans can identify about 3,000 different smells.

• Smell is processed by the part of the brain that also deals with taste, memory, and emotions.

LUNGS AND BREATHING

OXYGEN IS VITAL to every cell in the body. Without it, brain cells die in minutes. To keep up the supply of oxygen, we breathe air continuously into the lungs. From there the oxygen enters the bloodstream.

LUNGS

LUNG STRUCTURE

Humans have two lungs, each protected by the rib cage. As we breathe in, air rushes down the trachea (windpipe), and into the lungs via two branches, called bronchi. From there, air spreads through the smaller bronchioles. Around the end of each bronchiole are bunches of air sacs called alveoli.

Left lung has two lobes

OXYGEN EXCHANGE

As the air enters the alveoli, it seeps through the thin walls into the bloodstream. At the same time, carbon dioxide seeps from the blood back into the lungs, to be breathed out.

Bronchioles

Trachea, or windpipe, leads to lungs

Larynx consists of cartilage and contai vocal cords

Right lung h three lob

Bronchi

The base of each lung rests on the muscular diaphragm

Network of tiny capillary blood vessels

Each lung has 700 million microscopic alveoli, or air sacs

BREATHING

Lungs expand, drawing in air

Intercostal muscles contract

Lungs contract, forcing air out

Intercostal muscles relax

Ribs lift upward and outward

Ribs move downward and in

Diaphragm returns to natural arch shape

Diaphragm contracts and flattens

INHALATION

When we breathe in, the diaphragm contracts and the rib cage expands. Pressure in the chest cavity drops and draws air into the lungs.

EXHALATION

When we breathe out, the diaphragm and the rib cage relax. Pressure in the chest cavity rises and pushes air out of the lungs.

COMPOSITION OF INHALED AIR

Oxygen 21%

Nitrogen 78%

Carbon dioxide 0.03%

COMPOSITION OF EXHALED AIR

Oxygen 16%

Nitrogen 79%

Carbon dioxide 5%

AIR COMPOSITION

Every minute, we breathe in and out about 13 pints (6.5 liters) of air containing oxygen, nitrogen, and carbon dioxide. The air that we exhale contains about 100 times more carbon dioxide than the air we inhale.

BREATHING FACTS

• The average human takes 600 million breaths in a 70-year lifetime.

• If the lungs were opened out and laid flat, they would cover a tennis court.

• The lungs contain 1,490 miles (2,400 km) of airways.

• Humans can survive with only one fully working lung.

HEART AND BLOOD

THE BODY'S transportation network, the heart, blood, and blood vessels, is called the cardiovascular system. Blood carries oxygen to cells and also transports food, hormones, waste, and warmth.

HEARTBEAT CYCLE

1 During diastole (resting), both atria fill with blood and some flows into the ventricles below.

2 During atrial systole (pumping), the atria contract, forcing blood into the ventricles.

3 During ventricular systole, the ventricles contract, forcing blood out into the arteries.

Vena cava is main incoming blood vessel

Right atrium

Pulmonary artery is main blood vessel to lungs

Aorta is main outgoing blood vessel

Pulmonary valve

Left atrium

Right pulmonary vein

Left ventricle

Right ventricle

Valves stop blood from flowing backward.

HEART STRUCTURE
The heart is a pump with two sides. Each side has two chambers – the atrium above and the ventricle below. These contract and relax every 0.8 seconds to pump blood around the body.

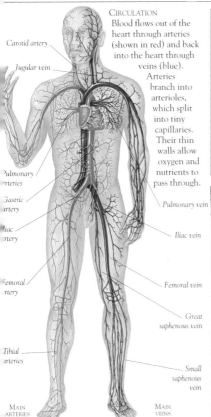

Carotid artery

Jugular vein

Pulmonary
arteries

Gastric
artery

Iliac
artery

Femoral
artery

Tibial
arteries

Pulmonary vein

Iliac vein

Femoral vein

Great
saphenous vein

Small
saphenous
vein

MAIN
ARTERIES

MAIN
VEINS

CIRCULATION

Blood flows out of the heart through arteries (shown in red) and back into the heart through veins (blue). Arteries branch into arterioles, which split into tiny capillaries. Their thin walls allow oxygen and nutrients to pass through.

HEART FACTS

- A human heart beats more than 30 million times a year.
- The heart rate increases with exercise to provide muscles with extra oxygen.
- With every heart beat, the heart pumps out about 2.8 fl oz (80 ml) of blood.

BLOOD

The liquid part of blood, called plasma, contains a rich mixture of blood cells, proteins, antibodies, hormones, and minerals. Red blood cells are button-shaped, and carry oxygen around the body. White cells, or leukocytes, fight infection. The tiny platelets help to plug leaks by forming blood clots.

DIGESTION

FOOD IS BROKEN down by
a process called digestion.
Once food has been
swallowed, it slips into the
alimentary canal, or gut,
which runs from mouth to
anus. As food passes through
the gut, it is gradually
digested and absorbed until
all that emerges at the far
end is waste.

Teeth soften
food by
chewing it

Saliva helps to
dissolve starch

Food is
swallowed
as a bolus

ALIMENTARY CANAL
The digestive tract runs
from the mouth to the
anus and is about 30 ft
(9 m) long. Food passes
from the mouth, down
the esophagus into the
stomach. From here, it
passses into the small
intestine, made up of
the duodenum, jejunum,
and ileum, and into the
large intestine, made up
of the colon and rectum.
Several organs and
glands are connected
to the gut to help
digestion.

Waves of muscular
action push food
down esophagus
into stomach

Liver

Stomach

Digestive enzymes in
duodenum break down
food into semifluid
called chyme

Ileum absorbs digested
minerals and nutrients
into bloodstream

Indigestible solids pass
on into colon, where
water is absorbed

Muscular rectum expels
waste through anus

Intestine — *Food*

Food slides forwards — *Muscle contracts behind food*

Contractions push food along

PERISTALSIS
The walls of the digestive tract contain strong muscle fibers that produce wave-like contractions to propel food along. This process is called peristalsis.

STOMACH ACTION
The stomach is a bag-like chamber that stores food. As the stomach fills with food, its walls stretch. Powerful muscles churn up the food, and gastric juices break it down so it can be digested. The food passes from the stomach into the intestines.

Undigested food enters the stomach

Gastric juices digest the food

Broken-down food is pushed into the duodenum

VILLI
The lining of the small intestine has millions of microscopic fingerlike villi that absorb nutrients.

Each villus measures 0.04 in (1 mm).

Capillaries

Mucus layer

Muscles

LIVER
The liver has many functions. It stores vitamins, turns digested food into blood proteins, and makes bile, which helps break fat into tiny globules.

Esophagus

Liver

Stomach

Bile duct secretes bile into intestine

Gallbladder stores bile

Pancreas supplies digestive chemicals

DIGESTION FACTS
• Food stays in the stomach for up to five hours, and spends up to 20 hours in the colon.

• So that the stomach does not digest itself, its walls are lined with protective mucus.

• The digestive process begins as soon as you take a bite of food.

URINARY SYSTEM

AS BLOOD FLOWS through the kidneys, they filter out waste and drain off excess water. This is expelled from the body as urine, via the ureter, bladder, and urethra. In this way the urinary system clears the blood of toxins and regulates its water content.

THE URINARY SYSTEM

Cortex

Adrenal gland

Any remaining water and waste drains into the collecting duct as urine

Medulla

Renal artery brings in blood for filtering

Renal vein takes away filtered blood

In the tubules most of the water and valuable amino acids, glucose, and salt are retrieved and returned to the blood

Urine drains from the kidneys via the ureter

KIDNEYS
The kidneys filter the blood in over a million filtering units called nephrons. In each nephron, water and tiny molecules are drawn off and channeled through little tubes called tubules. Inside these, valuable molecules and most of the water are retrieved and returned to the blood, leaving only a little water and waste to drain off as urine.

KIDNEY AND URINE FACTS
• The kidneys clean 2.7 pints (1.3 liters) of blood a minute.

• Urine is 95 percent water. The rest is toxic waste such as urea, which is produced in the liver.

HORMONES

ENDOCRINE glands secrete chemical messengers called hormones into the blood. These stimulate, regulate, and coordinate a whole range of body processes.

TESTOSTERONE
In men, the testes produce the hormone testosterone to control the development of sexual characteristics.

Testis

HORMONE FACTS

• Too much growth hormone can cause gigantism (excess growth); too little can cause slow growth.

• The hormone epinephrine can give short bursts of superhuman strength.

Pituitary gland sends out hormones that regulate other endocrine glands

Thyroid gland secretes thyroxine, which controls growth

Parathyroid glands secrete hormone that raises blood calcium levels

Adrenal glands secrete cortisone, which boosts metabolism, and epinephrine, which primes body for action

Pancreas secretes glucagon and insulin, which regulate blood sugar levels

Stomach and intestines secrete hormones that aid digestion

Ovaries in women make female sex hormones, estrogen and progesterone

REPRODUCTION

FROM PUBERTY ONWARD, the reproductive system in males and females is sufficiently developed for them to have sexual intercourse and potentially create new human beings. Pregnancy occurs when a woman's egg cell is fertilized by a man's sperm cell.

THE MALE REPRODUCTIVE SYSTEM

MALE REPRODUCTIVE SYSTEM
Male sex cells, or sperm, are made inside the testicles in tubes called seminiferous tubules. Sperm mature in tubes called the epididymides. When the penis is stimulated, muscles pump sperm from the epididymis along the vas deferens, where they mix with seminal fluid to make semen.

Bladder

Vas deferens

Prostate gland

Urethra

Penis

Testis

Epididymis

SINGLE SPERM

MALE SEX ORGANS

THE FEMALE REPRODUCTIVE SYSTEM

FEMALE REPRODUCTIVE SYSTEM
Female sex cells, or ova, are stored in the ovaries. Every 28 days or so, one ovum, or egg, is released during ovulation. The egg passes down one of two fallopian tubes to the uterus, or womb. If the ovum is fertilized, it is embedded in the womb lining. If not, both the ovum and lining are shed during menstruation.

Fallopian tube

SINGLE OVUM

Ova (eggs) stored in ovary

Uterus (womb)

Neck of womb called the cervix

Vagina

FEMALE SEX ORGANS

SEXUAL INTERCOURSE
During sexual intercourse, the man's penis fills with blood, becoming hard and erect. It fits into the woman's vagina, where semen is released (ejaculated). If one of the 300 million sperm reaches the egg, it may fertilize it.

Oral contraceptive pills

Diaphragm

Condom

CONTRACEPTIVES
Condoms and other contraceptives are used to stop conception during intercourse. They prevent sperm fertilizing the egg.

Penis inside vagina

Umbilical cord consists of three intertwined blood vessels

Amniotic sac contains amniotic fluid

The placenta is a spongy organ on uterine lining

Fetus turns head down during last few weeks of pregnancy

Pregnancy

Once the egg is fertilized, it becomes an embryo, which grows rapidly in the womb (uterus). Within eight weeks, it is a fetus, with recognizable features and all its internal organs. Fed through the umbilical cord with food and oxygen from the placenta, the fetus continues development. After 40 weeks, it is ready to be born.

GENES AND HEREDITY

STORED IN a cell's nucleus are packages called
chromosomes, made up of long spirals of the
molecule DNA. Each DNA molecule consists of
genes, which are responsible for characteristics
such as eye color.

*A chromosome has two identical
arms called chromatid*

Cell

GENES
Each DNA molecule consists of
millions of genes. Each gene provides
instructions to make a single protein,
used to build a new cell or to control
a cell's activities. Genes are passed on
to the next generation during
sexual reproduction.

Nucleus

*Each cell has 46 chromosomes,
except for sex cells, which have 23*

*Chromosome
unwinds*

MITOSIS
As the body grows, or
when worn-out cells
need replacing, the cells
divide into two by a
process called mitosis.
The normal number of
chromosomes in each
cell is 46. When the cells
divide, each new cell has
the same number of
chromosomes – 46.

*Cell copies
chromosomes
before it
divides*

MITOSIS

*Each new
cell has 46
chromosomes*

*Genes are
reshuffled
in original
cell*

MEIOSIS

MEIOSIS
Sex cells are produced during the cell
division called meiosis. The original
cell's genes are mixed and recombined
so that the new cells produced are
genetically unique.

*Each pair of
chromosomes
splits in half and
the two new cells
receive half each*

Chromatid

Each DNA strand is made up of sections called genes

Genes consist of linked pairs of four different chemicals called bases

Copies of the gene are made and tell tcell to make a particular protein

As the DNA unwinds, the genes are exposed

Each DNA molecule is made up of two spiral strands

GIRL OR BOY
A child's sex depends on the sperm that reaches the mother's egg; another X chromosome means a girl; a Y means a boy.

GENETIC FACTS
• DNA stands for deoxyribonucleic acid.
• Red blood cells have no nucleus and do not contain genes.
• Women have two X chromosomes. Men have one X chromosome paired with a Y chromosome.

HEREDITY
The passing on of characteristics via the genes is called heredity. A baby inherits half its genes from its mother and half from its father. The reshuffling of genes means that brothers and sisters inherit different genes, but there may be a resemblance.

Maternal grandfather's genes

Grandmother's genes

Paternal grandfather's genes

Sperm

Egg

Egg

Sperm

Mother inherits half her genes from each parent

Father inherits half of his genes from each parent

Child inherits half its genes from each parent

Child's genes include some from all four grandparents

FIGHTING INFECTION

IF BACTERIA or viruses enter the body and multiply, you can become ill. To fight infection, the body has a defense mechanism called the immune system.

Adenoid glands

Tonsils

Tonsils and adenoids produce antibodies to fight infection.

A single macrophage can ingest 100 bacteria

MACROPHAGE (BLUE) ENGULFING A YEAST CELL (YELLOW)

Spleen stores special white blood cells called lymphocytes

Small intestine contains lymph tissues that help fight infection

Bone marrow produces lymphocytes

Lymph capillaries drain tissue fluids into lymphatic system

SCAVENGER CELLS
Lymphocytes called phagocytes, and larger ones called macrocytes, roam through the blood, engulfing unwanted matter, such as the dirt in a cut.

IMMUNE FACTS

• A fever is caused when white blood cells release proteins called pyrogens, raising the body's temperature.

• Swollen glands are a sign of infection.

LYMPHATIC SYSTEM
Lymph fluid drains waste from the body's tissues into the ducts of the lymphatic system. Germs that enter the lymphatic system are swept towards lymph nodes, where there a cluster of lymphocytes is waiting to fight them.

TH LYMPHAT SYSTE

Virus

Antigen

Antibodies lock on to antigens

Antibody

IMMUNE RESPONSE

On certain bacteria and viruses there possess substances called antigens, which trigger the immune system into action. When the immune system first meets an antigen, it produces antibodies to fight it. Lymphocytes called B-cells make these antibodies, and each one targets a specific antigen.

Medicine

The body's immune system is remarkably effective at dealing with infection, but sometimes it breaks down or takes a long time to work. Modern drugs and traditional forms of medicine such as herbalism can help the body to combat illness.

IMMUNIZATION

Active or passive immunization by injection provides the body with protection from certain diseases.

ACTIVE IMMUNIZATION	PASSIVE IMMUNIZATION
Harmless extracts that cannot cause disease are injected into the body.	*People donate blood that contains antibodies.*
Vaccine causes B-cells to produce antibodies.	*Antibodies to a disease are injected into patient.*
Immune system will respond more quickly.	*If disease attacks, the antibodies will fight it.*

DRUGS

The drugs we use to treat illness and disease are made from plant extracts or from chemicals produced in a laboratory. They are commonly taken in the form of tablets, capsules, or liquid.

143

SCIENCE AND TECHNOLOGY

MATTER

FROM THE TINIEST speck of dust to giant stars, everything that exists in the universe is made up of matter. Most matter consists of minute particles called atoms. On Earth, matter usually occurs in one of three forms, or "states," called solid, liquid, or gas.

Electrode

Plasma streaks

PLASMA
A rare fourth state of matter called plasma forms when a gas becomes so hot electrons (see p.148) break away from atoms.

GAS
A gas has no fixed volume or shape. Gas particles are widely spaced and loosely bound, with the ability to move freely in all directions. A gas will expand to fill any container it is put in.

Gas dispersing from a chemical reaction

LIQUID
A liquid has a definite volume but no fixed shape. Liquid particles are more loosely bound than solid particles and can move over small distances. A liquid will flow and take the shape of its container.

Every liquid takes the shape of its container

Coins have a rigid shape

SOLID
A solid has a fixed shape and volume. Solid particles are tightly packed in regular patterns. Strong bonds allow the particles to vibrate, but keep them from moving.

CHANGING STATE

The particles of a substance are held together by bonds that weaken when heated and strengthen when cooled. Heat changes solids to liquids, and liquids to gases. When cooled sufficiently, gases condense to liquids, and liquids freeze to solids.

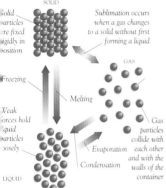

SOLID

Solid particles are fixed rigidly in position

Sublimation occurs when a gas changes to a solid without first forming a liquid

GAS

Freezing

Melting

Weak forces hold liquid particles loosely

Evaporation

Condensation

Gas particles collide with each other and with the walls of the container

LIQUID

Blocks of equal mass but unequal density

LEAD

WAX

BALSA

HIGH DENSITY   MEDIUM DENSITY   LOW DENSITY

MASS, VOLUME, AND DENSITY

The amount of matter in an object is its mass. Volume is the space it occupies. The object's density is its mass divided by its volume.

GAS LAWS

Pressure

Gas molecules

BOYLE'S LAW

At constant temperature (T), the volume of a gas (V) is inversely proportional to the pressure (P) (the gas contracts as the pressure rises): PV=constant.

PRESSURE LAW

At constant volume, the pressure of a gas is proportional to the temperature (increasing the temperature raises the gas's pressure): P/T=constant.

Temperature

CHARLES' LAW

At constant pressure, the gas's volume is proportional to the temperature (the gas expands if temperature rises): V/T=constant.

ATOMS

MATTER IS MADE UP of tiny particles called atoms.
Atoms form the building blocks for everything in
the universe. There are just over a hundred types of
atoms, which are themselves made up of even smaller
"subatomic" particles. Atoms and subatomic particles
are not solid – they are clouds of energy.

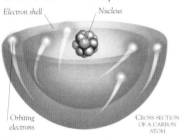

Electron shell   *Nucleus*

*Orbiting
electrons*

CROSS SECTION
OF A CARBON
ATOM

INSIDE THE ATOM
The center, or nucleus, of all but
the hydrogen atom contains
protons (positively charged) and
neutrons (with no charge).
Negatively charged particles
called electrons orbit the nucleus
at very high speeds, forming
layers or "shells."

CARBON–12 ATOM

NUCLEON NUMBER
The total number of protons and neutrons
contained in the nucleus of an atom is called
the nucleon number. The most common
form of carbon is referred to as carbon–12,
since it contains 6 protons and 6 neutrons.

CARBON–14 ATOM

Proton

Neutron

*Nucleus contain
6 protons and 6 neutron*

*Nucleus contains
6 protons and
8 neutrons*

ISOTOPES
All atoms of a particular element have the
same number of protons, but some forms of
the element may have different numbers of
neutrons. These variations are called isotope
The isotope carbon–14, for example, has two
more neutrons than the isotope carbon–12.

PARTICLE COLLISIONS
Scientists have discovered many new particles by smashing together subatomic particles at high speed. Most new particles exist for only a fraction of a second after the collision, but their movements can be recorded by computers.

PATHS OF PARTICLES CREATED
AFTER SUBATOMIC COLLISION

ATOM FACTS
• Protons and neutrons are 1,836 times heavier than electrons.

• Scientists have discovered more than 200 different subatomic particles.

• Specks of dust contain a trillion atoms.

QUARKS
Particles such as neutrons and protons are called hadrons. A hadron is made up of three smaller particles called quarks, which are stuck together by tiny particles called gluons. Quarks occur in two types: "down" quarks have one-third of a unit of negative electric charge, while "up" quarks have two-thirds of a unit of positive charge.

QUARKS IN A NEUTRON

A neutron has 1 up quark and 2 down quarks, giving an overall neutral charge.

QUARKS IN A PROTON

A proton has 2 up quarks and 1 down quark, giving an overall positive charge.

Gluon particles hold quarks together

up quark

NEUTRON

Down quark

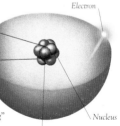

Electron

Nucleus

Neutron

BINDING FORCES
Atoms are held together by four fundamental forces, or interactions. Electrons are attracted to protons by electromagnetic force, while "strong" and "weak" nuclear forces bind together particles inside the nucleus. These basic forces, plus the pull of gravity, hold the entire universe together.

ELEMENTS

AN ELEMENT is a substance
made from only one type of atom.
The known elements are set out in a
chart called the periodic table. This chart
arranges elements into "groups"
(columns) and "periods" (rows).

Veins of pure gold

QUARTZ

NAME, NUMBER, AND SYMBOL
Each box carries basic details about
an element. The atomic number is
the number of protons in the nucleus
of one of the element's atoms.

Atomic number

Chemical symbol

Name of element

15
P
Phosphorus

1	2	3	4	5	6	7	8	9
1 H Hydrogen								
3 Li Lithium	4 Be Beryllium							
11 Na Sodium	12 Mg Magnesium							
19 K Potassium	20 Ca Calcium	21 Sc Scandium	22 Ti Titanium	23 V Vanadium	24 Cr Chromium	25 Mn Manganese	26 Fe Iron	27 Co Cobalt
37 Rb Rubidium	38 Sr Strontium	39 Y Yttrium	40 Zr Zirconium	41 Nb Niobium	42 Mo Molybdenum	43 Tc Technetium	44 Ru Ruthenium	45 Rh Rhodium
55 Cs Cesium	56 Ba Barium	57-71 Lanthanides	72 Hf Hafnium	73 Ta Tantalum	74 W Tungsten	75 Re Rhenium	76 Os Osmium	77 Ir Iridium
87 Fr Francium	88 Ra Radium	89-103 Actinides	104 Unq Unnil-quadium	105 Unp Unnil-pentium	106 Unh Unnil-hexium	107 Uns Unnil-septium	108 Uno Unnil-octium	109 Une Unnil-ennium

GROUP I   GROUP II

*The number of electron
shells circling the nuclei of
an element's atoms increases
down each group. Elements
in the same group have
similar chemical properties.*

57 La Lanthanum	58 Ce Cerium	59 Pr Praseo-dymium	60 Nd Neodymium	61 Pm Promethium	62 Sm Samarium
89 Ac Actinium	90 Th Thorium	91 Pa Protactinium	92 U Uranium	93 Np Neptinium	94 Pu Plutonium

TYPES OF ELEMENTS KEY

ALKALI METALS

ALKALINE-EARTH METALS

TRANSITION METALS

LANTHANIDES

ACTINIDES

POOR METALS

SEMIMETALS

NONMETALS

NOBLE GASES

GROUPS AND PERIODS
Each period starts on the left with a highly reactive alkali metal with an outer shell of one electron. It ends on the right with a stable noble gas in group 18 (0) with eight electrons in its outer shell. Elements in the same group have the same number of electrons in their outer shells.

As the atomic number increases by one along each period, the chemical properties of the element gradually change

18
2 **He** Helium

13	14	15	16	17
5 **B** Boron	6 **C** Carbon	7 **N** Nitrogen	8 **O** Oxygen	9 **F** Fluorine	10 **Ne** Neon
13 **Al** Aluminum	14 **Si** Silicon	15 **P** Phosphorus	16 **S** Sulfur	17 **Cl** Chlorine	18 **Ar** Argon

10	11	12	13	14	15	16	17
28 **Ni** Nickel	29 **Cu** Copper	30 **Zn** Zinc	31 **Ga** Gallium	32 **Ge** Germanium	33 **As** Arsenic	34 **Se** Selenium	35 **Br** Bromine	36 **Kr** Krypton
46 **Pd** Palladium	47 **Ag** Silver	48 **Cd** Cadmium	49 **In** Indium	50 **Sn** Tin	51 **Sb** Antimony	52 **Te** Tellurium	53 **I** Iodine	54 **Xe** Xenon
78 **Pt** Platinum	79 **Au** Gold	80 **Hg** Mercury	81 **Tl** Thallium	82 **Pb** Lead	83 **Bi** Bismuth	84 **Po** Polonium	85 **At** Astatine	86 **Rn** Radon

GROUP III GROUP IV GROUP V GROUP VI GROUP VII GROUP 0

An element's atomic number corresponds to the total number of electrons orbiting the nucleus of one of its atoms.

Two alternative number systems are used to group the elements

Lanthanides and actinides are set apart from the main table to make it easier to understand

63 **Eu** Europium	64 **Gd** Gadolinium	65 **Tb** Terbium	66 **Dy** Dysprosium	67 **Ho** Holmium	68 **Er** Erbium	69 **Tm** Thulium	70 **Yb** Ytterbium	71 **Lu** Luterium
95 **Am** Americium	96 **Cm** Curium	97 **Bk** Berkelium	98 **Cf** Californium	99 **Es** Einsteinium	100 **Fm** Fermium	101 **Md** Mendelevium	102 **No** Nobelium	103 **Lr** Lawrencium

MOLECULES AND BONDS

A GROUP OF ATOMS that are linked together is called a molecule. A molecule may be made up of a few or very many atoms. Molecules are formed when the electrical forces created by electron movement "bond" atoms together. Electron transfer between atoms occurs because some atoms require extra electrons to fill their outer shell.

WATER MOLECULE

CHEMICAL FORMULA
A chemical formula uses letters and numbers to show how elements combine in a compound. The formula for a water molecule is H_2O as it is made up of two atoms of hydrogen linked to a single atom of oxygen.

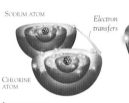

SODIUM ATOM

Electron transfers

CHLORINE ATOM

POSITIVELY CHARGED SODIUM ION

Both ions now have eight electrons in their outer shells

Ionic bond

IONIC BONDS
In ionic bonding, excess electrons transfer from the full outer shell of one atom to the outer shell of another that requires extra electrons to fill it. The transfer leaves both atoms as charged particles called ions. The atom losing the electron becomes a positively charged ion, or cation, and the atom gaining the electron becomes a negative ion, or anion. The force of attraction between the opposite charges binds the ions together.

NEGATIVELY CHARGED CHLORIDE ION

GIANT IONIC STRUCTURE

A crystal of salt (sodium chloride) contains sodium and chloride ions arranged in a regular, connected network that extends throughout the crystal. This network is called a giant ionic lattice.

Positive sodium ion (Na⁺)

Negative chloride ion (Cl⁻)

SODIUM CHLORIDE

itrogen atom
nds with
ree hydrogen
oms

Nitrogen atom

Hydrogen atom

Shared electrons form single bond between nitrogen and hydrogen atoms

itrogen
ucleus

Hydrogen nucleus

AMMONIA MOLECULE (NH₃)

COVALENT BONDS

Ionic bonds are formed between metals and nonmetals. In covalent bonds, nonmetals bind together by sharing electrons. Two atoms each "donate" an electron, and the electrons form a pair that orbits both nuclei, holding the atoms together as a molecule. In a double bond, each atom donates two electrons.

RGANIC CHEMISTRY

arbon compounds are extremely common ecause carbon atoms link up easily with toms of most other elements, and have the bility to form very stable bonds with other arbon atoms. All living things contain some ompounds of carbon. The study of substances ontaining carbon is known as rganic chemistry.

MATERIALS CONTAINING CARBON COMPOUNDS

Plants

Fuels (butane, gas)

Earthenware

Foods

Hydrogen atom

Carbon atom

MOLECULE OF CARBON COMPOUND BUTANE (C_4H_{10})

Textiles

Natural sponge

Plastics

Soaps

CHEMICAL REACTIONS

WHEN A CHEMICAL reaction occurs, new substances (called products) form from the original chemicals taking place in the reaction (called reactants). The atoms of the reactants rearrange themselves to form products.

Electron

ELECTRON TRANSFER
During the oxidation proces[s] atoms lose electrons and are "oxidized." During reductio[n] atoms gain electrons and are "reduced."

EXOTHERMIC REACTIONS
A reaction that gives out more heat than it takes in, such as burning, is called an exothermic reaction. Oxidation and reduction are both types of exothermic reaction. Oxidation occurs when a substance combines with oxygen. Reduction takes place when a substance loses oxygen.

Heat is produced, warming surrounding air

Log burns, combining with oxygen in an oxidation reaction

Heat is absorbed during cooking

ENDOTHERMIC REACTION
Reactions that take in more heat than they give out, such as those during cooking, are endothermi[c]

ACIDS
An acid is a compound that forms hydrogen ions when it dissolves in water. The greater the concentration of ions, the stronger the acid. Strong acids are corrosive and can burn skin and dissolve metals. The pH scale measures acidity; pH 1 is the strongest acid, pH 7 is neutral.

UNIVERSAL INDICATOR COLOR/pH CHART OF ACIDS						
DIGESTIVE JUICES	CAR BATTERY	LEMON JUICE	VINEGAR	ACID RAIN	TAP WATER	PURE WATER

Mixtures and compounds

Most substances are made of two or more elements, either mingled loosely as mixtures or, after chemical reactions, combined strongly as compounds.

CHLORINE (GAS)

+

SODIUM (METAL)

=

SODIUM CHLORIDE OR COMMON SALT

COMPOUNDS

A compound is a substance in which the atoms of two or more elements are combined together. Common salt (sodium chloride), for example, is a compound of sodium and chlorine atoms.

Potassium permanganate forms a solution in water

COLLOIDS

In a colloid, tiny particles of one substance are dispersed evenly throughout another. Hair gel is a colloid of solid fat particles suspended in water.

HAIR GEL

SOLUTIONS

A solution is a mixture of one substance (the solute) dissolved in another (the solvent). Many compounds dissolve in water, forming weak bonds with water molecules.

BASES AND ALKALIS

A base is a compound that neutralizes acidity. Alkalis are bases that dissolve in water. The pH scale for bases ranges from neutral pure water (pH 7) to strongest alkali (pH 14).

UNIVERSAL INDICATOR COLOR/pH CHART OF BASES

| PURE WATER | SOAP | BICARBONATE OF SODA | DISINFECTANT | HOUSEHOLD CLEANER | CALCIUM HYDROXIDE | OVEN CLEANER | SODIUM HYDROXIDE |

FORCE AND MOTION

ALL MOVEMENT, or motion, is caused by forces. A force is invisible, but its effects are observable. Forces push or pull, causing objects to start or stop moving, change speed or direction, bend, twist, or change shape.

ATHLETES ACCELERATING UNDER FORCE FROM MUSCLES

Cue strikes white ball, transmitting momentum that overcomes ball's inertia

Ball accelerates away

White ball strikes red ball, transferring some of its momentum

Transferred momentum accelerates red ball away

INERTIA AND MOMENTUM

The tendency of all objects to resist effort to change their state or motion, whether they are actually moving or at rest, is called inertia. Momentum is the transferable force possessed by an object moving in a line, circle, or back and forth. It is calculated by multiplying the object's mass by its velocity.

VELOCITY AND ACCELERATION

The speed of an object in a particular direction is called its velocity. A cornering motorcycle, for example, keeps a constant speed but changes velocity as the direction of motion shifts. An increase in the velocity of an object is called acceleration. As its velocity decreases, the object undergoes deceleration.

NEWTON'S LAWS OF MOTION

• **First Law**: An object will remain at rest or continue traveling at a uniform velocity unless a force acts on it.

• **Second Law:** An object's acceleration is equal to the force acting on it, divided by the object's mass.

• **Third Law:** When two objects act on each other, they experience equal forces in opposite directions.

Athlete pulls on hammer, producing centipetal force

entripetal rce pulls ammer ward

Hammer's direction changes constantly

Hammer's inertia pulls it outward

Hammer flies off when released

CIRCULAR MOTION
A whirling object, such as an athlete's hammer, tries to fly off in a straight line, but circular motion, or centripetal force, pulls it toward the center of the circle. This force constantly changes the object's direction, keeping it moving in a circle.

Gravity

A force of attraction between all objects is called gravity. The greater he object's mass, the stronger the ull. The large mass of Earth enerates a strong gravitational ull, keeping us on the ground.

Equal mass but different weight

ON THE MOON   ON EARTH

WEIGHT AND MASS
The force exerted on an object by gravity is called weight. Mass is the amount of matter an object contains.

EARTH   MOON

Force of gravity = X

Mass = Y

Force of gravity = X

Mass = Y

Force of gravity = X

Mass = Y

Moon half as far

NEWTON'S LAW OF GRAVITATION
According to Newton's law, the force of gravity between two objects is calculated by multiplying their masses and dividing the result by the square of the distance between them. For example, if the Moon was half its actual distance from Earth, the force of gravity between them would be four times as strong. If the Moon had twice as much mass, the gravity between Earth and the Moon would be twice as great.

SIMPLE MACHINES

MACHINES can make tasks easier by
changing the size or direction of a
force. Many machines magnify effort,
which is the level of force needed to
overcome a resisting force, or load.

Axle
turns with
greater
force

Eff
applied
wheel r
magnifi
by a

WHEEL AND AX
Effort applied to th
wheel rim is magnified b
the axle, which turns wi
greater force over
shorter distance. Applyir
effort to an axle turns th
wheel rim with less forc
over a greater distanc

INCLINED PLANE

An inclined plane is an angled surface,
or slope, that reduces the effort required
to move an object. Moving a car by
pulling it up a ramp, for example, is
easier than lifting it vertically.
The car must travel further, but
less effort is needed to move it.

*Force of tension
in rope pulls car
up slope*

Win
magnif
force appli
to a hand

*Car has to travel
farther than if
lifted vertically*

*Weight of
car pulls it
downward*

A winch i
form of whe
and ax

Ramp (inclined plane)

*Force
used to
wield axe
magnified and
transferred
into log,
pushing
it apart*

WEDGE

A wedge is a
moving inclined
plane that pushes
an object with more
force than the effort
needed to move the
wedge. Cutting
blades, such as axes,
make use of the
wedge.

*Screw
head*

*Screw
thread*

SCREW

A screw's spiral groove, or
thread, is a type of inclined
plane wrapped around a
shaft. When the screw head
is turned, the thread moves
the whole screw forwar
with more force
than the
turning effort.

SINGLE PULLEY

Pulley wheel changes direction of effort

Rope is pulled downward

Rope moves up, lifting load

Effort required to lift load registers at 10 newtons

10 newton load

Spring balance

DOUBLE PULLEY

Effort applied to rope registers at 5 newtons

Pulley wheels

10 newton load moves upward

PULLEY

A pulley is a grooved wheel, or set of wheels, around which a rope passes in order to move a load. A single-wheeled pulley helps lift a load by changing the direction of effort applied to the rope. A double pulley halves the effort required to lift the same load.

SIMPLE LEVER

A lever is a bar that exerts a force by turning on a pivot, or "fulcrum." A small effort moved through a great distance at one end moves a larger load through a shorter distance at the other end.

Small force is applied

Lever magnifies force

Fulcrum

Direction of movement

Large load to be moved

Rack

Linear (straight) motion

Pinion

Rotary (circular) motion

Worm gear (cog meshes with screw-threaded shaft)

Direction of motion

Spur gear

MACHINE FACTS

• A machine's force ratio (FR) shows how effective the machine is as a force magnifier. FR is the force of the load divided by the effort needed to move it.

• A machine's velocity ratio (VR) shows how effective the machine is as a distance magnifier. VR is the distance moved by the effort divided by the distance moved by the load.

• Units of force are called newtons (N).

GEARS

Intermeshing toothed wheels, or cogs, that transmit and direct force and motion are called gears. A gear system uses large cogs to turn small cogs with less force but greater speed, and small cogs to turn large cogs with more force but less speed.

ENERGY AND HEAT

THE ABILITY to cause an action is called energy. Light, sound, heat, and electricity are forms of energy. Human energy comes from the chemical energy in food. Movement energy is also called kinetic energy.

Jack h
kinetic ener

Spring in
box has
potential
energy

POTENTIAL ENERG
Stored energy
called potential energy
Squeezing or stretchir
an object makes it ga
potential energy, whic
is stored until the obje
is released. Dropping
raised object converts i
potential to fall to Ear
into kinetic energy

200 N

200 N

Total
weight is
400 N

Bar carries
two sets of
200 N
weights

Weights are
raised about
4.9 ft (1.5 m)

Weight lifter
raises weights
in two seconds

Raised
weights have
gravitational
potential energy

WORK AND POWER
Work is done
when a force
moves something.
Energy provides
the ability to do
work. When work
is done, energy
converts from one
form to another.
The rate at which
work is done, or
energy changed
from one form to
another, is
called power.

WEIGHT LIFTER
RAISING
WEIGHTS

WORK FACTS

• The **joule** (J) is the SI unit of energy and work: 1 J of energy is used when a force of 1 newton moves through a distance of 1 meter. A kilojoule (kJ) is 1,000 joules.

• The **watt** (W) is the SI unit of power: 1 W is the conversion of 1 joule of energy from one form to another in 1 second. A kilowatt (kW) is 1,000 watts.

Heat and temperature

The more energy an object's particles have, the hotter the object is. Heat is the total kinetic energy of an object's moving particles.

MEASURING TEMPERATURE

Temperature is a measure of the average kinetic energy of an object's moving particles. Most liquid and electronic thermometers measure temperature on the Celsius and Fahrenheit scales.

LIQUID THERMOMETER

Column of mercury or alcohol expands as temperature rises

Temperature

Liquid-crystal display

ELECTRONIC THERMOMETER

Heat-sensitive tip

Heat from feet conducts into stone, leaving feet feeling cold

CONDUCTION

Heat energy always passes from hot objects to cooler ones. Heat travels through solids by conduction. Particles in the heated part of the solid vibrate and excite neighboring particles.

CONVECTION AND RADIATION

Heat travels through liquids and gases by convection. Hot fluids are less dense than cold ones and float upward, sinking again as they cool. Matter can also lose or gain heat energy by radiation.

Swirling color trails show how heat spreads through liquid

Hot, colored water floats to top of jar

Bottle contains hot, colored water

SCALE OF TEMPERATURE

Temperatures are measured in degrees on the Celsius (C) and Fahrenheit (F) scales, and in Kelvins (K).

482°F, 250°C, 523K
Burning point of wood

424°F, 218°C, 491K
Explosion point of nitroglycerine

284°F, 140°C, 413K
Sauna bath

212°F, 100°C, 373K
Boiling point of water

134°F, 56.7°C, 329.7K
Midday heat in Death Valley, California

98.6°F, 37°C, 310K
Human body temperature

71.6°F, 22°C, 295K
Body temperature of spiny anteater

32°F, 0°C, 273K
Freezing point of pure water

–38°F, –39°C, 234K
Freezing point of mercury

–459°F, –273°C, 0K
Absolute zero

ELECTRICITY

THE MOVEMENT OF electrons between
atoms creates a form of energy called
electricity. A flow of electrons is
called a current. Electric currents
and certain materials generate
a force called magnetism.

BALLOON
CHARGED BY
RUBBING
(FRICTION)

ELECTROSTATIC INDUCTION
Electricity that does not flow in a
current is called static electricity.
A static charge can be produced by
rubbing a balloon against an object
such as a sweater. Friction causes
electrons to transfer from the
sweater's atoms to the balloon's
atoms; the balloon gains a negative
electric charge and the sweater a
positive one. The charged balloon
can also induce a static charge in
other objects.

*Negatively
charged
balloon repels
electrons in pieces of
paper, giving paper
a positive static
charge*

*Positively
charged
paper attracted
to negatively
charged balloon*

*Positive
charge*

*Negative
charge*

*"Sheet"
lightning
occurs between
positive and
negative charges
within clouds*

*Flash of forked lightning
discharges electricity*

LIGHTNING
Inside a thundercloud, positive and
negative charges separate between the
top and bottom of the cloud. The
negative charge at the bottom of
the cloud induces a positive charge to
build up in the ground below. "Forked"
lightning occurs when a strong pulse
of electric current suddenly flows
between the two opposite charges,
discharging from the cloud's base to
the ground and back again.

Electric current lights bulb

Carbon anode (positive electrode)

Zinc casing is cathode (negative electrode)

Electron flow

BATTERY

A battery is a device that produces and stores electric current. Many batteries produce current by using carbon and zinc conductors called electrodes and a chemical paste called an electrolyte. In a circuit, the current flows from the negative electrode (cathode) to the positive (anode). An electric current can be used to power anything from a light-bulb to a computer.

Battery

Current flows through wires

Electrical contacts

ELECTRIC MOTOR

A current flows through a wire coil between the poles of a magnet. The current creates a magnetic field around the coil that interacts with the field produced by the magnet, forcing the coil to turn.

Opposing magnetic fields cause coil to rotate

Rotating coil can be attached to a driveshaft or flywheel

Compass needles align with magnetic field

Iron filings show lines of magnetic force

Magnet

Unlike, or opposite, magnetic poles (a north pole and a south pole) attract each other. Like poles (two north or two south poles) repel each other. Iron filings scattered near the magnets show the lines of attraction and repulsion.

MAGNETISM

A magnet exerts an invisible field of magnetic force that attracts objects made of iron, and a few other metals. Every magnet has two ends, called its north and south poles, where the forces it exerts are strongest. An electromagnet is a piece of iron that exerts magnetic force when a current is passed through it.

South pole

ATTRACTION   North pole

Two South poles   REPULSION

LIGHT AND COLOR

THE FASTEST-MOVING form of energy is light. It travels in waves that are part of a range of radiation called the electromagnetic spectrum. Visible "white light" is a mixture of many different colors of light, each with its own frequency and wavelength.

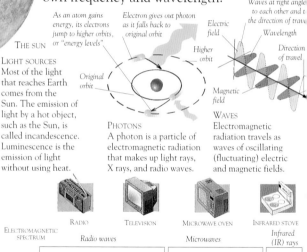

As an atom gains energy, its electrons jump to higher orbits, or "energy levels"

Electron gives out photon as it falls back to original orbit

Electric field

Waves at right angle to each other and t the direction of trave

Wavelength

Higher orbit

Direction of travel

THE SUN

Original orbit

Magnetic field

LIGHT SOURCES
Most of the light that reaches Earth comes from the Sun. The emission of light by a hot object, such as the Sun, is called incandescence. Luminescence is the emission of light without using heat.

PHOTONS
A photon is a particle of electromagnetic radiation that makes up light rays, X rays, and radio waves.

WAVES
Electromagnetic radiation travels as waves of oscillating (fluctuating) electric and magnetic fields.

| RADIO | TELEVISION | MICROWAVE OVEN | INFRARED STOVE |

ELECTROMAGNETIC SPECTRUM

| Radio waves | Microwaves | Infrared (IR) rays |

10^5 10^4 10^3 10^2 10 1 10^{-1} 10^{-2} 10^{-3} 10^{-4} 10^{-5} 10^{-}

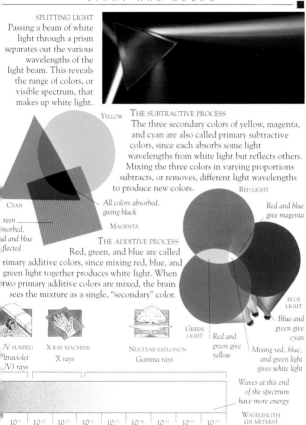

SPLITTING LIGHT
Passing a beam of white light through a prism separates out the various wavelengths of the light beam. This reveals the range of colors, or visible spectrum, that makes up white light.

YELLOW

THE SUBTRACTIVE PROCESS
The three secondary colors of yellow, magenta, and cyan are also called primary subtractive colors, since each absorbs some light wavelengths from white light but reflects others. Mixing the three colors in varying proportions subtracts, or removes, different light wavelengths to produce new colors.

CYAN

All colors absorbed, giving black

MAGENTA

reen
sorbed,
d and blue
flected

RED LIGHT

Red and blue give magenta

THE ADDITIVE PROCESS
Red, green, and blue are called rimary additive colors, since mixing red, blue, and green light together produces white light. When two primary additive colors are mixed, the brain sees the mixture as a single, "secondary" color.

BLUE LIGHT

Blue and green give cyan

GREEN LIGHT

Red and green give yellow

Mixing red, blue, and green light gives white light

UV SUNBED
ltraviolet
JV) rays

X RAY MACHINE
X rays

NUCLEAR EXPLOSION
Gamma rays

Waves at this end of the spectrum have more energy

WAVELENGTH (IN METERS)

| 10⁻⁹ | 10⁻¹⁰ | 10⁻¹¹ | 10⁻¹² | 10⁻¹³ | 10⁻¹⁴ | 10⁻¹⁵ | 10⁻¹⁶ | 10⁻¹⁷ |

SOUND

A SOUND source generates vibrations that pass though a material in waves. Our ears pick up sound waves traveling in the air around us. Sound waves can travel through solids, liquids, and gases, but not through a vacuum, since there are no particles of matter to carry vibrations.

DECIBELS	
140	EAR DAMAGE *Rocket lifting of*
120	PAIN THRESHO *Jet plane taking*
100	ROCK CONCER
80	BUSY TRAFFIC
60	NORMAL CONVERSATIO
30	PEOPLE WHISPER 18 FT (5 M) AW
10	LEAVES FALLIN 3.3 FT (1 M) AW
0	THRESHOLD O HUMAN HEARI (SOUND JUST AUDIBLE)

Tuning fork vibrates, causing pressure variations in surrounding air

High pressure (compression)

Low pressure (rarefaction)

Sound wave

SOUND WAVES
A sound source produces vibrations that squeeze and stretch surrounding air. Squeezing air molecules together creates high pressure, or "compression." Stretching air creates an area of low pressure, or "rarefaction." Alternating compressions and rarefactions travel through air as sound waves.

LOUDNESS
The greater the pressure changes between a sound wave's highest and lowest points (amplitude), the louder the sound. Loudnes is measured in decibels (dB). A 10-dB increase means the sound is ten times as loud.

HUMAN
HEARS: 20–20,000 Hz
MAKES: 85–1,100 Hz

PITCH
Pitch of a sound is how high or low a sound wave is. Pitch depends on frequency vibrations a second, measured in hertz (Hz).

NUCLEAR EXPLOSION
MAKES: 0.01 Hz

ELEPHAN
HEARS: 1–20,0
MAKES: 12 H

RECORDING SOUND

COMPACT
DISC

SOUND SYSTEMS

All sound recording
systems store sound
by making copies of
sound waves,
as spiral grooves
on a vinyl record,
magnetic patterns
on tape, or tiny,
laser-scanned pits
on a compact disc.

*Record
groove*

*Stylus picks
up sound
stored as
electrical
signals in
groove*

VINYL RECORD

*Pits pressed into
CD surface store
sound as a sequence
of binary numbers*

*Magnetic field
aligns particles
on tape to
reproduce
sound*

CASSETTE TAPE

MICROPHONE

In a moving-coil
microphone, sound
waves cause a wire coil
to vibrate, or move,
within a magnetic field.
This makes an electric
current flow through
the coil. The current
fluctuates in strength
as the sound waves
change, producing
electrical signals
that mirror the
sound waves.

*Permanent
magnet*

*Permanent
magnet*

*Wire coil
forms an
electromagnet*

*Diaphragm
of thin
plastic or
metal foil*

Electromagnet

Diaphragm

LOUDSPEAKER

Feeding electric signals to a loudspeaker
generates a varying magnetic field
around an electromagnet. The varying
field causes a diaphragm to vibrate,
producing sound waves.

DOG
HEARS: 15–50,000 Hz
MAKES: 450–1,080 Hz

BAT
HEARS: 1,000–120,000 Hz
MAKES: 10,000–120,000 Hz

ULTRASOUND SCANNER
MAKES AND RECEIVES:
3,500,000–7,500,000
Hz

PORPOISE
HEARS: 150–150,000 Hz
MAKES: 7,000–120,000 Hz

ELECTRONICS

Three layer "sandwich" of n- and p-type silicon

THE SCIENCE OF electronics is concerned with controlling and directing the movement of electrons. The complex operation of machines such as computers and jet aircraft is dependent on electronic technology.

SEMICONDUCTORS

A semiconductor is a material found in most electronic components that can vary its ability to conduct electricity. Adding impurities alters its electrical properties. Boron atoms in p-type silicon take up electrons from the outer shells of silicon atoms, leaving moving "holes" that carry current. In n-type silicon, extra electrons donated by added arsenic atoms carry current.

Hole in outer shell of silicon atom moves, carrying current

Extra electron moves, carrying current

P-TYPE SILICON (SEMICONDUCTOR)   *Boron atom*

N-TYPE SILICON (SEMICONDUCTOR)   *Arsenic atom*

TRANSISTOR

A transistor is a semi-conducting component that boosts or switches current. In computers, transistors switch on and off many times each second, enabling rapid information processing.

INTERNATIONAL ELECTRICAL COMPONENT SYMBOLS

CAPACITOR
Stores charge

DIODE
Permits current to flow in one direction only; can also be used to convert ac signals to dc (a rectifier)

LIGHT-EMITTING DIODE
Emits light when current flows through it

MICROPHONE
Converts sound waves into ac signals (and vice versa)

LOUDSPEAKER
Converts ac signals into sound waves

n-p-n TRANSISTOR
Amplifies electric current, and turns it on and off

p-n-p TRANSISTOR
Amplifies electric current, and turns it on and off

INTEGRATED CIRCUITS

An integrated circuit, or "microchip," a tiny piece, or "wafer," of silicon that contains a complete circuit of thousands of electronic components. Layers of n- and p-type semi-conductors and other materials are built up on the silicon wafer and linked by fine conducting wires.

MAGNIFIED OVERLAY OF AN INTEGRATED CIRCUIT

Circuits are "printed" onto wafer photographically through transparent overlay

Detailed overlay plans are made for each layer of the chip

Each plan is a different color

ON   ON   OFF   ON

2^3 2^2 2 1

$(1 \times 8) + (1 \times 4) + (0 \times 2) + (1 \times 1) = 13$

Microchips, or "chips," are encased in a tough plastic or ceramic capsule

ENCASED INTEGRATED CIRCUIT

Conducting pins can be soldered or plugged into a circuit board

ENCASED CHIP

A microchip is housed in a protective casing that dwarfs the tiny chip itself. An encased chip stores data as electrical signals in binary code, and uses logic gates (see right) to process that data. A microprocessor is a chip that can store instructions in an electronic memory.

BINARY CODE

Microchips store data as on/off electrical pulses called binary code. All information is broken down into sequences of ones (on) and zeros (off). The decimal number 13, for example, is 1101 in binary form.

LOGIC GATES

Microchips use patterns of transistors called logic gates to process binary code. Different types of gates switch on (open) or off (close) depending on the type of input received.

OUTPUT

AND GATE
Gives an output signal when a signal is applied to one input AND to the other input.

A   B

OUTPUT

OR GATE
Gives an output signal when a signal is applied to one input OR to the other input, OR to both.

A   B

OUTPUT

NOT GATE
Gives an output signal when a signal does NOT arrive at its input.

INPUT

COMPUTERS

A COMPUTER IS an electronic
machine that can perform a wide
variety of complex tasks very
quickly. Each task is reduced to a
series of simple calculations, which
enables rapid processing of data.

COMPUTER PROGRAM
A program is a set of
instructions that tells a
computer to carry out a
specific task. This set of
instructions may be
written as long sets of
numbers called
"machine code," or
in a computer
language such as
BASIC or FORTRAN.
Computer programs are
called "software."

PERSONAL COMPUTER
The most familiar
type of computer is
the personal computer
(PC), which can
only be used by one
person at a time.
The machinery that
makes up a PC, such
as the keyboard and
mouse, disk drive,
and monitor,
is called
"hardware."

Monitor displays data

Disk drive uses magnetic "floppy" disks to store and run software

Keyboard and mouse for inputting data

CENTRAL PROCESSING UNIT
A computer is controlled
by a central processing unit
(CPU), a single microchip
containing a large number
of circuits. The CPU
processes data from the
keyboard, ROM, and RAM.
It also sends information to
the RAM, outputs data
to the printer, and displays
software on the monitor.

ROM (read-only memory) is permanent and contains the operating system, a set of instructions that tells the computer how to work

Keyboard

RAM (random-access memory) temporarily stores programs that are currently being run

Ouput to monitor or printer

CPU

Input

SUPERCOMPUTER

Computers designed to perform complex tasks at the highest possible speeds are called supercomputers. The world's fastest computers use parallel processing. While conventional computers handle tasks one after another (in a series), parallel computers perform groups of operations at the same time. Their processing speed is also increased by cooling their components, which aids conductivity.

COMPUTER-AIDED DESIGN

Designers and architects test new ideas by using computer-aided design (CAD) to create 3-D graphic models on screen.

This computer is used in the study of particle physics

CRAY X-MP/48
SUPERCOMPUTER

COMPUTER FACTS

• Neural networks are computers designed to imitate the workings of the human brain.

• The world's largest computer manufacturer is American company IBM, employing up to 225,000 people.

CD-ROM

A form of compact disc adapted for use in computers, a CD for a CD-ROM can store 450 times more information than a standard floppy disk, including pictures, text, sound, and video.

CD-ROM
software page

VIRTUAL REALITY

A virtual-reality (VR) system enables the user to interact with a computer-generated "virtual" world. A headset supplies the user with 3-D images, while a "data glove" lets you "touch" what you see.

PRINTING TECHNOLOGY

THE PROCESS of reproducing words (text) and pictures (images) using ink is called printing. Printing presses enable numerous copies of text and images to be made very quickly. Modern print production uses computers at many stages in the printing process.

Paper fed through press

Colors are added one by one as paper comes into contact with the color plates

Adding yellow ink

Adding cyan ink

Adding magenta ink

Adding black ink

Each roller is equipped with a plate coated with a different colored ink

Full-color printed sheets emerge

PRINTING PRESS

PRINTING PRESS

A color press uses printing plates to print text and images. Light shined through the text film and color-separated image films photographically records their details onto the light-sensitive coating of the plates. After being attached to rollers, ink is then applied to the plates. Paper is pressed against the plates, printing the text and images.

PRINTED FULL-COLOR IMAGE

YELLOW   MAGENTA

CYAN   BLACK

COLOR PRINTING

Only four colors are used in color printing – yellow, magenta, cyan, and black. The image to be printed is scanned electronically, producing a separate piece of film for each color. The details of these "separations" are transferred onto color plates in the printing press. The separations are then printed on top of one another, reproducing the full-color image.

TELECOMMUNICATIONS

THE SCIENCE OF broadcasting sound and pictures
over long distances is called telecommunications.

WAVE MODULATION
Radio and television programs are
broadcast by radio waves, which must
first be modulated (coded) so that
they can carry sound and picture
signals. A steady radio wave is
modulated by a sound signal in one
of two ways. Its amplitude (strength)
may be modulated (AM) or its
frequency may change (FM).

AM RADIO WAVE

Wave strength
modulated

FM RADIO WAVE

Wave
frequency modulated

red, green,
and blue
electron
guns

Electro-
magnets

Circuits
amplify
signal   Electron
beams

Input from
TV antenna TELEVISION SET

HOW A TELEVISION WORKS
The antenna of a TV receives a modulated
carrier wave (carrying sound and picture
signals), which is then "demodulated" into
electrical signals and sent to a cathode-ray
tube. The tube contains three "electron
guns" that fire beams of electrons at the
phosphor-coated TV screen. Magnetic
fields cause the beams to scan the screen.
The picture builds as the electrons make
the phosphors glow.

LONG-RANGE COMMUNICATIONS
Low-frequency radio waves
can be sent long distances by
bouncing them between the
ionosphere (an ion-rich region
of the atmosphere) and the
ground. High-frequency waves
are transmitted through the
ionosphere to orbiting
communication satellites,
which relay the radio waves
to receiving stations on Earth.

Phosphors glow red,
blue, or green when
hit by electron beams

High-frequency
signals are sent
via satellite

Short waves
reflect off top
of ionosphere

Some radio waves
do not need to be
reflected

Low-frequency waves bounce
between ionosphere and ground

TRANSMITTING RADIO WAVES

MATHEMATICS

THE STUDY OF numbers and shapes is called mathematics. The different branches of mathematics enable us to create sophisticated machines, build structures, and run businesses. Algebra, for example, uses abstract symbols in place of numbers, while geometry deals with shapes and lines.

MATHEMATICAL SYMBOLS

=
EQUAL TO

−
SUBTRACTION

+
ADDITION

÷
DIVISION

×
MULTIPLICATION

TYPES OF NUMBERS
A written number consists of digits, or numerals; the number 313, for example, has 3 digits. A positive number is any number greater than zero, such as 6. A negative number is less than zero, such as −6. A prime number can only be divided by itself and 1.

ROTATION AND ANGLES

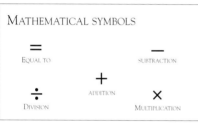

Obtuse angle
90°
130°
Reflex angle
45°
Acute angle
360° 0°
Right angle
Round angle
240°

CIRCLES AND CURVES

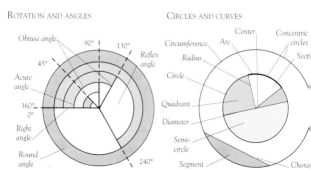

Center
Circumference
Arc
Concentric circles
Radius
Sector
Circle
Quadrant
Diameter
Semi-circle
Segment
Chord

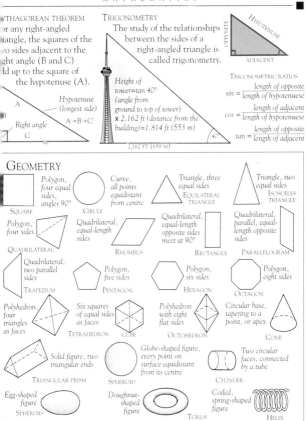

PYTHAGOREAN THEOREM

For any right-angled triangle, the squares of the two sides adjacent to the right angle (B and C) add up to the square of the hypotenuse (A).

Hypotenuse (longest side)

A

B

Right angle

C

$A^2 = B^2 + C^2$

TRIGONOMETRY

The study of the relationships between the sides of a right-angled triangle is called trigonometry.

HYPOTENUSE

OPPOSITE

ADJACENT

Height of tower=tan 40° (angle from ground to top of tower) x 2,162 ft (distance from the building)=1,814 ft (553 m)

40°

2,162 FT (659 M)

TRIGONOMETRIC RATIOS

$sin = \dfrac{length\ of\ opposite}{length\ of\ hypotenuse}$

$cos = \dfrac{length\ of\ adjacent}{length\ of\ hypotenuse}$

$tan = \dfrac{length\ of\ opposite}{length\ of\ adjacent}$

GEOMETRY

Polygon, four equal sides, angles 90°
SQUARE

Curve, all points equidistant from centre
CIRCLE

Triangle, three equal sides
EQUILATERAL TRIANGLE

Triangle, two equal sides
ISOSCELES TRIANGLE

Polygon, four sides
QUADRILATERAL

Quadrilateral, equal-length sides
RHOMBUS

Quadrilateral, equal-length opposite sides meet at 90°
RECTANGLE

Quadrilateral, parallel, equal-length opposite sides
PARALLELOGRAM

Quadrilateral, two parallel sides
TRAPEZIUM

Polygon, five sides
PENTAGON

Polygon, six sides
HEXAGON

Polygon, eight sides
OCTAGON

Polyhedron, four triangles as faces
TETRAHEDRON

Six squares of equal sides as faces
CUBE

Polyhedron with eight flat sides
OCTOHEDRON

Circular base, tapering to a point, or apex
CONE

Solid figure, two triangular ends
TRIANGULAR PRISM

Globe-shaped figure, every point on surface equidistant from its centre
SPHEROID

Two circular faces, connected by a tube
CYLINDER

Egg-shaped figure
SPHEROID

Doughnut-shaped figure
TORUS

Coiled, spring-shaped figure
HELIX

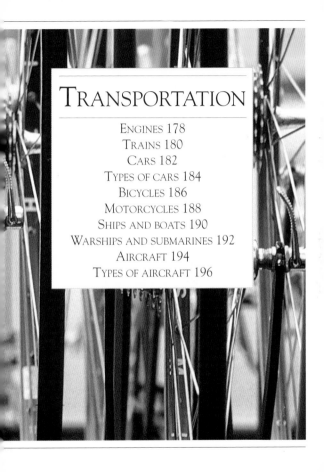

TRANSPORTATION

ENGINES

AN ENGINE harnesses one form of energy and converts it into motive force, or kinetic energy. Engines range in complexity from simple windmills to sophisticated turbofans.

WINDMILL
The sails of a windmill convert wind force into rotary motion, driving a central shaft that powers the milling machinery.

INTERNAL COMBUSTION
An internal combustion engine provides motive force by harnessing the energy released when a mix of fuel and air is burned (combusted) inside its cylinders. The stages of the combustion cycle are called strokes.

Distributor

Spring snaps valve shut

Camshaft controls opening and closing of valves

Rocker arm pushes valve open

Channels for cooling water

Valve

Piston

Fan belt drives cooling fan

Dipstick for checking level of lubricating oil

FOUR-CYLINDER GAS ENGINE

Cylinder

Flywheel

Clutch disconnects engine while driver changes gear

Crankshaft drives wheels via gearbox and clutch

Oilpan contains reservoir of oil for lubricating engine parts

Crankshaft bearing where crankshaft runs through engine block

FOUR-STROKE ENGINE CYCLE

Inlet valve opens

Cylinder

Piston slides down cylinder, sucking in mix of fuel and air (charge)

INDUCTION STROKE

Inlet valve shuts

Piston rises, compressing charge into small space

COMPRESSION STROKE

Spark plug ignites compressed charge

Expanding gases force piston down

Piston spins crankshaft

POWER STROKE

Exhaust valve opens

Rising piston pushes out hot gases

Cycle restarts

EXHAUST STROKE

Blades rotate and compress incoming air

Fan blade

Bypass air provides main thrust

Outer drive-shaft

Bypass air duct

Inner driveshaft

Fuel inlet

Fuel (kerosene) and air ignited

Turbine spins outer shaft, driving compressor

TURBOFAN

TURBOFAN JET ENGINE

A turbofan jet engine sucks in and compresses air, which is then mixed with fuel and ignited. The hot gases produced create forward thrust and drive air-circulating turbines that cool the engine.

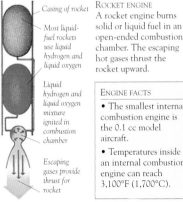

Casing of rocket

Most liquid-fuel rockets use liquid hydrogen and liquid oxygen

Liquid hydrogen and liquid oxygen mixture ignited in combustion chamber

Escaping gases provide thrust for rocket

ROCKET ENGINE

A rocket engine burns solid or liquid fuel in an open-ended combustion chamber. The escaping hot gases thrust the rocket upward.

ENGINE FACTS

• The smallest internal combustion engine is the 0.1 cc model aircraft.

• Temperatures inside an internal combustion engine can reach 3,100°F (1,700°C).

TRAINS

PEOPLE AND GOODS are
transported along railroads
in long trains of trucks and
carriages. These trains are
pulled by powerful engine
units called locomotives.

*The tracks rests on
concrete or wooden
beams known as
ties or sleepers*

*When a switch
takes place, short
sections of rail
swing across
to guide the
train on
to the new
track*

Ra...

Switc...
(poin...

STEAM TRAVEL

Water in a steam locomotive's boiler is heated
by a coal fire in the firebox, making steam.
Pressure from the steam moves a piston back
and forth; a connecting rod and crank linked
to the piston makes the wheels turn.
Steam locomotives were used to pull the
earliest trains, eventually being replaced by
electric and diesel locomotives in the 1960s.

TRACKS AND SWITCHES

Rails are often welded into one
continuous track as they are laid,
allowing trains to run smoothly.
Trains change tracks at pivoting
sections called switches, or points

Water tank   Coal space   Boiler   Crank

Coal burned   Coupling rod   Connecting   Pisto...
in firebox   rod drives wheels linked ...
                                                        connecting ro...

1808 BRITISH ENGINEER
RICHARD TREVITHICK BUILDS THE
FIRST STEAM LOCOMOTIVE

1829 ROBERT STEPHENSON'S
ROCKET HERALD'S THE AGE OF
THE PASSENGER TRAIN

1890 WORLD'S FIRST
ELECTRIC UNDERGROUND
RAILROAD OPENS IN UK

MONORAIL
Some trains run on or hang underneath a single (mono) electric rail. Monorails are fast and clean, and do not interfere with ground traffic.

Air-conditioned carriage

lectric otors drive heels of ower rs d ading rriage

Leading carriage

Pantograph picks up electric current from overhead cables

Power cars at each end of TGV drive train

Radio keeps driver in touch with signaling center and other trains

Computer in driver's cab checks for faults on train

ARTS OF A TRAIN
he high-speed French rain à Grand Vitesse TGV) runs on specially uilt tracks with gentle urves and slopes. rst introduced in 1981, e TGV has a top speed 186 mph (300 km/h).

Streamlined shape reduces air resistance, enabling TGV to travel at high speed

Trucks of four or more wheels enable train to go around curves

938 MALLARD SETS WORLD SPEED CORD FOR A STEAM LOCOMOTIVE AT 126 MPH (203 KM/H)

1934 PIONEER ZEPHYR DIESEL-ELECTRIC TRAIN INTRODUCED IN US

1990S FRENCH TGV SETS WORLD SPEED RECORD FOR AN ELECTRIC LOCOMOTIVE

CARS

MODERN CARS use a variety of mechanical and
electrical systems to provide the transportation we
take for granted. Car manufacturers are always
looking for new ways to make cars
safer and more efficient.

*Gearshift changes gears
which enable the engine to run
at efficient speeds while the
car slows down or speeds up*

ENGINE LAYOUTS

FRONT ENGINE,
REAR-WHEEL DRIVE

REAR ENGINE,
REAR-WHEEL DRIVE

FRONT ENGINE,
FRONT-WHEEL DRIVE

MIDENGINE,
REAR-WHEEL DRIVE

Design features
Compromise
between traction
(roadgrip),
handling, and
internal space
requirements.

Provides
maximum
traction, but
reduces amount
of internal space.

Maximizes
internal space,
and provides
good traction.
Used by most
family cars.

Good handling
and traction, but
little internal
space. Fast sports
cars use this
engine layout.

Fuel tank

Sunroof

*Rear drive
wheel*

*Hand brake
and ratchet*

*Driveshaft transmits
the movements of the
engine to the wheels*

THE ANATOMY OF A CAR
Most cars have four wheels, an
engine at the front, and room for at
least two passengers. This illustration
shows the main features of a rear-
wheel drive hatchback.

Disk

Brake
shoe

Drum

Calliper
holding
brake pads

DISK
BRAKE

DRUM
BRAKE

Types of Brakes
Modern disk brakes use hydraulic pressure to squeeze a steel disk attached to the wheel between two brake pads, slowing the car. In older drum brakes, curved brake "shoes" push against the inside of a metal drum attached to the wheel.

Ball joint

V-shaped
"wishbone"
arms

Lower
arm

Spring/damper
strut

FRONT SUSPENSION

Spring

Damper unit

Lower arm

Ball joint

MACPHERSON STRUT

Suspension isolates the wheels from the rest of the car, providing a smoother ride. Front suspension uses hinged, swiveling V-shaped arms that enable the steered wheels to go up and down as well as swivel. A MacPherson Strut is a swiveling coil and damper unit that gives lighter suspension for front or rear wheels.

Rear-view mirror

Windshield

Steering wheel connected
to rod that swivels the
front wheels

Air filter cleans air
before it is mixed
with fuel

Battery

Headlights

Front
bumper

Radiator cools
water flowing
around the
engine

Distributor
ensures that
spark plugs fire
in sequence

Generator produces
electricity when the
engine is running;
this electricity is
stored in the battery

Fan helps
cool water in
the radiator

Types of cars

Since 1901, when the Oldsmobile became the first mass-produced motor vehicle, car design has changed drastically. Today, there are many different designs to suit a wide variety of purposes, from driving to work, to racing.

1898 BENZ VELO

1898 BENZ VELO
German engineer Karl Benz produced the first car to be sold to the public in 1885. The Benz Velo, introduced in 1894, was the first car to sell in significant numbers.

1903 DE DION BOUTON MODEL Q
Produced by the French De Dion Bouton company, the 698 cc Model Q is typical of the light, reliable cars popular in the early years of the 20th century.

1903 DE DION BOUTON MODEL Q

Coach-type leaf-spring suspension

Wooden spoked wheels inherited from the horse cart

Solid rubber tire

Propeller shaft carrying drive from gearbox to final-drive

Folding hood

Folding windshield for rear-seat passenger

1909 ROLLS-ROYCE SILVER GHOST
Demand for more luxurious cars led to the manufacture of quality vehicles such as the Rolls-Royce Silver Ghost.

"Spirit of Ecstasy" mascot added in 1911

1909 ROLLS-ROYCE SILVER GHOST

Air-filled "pneumatic" tires

'57 MERCEDES-BENZ 300SL GULL WING
The futuristic design of the 300SL sports car features upward-swinging doors that resemble the wings of a seagull.

"Gull wing" doors

CAR FACTS

• The Aston Martin Lagonda was the first car with all-electronic instruments.

• The jet-engined car Thrust 2 holds the Land Speed Record, reaching 633.5 mph (1019.2 km/h) in 1983.

Rear wing forces wheels onto ground

Ferrari Boxer 312 12-cylinder engine

Light fiberglass body shell

Driver's cockpit

1979 FERRARI 312T4
Powerful engines and road-gripping wide tires allow Formula One racing cars to travel at over 190 mph (300 km/h).

CONTEMPORARY CARS

Modern cars are designed to cater to specific driving requirements.

FOUR-WHEEL DRIVE OFF-ROAD VEHICLE, SUZUKI VITARA

MULTI-PURPOSE VEHICLE (MPV), FIAT ULYSSES

COMPACT CITY CAR, RENAULT TWINGO

FOUR-WHEEL DRIVE, LUXURY SEDAN, AUDI A8

BICYCLES

APART FROM WALKING there is no simpler and cheaper way to travel than on a bicycle. Bicycles were invented in Europe little more than 200 years ago, but today they are popular worldwide for both transportation and leisure.

MODERN RACING BIKE
Air-filled tires, an efficient gearing system, and a cushioned saddle make modern bicycles more comfortable and easier to ride than their predecessors

Crossbar

Saddle

Fro...
derailleu...

Brake block

Spoke

Tire

Chainrin...

Rim

Rear derailleur
(gear changer)

Sprockets or cogs

TYPES OF BICYCLES

RACING BIKE
FOR ROAD
RACES

BMX FOR
ROUGH
TERRAIN

MOUNTAIN
BIKE

TANDEM FOR TWO PEOPLE

1790 THE COMTE DE SIVRAC BUILDS THE *CELERIFERE*

1813 CARL VON DRAIS BUILDS THE *DRAISIENNE*

1839 "BONESHAKER" IS FIRST BIKE WITH PEDAL-DRIVEN BACK WHEEL

1861 FIRST BIKE WITH PEDAL-DRIVEN FRONT WHEEL

Tour de France
Cycle races range from
track sprints held over
1,094 yd (1,000 m) to
multistage events lasting
several weeks. One of the
most famous road races is
the 24-day Tour de France.

Brake
cable

Handlebar

Brake lever

Stem

Gearshift

Fork blade

Pedal

Large cogs
used for
climbing
uphill

Small cogs
allow fast
travel
downhill or
on flat
ground

Chain

Pedal

Hub axle
or spindle

Valve

Gear systems
Many bicycles have
gear systems that enable
the cyclist to travel quickly
or slowly while pedaling at a
comfortable rate. By moving the
gearshift, the cyclist lifts the
chain from one cog to another.

c.1870 THE "PENNY
FARTHING" FIRST
APPEARS

1839 THE "BICYCLETTE"
IS THE FIRST
COMMERCIAL BICYCLE

1959 THE "MOULTON"
IS FIRST NEW BIKE
DESIGN FOR 50 YEARS

1990s "HPV"
HUMAN-POWERED
VEHICLE

MOTORCYCLES

THE SMALLEST and lightest form of motorized transportation, motorcycles range from small-engined commuter mopeds to racers that can reach speeds of more than 300 mph (500 km/h).

TYPES OF MOTORCYCLES

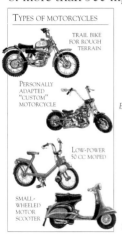

TRAIL BIKE FOR ROUGH TERRAIN

PERSONALLY ADAPTED "CUSTOM" MOTORCYCLE

LOW-POWER 50 CC MOPED

SMALL-WHEELED MOTOR SCOOTER

PARTS OF A MOTORCYCLE
A motorcycle is essentially a bicycle powered by an engine. Motorcycle engine sizes range from 50 cc (cubic capacity) to more than 1,000 cc.

Saddle

Exhaust

Brake disk

Drive chain

Four-cylinder 1,002 cc engine

1885 MAYBACH AND DAIMLER'S WOODEN MOTORCYCLE

1892 FIRST COMMERCIALLY PRODUCED MOTORCYCLE

1901 WERNER COMPANY PRODUCES ONE OF FIRST PRACTICAL MOTORCYCLES

1904 FIRST HARLEY-DAVIDSON MOTORCYCLE, THE SILENT GRAY FELLOW, PRODUCED

CORNERING
Motorcyclists lean
over on curves to
prevent the
motorcycle's
momentum
from overturning
the bike.

Brake
levers

Mirror

Fuel
tank

Windshield

1992 YAMAHA FZR 1000 EXUP

Fairing (front
enclosure)

Throttle connected
to handlebar grip

Telescopic
suspension
forks

The fairing
moved to
show engine

Radiator

Three-spoke
wheels

Exhaust
port

TWO-STROKE ENGINE
Smaller motorcycles often
use valveless two-stroke
engines. Fuel enters and
exhaust is ejected through
cylinder openings called
ports. The moving piston
opens and closes the ports.

1910 FIRST
POPULAR MOTORCYCLE
SIDECARS

1959 TRIUMPH COMPANY
INTRODUCES THE HIGH
PERFORMANCE *BONNEVILLE*

1978 MOTORCYCLE SPEED
RECORD OF 318 MPH (512 KM/H)
SET BY DONALD VESCO

1990s BMW
COMPANY LAUNCHES
COMPUTERIZED R1100

SHIPS AND BOATS

BOATS AND SHIPS have been
used to transport people and
goods across rivers, lakes,
and oceans for thousands
of years. From the first
dugout canoes to ocean
liners, boats have played
a major role in world trade.

Bipod or
"double" mast

Lugsail
made from
reed

TITICACA RA[...]
The elega[...]
rafts made [...]
the people [...]
Lake Titica[...]
in the And[...]
mountai[...]
are bu[...]
from re[...]
that grow [...]
the lak[...]

ALGONQUIN TRANSPORTATION
Birch bark canoes were used by the native Canadian
Algonquins to traverse the St. Lawrence River,
in what is now called Ontario. The boats
ranged in length from 10 ft (3 m)
vessels to 35 ft (10.5 m)
war canoes.

Yard   Mast

Batt[...]
keep [...]
sta[...]

Fo[...]
sided[...]

Cross-strut
strengthens
canoe

Birch bark hull

CHINESE
JUNK
Traditional
Chinese
vessels, or
"junks," have
four-sided sails
that hang from a
yard that crosses the mast at an angle.

OCEAN LINER
From the early 1900s to the 1950s, huge,
luxurious liners carried many passengers
across the oceans. Cheap, fast air travel
caused their popularity to decline.

CUNARD LINE[R]
MAURETANIA

Bridge

Funnels expel exhaust
fumes from boiler rooms

D[...]
[...]

ACKING

boat cannot sail
raight into the wind,
d so must cut a zigzag
urse when heading
wind. This is called
cking. Turning when
e wind is behind the
at is called jibing.

Wind

Destination

Second tack

Start   First tack

FFSHORE RACING YACHT

Forestay

Mast

Pulpit

Bow
(Front)

rt
ft-hand side)

Watertight
hatch

Vang (kicking
strap) holds the
boom down

Halyards
hoist (raise)
or lower sails

Steering
compass

om

eet (cable)
trols
sition of
relative
wind

der
trols
lder

ckstay

nsom

Winch

Guard
rails

Deck

Gunwales
(tops of the
boat's sides)

Hull (main
body of boat)

Genoa sheet

Blocks enclose
rotating pulleys

Cockpit

Cleat

Pushpit

Navigation
light

Starboard
(right-hand
side)

rn
ck)

ARTS OF A BOAT

iling has its own language, with special terms
describe many of the features found on boats.
is racing yacht shows most of the parts
a modern boat.

SHIP FACTS

• The world's largest
ship is the Norwegian
oil tanker *Jahre Viking*,
which is 1,503 ft
(458 m) long.

• About 92% of the
world's trading goods
are transported
by ships.

WARSHIPS AND SUBMARINES

THERE ARE MANY types of
fighting vessel, from light,
speedy destroyers, to huge
aircraft carriers
and nuclear
submarines.

Mizzen topgallant sail

Main topgallant sail

Fore mast topgallant sail

Fore m...

Fore tops...

Fore tops...

Jib s...

Mizzen topsail

1700s "MAN-OF-WAR"
By the 18th century,
sailing ships had become
floating fortresses.
Rival northern European
powers built heavily
armed fighting ships
called "men-of-war."

1700S 74-GUN SHIP

Main topsail

Gun ports

Sp...

tops...

TYPES OF WARSHIPS

AIRCRAFT CARRIER
The largest warship, a
carrier houses 100 aircraft
and a crew of over 2,000.

DESTROYER
Armed with guided missiles,
the destroyer's role is to
defend the fleet.

MINESWEEPER
This small
vessel carries
special equipment
for locating and
destroying mines.

CRUISER
The cruiser is designed for
speed and endurance at sea.

BATTLESHIP
Most heavily armed battleships
have been replaced by carriers.

PARTS OF A WARSHIP

Modern warships are armed with guns and guided missiles for attack and defense. Most vessels are also equipped with advanced electronic equipment for tracking and hitting targets.

Surveillance radar

Lynx helicopter

Seacat missile launcher

Funnel

Mast

Sonar torpedo decoy

Exocet missile launcher

Gun turret

Rudder

Variable pitch propeller

Antisubmarine torpedo tube

Liferaft cylinder

Rocket launcher

Pennant number

Sonar bulge

4.4 in (11 cm) gun

MODERN WARSHIP

MILITARY SUBMARINES

There are two main types of underwater warships. Patrol submarines seek and destroy other vessels, while missile-carrying submarines are equipped with nuclear warheads aimed at enemy cities and military targets.

Periscope

Senior enlisted man's mess

Stabilized fin

Aft hydroplane

Main turbine

Control room

Conning tower

Galley

Officers' mess

Propeller

Lower rudder

Diesel motor compartment

Nuclear reactor

Junior enlisted man's mess

Torpedo compartment

Torpedo tube

NUCLEAR-POWERED SUBMARINE

AIRCRAFT

THE FIRST PLANE flew
in only 1903, yet today
millions of people fly
each year. Airplanes are
heavier-than-air aircraft
with fixed wings, usually
powered by propellers
or jet turbines.

Lift (upward force)

Drag (backward force)

HOW A WING WORKS

Air passing over the curved
upper surface of a wing, or airfoil, travel
faster than the air passing beneath the
flatter underside. The lower pressure of
the fast air above the wing in relation to
the slower air beneath
it creates lift.

Wings covered with thin aluminum sheeting

Fuel tanks in wings and wing tips hold 70 gallons (320 liters) of fuel

Fin stops plane from swinging from side to side

Rudd
stee
pla

Fuselage

Pilot's seat

Elevat
control plane
ascent a
desce

Tailplane

Metal cables run from pilot's control stick and pedals to control surfaces

Ailerons cont
plane's balan
and, togeth
with rudd
steer pla

Engine

Spinner

Main landing gear

Fixed flap

Hinged aileron flap

Propeller

Nose landing gear

PIPER CHEROKEE

PARTS OF AN AIRCRAFT

This small, propeller-driven light aircraft shows the features o
a typical airplane. Its main structures are the fuselage, wings,
tailplane, and fin, which together are called the airframe.

The airframe of a jet airliner has to be capable of withstanding the stresses of high-speed flight and pressurization and depressurization of the passenger cabin. Airliners are built from light, strong materials such as aluminum alloys, titanium, and carbon fiber.

Brackets for overhead luggage lockers

Sound-proofing insulation

Luggage hold

Aluminum alloy skin

Stringers give fuselage extra strength

Hydraulic control pipes

Electric control wires

Floor panels

FUSELAGE SECTION

CONTROLLING THE PLANE

The wings and tail of an airplane are equipped with hinged flaps, or control surfaces, that allow it to pitch up or down, roll from side to side, or yaw left and right. To turn, the plane is banked, rolling and yawing at the same time.

Nose comes up

Elevators raised, pushing down the tail

Wing meets air at a sharper angle, increasing lift

PITCHING UP

To pitch up and climb, pilot pulls control column backward

Left aileron rises, reducing lift on left wing

Right aileron lowers, increasing lift on right wing

ROLLING LEFT

Pilot pushes control column to left

Rudder swings left, causing plane to yaw (swerve) to the left

Aircraft banks into left turn, rolling and yawing at same time

Left aileron rises

Right aileron lowers

TURNING LEFT

Pilot pushes control column to left while pushing rudder pedal with left foot

Types of aircraft

An aircraft is essentially any machine that enables people to fly. Powered airplanes and helicopters, hot-air balloons, gas-filled airships, and unpowered gliders are all different types of aircraft. There are many different types of aircraft for different uses, including transportation, warfare, and recreation.

HELICOPTERS
A helicopter uses rotating blades to take off vertically, hover, and move in any direction. Helicopter functions range from crop spraying to military operations.

Rotor blades

Tail rotor

Swivel joint allows blades to change pitch

Landing skids

Swashplate controlling pitch (angle) of rotor blade

SCHWEIZER 500C HELICOPTER

TORNADO FIGHTER/BOMBER
The most powerful military plane used by NATO forces, the Tornado is built in two forms. The fighter version intercepts enemy aircraft, while the bomber carries guided weapons and bombs for ground attack.

Radome containing ground mapping, attack, an terrain-following rada

Port outboard stores pylon

Air data probe

PANAVIA TORNADO GR1A

Upper rudder

Dorsal fin

Passenger window

Flight deck windshield

Nose in drooped position

THE CONCORDE
The Anglo-French Concorde is the world's only successful supersonic passenger airliner, reaching speeds of 1,550 mph (2,494 km/h).

Radome

THE CONCORDE

Strengthened glass
fiber nose cone

Elevator flaps to help
climbing or diving

Gas-filled
envelope

Crew and
passenger cabin,
or "gondola"

Propellers

Rudder
for steering

SKYSHIP 500HL AIRSHIP

Nylon load
tapes attach
cables to
envelope

Envelope
fills with
hot air

Stainless-
steel cables

Twin gas
burners
provide
hot air

Burner
frame

Basket

HOT-AIR BALLOON
AND BASKET

BALLOONS AND AIRSHIPS

Heated air rises, and when trapped in an envelope,
or balloon, it provides lift. Hot-air balloons were the
earliest aircraft, first appearing in the late 1700s.
Gas-filled airships, powered by propellers, were a
popular form of passenger air travel in the early 20th
century, but are now used mainly for advertising.

Tow rope
attachment

Streamlined
cockpit

Aileron

Slim, tapering
fuselage

T-shaped
tail improves
aerodynamics

EVW

Rudder

SCHELICHER K25 GLIDER

Fabric wings
allow hang
glider to ride
thermals

GLIDERS AND HANG GLIDERS

A glider is an unpowered plane with a
wide wingspan that uses currents of hot,
rising air (thermals) to stay aloft.
Gliders are tugged into the air by a winch
or towing vehicle. Hang gliders are made of
material stretched across a simple frame, forming
wings, and are launched from a hilltop or cliff.

Pilot hangs
from harness

HANG GLIDER

THE WORLD

HOW TO USE THIS SECTION

THESE PAGES SHOW YOU how to use the World
section of the encyclopedia. The maps are organized
by continent: North America, Central and South
America, Europe, Africa, North and West Asia,
South and East Asia, and Australasia. Information-
packed country fact pages separate the maps.

KEY TO ICONS
All the icons used on the
maps are listed below.

🎵 THE ARTS

☁ CLIMATE

🏭 COMMUNICATIONS

✂ ENVIRONMENT

🦋 FLORA AND FAUNA

🏛 HISTORY

🏭 INDUSTRY

⛰ NATURAL
FEATURES

👥 PEOPLE

Running head

Heading

Locator map

Introduction

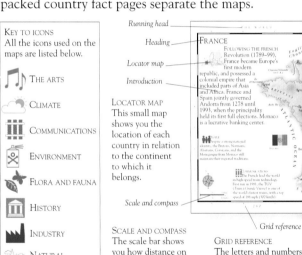

Scale and compass

Grid reference

LOCATOR MAP
This small map
shows you the
location of each
country in relation
to the continent
to which it
belongs.

SCALE AND COMPASS
The scale bar shows
you how distance on
the map relates to
miles and kilometers.
The compass points
show you north,
south, east, and west.

GRID REFERENCE
The letters and numbers
around this grid help you
locate places listed in the
gazetteer index. See page
470 for an explanation
on how to use this grid.

Flag

COUNTRY FACT PAGES
The fact pages give every country's facts and figures.

FLAGS
Every country's flag is shown by its side.

GAZETTEER INDEX
A gazetteer index at the back of the book lists major towns, cities, rivers, lakes, and mountain ranges that appear on the map pages.

KEY TO FACT SYMBOLS
These symbols are used on all the country fact pages.

⊙ CAPITAL CITY

✧ AREA

♦ POPULATION

💰 CURRENCY

♀ MAIN LANGUAGE

▲ GOVERNMENT

● LIFE EXPECTANCY

KEY TO MAPS

INTERNATIONAL BORDER	
DISPUTED BORDER	
STATE BORDER	
CAPITAL CITY	SHING D.C.
STATE OR ADMINISTRATIVE CAPITAL	LANTA
MAJOR TOWN	arlesto
AIRPORT	⊕
SEAPORT	
RIVER	
CANAL	
WADI	
LAKE	
SEASONAL LAKE	

GUIDE TO MAP PAGES

EUROPE
pp. 246–289

NORTH AND
WEST ASIA
pp. 314–329

SOUTH AND
EAST ASIA
pp. 330–349

AFRICA
pp. 290–313

*INDIAN
OCEAN*

*ATLANTIC
OCEAN*

AUSTRALAS
AND OCEAN
pp. 350–359

*SOUTHERN
OCEAN*

ARCTIC OCEAN

Arctic Circle

ATLANTIC OCEAN

NORTH AMERICA
pp. 204–227

PACIFIC OCEAN

Tropic of Cancer

Equator

PACIFIC OCEAN

CENTRAL AND
SOUTH AMERICA
pp. 228–245

Tropic of Capricorn

ATLANTIC OCEAN

NORTH AMERICA

ARCTIC OCEAN

BEAUFORT SEA

Alaska

CANADA

GULF OF ALASKA

PACIFIC OCEAN

UNITED STAT

MEX

Hawaii

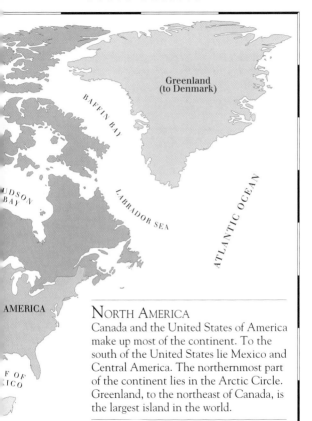

Greenland
(to Denmark)

BAFFIN BAY

HUDSON BAY

LABRADOR SEA

ATLANTIC OCEAN

AMERICA

GULF OF
MEXICO

NORTH AMERICA
Canada and the United States of America
make up most of the continent. To the
south of the United States lie Mexico and
Central America. The northernmost part
of the continent lies in the Arctic Circle.
Greenland, to the northeast of Canada, is
the largest island in the world.

ALASKA AND
WESTERN CANADA

AT THE END OF the last ice age, people traveled from Asia into North America over the Bering land bridge, which connected the continents at present-day Alaska.

ARCTIC OCEAN

Bering Strait

Prudhoe Bay

BROOKS RANGE

BEAUF

St. Lawrence I.

Nunivak I.

St. Matthew I.

BERING SEA

Aleutian Islands

Umnak I.
Unalaska I.
Unimak I.

Bristol Bay

ALASKA (U.S.A.)

Porcupine

Yukon

Fairbanks

Dawson

ALASKA RANGE

Anchorage

Kodiak I.

Gulf of Alaska

PACIFIC

ROCKY MO

WHITEHORSE

JUNEAU

Queen Charlotte Is.

BRI
COLA

Vancouver I.

Vancou

VICTO

ALASKA

⚑ 550,043

🏭 INDUSTRY
Fishing, oil, minerals, timber.
Railroads were the key to the
development of farming in western
Canada. The USA's biggest oil field
is at Prudhoe Bay, Alaska.

🏛 HISTORY
The U.S.A.
bought Alaska from
Russia in 1867 for
$7.2 million. Many
Americans thought this
was a waste of money until
gold was discovered there in
1896 and oil in 1968.

☁ CLIMATE
A polar climate prevails
in the north; the south is warmer.
The Pacific coast, near Vancouver,
has the warmest winters, and
temperatures rarely fall below freezing.

WESTERN CANADA

PEOPLE
The Inuit arrived in the area about 5,000 years ago. In 1999, they will become the first native North Americans to gain independence when they start to govern the Nunavut area in the eastern part of the Northwest Territories.

Nares Strait

Ellesmere I.

Axel
Heiberg
I.

Queen Elizabeth Islands

Baffin Bay

Devon I.

'Clure Strait   Melville I.   Lancaster Sound

Viscount Melville   Somerset
Sound   I.

Banks I.

Prince
of Wales
I.

Baffin I.

Davis Strait

Victoria I.

Gulf of Boothia

'n Gulf

King
William I.

Foxe Basin

Iqaluit

'ORTHWEST TERRITORIES

Southampton
I.

Hudson Strait

eat Bear

YELLOWKNIFE

at Slave L.

Hudson Bay

N   A   D   A

Churchill

FLORA AND FAUNA
Alaskan wildlife includes fur seals, moose, caribou, and many kinds of bear, including the kodiak, or Alaskan brown bear – the world's largest carnivorous land mammal.

L. Athabasca

Fort McMurray

Churchill

Nelson

MANITOBA

'BERTA

EDMONTON

SASKATCHEWAN

Saskatoon

L. Winnipeg

Calgary

Winnipegosis

REGINA

WINNIPEG

'TED STATES OF AMERICA

N

0   400   800km

0   200   400miles

EASTERN CANADA

THE SECOND LARGEST country in the world, Canada has a relatively small population. Most people live within 100 miles (160 km) of the USA border. Snowbound for most of the year, the Hudson Bay area is a wilderness of forests, rivers, and lakes.

PEOPLE
The Vikings were the first Europeans to visit eastern Canada, in about 986 B.C. They settled for only a short time before Native Americans drove them away.

INDUSTRY
Wood industries, oil, zinc, nickel, hydroelectricity, uranium. The area off the east coast, called the Grand Banks, is one of the world's richest fishing areas. A major export from the Atlantic provinces is newsprint, made from wood pulp.

Salis
Nottingham I.
Mansel I.

Inukjuak

Hudson Bay

Belche

MANITOBA

Severn

Winisk

C. Henrietta Maria

Attawapiskat

James Bay

Attawapiskat

Albany

ONTARIO

C A N

Lake of the Woods

L. Nipigon

Thunder Bay

Timmins

UNITED STATES OF AMERICA

Lake Superior

Sault Sainte Marie

Sudbury

Lake Michigan

Lake Huron

TORONTO

Hamilton

London

Windsor

L. Erie

Nia
Fall

UNI

E F G H

1

Davis Strait

Akpatok I. C. Chidley

ière aux
ailles Ungava Bay

2

Kuujjuaq

Nain

L A B R A D O R S E A

le Rivière
Baleine Smallwood
Reservoir LABRADOR

3

CLIMATE
January temperatures average
below 0°F (–18°C) in more than two-
thirds of Canada. Summers are short and
cool in the north, but warm enough for
farming in the south.

HISTORY
In the 15th and 16th
centuries, two expeditions, from
England and France, reached
Canada and each claimed it.
The struggle for territory
led to war and France
was forced to give up
its territories to
Great Britain in 1763.

L. Caniapiscau

**Churchill
Falls** **Goosebay**

rande Rivière
Project

Caniapiscau

Manicouagan
Res.

A
L. Mistassini

Île d'Anticosti

Newfoundland

4

Gulf of St.Lawrence

ST JOHN'S⊕⊕⊕

C. Race

Q U É B E C

St. Lawrence

Cabot Strait

ST PIERRE & MIQUELON
(to France)

5

QUÉBEC

PRINCE
EDWARD
ISLAND

NEW
BRUNSWICK **CHARLOTTE-
TOWN**

FREDERICTON

A T L A N T I C O C E A N

6

NOVA
SCOTIA

Montréal

HALIFAX

Bay of Fundy

C. Sable

7

A T E S O F A M E R I C A

way (Canal)

Lawrence
way (Canal)

COMMUNICATIONS
With the completion
of the Canadian Pacific
Railway in 1885, Canada's
east and west coasts were
linked for the first time.
The country is so vast that
there are six time zones
within its borders.

N

8

0 200 400km

0 100 200miles

EASTERN CANADA

E F G H

NORTHEASTERN STATES

WITH ITS RICH MINERAL resources and safe harbors, the Northeast was the first area on the continent to be colonized by Europeans. In 1620, English pilgrims sailed on the *Mayflower* to settle in a region that is still called New England. During the mid-19th century, European immigrants settled in New York City and in other East Coast cities. Today, this region is the most densely populated and heavily industrialized area of the USA.

CLIMATE
This area of the U.S.A has a temperate climate, with warm and humid summers. However, the northeastern region, in particular, can experience very heavy snowfall from November to April.

NORTHEASTERN STATES
♦ 51.5 million

PEOPLE
Northeastern Native American tribes, such as the Wampanoag, the Algonquin, and the tribes of the Iroquois League, were the first to come into contact with European settlers and explorers.

INDUSTRY
Oil, iron, steel, chemicals, maple sugar, blueberries, cranberries, fishing, tourism. Vermont is the main producer of maple syrup in the USA. The stock exchange on Wall Street, New York City, is the largest in the world.

E F G H

NATURAL FEATURES
Lying on the border
ween the USA and Canada,
agara Falls were formed about
,000 years ago. About 180,000
ns (tonnes) of water go over
e falls every minute.

1

2

CANADA

3

L. Champlain

Moosehead L.

ADIRONDACK MTS.
MONTPELIER WHITE MTS.

AUGUSTA

ester

Syracuse
er Lakes
NEW YORK
Mohawk

ALBANY

CATSKILL MTS.

MASSACHUSETTS

CONCORD

4

Springfield Worcester Cape Cod
Waterbury HARTFORD
New Haven CONNECTICUT
Bridgeport Nantucket I.
Martha's Vineyard

BOSTON
PROVIDENCE
RHODE ISLAND

5

HISTORY
In 1621, the
Mayflower pilgrims
celebrated their first
successful harvest.
Thanksgiving is now
an annual holiday,
observed on the
last Thursday
in November.

Susquehanna

Paterson
allentown Newark New York City
HARRISBURG TRENTON Long I.
Innington Philadelphia
NEW JERSEY
LAND Newark

6

ATLANTIC OCEAN

DOVER
DELAWARE

7

FLORA AND FAUNA
The Appalachian
Mountains are home to the
opossum, North America's
only species of marsupial,
or pouched mammal.

N

0 100 200km
0 50 100miles

8

E F G H

SOUTHERN STATES

BY THE 19TH CENTURY, the wealth of the South was based on crops like tobacco, indigo, rice, and especially cotton, which was grown on large plantations by African slaves. The area is known today for New Orleans' jazz, Florida's Disney World, and the Kentucky Derby. The city of Washington, in the District of Columbia, was made the US capital in 1800.

Mississippi Delta

CLIMATE
Summers are long and hot; winters are mild, but temperatures are generally warmer on the coast than inland. Southern Florida is tropical.

INDUSTRY
Soybeans, coal, peanuts, cotton, citrus fruits, tobacco, oil, tourism. Georgia grows half of the USA's peanuts – most are used to make peanut butter.

THE ARTS
The French brought Mardi Gras to America in the early 170[?] Celebrated in many of the south[ern] states, the most famous festival is held in New Orleans, where para[des] last for a week before Mardi Gras Day, the day before Lent starts.

Louisville FRANKFORT WEST WASHINGTON ANNAPOLIS
INDIANA OHIO VIRGINIA D.C. DELAWARE
CHARLESTON Baltimore
KENTUCKY ALLEGHENY MTS. VIRGINIA MARYLAND
NASHVILLE RICHMOND
TENNESSEE Roanoke
CUMBERLAND PLATEAU APPALACHIAN MTS. Newport News C. Charles
Tennessee Winston-Salem Norfolk
ntsville Chattanooga NORTH Durham
CAROLINA RALEIGH
Alabama ATLANTA Charlotte C. Hatteras
Birmingham COLUMBIA
MONTGOMERY SOUTH C. Fear
ALABAMA CAROLINA
Columbus GEORGIA Savannah Charleston
Chattahoochee Savannah
Flint Savannah

Okefenokee
Swamp

LLAHASSEE
Jacksonville
Gulf
of
Mexico FLORIDA

Orlando C.
Tampa Canaveral
St. Petersburg
L. Okeechobee

SOUTHERN STATES The Everglades
64.6 million Hollywood
Miami

Florida Keys Straits of Florida

III COMMUNICATIONS
The Mississippi River is
the longest and busiest
waterway in America. Barges
transport heavy cargo from
industrial and agricultural
regions near the Great Lakes
to the Gulf of Mexico.

N

0   150   300km
0   75   150miles

213

THE GREAT LAKES

THE STATES OF Indiana, Illinois, Michigan, Ohio, Wisconsin, and Minnesota, all of which border on one or more of the five Great Lakes, are often called the industrial and agricultural heartland of the United States. The region is rich in natural resources, with large areas of fertile farmland on flat plains called prairies.

Lake of the Woods

Upper Red

Lower Red L.

Leech L.

NORTH DAKOTA

SOUTH DAKOTA

MINNESOTA

Mississippi

Minneapo

ST P

CLIMATE
The region around the Great Lakes has warm summers but quite severe winters, and parts of the lakes can freeze over. Minnesota, in particular, suffers from heavy snowstorms.

GREAT LAKES STATES
♦ 46.4 million

ENVIRONMENT
The Great Lakes – Ontario, Huron, Superior, Michigan, and Erie – together form the largest area of freshwater in the world. Heavy industry has caused severe water pollution, and in some areas it is dangerous to eat the fish or swim.

INDUSTRY
Vehicles, coal, iron, grains, cherries. Nearly half of the world's corn crop and a thir of the cherry crop are grown in the Great Lakes region. Detroit is known as "motor city" because it is the center of the US car industry.

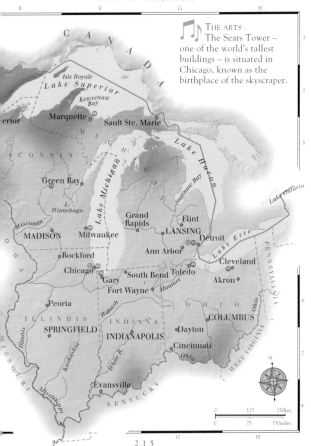

E   F   G   H

C   A   N   A   D   A

THE ARTS
The Sears Tower –
one of the world's tallest
buildings – is situated in
Chicago, known as the
birthplace of the skyscraper.

Isle Royale

Lake Superior

Keweenaw
Bay

perior

Marquette

Sault Ste. Marie

Lake Huron

M   I   C   H   I   G   A   N

W   I   S   C   O   N   S   I   N

Green Bay

L.
Winnebago

Lake Michigan

Saginaw Bay

Lake Ontario

Grand
Rapids

Flint

Wisconsin

MADISON

Milwaukee

LANSING

Detroit

Lake Erie

I   O   W   A

Rockford

Ann Arbor

Cleveland

PENNSYLVANIA

Chicago

South Bend

Toledo

Gary

Akron

Fort Wayne

Maumee

Peoria

Wabash

Illinois

I   L   L   I   N   O   I   S

SPRINGFIELD

I   N   D   I   A   N   A

O   H   I   O

Ohio

COLUMBUS

Dayton

INDIANAPOLIS

Cincinnati

WEST VIRGINIA

M   I   S   S   O   U   R   I

Kaskaskia

White R.

Ohio

N

Evansville

Mississippi

K   E   N   T   U   C   K   Y

0   125   250km

0   75   150miles

G   H

CENTRAL AND MOUNTAIN STATES

THE GREAT Plains, the Rocky Mountains, and the Mississippi lowlands dominate the landscape of the Midwest. Once home to Native Americans and herds of bison, the Great Plains were settled in the 19th century by Europeans, who forced the Native Americans onto reservations and slaughtered the bison to near-extinction.

HISTORY

Pioneers traveling to the West had to cross the Great Plains, which were known as the "Great American Desert." The last region to be settled, it is now a wealthy agricultural region.

CLIMATE

Summers are cooler and winters warmer than they are east of the Rockies. The Great Plains have an extreme climate, which can change quite suddenly and violently – blizzards, hail, thunderstorms, and tornadoes may occur.

CENTRAL AND
MOUNTAIN STATES
♦ 18.7 million

NATURAL FEATURES

The Rocky Mountains exte through Canada and the USA for more than 3,000 miles (4,800 km) Dividing North America, they separate the rivers flowing west to the Pacific from those flowing east to the Atlantic.

E   F   G   H

FLORA AND FAUNA
Grizzly bears were
once found west of the Black
Hills in South Dakota. So
many have been hunted that
there are probably fewer than
800 grizzly bears left. Most
are found in the mountains
of Idaho and Wyoming.

D   A

Peck L.
Missouri

L. Sakakawea

NORTH DAKOTA   Fargo

BISMARCK

MINNESOTA

SOUTH DAKOTA

Cheyenne

PIERRE

BLACK
HILLS

White R.

James

Missouri

WISCONSIN

Cedar

Sioux Falls

Cedar Rapids

Casper

Niobrara

IOWA

I L L I N O I S

OMING

NEBRASKA

North Platte

DES MOINES

EYENNE

Platte

LINCOLN

Omaha

Missouri

COLORADO

MISSOURI

Mississippi

SMOKY HILLS

Kansas City

St Louis

Smoky Hill

K A N S A S

TOPEKA

JEFFERSON
CITY

Wichita

Springfield

OZARK PLATEAU

Arkansas

KENTUCKY

Tulsa

A R K A N S A S

TENNESSEE

NEW
MEXICO

OKLAHOMA

OKLAHOMA
CITY

Canadian

N

INDUSTRY
Cattle, wheat, corn,
coal, natural gas, gold.
ming on the Great Plains of the
dwest is large-scale and mechanized.
oser to the Rockies, rainfall decreases and
ble farming gives way to cattle ranching.

Red R.

T E X A S

0   200   400km

0   100   200miles

E   F   G   H

SOUTHWESTERN STATES

THE FIRST Europeans in the Southwest were the Spanish, who traveled north from Mexico. This resulted in a mingling of Spanish and Native American cultures in this region. Gold and silver mining and cattle-ranching attracted other settlers in the mid 19th century, when this area became part of the USA after the Mexican War.

NATURAL FEATURES

The Colorado plateau has some unusual landforms, including natural bridges and arches of solid rock. Over the last million years, the Colorado River has cut away the plateau, forming the world's largest river gorge – the Grand Canyon.

HISTORY

At the end of the Mexican War (1846–48), the USA acquired Utah, Nevada, California, and parts of Arizona, New Mexico, Colorado, and Wyoming. One of the causes of the war was a border dispute between Texas and Mexico.

SOUTHWESTERN STATES

♦ 28.4 million

PEOPLE

Some of the earliest Native Americans lived in the Nevada area. Bones and ashes discovered near Las Vegas indicate that they may have lived there more than 20,000 years ago. Today, the region has the largest concentration of Native Americans in the country.

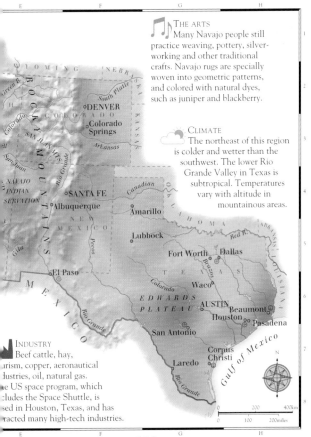

♫ THE ARTS
Many Navajo people still practice weaving, pottery, silver-working and other traditional crafts. Navajo rugs are specially woven into geometric patterns, and colored with natural dyes, such as juniper and blackberry.

CLIMATE
The northeast of this region is colder and wetter than the southwest. The lower Rio Grande Valley in Texas is subtropical. Temperatures vary with altitude in mountainous areas.

INDUSTRY
Beef cattle, hay, tourism, copper, aeronautical industries, oil, natural gas. The US space program, which includes the Space Shuttle, is based in Houston, Texas, and has attracted many high-tech industries.

WYOMING   NEBRASKA

Green R.

South Platte

ROCKY MOUNTAINS

COLORADO   DENVER   KANSAS

Colorado Springs

Colorado

Arkansas

SAN JUAN MTS.

San Juan

Rio Grande

NAVAJO INDIAN RESERVATION

SANTA FE   Canadian   OKLAHOMA   ARKANSAS

Albuquerque   Amarillo

NEW MEXICO   Red R.

Pecos   Lubbock

Gila   Fort Worth   Dallas

El Paso   T E X A S

MEXICO   Colorado   Waco

Brazos

EDWARDS PLATEAU   AUSTIN   Beaumont

Houston   Pasadena

San Antonio

Rio Grande   Corpus Christi

Laredo

Gulf of Mexico

Rio Grande

LOUISIANA

N

0   200   400km
0   100   200miles

E   F   G   H

PACIFIC STATES

ALL THREE STATES on the West Coast are major agricultural producers – Washington and Oregon supply one-third of the softwood timber for the USA, and California produces half of the country's fruit and vegetables. Situated where two of the Earth's plates meet, the area suffers from earthquakes and volcanic activity. Mount St. Helens, dormant since 1857, erupted in 1980, losing some 1,300 ft (400 m) off its height.

NATURAL FEATURES
The lowest point in the western hemisphere is in Death Valley, 282 ft (86 m) below sea level. One of the driest, hottest places on Earth, the highest temperature, 135°F (57°C), was recorded there in 1913, and its average rainfall is only 1.5 in (38 mm) per year.

Climate varies from the moderate coast to the snow-capped Sierra Nevada mountains. Much of California is arid desert.

INDUSTRY
Timber, aerospace industries, wine. The Santa Clara Valley, or Silicon Valley, specializes in high-tech industry. Hollywood is considered the center of the US film industry, although many major studios are no longer located there.

FLORA AND FAUNA
Redwoods are believed to be the tallest and oldest trees in the world. They are found along the West Coast from central California to southern Oregon and rarely occur more than 50 miles (80 km) inland.

PACIFIC STATES
37.5 million

MEXICO

THE ANCIENT empires of the Maya and Aztec flourished for centuries before the Spanish invaded Mexico in 1519, lured there by legends of hoards of gold and silver. Mexico gained its independence in 1810, after 300 years of Spanish rule. Today, most Mexicans are *mestizo*, a mix of Spanish and Native American. Although Spanish is the official language, Native American languages such as Maya, Nahuatl, and Zapotec are also widely spoken.

Tijuana Mexicali

UNITED STAT

BAJA CALIFORNIA

Angel de la Guarda I.

Cedros I.

Hermosillo

Tiburón I.

Nogal

Gulf of California

Culi

La Paz

CLIMATE
The Mexican plateau and mountains are warm for most of the year. The Pacific coast has a tropical climate.

MEXICO

NATURAL FEATURES
The plateau of Mexico is enclosed to the west and east by the Sierra Madre mountain ranges which occupy 75 percent of the total land area. Mexico is so mountainous and arid in parts that only 12 percent of the land is arab

FLORA AND FAUNA
The Mexican beaded lizard and the gila monster are the only two poisonous lizards known. The largest of all cacti is the giant saguaro, which grows in the Sonora Desert to a height of more than 60 ft (18 m).

1

ENVIRONMENT
Poor air quality is a problem in Mexico City because it is surrounded by mountains, which stop fumes released by cars and factories from escaping.

2

HISTORY
The remains of Mayan and Aztec cities are found all over Mexico and Central America. Mexico City is built on the ruins of the Aztec capital, Tenochtitlán.

3

INDUSTRY
Oil, natural gas, tourism, minerals, brewing, agriculture. Tourism employs nine percent of the workforce. Mexico is one of the largest oil producers and supplies one-fifth of the world's silver.

4

A M E R I C A

dad
ez

Bravo del Norte

ihuahua

Rio Grande

os

M E X I C O

SIERRA MADRE ORIENTAL

Monterrey

ENTAL

San Luis Potosí

Aguascalientes

Ciudad
Madero

León

Guadalajara   Poza Rica

L. Chapala

Gulf of Mexico

Mérida

MEXICO CITY □   L. Tezcoco

Campeche   Cozumel I.

Puebla

Bay of Campeche

YUCATÁN PENINSULA

Bahías

SIERRA MADRE DEL SUR

Villahermosa

Acapulco

Coatzacoalcos

Oaxaca

Tuxtla Gutiérrez

BELIZE

CIFIC   OCEAN

N

Gulf of Tehuantepec

GUATEMALA

Tapachula

200   400km

100   200miles

E   F   G   H

North America facts

UNITED STATES OF AMERICA

- The US economy is the largest in the world.
- The nation is made up of 50 states plus the District of Columbia.
- The world's leading computer software is produced in the US.

ESSENTIAL FACTS

- ⊙ Washington, DC
- ⚲ 3,618,760 sq miles (9,372,610 sq km)
- �141 257.8 million
- ☙ American dollar
- ♀ English
- ▲ Multiparty republic
- ♦ 76 years

BEAUTIFUL BIRD
The American national symbol is the bald eagle

WYOMING LANDSCAPE
The varied American scenery ranges from arid desert in Arizona through to areas of mountainous lakes in Wyoming.

SOUTHWESTERN STATES

ARIZONA
⊙ Phoenix
♦ 3.6 million

NEVADA
⊙ Carson City
♦ 1.1 million

TEXAS
⊙ Austin
♦ 17 million

COLORADO
⊙ Denver
♦ 3.3 million

NEW MEXICO
⊙ Santa Fe
♦ 1.5 million

UTAH
⊙ Salt Lake City
♦ 1.7 million

COWBOYS
Cattle ranching still big business Texas today.

NORTHEASTERN STATES

CONNECTICUT
⊙ Hartford
♣ 3.2 million

NEW JERSEY
⊙ Trenton
♣ 7.7 million

DELAWARE
⊙ Dover
♣ 673,000

NEW YORK
⊙ Albany
♣ 18 million

MAINE
⊙ Augusta
♣ 1.2 million

PENNSYLVANIA
⊙ Harrisburg
♣ 12 million

MASSACHUSETTS
⊙ Boston
♣ 6 million

RHODE ISLAND
⊙ Providence
♣ 998,000

NEW HAMPSHIRE
⊙ Concord
♣ 1.1 million

VERMONT
⊙ Montpelier
♣ 567,000

PACIFIC STATES

CALIFORNIA
⊙ Sacramento
♣ 29.1 million

WASHINGTON
⊙ Olympia
♣ 4.8 million

OREGON
⊙ Salem
♣ 2.8 million

BASEBALL IS THE
NATIONAL SPORT
OF THE US

THE STATUE
OF LIBERTY
New York's
famous statue
was given to
the US by
France in 1884.

OUTLYING STATES

ALASKA
⊙ Juneau
♣ 527,000

HAWAII
⊙ Honolulu
♣ 1.1 million

GREAT LAKES

ILLINOIS
⊙ Springfield
♣ 11.7 million

MICHIGAN
⊙ Lansing
♣ 9.3 milllion

OHIO
⊙ Columbus
♣ 10.9 million

INDIANA
⊙ Indianapolis
♣ 5.6 million

MINNESOTA
⊙ St. Paul
♣ 4.4 million

WISCONSIN
⊙ Madison
♣ 4.9 million

NORTH
AMERICAN
MOOSE

DETROIT,
MICHIGAN, IS
THE CENTER
OF THE
CAR
INDUSTRY IN
THE US

CENTRAL AND MOUNTAIN STATES

IDAHO
- ⊙ Boise
- ♦ 1 million

IOWA
- ⊙ Des Moines
- ♦ 2.8 million

KANSAS
- ⊙ Topeka
- ♦ 2.5 million

MISSOURI
- ⊙ Jefferson City
- ♦ 5.2 million

MONTANA
- ⊙ Helena
- ♦ 806,000

NEBRASKA
- ⊙ Lincoln
- ♦ 1.6 million

NORTH DAKOTA
- ⊙ Bismarck
- ♦ 660,000

OKLAHOMA
- ⊙ Oklahoma City
- ♦ 3.2 million

SOUTH DAKOTA
- ⊙ Pierre
- ♦ 715,000

WYOMING
- ⊙ Cheyenne
- ♦ 475,000

POPCORN
Corn products are an export of the midwestern states.

SOUTHERN STATES

MALABAMA
- ⊙ Montgomery
- ♦ 4.1 million

ARKANSAS
- ⊙ Little Rock
- ♦ 2.4 million

FLORIDA
- ⊙ Tallahassee
- ♦ 12.7 million

GEORGIA
- ⊙ Atlanta
- ♦ 6.4 million

KENTUCKY
- ⊙ Frankfort
- ♦ 3.7 million

LOUISIANA
- ⊙ Baton Rouge
- ♦ 4.4 million

MARYLAND
- ⊙ Annapolis
- ♦ 4.7 million

MISSISSIPPI
- ⊙ Jackson
- ♦ 2.6 million

NORTH CAROLINA
- ⊙ Raleigh
- ♦ 6.6 million

TENNESSEE
- ⊙ Nashville
- ♦ 4.9 million

SOUTH CAROLINA
- ⊙ Columbia
- ♦ 3.5 million

VIRGINIA
- ⊙ Richmond
- ♦ 6.1 million

WEST VIRGINIA
- ⊙ Charleston
- ♦ 1.9 million

Peanut butter

Peanut

GEORGIA GROWS NEARLY HALF THE TOTAL PEANUT CROP OF THE US

CANADA

- The CN Tower in Toronto is the tallest freestanding structure in the world.
- French-speaking Québec's claim for independence from the rest of the country is a key constitutional issue.
- Forests and lakes cover 40% of Canada.

ESSENTIAL FACTS

⊙ Ottawa

◷ 3,851,788 sq miles (9,976,140 sq km)

♦ 27.3 million

🖀 Canadian dollar

♀ English, French

▲ Multiparty democracy

♦ 77 years

NATIVE CANADIANS Kwakiutls displayed their status on posts carved with animal and human figures.

SWEET SYMBOL The leaf of the sugar maple tree is Canada's national symbol.

SPOOKY FESTIVAL Imaginative skeletons are seen everywhere during Mexico's Day of the Dead.

MEXICO

- The Mexican landscape ranges from snow-capped mountains to tropical rain forests.
- Mexico City is the world's largest city.
- More people emigrate from Mexico than any other country in the world.

ESSENTIAL FACTS

⊙ Mexico City

◷ 756,061 sq miles (1,958,200 sq km)

♦ 90 million

🖀 Mexican new peso

♀ Spanish

▲ Multiparty republic

♦ 70 years

CENTRAL AND SOUTH AMERICA

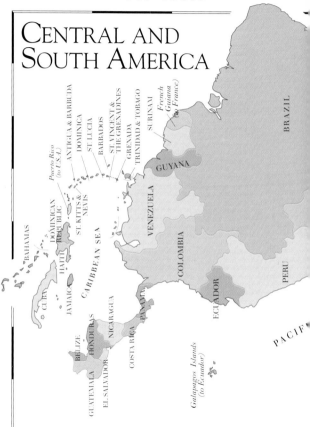

BRAZIL

ANTIGUA & BARBUDA
DOMINICA
ST LUCIA
BARBADOS
ST VINCENT &
THE GRENADINES
GRENADA
TRINIDAD & TOBAGO
SURINAM
French Guiana (to France)

Puerto Rico (to U.S.A.)

GUYANA

DOMINICAN REPUBLIC
HAITI
ST KITTS & NEVIS

VENEZUELA

BAHAMAS

CUBA

JAMAICA

CARIBBEAN SEA

COLOMBIA

PERU

ECUADOR

BELIZE
HONDURAS
NICARAGUA

PANAMA

GUATEMALA
EL SALVADOR
COSTA RICA

PACIFIC

Galapagos Islands (to Ecuador)

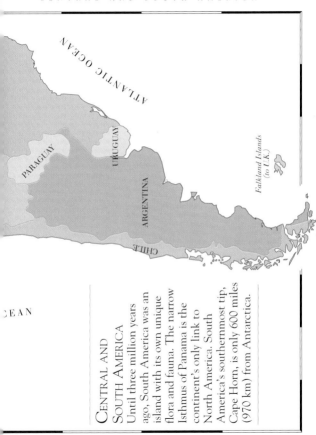

ATLANTIC OCEAN

PARAGUAY

URUGUAY

ARGENTINA

CHILE

*Falkland Islands
(to U.K.)*

...CEAN

CENTRAL AND SOUTH AMERICA

Until three million years ago, South America was an island with its own unique flora and fauna. The narrow Isthmus of Panama is the continent's only link to North America. South America's southernmost tip, Cape Horn, is only 600 miles (970 km) from Antarctica.

CENTRAL AMERICA AND THE CARIBBEAN

CENTRAL AMERICA FORMS a narrow land
bridge joining North and
South America. To the east
lie the Caribbean islands, many
of which are
uninhabited.

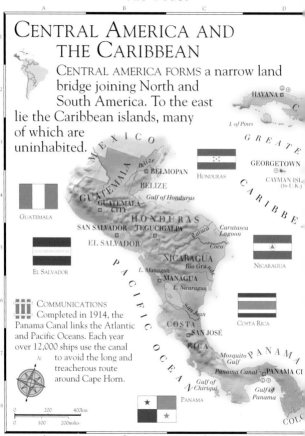

HAVANA

I. of Pines

GREATE

GEORGETOWN

HONDURAS

CAYMAN ISL.
(to U.K.)

CARIBBE

MEXICO

Belize

BELMOPAN

BELIZE

GUATEMALA

Gulf of Honduras

GUATEMALA
CITY

HONDURAS

SAN SALVADOR   TEGUCIGALPA

Patuca

Caratasca
Lagoon

GUATEMALA

EL SALVADOR

Coco

EL SALVADOR

NICARAGUA

Rio Grande

L. Managua

MANAGUA

NICARAGUA

L. Nicaragua

PACIFIC

San Juan

COSTA

COSTA RICA

SAN JOSÉ

COMMUNICATIONS
Completed in 1914, the
Panama Canal links the Atlantic
and Pacific Oceans. Each year
over 12,000 ships use the canal
to avoid the long and
treacherous route
around Cape Horn.

OCEAN

RICA

Mosquito
Gulf

PANAMA

PANAMA CI

Panama Canal

N

Gulf of
Chiriqui

Gulf of
Panama

PANAMA

0   200   400km

0   100   200miles

COL

230

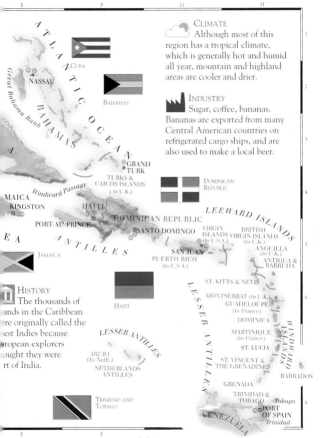

ATLANTIC OCEAN

CUBA

NASSAU

Great Bahama Bank

BAHAMAS

B A H A M A S

CLIMATE
Although most of this region has a tropical climate, which is generally hot and humid all year, mountain and highland areas are cooler and drier.

INDUSTRY
Sugar, coffee, bananas. Bananas are exported from many Central American countries on refrigerated cargo ships, and are also used to make a local beer.

GRAND TURK
TURKS & CAICOS ISLANDS (to U.K.)

MAICA
KINGSTON

Windward Passage

HAITI

PORT-AU-PRINCE

DOMINICAN REPUBLIC

DOMINICAN REPUBLIC

SANTO DOMINGO

LEEWARD ISLANDS

VIRGIN ISLANDS (to U.S.A.)

BRITISH VIRGIN ISLANDS (to U.K.)

ANGUILLA (to U.K.)

SAN JUAN
PUERTO RICO (to U.S.A.)

ANTIGUA & BARBUDA

E A   A N T I L L E S

JAMAICA

ST. KITTS & NEVIS

HISTORY
The thousands of
ands in the Caribbean
ere originally called the
est Indies because
ropean explorers
ought they were
rt of India.

HAITI

MONTSERRAT (to U.K.)
GUADELOUPE (to France)

DOMINICA

MARTINIQUE (to France)

ST. LUCIA

LESSER ANTILLES

ARUBA (to Neth.)

NETHERLANDS ANTILLES

ST. VINCENT & THE GRENADINES

WINDWARD ISLANDS

BARBADOS

GRENADA

TRINIDAD & TOBAGO

Tobago

PORT OF SPAIN

TRINIDAD AND TOBAGO

Trinidad

VENEZUELA

L E S S E R   A N T I L L E S

Central America facts

NICARAGUA

• Lake Nicaragua is the only freshwater lake in the world to contain ocean animals.

ESSENTIAL FACTS

⊙ Managua
◷ 50,193 sq miles (130, 000 sq km)
♦ 4.1 million
☙ New córdoba
♀ Spanish

HONDURAS

• The swampy Caribbean shoreline of Honduras is known as the Mosquito Coast.

ESSENTIAL FACTS

⊙ Tegucigalpa
◷ 43,278 sq miles (112,090 sq km)
♦ 5.6 million
☙ Lempira
♀ Spanish

QUETZAL
Inca headdresses were decorated with the colorful tail feathers of the quetzal bird.

COTTON
The export of cotton is a major Nicaraguan industry.

BANANAS
Honduras has huge banana plantations. The work is hard and the pay is low.

GUATEMALA

• The ruined remains of temples and pyramids built by the ancient Mayans can still be seen in the forests of Guatemala.

ESSENTIAL FACTS

⊙ Guatemala City
◷ 42,043 sq miles (108,890 sq km)
♦ 10 million
☙ Quetzal
♀ Spanish

EL SALVADOR

• Coffee accounts for 90% of the country's exported goods.
• El Salvador means "the saviour," referring to Christ.

ESSENTIAL FACTS

⊙ San Salvador
◷ 28,124 sq miles (1,040 sq km)
♦ 5.4 million
☙ Salvadorean colón
♀ Spanish

COSTA RICA

• The constitution of Costa Rica is the only one in the world to ban National Armies.
• The name Costa Rica means "rich coast" in Spanish.

ESSENTIAL FACTS

⊙ San José
◔ 19,730 sq miles (51,100 sq km)
♦ 3.3 million
⛁ Costa Rican colón
♀ Spanish

MAHOGANY
Costa Rica's forests have been devastated by excessive felling of trees, such as mahogany and cedar, for timber. Today, much forested land is protected.

CUBAN BEE HUMMINGBIRD

PANAMA

• Many rare bird and animal species are threatened by the wholesale destruction of Panama's rain forests.

ESSENTIAL FACTS

⊙ Panama City
◔ 29,761 sq miles (77,080 sq km)
♦ 2.6 million
⛁ Balboa
♀ Spanish

BELIZE

• The Belizean barrier reef is the second largest in the world.
• Belize was formerly known as British Honduras, gaining independence in 1981.

ESSENTIAL FACTS

⊙ Belmopan
◔ 8,865 sq miles (22,960 sq km)
♦ 200,000
⛁ Belizean dollar
♀ English

CUBA

• As a result of fuel shortages, the bicycle is the main form of public transportation.
• Cuba is the only communist country in the Americas.

ESSENTIAL FACTS

⊙ Havana
◔ 42,803 sq miles (110,860 sq km)
♦ 10.9 million
⛁ Cuban peso
♀ Spanish

EXPORTS
Belize exports grapefruit. Sugar is made from cane, which grows in Panama.

Caribbean facts

DOMINICAN REPUBLIC

• Founded in 1496 by Christopher Columbus's brother, Santo Domingo is the oldest American city.

ESSENTIAL FACTS

⊙ Santo Domingo

◔ 18,815 sq miles (48,730 sq km)

♦ 7.6 million

🐚 Dominican Republic peso

♡ Spanish

HAITI

• Many Haitians still practice the folk religion of voodoo.
• Haiti became the first independent black republic in 1804.

ESSENTIAL FACTS

⊙ Port-au-Prince

◔ 10,714 sq miles (27,750 sq km)

♦ 6.9 million

🐚 Gourde

♡ French, Creole

Molasses

Rum, ma from ca ju

Sugar cane

CANE PRODUCTS
Sugar cane thrives in the tropical Caribbean

JAMAICA

• Reggae music originated in Jamaica.
• The Rastafarians of Jamaica worship Haile Selassie, the late emperor of Ethiopia.
• Large areas of Kingston are ruled by gang leaders, or *Dons*.

ESSENTIAL FACTS

⊙ Kingston

◔ 4,243 sq miles (10,990 sq km)

♦ 2.5 million

🐚 Jamaican dollar

♡ English

Wooden maracas

Steel drum, made from an oil drum

Guiora, percussion instrument

ISLAND SOUNDS
Caribbean music, such as calypso and reggae, shows a strong African influence.

GRENADA
- St. George's
- 91,000
- English, Creole

ST. LUCIA
- Castries
- 156, 000
- English, French

THE BAHAMAS
- Nassau
- 300,000
- English, Creole

DOMINICA
- Roseau
- 72,000
- English, French

ISLE OF SPICES Many varieties of spice are grown on the island of Grenada.

Cloves

Mace

Bay leaf

Saffron

Cinnamon stick

Ground cinnamon

ST. KITTS & NEVIS
- Basseterre
- 44,000
- English, Creole

ST. VINCENT & THE GRENADINES
- Kingstown
- 109,000
- English, Creole

BARBADOS
- Bridgetown
- 260,000
- English, Creole

TRINIDAD & TOBAGO
- Port-of-Spain
- 1.3 million
- English

ANTIGUA & BARBUDA
- St. John's
- 200,000
- English, Creole

STORMY WEATHER The Caribbean islands are often subject to extreme weather, such as hurricanes and typhoons.

NORTHERN SOUTH AMERICA

THE INCAS RULED MUCH of this area in the 15th century, and today large numbers of their descendants live in Peru, Ecuador, and Bolivia. In 1533, the last Incan emperor was executed by the Spanish, who colonized this region. Countries east of Venezuela were later settled by the French, Dutch, and British, although all but French Guiana are now independent.

Coastal areas are hot and humid. The Andes are divided into three climatic zones – cold highlands, which have springlike weather all year round, temperate uplands, and hot lowlands.

INDUSTRY
Oil, bauxite, rice, coal, coffee, bananas, gold, silver, tin. Colombia and Bolivia are the largest exporters of the illegal drug cocaine, made from the leaves of the coca bush.

BOLIVIA

ECUADOR

NATURAL FEATURES
Lake Titicaca, the world's highest navigable lake, lies in the Andes at 12,497 ft (3,809 m) above sea level. Wood is scarce, so native South Americans make boats from the reeds that grow around the lake.

PERU

BRAZIL

BOLIVIA

PERU

CHILE

ARGENTINA

PARAGUAY

Guayaquil
Piura
Chiclayo
Trujillo
Chimbote
Iquitos
Callao
LIMA
Ica
Huancayo
Arequipa
Tacna
Oruro
LA PAZ
L. Titicaca
Cochabamba
Sucre
Santa Cruz
San Miguel
Marañón
Amazon
Ucayali
Madre de Dios
Beni
Mamoré

N

0   150   300
0   300   600km
0   400miles

Northern South America facts

SURINAM

• Jaguars, pumas, ocelots, and iguanas live wild in Surinam.

ESSENTIAL FACTS

⊙ Paramaribo

◔ 63,039 sq miles (163,270 sq km)

♦ 400,000

☙ Surinam guilder

♡ Dutch

COLOMBIA

• The country of Colombia produces two-thirds of the world's emeralds.

ESSENTIAL FACTS

⊙ Bogotá

◔ 439,620 sq miles (1,138,910 sq km)

♦ 34 million

☙ Colombian peso

♡ Spanish

▲ Multiparty republic

♦ 69 years

Uncut gem

Rock

COLOMBIAN EMERALD

PERU

• The Morochocha railway in Peru has the world's highest section of railway track.
• Peru is a strongly patriarchal, or male-dominated, society.

ESSENTIAL FACTS

⊙ Lima

◔ 496,223 sq miles (1,285,220 sq km)

♦ 22.9 million

☙ New sol

♡ Spanish, Quechua, and Aymará

ECUADOR AND THE GALÁPAGOS

• Charles Darwin's studies on the Galápagos Islands in 1856 helped formulate his theories on the evolution of species.
• Ecuador's landscape features low coastal regions, high Andean peaks, and dense jungle.

ESSENTIAL FACTS

⊙ Quito

◔ 109,483 sq miles (283,560 sq km)

♦ 11.3 million

☙ Sucre

♡ Spanish, Quechua

GALÁPAGOS TORTOISE

THE GALÁPAGOS

These islands lie 603 miles (970 km) west of Ecuador. Many of the islands' animals are unique.

Wing span of more than 10 ft (3m)

ANDEAN
CONDOR
The heaviest
bird of prey in the
world, the condor lives
in the highest parts
of the Andes.

BOLIVIA

• La Paz is the
highest capital city
in the world.
• Many Bolivian
farmers are very poor,
growing just enough
food for their families
to live on.
• Bolivia has the
world's highest golf
course and ski run.

ESSENTIAL FACTS

⊙ La Paz
⊘ 424,162 sq miles
(1,098,580 sq km)
✦ 7.8 million
☷ Boliviano
♡ Spanish, Quechua,
and Aymará

VENEZUELA

• Many Venezuelan
people live in poverty.
• Venezuela is the most
urbanized country in
South America.
• Angel Falls, the
highest waterfall in
the world, lies in
southern Venezuela.

ESSENTIAL FACTS

⊙ Caracas
⊘ 352,143 sq miles
(912,050 sq km)
✦ 20.6 million
☷ Bolívar
♡ Spanish

CAYENNE PEPPER
Crushed South
American
chilies are
used to make
cayenne
pepper.

GUYANA

• The Guyanese nation
is the only English-
speaking country in
South America.
• Guyana means
"land of many waters."

ESSENTIAL FACTS

⊙ Georgetown
⊘ 83,000 sq miles
(214,970 sq km)
✦ 800,000
☷ Guyana dollar
♡ English, Creole

FRENCH GUIANA

• The European Space
Agency conducts its
rocket launches
from French Guiana.
• The territory of
French Guiana is the
last remaining colony
in South America.

ESSENTIAL FACTS

⊙ Cayenne
⊘ 35,135 sq miles
(90,996 sq km)
✦ 114,800
☷ French franc
♡ French

BRAZIL

OCCUPYING NEARLY HALF of South America, Brazil has the largest river basin in the world. Many Brazilians are descendants of Portuguese, who colonized Brazil in the 16th century and Africans, who were brought to work on sugar plantations. Brazil's Native American tribes have little contact with the outside world. In 1992, the United Nations held its first Earth Summit in Rio, partly to highlight the destruction of the Amazon rainforest, the largest rainforest in the world.

PEOPLE

There were once about two million indigenous people living in Amazonia. Today only 50,000 remain. The survival of many tribes and their way of life is threatened by the destruction of the Amazon rainforest.

ATLANTIC OCEAN

Fortaleza

Teresina

São Luís

Belém

FRENCH
GUIANA
(to France)

SURINAM

GUYANA

VENEZUELA

COLOMBIA

Negro

Manaus

Balbina
Res.

Madeira

Santarém

SERRA PELADA

Xingu

Tapajós

Purus

Amazon

CLIMATE
The Amazon basin has an equatorial climate, with consistently high temperatures and rainfall. In the rest of Brazil, the climate varies – the northeast is extremely dry, while the southern states have hot summers and cool winters, when frost may occur.

NATURAL FEATURES
Covering about two-thirds of Brazil, the Amazon rainforest is the most complex ecosystem known. The Amazon River, the longest in South America, meets the Atlantic at the equator with such force that from the air its waters appear as a long, muddy stain in the sea.

INDUSTRY
Cars, steel, iron, coffee, cattle, citrus fruit, sugar. Brazil is the world's largest coffee producer and supplies 85 percent of the world's orange juice.

BRAZIL

N

0   400   800km
0   200   400miles

SOUTHERN SOUTH AMERICA

THE LANDSCAPE OF this region of South America varies from snow-capped volcanoes in the Andes to the wastelands of Patagonia. In the heart of Argentina lie the Pampas, fertile grasslands where vast herds of cattle graze. In parts, grasses grow up to 10 ft (3 m) high. Chile is separated from the rest of the region by the Andes, which run the length of the continent.

CLIMATE

Paraguay is subtropical, farther south is temperate. The Andes have snow year-round, while parts of the Atacama desert in Chile have had no rain for 400 years.

URUGUAY

PARAGUAY

Map labels

BRAZIL

Ciudad
del Este

ASUNCIÓN

Paraguay

Pilcomayo

Bermejo

Paraná

Posadas

Corrientes

Formosa

Resistencia

PARAGUAY

GRAN CHACO

Salado

L. Mar

San Salvador
de Jujuy

Salta

San Miguel
de Tucumán

Santiago
del Estero

BOLIVIA

A N D E S

ATACAMA DESERT

Copiapó

C H I L E

Arica

PERÚ

PACIFIC OCEAN

INDUSTRY
Copper, wool, beef, wheat. Chile is the world's largest copper producer, and Uruguay is the second-largest wool exporter.

ARGENTINA

HISTORY
Before the discovery of Cape Horn at the tip of the continent in 1616, ships used the dangerous Straits of Magellan to travel between the Atlantic and the Pacific Oceans. Today, ships use the Panama Canal.

NATURAL FEATURES
The longest chain of mountains in the world, the Andes are 4,500 miles (7,240 km) in length. They are the most recently formed mountains on Earth, and the area suffers from earthquakes and volcanic activity. Glaciers, fjords, lakes, and deep-sea channels are features of the southern Andes.

ATLANTIC OCEAN

Plate

BUENOS AIRES

Mar del Plata

Bahía Blanca

Colorado

Negro

Gulf of San Matías

Valdés Peninsula

P A M P A S

Comodoro Rivadavia

Chubat

Deseado

P A T A G O N I A

L. Colhué Huapi
L. Musters

L. Nahuel Huapi

Coihaique

L. Buenos Aires

Puerto Santa Cruz

Santa Cruz

Chico

Puerto Montt

Chiloé I.

Osorno

Valdivia

Temuco

Los Angeles

Concepción

Bío-Bío

Talcahuano

Chillán

San Bernardo

SANTIAGO

Viña del Mar

Valparaíso

Santa Cruz

A N D E S

C H I L E

TORRES DEL PAINE

L. Argentino

L. Viedma

Strait of Magellan

Punta Arenas

TIERRA DEL FUEGO

Cape Horn

CHILE

N

0   150   300
0   300   600 km
0   300 miles

Southern South America Facts

CHILE

- Democracy was restored in Chile in 1989 after 12 years of military rule under General Pinochet.
- The Atacama Desert in northern Chile is the driest place on Earth.

ESSENTIAL FACTS

⊙ Santiago

◔ 292,258 sq miles (756,950 sq km)

♦ 13.8 million

🐚 Chilean peso

♥ Spanish

▲ Multiparty republic

♦ 72 years

TREE OF MYSTERY
The Chile pine, also known as the monkey puzzle tree, is native to the Andes, the world's longest mountain range.

URUGUAY

- The country of Uruguay is the smallest in South America.
- Almost half of the population lives in Montevideo.
- Hydroelectric power generates 86% of the country's electricity.
- Uruguay is tolerant of all forms of religion.

ESSENTIAL FACTS

⊙ Montevideo

◔ 68,498 sq miles (177,410 sq km)

♦ 3.1 million

🐚 Uruguayan peso

♥ Spanish

PARAGUAY

- The majority of Paraguayans are *mestizo* – a mixture of native Guaraní Indian and Spanish blood.
- Half the work force is employed in agriculture.

ESSENTIAL FACTS

⊙ Asunción

◔ 157,046 sq miles (406,750 sq km)

♦ 4.5 million

🐚 Guaraní

♥ Spanish, Guaraní

WOOLEN SCARF

TEXTILES
Uruguay is a major exporter of handmade wool products.

GAUCHO
Argentinian cowboys are known as gauchos.

ARGENTINA

• Crop production and cattle and sheep rearing produce three-quarters of the nation's income.
• The Argentinian daily drink is a tea called *maté*.
• The tango, a dance, originated in Buenos Aires in the late 19th century.

ESSENTIAL FACTS
⊙ Buenos Aires
◷ 1,068,296 sq miles (2,766,890 sq km)
♦ 33.5 million
♻ Argentinian peso
♡ Spanish
▲ Multiparty republic
♦ 71 years

PUDU
Southern Argentina's Patagonia region is home to the pudu, the world's smallest deer.

BRAZILIAN SOCCER
Soccer is Brazil's favorite sport, with more than 0,000 teams.

BRAZIL

• São Paulo is the world's second largest city, with 17 million inhabitants.
• Rio de Janeiro's *Mardi Gras* carnival is a major tourist attraction.
• Brazil has rich gold and diamond reserves.
• Many Brazilians live in poverty, despite the country's resources.

ESSENTIAL FACTS
⊙ Brasília
◷ 3,286,472 sq miles (8,511,970 sq km)
♦ 156.6 million
♻ Reál
♡ Portuguese
▲ Multiparty republic
♦ 66 years

EUROPE

Jan Mayen I.
(to Norway)

ICELAND

Faeroe Islands
(to Denmark)

NORWEGIAN SE

NORWAY

NORTH
SEA

DENMARK

UNITED KINGDOM

REPUBLIC OF
IRELAND

GERMANY

1
2
3

FRANCE

4
5

AU

6
7

9

8

PORTUGAL

SPAIN

Gibraltar
(to U.K.)

MA

MEDIT

EUROPE

The Alps and the Pyrenees roughly divide the continent into north and south, forming a barrier that protects warm southern countries, such as Spain and Italy, from cold northern winds. Parts of Europe are moderated by the Gulf Stream, which circulates warm waters from the Caribbean, and even seas in the Arctic Circle stay ice-free in winter.

BARENTS SEA

FINLAND

ARCTIC SEA

ESTONIA

LATVIA

LITHUANIA

RUSSIAN
FEDERATION

BELARUS

POLAND

SLOVAKIA

HUNGARY

UKRAINE

16

ROMANIA

13

BULGARIA

BLACK SEA

GEORGIA

AZERBAIJAN

ARMENIA

14

5

GREECE

TYRRHENIAN SEA

1 NETHERLANDS
2 BELGIUM
3 LUXEMBOURG
4 LIECHTENSTEIN
5 SWITZERLAND
6 ANDORRA
7 MONACO
8 VATICAN CITY
9 SAN MARINO
10 SLOVENIA
11 CROATIA
12 BOSNIA/HERZEGOVINA
13 YUGOSLAVIA
14 MACEDONIA
15 ALBANIA
16 MOLDOVA

SCANDINAVIA AND FINLAND

DURING PAST ICE AGES, much of Scandinavia and Finland were covered in glaciers that carved out the land, leaving steep-sided valleys, fjords, and lakes. The Finns, originally from the east via Russia, differ from Scandinavians in culture and language.

CLIMATE
Norway's west coast is warmed by the Gulf Stream. Northern temperatures fall to −22°F (−30°C) during the six-month winter; the south is milder.

INDUSTRY
Fishing, timber, wood-pulp, paper, oil, gas, car manufacture. Norway is western Europe's largest producer of oil.

FINLAND

NORWAY

ARCTIC OCEAN

North Cape

Hammerfest

Tromsø

RUSSIAN FEDERATION

L. Inari

Paatsjoki

FINLAND

Ounas

Muonio

Torne

Oulu

L. Uddjaur

Lule

Torne

SCANDINAVIA

Lofoten Islands

NORWEGIAN SEA

NATURAL FEATURES
In the far north, the sun never sets during the 73 days of midsummer. In winter in Lappland, the sun remains below the horizon for one week; farther north, the darkness lasts for two months.

SWEDEN

THE ARTS
Swedish chemist Alfred Nobel, who invented dynamite, left his money to fund prizes to promote peace. Since 1901, Nobel prizes have been awarded for physics, chemistry, medicine, literature, economics, and peace.

DENMARK

L. Vienan
L. Oni
Vaasa
L. Saimaa
HELSINKI
Tampere
Turku
Gulf of Finland
Åland Is.
Gulf of Bothnia
BALTIC SEA
Fårö
Uppsala
Ljusnan
Ljungan
Norrköping
Linköping
Gotland
STOCKHOLM
Västerås
Örebro
Jönköping
Öland
L. Vätter
Gothenburg
Borås
Helsingborg
L. Väner
Malmö
Bornholm
Klarälven
OSLO
L. Mjösa
L. Femund
Glåma
Skagerrak
Kattegat
DENMARK
Helsingør
COPENHAGEN
Bergen
Ålborg
JUTLAND
Århus
Odense
GERMANY

Northern Europe facts

ICELAND

- The remote interior of Iceland can only be reached by special vehicle, pony, or small plane.
- Iceland has the lowest population in Europe.
- Heating is provided by geothermal power.

ESSENTIAL FACTS

- ⊙ Reykjavik
- ◷ 139,770 sq miles (103,000 sq km)
- ♦ 300,000
- ⚉ New Icelandic krona
- ♡ Icelandic
- ▲ Multiparty republic
- ♦ 78 years

ICELANDIC COD
More than a third of the world's cod-liver oil is produced in Iceland.

NORWAY

- According to Norway's constitution, the government's duty is to create conditions enabling every person to find work.

ESSENTIAL FACTS

- ⊙ Oslo
- ◷ 125,060 sq miles (323,900 sq km)
- ♦ 4.2 million
- ⚉ Norwegian krone
- ♡ Norwegian
- ▲ Multiparty democracy
- ♦ 77 years

GRASS ROOFS
Some Norwegian vacation homes have turf-covered roofs.

LAND OF LEGO
Lego building blocks, known by children worldwide, were invented in Denmark.

DENMARK

- Single parents and cohabiting couples raise 40% of Danish children.
- Denmark is Europe's oldest monarchy, dating back to the 1100s.

ESSENTIAL FACTS

- ⊙ Copenhagen
- ◷ 16,629 sq miles (43,069 sq km)
- ♦ 5.2 million
- ⚉ Danish krone
- ♡ Danish
- ▲ Multiparty democracy
- ♦ 75 years

SWEDEN

- Over 50% of Swedish women go out to work.
- Sweden has maintained a position of armed neutrality since 1815.
- Swedish law requires cars to travel with their headlights on at all times.
- Many Swedes invest in overseas property.

ESSENTIAL FACTS

- ⊙ Stockholm
- ◑ 173,730 sq miles (449,960 sq km)
- ♦ 8.7 million
- ✸ Swedish krona
- ♥ Swedish
- ▲ Multiparty democracy
- ● 78 years

SMÖRGÅSBORD
A Swedish smörgåsbord, meaning "sandwich table," is a spread of local delicacies served cold.

GREENLAND

Dependency of Denmark
Atlantic Ocean, pp.360–361)

- ◑ Nuuk
- ♦ 55,385
- ♥ Inuit, Danish

FINNISH TIMBER
Most of Finland's wealth is provided by its timber exports.

Ladle

Sauna
bucket

STEAM CLEANING
The Finns invented the steam bath, or sauna, over 1,000 years ago.

FINLAND

- Over half of Finland's population lives in the five districts around Helsinki.
- Finland was the first country to allow women to run for parliament.
- Finland's inland waterway system is the largest in Europe.

ESSENTIAL FACTS

- ⊙ Helsinki
- ◑ 130,552 sq miles (338,130 sq km)
- ♦ 5 million
- ✸ Markka
- ♥ Finnish, Swedish
- ▲ Multiparty republic
- ● 75 years

THE BRITISH ISLES

LYING OFF THE COAST of mainland Europe, the British Isles consist of two main islands, Ireland and Great Britain, and many smaller islands. England, Scotland, Wales, and Northern Ireland form the United Kingdom (U.K.). The Republic of Ireland became independent of the U.K. in 1921.

UNITED KINGDOM

NORTH S

NATURAL FEATURES
The highest point in the British Isles is Ben Nevis in Scotland, at a height of 4,406 ft

HIGHLANDS

GRAMPIAN MTS

Aberdeen

Edinburgh

Glasgow

Arran

Kintyre

Mull

Jura

Islay

Colonsay

Coll

Tiree

Skye

Lewis

North Uist

South Uist

Barra

Outer Hebrides

Shetland Is.

Orkney Is.

ATLANTIC OCEAN

THE LOW COUNTRIES

BELGIUM, THE NETHERLANDS, and Luxembourg are known as the "Low Countries" because they are flat and low-lying. Much of the Netherlands lies below sea level and has been reclaimed from the sea. The Low Countries, also called "Benelux," are Europe's most densely populated countries.

CLIMATE
The region is mostly temperate. Coastal areas are mildest, warmed by the Gulf Stream. Luxembourg's winters are cold

NETHERLANDS

GERMANY

Groningen
Leeuwarden
Assen
West Frisian Is.
Waddenzee
IJsselmeer
Zwolle
IJssel
Flevoland
Enschede
Apeldoorn
Arnhem
Rhine
Nijmegen
's-Hertogenbosch
Haarlem
AMSTERDAM
Utrecht
The Hague
Rotterdam
Dordrecht
NORTH SEA

COMMUNICATIONS
Belgium can be crossed within four hours by car or train. Its highway network is so extensive and so well lit that, like the Great Wall of China, it can be seen from space.

LUXEMBOURG

N

0   15   70km
0   20   40miles

GERMANY

Maastricht

Albert Canal

Ghent

Scheldt

BRUSSELS

Liège

Namur

Charleroi

Sambre

Mons

Meuse

B E L G I U M

F R A N C E

A R D E N N E S

Our the

Sûre

Our

LUXEMBOURG

Arlon

LUXEMBOURG

INDUSTRY
High-tech industries, cheese, flowers, metal products, banking. Many of the world's diamonds are cut, polished, and sold in Antwerp and Amsterdam. Luxembourg is a banking center and tax haven.

HISTORY
The European Union (EU) was set up in 1957 with Brussels as its administrative capital. The European Court of Justice and Investment Bank are in Luxembourg.

ENVIRONMENT
To prevent coastal areas from flooding, the Dutch built windmills to pump excess water into canals. Amsterdam was encircled by 900 windmills. Today, the Dutch use a giant infrastructure of canals, dykes, and dunes.

BELGIUM

Northwest Europe facts

UNITED KINGDOM

- London's theaters, art galleries, and historical buildings are a major tourist attraction.
- British people meet to talk and drink in public houses (pubs).
- Scotland retains a distinct educational and legal system that differs from the rest of the UK.

ESSENTIAL FACTS

- ⊙ London
- ◔ 94,550 sq miles (244,880 sq km)
- ✚ 57.8 million
- ✤ Pound sterling
- ♡ English
- ▲ Multiparty democracy
- ♦ 76 years

TALL BOY
Big Ben, the Houses of Parliament's clock, is one of London's major landmarks.

SPORTS EXPORTS
Many sports invented in the UK are now played worldwide.

Rugby ball

Cricket ball

Soccer ball

IRISH HARP
An instrument used in traditional Irish music, the harp has been played in Ireland since the 1100s.

REPUBLIC OF IRELAND

- The nation gained full sovereignty from the UK in 1937.
- Ireland has the lowest consumption of alcohol per person in the European Union.
- Irish Gaelic is used as an everyday language by around 20,000 people.

ESSENTIAL FACTS

- ⊙ Dublin
- ◔ 27,135 sq miles (70,280 sq km)
- ✚ 3.5 million
- ✤ Irish punt (pound)
- ♡ Irish, English
- ▲ Multiparty republic
- ♦ 75 years

BELGIUM

The cultural mix of French-speaking Walloons and Flemings forms the national entity of Belgium. Belgium's highway network is so extensive and well lit that it can be seen from space. The country is the world's third largest producer of chocolate.

ESSENTIAL FACTS

⊙ Brussels

◔ 12,780 sq miles (33,100 sq km)

♦ 10 million

☷ Belgian franc

♡ French, Dutch, Flemish

▲ Multiparty democracy

♦ 76 years

SPACE-AGE STRUCTURE
The design of Belgium's futuristic Atomium building is based on the molecular structure of an iron crystal.

NETHERLANDS

• Dutch laws on sexuality and drugs are less strict than in other parts of Europe.
• Rotterdam is the world's largest port.

ESSENTIAL FACTS

⊙ Amsterdam, The Hague

◔ 14,410 sq miles (37,330 sq km)

♦ 15.3 million

☷ Guilder

♡ Dutch

▲ Multiparty democracy

♦ 77 years

LUXEMBOURG

⊙ Luxembourg City

♦ 400,000

♡ Letzeburgish

LUXEMBOURG BANKING
The nation of Luxembourg is a center of international banking and finance.

DUTCH TULIPS
The Netherlands is Europe's largest producer of flowers. The cultivation of bulbs such as daffodils and tulips is a specialty.

SPAIN AND PORTUGAL

SUPREME SKILL IN shipbuilding and navigation enabled both Spain and Portugal to become the most powerful empires of the 16th century. Both have a seafaring history; Christopher Columbus sailed to America in 1492, and Vasco da Gama, the Portuguese explorer, was the first to sail around Africa to India in 1497.

INDUSTRY
Fishing, car manufacture, olives, cork, ship building, citrus fruit, tourism. Spain and Portugal are famous for fortified wines. Sherry is named after Jerez de la Frontera, Spain, and Port after Porto, Portugal.

CLIMATE
Spain's coastal areas are milder than the central plateau, which has a more extreme temperature range. Almeria, Spain, contains Europe's only desert. Portugal's Mediterranean-like climate is moderated by the Atlantic.

PORTUGAL

SPAIN

Bay of Biscay

Santander

Basque provinces

Vitoria
Pamplona
Logroño

F   R   A   N   C   E

ANDORRA

P   Y   R   E   N   E   E   S

adolid Duero

Ebro

Zaragoza

Catalonia

Barcelona

Mequinenza
Res.

DE GUADARRAMA

MADRID

Toledo

Valencia

Valencia

Júcar

Balearic Islands

Minorca

Majorca

Palma de
Mallorca

Ibiza

diana

Segura

SIERRA DE SEGURA

Murcia

ENA
uivir

alusia

SIERRA NEVADA

Málaga

M   E   D   I   T   E   R   R   A   N   E   A   N   S   E   A

N

PEOPLE
The Spanish are fiercely
regional and each province has
its own language and literature –
Catalonia, Galicia, and the
Basque Provinces are the
largest. The Basques, who live
in the Pyrenees, now have
their own parliament.

0   100   200km
0   50   100miles

E   F   G   H

FRANCE

FOLLOWING THE FRENCH Revolution (1789–99), France became Europe's first modern republic, and possessed a colonial empire that included parts of Asia and Africa. France and Spain jointly governed Andorra from 1278 until 1993, when the principality held its first full elections. Monaco is a lucrative banking center.

English Channel

Cherbourg
Le Hav
Channel Islands
(to U.K.)
Caen
NORMA

Île d'Ouessant
Brest
B R I T T A N Y
Rennes
Le M

Belle Île
Loire
Nantes

A T L A N T I C   O C E A N

Po

Bordeaux

PEOPLE
Despite a strong national identity, the Bretons, Normans, Alsatians, Corsicans, and the Monegasque from Monaco still maintain their regional traditions.

ANDORRA

COMMUNICATIONS
The French lead the world in high-speed train technology. First run in 1981, the TGV (*Train à Grande Vitesse*) is one of the world's fastest trains, with a top speed of 186 mph (300 km/h).

PYREN
S P A

N

| 0 | 75 | 150km |
| 0 | 50 | 100miles |

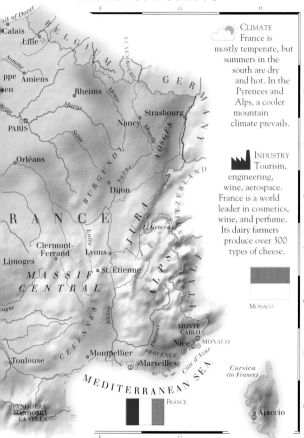

F G H

1

Strait of Dover
Calais
Lille

BELGIUM

LUXEMBOURG

GERMANY

Somme
Amiens
Dieppe
Rouen
Seine

Rheims

Marne

Nancy

Strasbourg

PARIS

Seine

Meuse

Moselle

VOSGES

Orléans

BURGUNDY

Loire

Dijon

Saône

JURA

FRANCE

SWITZERLAND

L. Geneva

Clermont-
Ferrand

Lyons

Limoges

Dordogne

MASSIF
CENTRAL

St. Étienne

Rhône

ALPS

ITALY

CÉVENNES

Durance

MONTE
CARLO
Nice
MONACO

Toulouse

Montpellier

PROVENCE

Marseilles

Côte d'Azur

ANDORRA
ANDORRA
LA VELLA

MEDITERRANEAN SEA

Corsica
(to France)

Ajaccio

CLIMATE
France is mostly temperate, but summers in the south are dry and hot. In the Pyrenees and Alps, a cooler mountain climate prevails.

INDUSTRY
Tourism, engineering, wine, aerospace. France is a world leader in cosmetics, wine, and perfume. Its dairy farmers produce over 300 types of cheese.

MONACO

FRANCE

ITALY AND MALTA

THE BOOT-SHAPED PENINSULA of Italy stretches from the Alps to the Ionian Sea and includes Sardinia, Sicily, and other small, offshore islands. Italy also contains two independent enclaves – the Vatican City in Rome and the Republic of San Marino near Rimini. The Romans, Arabs, French, Turks, Spanish, and British have all fought for or colonized Malta, which has been independent since 1964.

PEOPLE

Venetians were a seafaring people, whose ships carried silks and spices from Asia. The Venetian trader and explorer Marco Polo is said to have brought the recipe for pasta from China.

HISTORY

Italy was once a collection of small kingdoms and city-states, which were vulnerable to internal wars. It was united in 1870, through the efforts of the soldier Giuseppe Garibaldi and the politician

CLIMATE
Southern Italy and Malta have a Mediterranean climate with hot summers and mild winters. Northern Italy is cooler and wetter.

INDUSTRY
Cars, olives, wine, tourism. Italy is a leader in industrial design, textiles, and household goods and is the world's largest wine producer. Tourism is Malta's chief source of income.

Southwest Europe facts

SPAIN

- Young Spanish men tend to live at home until their late 20s.
- Spanish public hospitals are generally considered to be better than private ones.
- Over 3,000 festivals and feasts take place every year in Spain.

ESSENTIAL FACTS

⊙ Madrid

◔ 194,900 sq miles (504,780 sq km)

✚ 39.2 million

✸ Peseta

♀ Spanish

▲ Multiparty democracy

● 77 years

PORTUGUESE CORK
More than half the world's cork is supplied by Portugal, the main product being the bottle stopper.

SPANISH SIX-STRING
The classical guitar is Spain's national instrument.

Tuning pegs

Nut

Neck

Frets

Sound hole

Bridge

Hollow body

Strings

PORTUGAL

- Family ties are a major part of Portuguese life.
- Over 40% of the population has private health insurance.
- Portugal has few natural resources.

ESSENTIAL FACTS

⊙ Lisbon

◔ 35,670 sq miles (92,390 sq km)

✚ 9.9 million

✸ Escudo

♀ Portuguese

▲ Multiparty republic

● 74 years

ANDORRA

⊙ Andorra la Vella

✚ 58,000

♀ Catalan

ITALY

- Tourists have visited Italy since the 1500s.
- Italy is a world leader in product design and the fashion industry.
- Venice is such a popular place to visit that pedestrians have to use one-way systems in the summer.
- Most Italians live at home before marriage.

ESSENTIAL FACTS

- ⊙ Rome
- ◔ 116,320 sq miles (301,270 sq km)
- ♦ 57.8 million
- ✎ Italian lira
- ♡ Italian
- ▲ Multiparty republic
- ♦ 77 years

VENETIAN MASKS
Masks are traditionally worn during the February carnival in Venice.

SAN MARINO	VATICAN CITY	MALTA	MONACO
⊙ San Marino	⊙ Vatican City	⊙ Valletta	⊙ Monaco
♦ 23,000	♦ 1,000	♦ 400,000	♦ 28,000
♡ Italian	♡ Italian, Latin	♡ Maltese, English	♡ French

FRANCE

- Paris is the most visited European city.
- The French wine industry dates back to 600 B.C.
- More medicine is consumed per person in France than in any other country.
- Most French people spend their vacations in France, rather than traveling abroad.

ESSENTIAL FACTS

- ⊙ Paris
- ◔ 212,930 sq miles (551,500 sq km)
- ♦ 57.4 million
- ✎ Franc
- ♡ French
- ▲ Multi-party republic
- ♦ 77 years

PEDAL POWER
The *Tour de France* bicycle race is the most famous in the world.

CENTRAL EUROPE

HISTORICALLY AN unstable part of the continent, central Europe became part of the Eastern Bloc after World War II. Czechoslovakia and Poland had governments with strong ties to the former U.S.S.R. In 1989, they broke away from communism, and in 1993 Czechoslovakia split into the Czech Republic and Slovakia. Poland is still moving slowly toward a market economy.

CZECH REPUBLIC

CLIMATE
Central Europe has a continental climate, with wet springs, late summers, and cold winters. Snow can cover eastern Poland for almost three months of each year.

BALTI

Pomeranian Bay

POMERANI

POMERA

Odra

Warta

Poznań

Odra

Wroc

SUDETEN MOUN

Ohře

Labe

PRAGUE (PRAHA)

Plzeň

CZECH REPUBL

L. Vltava

BOHEMIA

Jihlava

Lužnice

MOR

B

Tihlava

AUSTRIA

BRATISLAV

N

0   75   150km

0   50   100miles

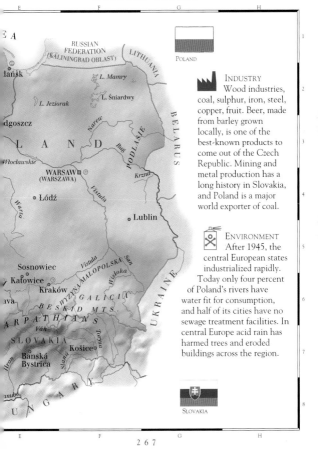

POLAND

INDUSTRY

Wood industries, coal, sulphur, iron, steel, copper, fruit. Beer, made from barley grown locally, is one of the best-known products to come out of the Czech Republic. Mining and metal production has a long history in Slovakia, and Poland is a major world exporter of coal.

ENVIRONMENT

After 1945, the central European states industrialized rapidly. Today only four percent of Poland's rivers have water fit for consumption, and half of its cities have no sewage treatment facilities. In central Europe acid rain has harmed trees and eroded buildings across the region.

SLOVAKIA

RUSSIAN FEDERATION (KALININGRAD OBLAST)
LITHUANIA
lańsk
L. Mamry
L. Jeziorak
L. Śniardwy
BELARUS
dgoszcz
P O L A N D
Narew
Bug
PODLASIE
Włocławskie
WARSAW (WARSZAWA)
Wisła
Krzna
Łódź
Warta
Lublin
Sosnowiec
Wisła
MAŁOPOLSKA
San
Kałowice
Kraków
Wisłoka
GALICIA
ava
B E S K I D   M T S.
UKRAINE
A R P A T H I A N S
Vah
S L O V A K I A
Torysa
Košice
Banská Bystrica
Slaná
Hron
nube
H U N G A R Y

GERMANY

IT WAS NOT UNTIL 1871 that many small independent states were united under Prussia to form Germany. After 1945, the country was divided again, into a democratic West Germany and a Soviet-dominated East Germany. Reunified in 1990, Germany is, like France, a leading member of the European Union and is currently Europe's strongest economic power.

INDUSTRY
Cars, heavy and precision engineering, electronics, chemicals. Germany has a strong industrial sector and is Europe's main car producer.

POLAND

BERLIN
Potsdam
Rügen
Rostock
L. Müritz
Oder
Mecklenburg Bay
BALTIC SEA
Kiel
Lübeck
Schwerin
Hamburg
Magdeburg
Brunswick
SAXONY
Mittelland Canal
HARZ
Hanover
Bremen
Bielefeld
DENMARK
Kiel Canal
Helgoland
North Frisian Is.
East Frisian Is.
NORTH SEA
Dortmund-Ems Canal
Ems
Münster
NETHERLANDS

GERMANY

CLIMATE

The Rhine Valley is mild and is suitable for wine-making. The Bavarian Alps and Black Forest are much colder, with heavy snowfalls in winter.

HISTORY

After World War II, Berlin was shared among the Allies. In 1955, Berlin was divided between East and West Germany. The Berlin Wall was built in 1961 to prevent people from defecting to the West.

ENVIRONMENT

Germany has strict pollution controls, recycling most paper, glass, and used tires. Acid rain is damaging many of Germany's forests and the Rhine is heavily polluted by industry.

Map labels

CZECH REPUBLIC
ERZGEBIRGE
Chemnitz
Erfurt
Thuringian Forest
BELGIUM
Aachen
Bonn
RHINELAND
Rhine
Wiesbaden
Mainz
Main
Frankfurt
Nuremberg
FRANKONIAN JURA
Danube
Augsburg
Munich
BAVARIA
BAVARIAN ALPS
AUSTRIA
LUXEMBOURG
Saarbrücken
Mannheim
Karlsruhe
Stuttgart
Black Forest
Neckar
Danube
SWABIAN JURA
L. Constance
SWITZERLAND
Rhine
FRANCE

153km
80miles
0   40   75

SWITZERLAND AND AUSTRIA

ONCE THE CENTER OF the vast Hapsbur Empire, the Republic of Austria was created after World War I. Switzerland has been a neutral country since 1815, and many international organizations such as the Red Cross have their headquarters there. Liechtenstein is closely allied to Switzerland, which handles its foreign relations.

LIECHTENS

SWITZERLAND

N

COMMUNICATIONS
The St. Gotthard road tunnel runs under the Swiss Alps. At over 10 miles (16 km) in length, it is the world's longest road tunnel.

CLIMATE
Altitude determines climate, ch alpine areas experiencing der temperatures and re rainfall. South of e Alps is nsiderably rmer and nnier.

Czech Republic

Slovakia

Linz

Danube

St. Pölten

VIENNA

AUSTRIA

L. Neusiedler

Eisenstadt

L. Atter

L. Traun

Salzburg

Enns

NIEDERE TAUERN

HOHE TAUERN

HUNGARY

Graz

nsbruck

INN

ZILLERTAL ALPS

Klagenfurt

Drau

SLOVENIA

AUSTRIA

♪ THE ARTS
Many famous musicians, such Beethoven, Mozart, Schubert, and ahms, lived and worked in Vienna.

NATURAL FEATURES
The Alps form part of an almost ntinuous mountain-belt, stretching m the Pyrenees in France to the malayas in Asia. They are also e source of Europe's largest rivers – e Rhine, Rhône, and Danube.

INDUSTRY
Pharmaceuticals, financial services, tourism, chemicals, electrical engineering. Liechtenstein is the center of world dental manufacture. False teeth and dental materials are exported to over 100 countries.

Central Europe facts

SWITZERLAND

- Three-quarters of Switzerland consists of mountains, forests, and ice.
- Swiss inventions include baby food and condensed milk.
- The banks of Switzerland attract investors worldwide.

ESSENTIAL FACTS

- ⊙ Bern
- ◓ 15,940 sq miles (41,290 sq km)
- ♦ 6.9 million
- ☻ Swiss franc
- ♡ German, French, Italian
- ▲ Multiparty republic
- ♦ 78 years

QUALITY TIME
Swiss watchmakers are famous for the quality and craftmanship of their products.

GERMANY

- The rivers and canals of Germany carry as much freight as its roads.
- The best-known beer festival in Europe, the *Oktoberfest*, is held annually in the city of Munich.

ESSENTIAL FACTS

- ⊙ Berlin
- ◓ 137,800 sq miles (356,910 sq km)
- ♦ 80.6 million
- ☻ Deutschmark
- ♡ German
- ▲ Multiparty republic
- ♦ 76 years

AUSTRIA

- University degrees take six years or more to complete in Austria.
- Salzburg's summer music festival is a major tourist attraction.

ESSENTIAL FACTS

- ⊙ Vienna
- ◓ 32,375 sq miles (83,850 sq km)
- ♦ 7.8 million
- ☻ Austrian schilling
- ♡ German
- ▲ Multiparty republic
- ♦ 76 years

GERMAN BEER STEIN

VIENNESE WHIRL
Austrian composer Johann Strauss (1825–1899) composed a famous waltz, "The Blue Danube."

CZECH REPUBLIC

• The Czech homeland was originally called Bohemia.
• Prague's gilded church roofs gave the city the name *zlata Praha*, or "golden Prague."
• The Czech Republic is the most polluted country in Europe.

ESSENTIAL FACTS

⊙ Prague

◑ 30,260 sq miles
(78,370 sq km)

♦ 10.4 million

❦ Czech koruna

♡ Czech

▲ Multiparty republic

♦ 71 years

SLOVAKIA

• Separation from the Czech Republic in 1993 resulted in full independence for Slovakia for the first time in over 1,000 years.

ESSENTIAL FACTS

⊙ Bratislava

◑ 19,100 sq miles
(49,500 sq km)

♦ 5.3 million

❦ Slovak koruna

♡ Slovak

LIECHTENSTEIN

⊙ Vaduz

♦ 29,000

♡ German, Alemannish

POLAND

• The largest remaining herds of European bison are found in the eastern forests of Poland.
• Poland has seven international borders.
• Polish women hold prominent policy-making posts in politics and business.

ESSENTIAL FACTS

⊙ Warsaw

◑ 120,720 sq miles
(312,680 sq km)

♦ 38.5 million

❦ Zloty

♡ Polish

▲ Multiparty republic

♦ 72 years

PRAGUE, CZECH REPUBLIC
Dating from medieval times, the beautiful capital city of Prague is now a popular tourist destination. The city lies on both banks of the Vltava River and is connected by a series of bridges. It is often called "city of a hundred spires" because it has so many churches

SOUTH CENTRAL EUROPE

FOR CENTURIES the countries of this region have had strong ties with Europe. In the early 1990s Slovenia, Croatia, and Bosnia and Herzegovina declared their independence from Yugoslavia, to which they had been annexed after World War 1. This area boasts the snow-capped Alps, the sunny Adriatic Sea in the south, as well as Hungary's fertile plain.

SLOVENIA   CROATIA

CLIMATE
The climate in the region is just as varied as its geography. The interior has a continental climate, with warm summers and bitterly cold winters. Coastal areas in Croatia benefit from Mediterranean temperatures suitable for growing plums, apricots, and grapes.

N

0   75   150km
0   50   100miles

INDUSTRY
Mercury ore, timber, tourism, paprika. Hungary's workforce is skilled in science and engineering. Elsewhere, industry has been affected by the conflict in Yugoslavia, but tourists are now returning to the lakes and coasts of Croatia.

PEOPLE
Historically, this region has been at the crossroads of many different empires, each influencing the language, religion, and customs of the people. Although this has created problems, the Slovenes, Croatians, and Muslims still maintain their own traditions.

HUNGARY

BOSNIA–HERZEGOVINA

SOUTHEAST EUROPE

THIS REGION IS often referred to as the Balkans, from the Turkish word for "mountain." It is made up of countries that have a long history of invasion and occupation. From its source in the Alps, the mighty Danube River flows eastward through Romania and Bulgaria, before pouring into the Black Sea.

YUGOSLAVIA

ROMANIA

BLACK

BULGARIA

TURKEY

Tundzha

Shumen

Varna

Burgas

Sliven

B U L G A R I A

Maritsa

BALKAN MTS

Stara Zagora

Plovdiv

SOFIA
(SOFIYA)

RHODOPE MTS.

Struma

G R E E C E

BALKAN MTS

KOPAONIK

Leskovac

Kosovska
Mitrovica

Priština

Peć

Prizren

NORTH ALBANIA

Drin
Gulf

TIRANA
(TIRANË)

A L B A N I A

Vlorë

A D R I A T I C   S E A

Kumanovo

SKOPJE

Vardar

MACEDONIA

Gostivar

Tetovo

L. Ohrid

Bitola

L. Prespa

Crni Drim

Montenegro

Podgorica

HISTORY

Over the past decade all the countries in this region have gained independence from the Russian communist bloc. This led to the breakup of the former Yugoslavia in 1991. When the states of Serbia and Montenegro combined to form the new Federal Republic of Yugoslavia, it resulted in a war which lasted from 1991-95.

MACEDONIA

ALBANIA

INDUSTRY

Coal, wine, tobacco, iron ore, tourism. Black Sea tourism is being developed in Romania to generate income to help improve the lives of the people. Most of the world's rose oil is produced in the foothills of the Balkan Mountains in Bulgaria.

CLIMATE

Hot or cold winds from Russia can bring spells of extreme weather in Romania and Bulgaria. Snow may even stay on the peaks until midsummer. Yugoslavia and Macedonia have warm summers that are good for growing early fruit crops.

N

250km

150miles

0   125

0   75

A   B   C   D   E   F   G   H

5   6   7   8

GREECE

SURROUNDED BY THE Aegean, Ionian, and Cretan seas, no part of Greece is more than 85 miles (137 km) from the coast. Its territory includes the mainland on the Balkan peninsula, and over 1,400 islands. The country is mountainous and less than one-third of the land is cultivated. Greece gained its independence in 1830 after a long and fierce war, ending 400 years of Turkish rule.

CLIMATE
Northwestern Greece is alpine, while parts of Crete are almost subtropical. The islands and the large central plain of the mainland have a Mediterranean climate, with high summer temperatures and mild winters.

GREECE

ENVIRONMENT
Athens suffers from smog, known as *nefos*, which damages its ancient monuments. The Parthenon, on the Acropolis, has suffered more erosion in the previous two decades than in the previous two thousand years.

HISTORY
Regarded as the founders o democracy, the ancient Greeks were advanced for their time. They were the first to study medicine, geometry, and physics (on a scientific basis), and Greec was home to great thinkers such Plato, Aristotle, and Socrates.

BULGARIA

THRACE

TURKEY

Thasos

Thessaloniki

Samothraki

Thermaic Gulf

arisa

Limnos

Sporades

AEGEAN SEA

Skiros

Lesvos

Evvoia

Chios

ATHENS
Piraeus

Andros

Samos

NNESE

Kea

Kithnos

Cyclades

Serifos   Paros

Sifnos

Naxos

Kos

Dodecanese

Ios

Milos

Rhodes

Kithira

Thira

Rhodes

SEA OF CRETE

Karpathos

Iraklion

Crete

N

MEDITERRANEAN SEA

INDUSTRY
Tourism, olives, fishing, citrus fruit, currants, sultanas, wine. Greece owns the world's largest shipping fleet and is one of Europe's major tourist spots. Olives and olive oil are major exports.

COMMUNICATIONS
Boats, ferries, and hydrofoils are commonly used for travel between the islands and the mainland. Greece has 444 ports; 123 handle heavy passenger and freight traffic. Piraeus is the country's main port.

0   100   200km

0   50   100miles

E   F   G   H

Southern Europe facts

CROATIA

- One-third of Croatia is held by the Serbs.
- The Adriatic coastline of Croatia was a popular tourist destination before the recent civil war.

ESSENTIAL FACTS

- ⊙ Zagreb
- ◔ 21,830 sq miles (56,540 sq km)
- ♦ 4.9 million
- 🛇 Kuna
- ♡ Croatian

DALMATIANS
The Dalmatian dog is named after its first known home, the Dalmatian coastal region of Croatia.

YUGOSLAVIA

- Settlers have lived on the site of present-day Belgrade for 7,000 years

ESSENTIAL FACTS

- ⊙ Belgrade
- ◔ 9,929 sq miles (25,715 sq km)
- ♦ 10.6 million
- 🛇 New Yugoslav dinar
- ♦ Serbian

BOSNIA AND HERZEGOVINA

- The Bosnian civil war made over two million people homeless by the year 1995.

ESSENTIAL FACTS

- ⊙ Sarajevo
- ◔ 19,741 sq miles (51,130 sq km)
- ♦ 4.5 million
- 🛇 Bosnian dinar
- ♡ Serbo-Croat

ALBANIA

- The Albanian's name for their nation is *Shqipërisë*, which means "land of the eagle."

ESSENTIAL FACTS

- ⊙ Tirana
- ◔ 11,100 sq miles (28,750 sq km)
- ♦ 3.3 million
- 🛇 New lek
- ♡ Albanian

SLOVENIA

- The average wage in Slovenia is the highest among the former Yugoslav republics.

ESSENTIAL FACTS

- ⊙ Ljubljana
- ◔ 7,820 sq miles (20,250 sq km)
- ♦ 2 million
- 🛇 Tolar
- ♡ Slovene

SLOVENIA IS A MAJOR PRODUCER OF MERCURY, WHICH IS USED IN THERMOMETERS

ROMANIA

- The tuberculosis rate in Romania is the highest in Europe.
- The Romanian Danube delta is to be used as a site for a biosphere reserve.

ESSENTIAL FACTS

⊙ Bucharest

◔ 91,700 sq miles (237,500 sq km)

♦ 23.4 million

💰 Leu

♀ Romanian

GREECE

- People throughout the Greek Islands use the flat roofs of their houses to dry fruit in summer and collect rain in winter.

ESSENTIAL FACTS

⊙ Athens

◔ 50,961 sq miles (131,990 sq km)

♦ 10.2 million

💰 Drachma

♀ Greek

▲ Multiparty republic

♦ 77 years

GREEK MUSIC
The bouzouki
is a traditional
Greek stringed
instrument.

MACEDONIA

- Lake Ohrid in Macedonia is the deepest lake in Europe.

MACEDONIA FACTS

⊙ Skopje

◔ 9,929 sq miles (25,715 sq km)

♦ 1.9 million

💰 Denar

♀ Macedonian

HUNGARY

- The Hungarian language has features not found in any other western language.
- The city of Budapest was originally Buda and Pest, two towns located on either side of the Danube River.

BULGARIA

- In Bulgaria there is a national museum devoted entirely to humor and satire.
- Bulgarians nod for "no" and shake their heads for "yes."
- People in Sofia travel by trolleybuses that get their power from overhead electric cables.

ESSENTIAL FACTS

⊙ Sofia

◔ 42,822 sq miles (110,910 sq km)

♦ 8.9 million

💰 Lev

♀ Bulgarian

▲ Multiparty republic

♦ 72 years

ESSENTIAL FACTS

⊙ Budapest

◔ 35,919 sq miles (93,030 sq km)

♦ 10.5 million

💰 Forint

♀ Hungarian

▲ Multiparty republic

♦ 70 years

THE BALTIC STATES AND BELARUS

LITHUANIA, ESTONIA, AND LATVIA – the three Baltic States – were the first republics to declare their independence from the Soviet Union in 1990-91. Economic reform has been slow and problems such as food shortages still remain. Many areas of Belarus are still affected by the 1986 Chernobyl nuclear disaster. The cleanup will take decades, and is a major drain on the nation's finances.

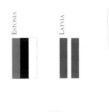

ESTONIA

LATVIA

BELARUS

PEOPLE
Russians, Belorussians, and Ukrainians resettled in Latvia when it was part of the USSR. Today Latvians make up only about half of the whole population, and they are a minority in the capital.

Gulf of Finland

RUSSIA

Narva

L. Peipus

☆ TALLINN

ESTONIA

Tartu

Võrtsjärv

Pärnu

Hiiumaa

Saaremaa

Gulf of Riga

□ RIGA

Venta

B a l t i

LITHUANIA

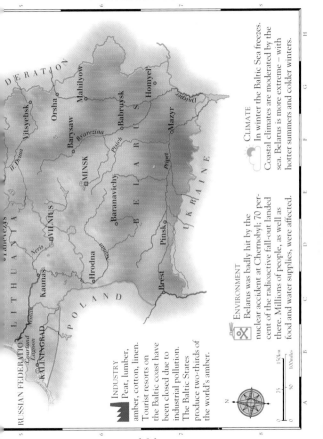

INDUSTRY

Peat, lumber, amber, cotton, linen. Tourist resorts on the Baltic coast have been closed due to industrial pollution. The Baltic States produce two-thirds of the world's amber.

ENVIRONMENT

Belarus was badly hit by the nuclear accident at Chernobyl; 70 percent of the radioactive fall-out landed there. Millions of people, as well as food and water supplies, were affected.

CLIMATE

In winter the Baltic Sea freezes. Coastal climates are moderated by the sea. Belarus is more extreme – with hotter summers and colder winters.

RUSSIAN FEDERATION

Courland Lagoon

KALININGRAD

L I T H U A N I A

Nemunas

Kaunas

Neris

VILNIUS

Hrodna

Nieman

P O L A N D

Brest

Pinsk

Pripet

U K R A I N E

Mazyr

Homyel

Babruysk

Byarezina

Baranavichy

MINSK

Ptsich

Barysaw

Vilsyebsk

Orsha

Mahilyow

B E L A R U S

Dniester

W. Dvina

DERATION

N

0 75 150km
0 50 100miles

EUROPEAN RUSSIA

SPANNING THE TWO continents of Europe and Asia, the Russian Federation is the world's largest country. In 1917 the world's first communist government took power, and in 1923 Russia became the USSR, which included many territories that were once part of the Russian Empire. Economic reforms in the 1980s led to changes that resulted in the fall of communism in 1991.

INDUSTRY
Oil, gas, gold, diamonds, hydrocarbons, precious metals. Russia has large reserves of iron, coal, and nickel. Huge factories, which have grown without environmental controls, are causing pollution problems.

**Map labels:** Novaya Zemlya · KARA SEA · Kara Strait · Kara Vaygach I. · S N · Yugorskiy · Vorkuta · Usa · BARENTS SEA · Pechora · Murmansk · Kolguyev I. · L. Imandra · KOLA PENINSULA · Arkhangel'sk · L. Pyaozero · WHITE SEA · L. Topozero · L. Segozero · FINLAND · L. Onega · L. Ladoga · St. Petersburg · ESTONIA

Some believe that Russia took its name from a Viking tribe called *Varangian Russes*. The first Russian state was established at Kiev in A.D. 800.

CLIMATE
Russia has a cold continental climate, open to influence by the Arctic and Atlantic Oceans. Snow covers more than half the country for six months of the year.

COMMUNICATIONS
The Trans–Siberian Railroad, started in 1881 and completed in 1916, is the longest continuous rail line in the world. The 5,785-mile-(9,310-km) journey from Moscow to Vladivostok takes seven days.

EUROPEAN RUSSIA

THE ARTS
The Hermitage Musuem in St. Petersburg contains 2.5 million objects in 1,000 rooms. Its buildings include the Winter Palace, which was stormed in the 1917 Revolution by Lenin's Bolshevik forces.

RUSSIAN FEDERATION

BELARUS

MOSCOW
Tula
Voronezh
Ryazan'
Penza
Nizhniy Novgorod
Simbirsk
Saratov
Kazan'
Tol'yatti
Samara
Ufa
Naberezhnyye Chelny
Izhevsk
Perm'
Orenburg

Kama Res.

Vyatka

Volga

UKRAINE
Rostov-na-Donu
Krasnodar
Volgograd
Astrakhan

Don
Tsimlyansk Res.

Kuma

Sea of Azov
CAUCASUS MTS.
BLACK SEA
GEORGIA
AZERBAIJAN
Kuban

CASPIAN SEA

KAZAKHSTAN

0   300   600 km
0   150   300 miles

N

UKRAINE AND
THE CAUCASUS

SEPARATED FROM
the Russian
Federation by the Caucasus
mountains, the newly
independent Caucasian
Republics – Armenia,
Azerbaijan, and
Georgia – are rich in
natural resources. The
Ukraine, Europe's largest country, is
dominated by a flat and fertile plain.

ENVIRONMENT
As a result of the 1986 Chernobyl
nuclear disaster, 4 million Ukrainians
live in radioactive areas. In 1994,
reactors from the Chernobyl plant were
still being used to provide nuclear power.

MOLDOVA

CLIMATE
The Ukraine and
Moldova have a continental
climate, with distinctive
seasons. Armenia,
Azerbaijan, and Georgia
are protected from cold
air from the north by the
Caucasus mountains.

INDUSTRY
Coal, iron, cars, win
citrus fruit, cotton, minera
The Ukraine was known a
the breadbasket of the Sov
Union because its flat step
were extensively cultivate
Georgia's known oil reserv
are as yet unexploited.

N

0   150   300km.
0   75   150miles

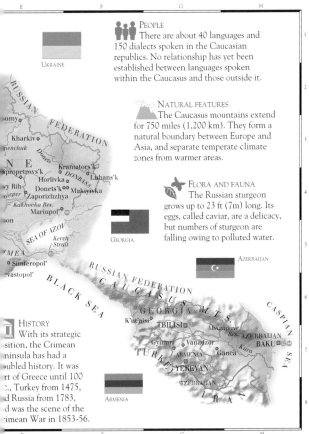

UKRAINE

PEOPLE
There are about 40 languages and 150 dialects spoken in the Caucasian republics. No relationship has yet been established between languages spoken within the Caucasus and those outside it.

NATURAL FEATURES
The Caucasus mountains extend for 750 miles (1,200 km). They form a natural boundary between Europe and Asia, and separate temperate climate zones from warmer areas.

FLORA AND FAUNA
The Russian sturgeon grows up to 23 ft (7m) long. Its eggs, called caviar, are a delicacy, but numbers of sturgeon are falling owing to polluted water.

GEORGIA

AZERBAIJAN

HISTORY
With its strategic position, the Crimean Peninsula has had a troubled history. It was part of Greece until 100 B.C., Turkey from 1475, and Russia from 1783, and was the scene of the Crimean War in 1853-56.

ARMENIA

Map labels

RUSSIAN FEDERATION

Kharkiv
Sumy
Dnieper
nenchuk
Kramators'k
ipropetrovs'k
Horlivka
DONBASS
Luhans'k
y Rih
Donets'k
Makiyivka
iieper
Zaporizhzhya
Kakhovka Res.
Mariupol'
son
SEA OF AZOV
Kerch'
Strait
MEA
Simferopol'
vastopol'
BLACK SEA
RUSSIAN FEDERATION
CAUCASUS
GEORGIA
M.T.S.
K'ut'aisi
TBILISI
Mingäçevir
Res.
Gyumri
Vanadzor
AZERBAIJAN
BAKU
TURKEY
ARMENIA
Gäncä
Kura
YEREVAN
AZERBAIJAN
IRAN
CASPIAN SEA

Northeast Europe facts

EUROPEAN RUSSIA

(See **Russian Federation** ESSENTIAL FACTS, p.329)

• Many Russians now have satellite dishes and tune in to Western TV channels for news and entertainment.
• Hospital food is normally provided by patients' families due to lack of funds.

ST. BASIL'S CATHEDRAL
This 16th century Russian building, with its nine great domes, is situated within Moscow's Kremlin fortress.

LATVIA

• The national flag is said to represent a sheet stained with the blood of a 13th-century Latvian hero.
• Latvia is the most built-up Baltic State.

ESSENTIAL FACTS

⊙ Riga
◕ 24,938 sq miles (64,589 sq km)
♦ 2.7 million
🛢 Lats
♡ Latvian

ESTONIA

• The standard of living in Estonia is higher than in any former Soviet republic.

ESSENTIAL FACTS

⊙ Tallinn
◕ 17,423 sq miles (45,125 sq km)
♦ 1.6 million
🛢 Kroon
♡ Estonian

LITHUANIA

• Most of the Baltic States' amber is found on Lithuania's Amber Coast.

ESSENTIAL FACTS

⊙ Vilnius
◕ 25,174 sq miles (65,200 sq km)
♦ 3.8 million
🛢 Litas
♡ Lithuanian

BELORUS

• Cancer cases have increased dramatically since the Chernobyl nuclear disaster in 1986.

ESSENTIAL FACTS

⊙ Minsk
◕ 80,154 sq miles (207,600 sq km)
♦ 10.3 million
🛢 Belorussian rouble
♡ Belorussian

GEORGIA

Most Georgians live
n poverty.
In Greek mythology,
he legendary Golden
leece was found in
estern Georgia.

ESSENTIAL FACTS

⊙ Tbilisi

◔ 26,911 sq miles
(69,700 sq km)

♦ 5.5 million

⛃ Coupon

♡ Georgian

ARMENIA

• In the fourth century,
Armenia became the
first country in the
world to adopt
Christianity as its
state religion.

ESSENTIAL FACTS

⊙ Yerevan

◔ 11,505 sq miles
(29,000 sq km)

♦ 3.6 million

⛃ Armenian dram

♡ Armenian

AZERBAIJAN

• The nation of
Azerbaijan became the
first of the former
Soviet republics to
declare independence
from Moscow in 1991.

ESSENTIAL FACTS

⊙ Baku

◔ 33,436 sq miles
(86,600 sq km)

♦ 7.3 million

⛃ Manat

♡ Azerbaijani

UKRAINE

Western Ukrainians
ppose their eastern
ounterparts' proposed
loser ties with Russia.
The name Ukraine
neans "frontier."

ESSENTIAL FACTS

⊙ Kiev

◔ 233,090 sq miles
(603,700 sq km)

♦ 52.2 million

⛃ Karbovanets
(coupons)

♡ Ukrainian

▲ Multiparty
republic

♦ 70 years

Sour cream

rscht

*Pierogi
umplings)*

BORSCHT
Russia's famous
beet soup, *borscht*,
comes from
the Ukraine.

MOLDOVA

• The underground
wine vaults of Moldova
contain entire "streets"
of bottles built into
rock quarries.
• Moldova was part of
Romania until Soviet
incorporation in 1940.

ESSENTIAL FACTS

⊙ Kishinev

◔ 13,000 sq miles
(33,700 sq km)

♦ 4.4 million

⛃ Moldovan leu

♡ Romanian

AFRICA

MEDITERRANEAN SEA

RED SEA

ERITREA

DJIBOUTI

EGYPT

SUDAN

LIBYA

CHAD

TUNISIA

NIGER

NIGERIA

NO

ALGERIA

MALI

BENIN

TOGO

GHA

BURKINA
FASO

MOROCCO

CÔTE

MAURITANIA

WESTERN
SAHARA

SENEGAL

GAMBIA

GUINEA-BISSAU

GUINEA

SIERRA

Madeira
(to Portugal)

Canary Islands
(to Spain)

SEYCHELLES

COMOROS

MADAGASCAR

BURUNDI

TANZANIA

RWANDA

MALAWI

MOZAMBIQUE

CONGO
(ZAIRE)

ZAMBIA

ZIMBABWE

SWAZILAND

CONGO

ANGOLA

BOTSWANA

LESOTHO

GABON

NAMIBIA

SOUTH
AFRICA

ATLANTIC OCEAN

AFRICA

Both tropics and the equator
run through Africa, the
warmest of all the continents.
The land around the tropics
is starved of rain, creating great
deserts such as the Sahara
and the Kalahari. In contrast,
high rainfall around the
equator has produced lush
tropical rainforests.

WEST AFRICA

BY 1914, MANY European countries, such as France, Britain, and Portugal, had divided up almost all of Africa between them. Despite independence, foreign companies still own many of the coffee and cocoa plantations in the region.

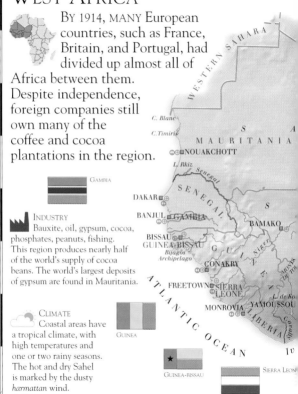

GAMBIA

INDUSTRY
Bauxite, oil, gypsum, cocoa, phosphates, peanuts, fishing. This region produces nearly half of the world's supply of cocoa beans. The world's largest deposits of gypsum are found in Mauritania.

CLIMATE
Coastal areas have a tropical climate, with high temperatures and one or two rainy seasons. The hot and dry Sahel is marked by the dusty *harmattan* wind.

GUINEA

GUINEA-BISSAU

SIERRA LEON

*Map labels:*
WESTERN SAHARA
C. Blanc
C. Timiris
S
A
MAURITANIA
NOUAKCHOTT
L. Rkiz
Senegal
SENEGAL
DAKAR
BANJUL
GAMBIA
BAMAKO
BISSAU
GUINEA-BISSAU
Bijagós Archipelago
G U I N E A
Niger
CONAKRY
ATLANTIC OCEAN
FREETOWN
SIERRA LEONE
L. de Ko
YAMOUSSOU
MONROVIA
LIBERIA

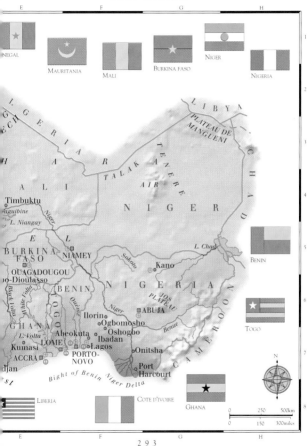

SENEGAL

MAURITANIA

MALI

BURKINA FASO

NIGER

NIGERIA

LIBYA

PLATEAU DE MANGUENI

ALGERIA

NIGER

SAHARA

TALAK TÉNÉRÉ

AIR

CHAD

Timbuktu

Faguibine

L. Niangay

Niger

MALI

BURKINA FASO

NIAMEY

OUAGADOUGOU

Bobo-Dioulasso

L. Chad

BENIN

Sokoto

Kano

NIGERIA

Black Volta

White Volta

BENIN

TOGO

Ilorin

Niger

JOS PLATEAU

ABUJA

Ogbomosho

Benue

TOGO

GHANA

L. Volta

LOME

Abeokuta

Oshogbo

Ibadan

Onitsha

CAMEROON

Kumasi

ACCRA

PORTO-NOVO

Lagos

Port Harcourt

Abidjan

Coast

Bight of Benin

Niger Delta

N

LIBERIA

COTE D'IVOIRE

GHANA

0   250   500km

0   150   300miles

NORTHWEST AFRICA

SPANNING THE continent of Africa from the Atlantic to the Red Sea, the Sahara is the world's largest desert, covering 3.5 million sq miles (9 million sq km). Drought and the overuse of land for farming are causing the Sahara to spread into the Sahel (semiarid grasslands). Italy, the UK, Spain, and France have had colonies in this region.

Morocco occupied the whole of Western Sahara in 1979.

MOROCCO

INDUSTRY
Oil, gas, phosphates, tourism, olives, dates, fruit. Morocco and Tunisia attract millions of tourists every year and are also leading phosphate producers. Algeria and Libya have significant oil reserves.

CLIMATE
Coastal areas have a temperate climate with hot, dry summers and wet winters. Mountain areas are cooler. Most areas are affected by the many different kinds of Sahara wind, such as the *sirocco*, the *chergui*, and the *chili*.

NATURAL FEATURES
The Atlas Mountains exte[n]d over 1,500 miles (2,410 km) from the Canary Islands in the Atlanti[c] to Tunisia. Like the Alps, the At[las] Mountains were formed when the continental plates of Europe and Africa pushed together.

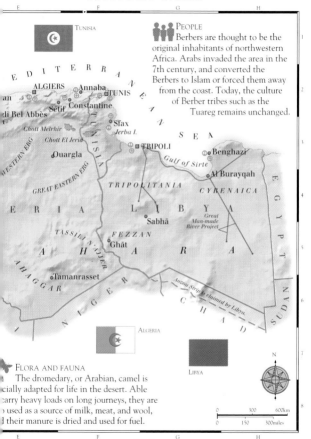

E F G H

TUNISIA

PEOPLE
Berbers are thought to be the original inhabitants of northwestern Africa. Arabs invaded the area in the 7th century, and converted the Berbers to Islam or forced them away from the coast. Today, the culture of Berber tribes such as the Tuareg remains unchanged.

M E D I T E R R A N E A N   S E A

ALGIERS Annaba TUNIS

di Bel Abbès Sétif Constantine

an

Chott Melrhir Sfax

Chott El Jerid Jerba I.

WESTERN ERG Ouargla TRIPOLI Benghazi

Gulf of Sirte Al Burayqah

GREAT EASTERN ERG TRIPOLITANIA CYRENAICA

E R I A L I B Y A E

Sabhā Great
Man-made
River Project

TASSILI N'AJJER FEZZAN Ghāt

A H A R A

A H A G G A R

Tamanrasset

N I G E R Aozou Strip is claimed by Libya.

C H A D D

S U D A N

ALGERIA

LIBYA

N

0   300   600km
0   150   300miles

FLORA AND FAUNA
The dromedary, or Arabian, camel is cially adapted for life in the desert. Able carry heavy loads on long journeys, they are used as a source of milk, meat, and wool, their manure is dried and used for fuel.

West Africa facts

Peanut
rip
und
grou

IVORY COAST

- Yamoussoukro's giant Christian basilica is the second largest church in the world.
- The Ivory Coast is home to 66 different West African tribes.
- Most people live on the sandy coastal strip.

ESSENTIAL FACTS

- ⊙ Yamoussoukro
- ◔ 124,503 sq miles (322,463 sq km)
- ♦ 13.4 million
- ☷ CFA franc
- ♀ French, Akran

GROUNDNUT PLANT
Peanuts, or groundnuts, are a major crop in West Africa.

LIBERIA

- The country of Liberia was founded in 1847 as a home for freed slaves from the US.
- Human rights have have frequently been abused in Liberia, with citizens being massacred or forced to flee to neighboring states.

ESSENTIAL FACTS

- ⊙ Monrovia
- ◔ 43,000 sq miles (111,370 sq km)
- ♦ 2.8 million
- ☷ Liberian dollar
- ♀ English

Animal skin

Leather thongs

Squeezing the "waist" changes the drum's sound

WEST AFRICAN KALUNGU, OR "TALKING DRUM"

WESTERN SAHARA

- ⊙ No capital
- ♦ 200,000
- ♀ Varied Arab dialects

SENEGAL

- The name Senegal comes from the Islamic Zenegar Berbers, who invaded the region in the 1300s.
- Senegal produced the first satirical journal in Africa with the founding of the publication *Le Politicien* in 1978.

ESSENTIAL FACTS

- ⊙ Dakar
- ◔ 75,950 sq miles (196,720 sq km)
- ♦ 7.9 million
- ☷ CFA franc
- ♀ French

GHANA

• Mining has polluted the environment and destroyed areas of land.
• Ghana was the first British colony in Africa to gain independence.

ESSENTIAL FACTS
⊙ Accra
◔ 92,100 sq miles (238,540 sq km)
♦ 16.4 million
♖ Cedi
♕ English

SIERRA LEONE

• The citizens of Freetown are largely descended from slaves freed from Britain and the US.
• Sierra Leone is one of the world's poorest nations.

ESSENTIAL FACTS
⊙ Freetown
◔ 27,699 sq miles (71,740 sq km)
♦ 4.5 million
♖ Leone
♕ English

BENIN

• Positions of power in Benin's retail trade are often held by women.

ESSENTIAL FACTS
⊙ Porto-Novo
◔ 43,480 sq miles (112,620 sq km)
♦ 5.1 million
♖ CFA franc
♕ French

MAURITANIA

• Slavery, although officially illegal, still persists in Mauritania.

ESSENTIAL FACTS
⊙ Nouakchott
◔ 395,953 sq miles (1,025,520 sq km)
♦ 2.2 million
♖ Ouguiya
♕ French

COCOA
West Africa grows half the world's cocoa.

BURKINA

• Droughts and poor soils in Burkina force many men to migrate seasonally to Ghana and the Ivory Coast for work.

ESSENTIAL FACTS
⊙ Ouagadougou
◔ 105,870 sq miles (274,200 sq km)
♦ 9.8 million
♖ CFA franc
♕ French

MALI

• The Malian town of Timbuktu was the center of the huge Malinke empire in the 14th century.
• Malians strongly disapprove of flaunted wealth.

ESSENTIAL FACTS
⊙ Bamako
◔ 478,837 sq miles (1,240,190 sq km)
♦ 10.1 million
♖ CFA franc
♕ French

West Africa facts

NIGER

• The threat of drought and desertification is Niger's primary concern.

ESSENTIAL FACTS

⊙ Niamey
◎ 489,188 sq miles (1,267,000 sq km)
♦ 8.5 million
☷ CFA franc
♀ French

CAPE VERDE

(Atlantic Ocean, pp.360–361)
⊙ Praia
♦ 400,000
♀ Portuguese, Creole

GAMBIA

⊙ Banjul
♦ 900,000
♀ English

GUINEA

• The three bright colors of Guinea's flag represent the national motto of "work, justice, solidarity."

ESSENTIAL FACTS

⊙ Conakry
◎ 94,926 sq miles (245,860 sq km)
♦ 6.3 million
☷ Guinea franc
♀ French

TOGO

• The retail trade in Togo is dominated by the "Nana Benz" or market women, of Lomé.

ESSENTIAL FACTS

⊙ Lomé
◎ 21,927 sq miles (56,290 sq km)
♦ 3.9 million
☷ CFA franc
♀ French, Kabye, Ewe

GUINEA-BISSAU

⊙ Bissau
♦ 1 million
♀ Portuguese

NIGERIA

• Modern medicine is not available in rural Nigeria; the health service is concentrated in urban areas.
• Nigeria is the most heavily populated country in Africa.

ESSENTIAL FACTS

⊙ Abuja
◎ 356,668 sq miles (923,770 sq km)
♦ 119 million
☷ Naira
♀ English
▲ Military regime
♦ 52 years

NIGERIAN TWINS

All twins in Nigeria, boys and girls, are given the same names. The firstborn is called Taiwo, the second Kehinde.

Northwest Africa facts

TUNISIA

• The Berber village of Matmata was a location for the planet Tatooine in the 1977 film *Star Wars*.
• Esparto grass grown on the plains of Tunisia is used to make quality paper.
• Tunisians use falcons to hunt partridge, quail, and hare in the summer.

ESSENTIAL FACTS

⊙ Tunis
◔ 63,170 sq miles (163,610 sq km)
♦ 8.6 million
🕮 Tunisian dinar
♡ Arabic

ALGERIA

• The Algerian population is mainly Arab, under 30 years of age, and urban.
• The highest sand dunes in the world are found in east central Algeria.
• More than 80% of Algeria lies within the Sahara desert.

ESSENTIAL FACTS

⊙ Algiers
◔ 919,590 sq miles (2,381,740 sq km)
♦ 27.1 million
🕮 Dinar
♡ Arabic

PATTERNED LEATHER BAG

LEATHER GOODS
Morocco and Tunisia produce quality leather goods for tourists to buy.

MOROCCO

• The Karueein University at Fès, which was founded in A.D. 859, is the world's oldest existing educational institution.

ESSENTIAL FACTS

⊙ Rabat
◔ 6269,757 sq miles (98,670 sq km)
♦ 27 million
🕮 Moroccan dirham
♡ Arabic

LIBYA

• The West has ignored Libya due to its past links with terrorist groups.
• Libyan oil contains no sulfur, resulting in little pollution when it is burned.

ESSENTIAL FACTS

⊙ Tripoli
◔ 679,358 sq miles (1,759,540 sq km)
♦ 5.5 million
🕮 Libyan dinar
♡ Arabic

NORTHEAST AFRICA

THE NILE, THE LONGEST river in the world, carries rich mud from the highlands of Sudan into Egypt, creating some of the most fertile land in the world. About 99 percent of Egypt's population live on the river's banks. Ethiopia, Somalia, and Sudan have been beset by drought, famine, and war, so about half of Africa's 4.5 million refugees come from this area.

EGYPT

HISTORY
Hieroglyphics were a set of mysterious symbols until the discovery of the Rosetta Stone in 1799. The Stone is inscribed in three different scripts: ancient Greek, demotic, and hieroglyphs. By comparing the royal names in the scripts, hieroglyphs were finally deciphered 25 years later.

ERITREA

COMMUNICATIONS
Opened in 1869, the Suez Canal connects the Mediterranean and the Red Seas, shortening the route from Europe to the Far East. More than 17,000 ships use it each year.

SOMALIA

DJIBOUTI

ETHIOPIA

SUDAN

*Labels on map:*

S O M A L I A

Gulf of Aden

HORN OF AFRICA

DJIBOUTI
DJIBOUTI

Berbera
Hargeysa

ERITREA *Dahlak Archipelago*

ASMARA

E T H I O P I A N

Gonder
L. Tana

Atbara

Dire
Dawa

Shebeli

Genale

ADDIS ABABA

H I G H L A N D S

East

Omo

L. Abaya

L. Turkana

Southeast Sudan is administered by Kenya

MOGADISHU

Juba

Kismaayo

K E N Y A

I N D I A N   O C E A N

Mbara

Khartoum North

OMDURMAN
KHARTOUM

Wad Medani

El Obeid

S U D A N

Blue Nile

White Nile

U G A N D A

Z A I R E

CENTRAL AFRICAN REPUBLIC

C H A D

Scale:
0   250   500km
0   150   300miles

N

301

CENTRAL AFRICA

MUCH OF THIS region is covered in dense tropical rainforest, drained by the Congo (Zaire) River, which flows in a huge arc on its way to the Atlantic. In the 16th century Portugal and Spain set up trading posts on the west coast as part of the slave trade. Millions of Africans from this region were sent as slaves to the New World. Many people in coastal areas still speak Spanish and Portuguese.

CHAD

INDUSTRY
Lumber, oil, iron, cocoa, coffee, copper. Bélinga, Gabon, contains the world's largest iron ore deposits. Many central African countries have unexploited oil and gas reserves.

CENTRAL AFRICAN REPUBLIC

CAMEROON

EQUATORIAL

L I B Y A

Aozou Strip, claimed by Libya

N I G E R

C H A D

T I B E S T I

S U D

L. Chad

NDJAMENA

Kousséri

Maroua

Ergérig

Logone

Chari

Garoua

Salamat

Garb

CLIMATE
Central Africa covers three climatic zones. Equatorial areas are hot and humid with little distinction between seasons. Farther north lies the semiarid Sahelian belt, and the far north lies within the Sahara desert.

SAO TOME AND PRINCIPE

CONGO

GABON

CENTRAL EAST AFRICA

LARGE AREAS OF savanna, or grassland, in central Africa provide grazing for domestic and wild animals alike. Industry is poorly developed in the region – Zambia, Rwanda, Burundi, and Uganda suffer from having no seaports. Lake Victoria is the largest lake in Africa, and a source of the Nile River.

UGANDA

RWANDA

R

KENYA

FLORA AND FAUNA
Poaching remains a major problem in this area. To combat this, all the countries in this region have set up wildlife parks to protect animals such as elephants and zebra.

INDUSTRY
Tobacco, coffee, tea, tourism, cloves, copper. Zambia is the world's fifth-largest producer of copper. Wildlife parks in this region

SOMALIA

ETHIOPIA

SUDAN

KENYA

CHALBI DESERT

Yaata

L. Turkana

Southern Sudan is administered by Kenya

NAIROBI

MERU RANGE

Great Rift Valley

Galana

UGANDA

L. Kyoga

Albert Nile

Victoria Nile

L. Albert

KAMPALA

Lake Victoria

Mwanza

L. Edward

KIGALI

RWANDA

BUJUMBURA

BURUNDI

ZAIRE

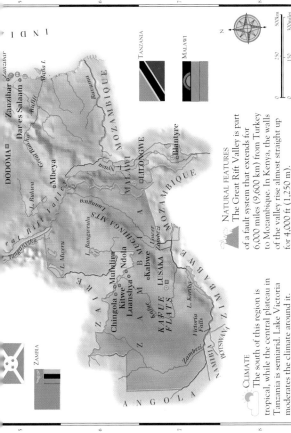

NATURAL FEATURES

The Great Rift Valley is part of a fault system that extends for 6,000 miles (9,600 km) from Turkey to Mozambique. In Kenya, the walls of the valley rise almost straight up for 4,000 ft (1,250 m).

CLIMATE

The south of this region is tropical, while the central plateau in Tanzania is semiarid. Lake Victoria moderates the climate around it.

TANZANIA

MALAWI

ZAMBIA

305

Northeast Africa facts

EGYPT

• Overpopulation is a major problem in Eygpt, where it is estimated a baby is born every 24 seconds.
• The ancient pyramids were built to house the mummified bodies of Egyptian kings.

ESSENTIAL FACTS

⊙ Cairo
◔ 386,660 sq miles (1,001,450 sq km)
♦ 56.1 million
⚜ Egyptian pound
♀ Arabic
▲ Multiparty republic

GREAT PYRAMIDS AT GIZA, EGYPT

ETHIOPIA

• Famines are a regular occurrence in Ethiopia.

ESSENTIAL FACTS

⊙ Addis Ababa
◔ 435,605 sq miles (1,228,221 sq km)
♦ 51 million
⚜ Ethiopian birr
♀ Amharic, English

DJIBOUTI

⊙ Djibouti
♦ 500,000
♀ Arabic, French

SUDAN

• The Sudd plain in Sudan contains the world's largest swamp.

ESSENTIAL FACTS

⊙ Khartoum
◔ 967,493 sq miles (2,505,815 sq km)
♦ 27.4 million
⚜ Sudanese dinar
♀ Arabic

ERITREA

• Three-quarters of Eritrea's people are dependent on food aid.

ESSENTIAL FACTS

⊙ Asmara
◔ 36,170 sq miles (93,680 sq km)
♦ 3.5 million
⚜ Ethiopian birr
♀ Tigrinya, Arabic

SOMALIA

• In 1992, civil war in Somalia led to the UN's worst refugee crisis.

ESSENTIAL FACTS

⊙ Mogadishu
◔ 246,200 sq miles (637,660 sq km)
♦ 9.5 million
⚜ Somali shilling
♀ Somali, Arabic

Central East Africa facts

KENYA

- Ethnic violence is the main political issue.
- Kenya has over 40 national parks and game reserves, and two marine parks in the Indian ocean.

ESSENTIAL FACTS

- ⊙ Nairobi
- △ 224, 081 sq miles (580,370 sq km)
- ♦ 26.1 million
- ✽ Kenya shilling
- ♡ Swahili

RWANDA

- ⊙ Kigali
- ♦ 7.5 million
- ♡ Kinyarwanda, French

MASAI WARRIORS
The Masai are a tribe of nomadic herders who live on the borders of Kenya and Tanzania.

GORILLAS OF RWANDA
Rwanda is one of the last remaining sanctuaries of the mountain gorilla.

BURUNDI

- ⊙ Bujumbura
- ♦ 5.8 million
- ♡ Kirundi, French

UGANDA

- The rugged Ruwenzori mountains of Uganda arealso known as the "Mountains of the Moon."

ESSENTIAL FACTS

- ⊙ Kampala
- △ 91,073 sq miles (235,880 sq km)
- ♦ 19.2 million
- ✽ New Uganda shilling
- ♡ English

TANZANIA

- One-third of Tanzania is national park or game reserve.
- The use of Swahili as a universal language has reduced ethnic rivalries.

ESSENTIAL FACTS

- ⊙ Dodoma
- △ 364,900 sq miles (945,090 sq km)
- ♦ 28.8 million
- ✽ Tanzanian shilling
- ♡ English, Swahili

Central Africa facts

ZAMBIA

• Victoria Falls in Zambia is called *Musi-o-Tunyi* by African people; this means "the smoke that thunders."

ESSENTIAL FACTS

⊙ Lusaka

◔ 290,563 sq miles (752,610 sq km)

♦ 8.9 million

🐚 Zambian kwacha

♡ English, Bemba, Tonga

CHAD

• The tropical, cotton-producing south is Chad's most heavily populated region.
• The Tibesti plateau is a site of prehistoric rock painting.

ESSENTIAL FACTS

⊙ N'Djamena

◔ 495,752 sq miles (1,284,000 sq km)

♦ 6 million

🐚 CFA franc

♡ French, Sara, Maba

FISH FOOD
Lake Chad's fish, such as this tilapia, are a major source of food for people who live in the region.

EQUATORIAL GUINEA

⊙ Malabo

♦ 400,000

♡ Spanish, Fang

Alluvial diamond

LITTLE GEMS
Congo (Zaire) is the world's largest producer of diamonds used in industry.

CONGO (ZAIRE)

• The rain forests of Congo (Zaire) comprise almost 50% of Africa's remaining woodlands.

ESSENTIAL FACTS

⊙ Kinshasa

◔ 905,563 sq miles (2,345,410 sq km)

♦ 41.2 million

🐚 New zaire

♡ French

CENTRAL AFRICAN REPUBLIC

• Hunting of elephants in the CAR was finally banned in 1985.

ESSENTIAL FACTS

⊙ Bangui

◔ 240,530 sq miles (622,980 sq km)

♦ 3.3 million

🐚 CFA franc

♡ French

CONGO

• In 1970, Congo became the first declared communist state in Africa.
• Congo has been used in the past as a dump for Western toxic waste.

ESSENTIAL FACTS

⊙ Brazzaville
◔ 132,040 sq miles (342,000 sq km)
♦ 2.4 million
☷ CFA franc
♀ French

CAMEROON

• The Portuguese explorers who colonized Cameroon fished for shrimp called *camaroes*, from which the country derived its name.

ESSENTIAL FACTS

⊙ Yaoundé
◔ 183,570 sq miles (475,440 sq km)
♦ 12.5 million
☷ CFA franc
♀ English, French

RESPECT FOR THE DEAD
This wooden figure from Cameroon was made to honor an ancestor.

SÃO TOMÉ & PRÍNCIPE

⊙ São Tomé
♦ 121,000
♀ Portuguese

SPIRITED FIGURE
Central African folk religions believe fetish figures like this are inhabited by spirits.

GABON

• Libreville was founded as a settlement for freed French slaves in 1849.
• Menial jobs in Gabon are done by immigrant workers.

ESSENTIAL FACTS

⊙ Libreville
◔ 103,347 sq miles (267,670 sq km)
♦ 1.3 million
☷ CFA franc
♀ French

MALAWI

• Lake Malawi contains at least 500 species of fish.
• Malawi's name means "the land where the sun is reflected in the water like fire."

ESSENTIAL FACTS

⊙ Lilongwe
◔ 45,745 sq miles (118,480 sq km)
♦ 10.7 million
☷ Kwacha
♀ English, Chewa

SOUTHERN AFRICA

THE RICHEST DEPOSITS of valuable minerals in Africa, such as gold and diamonds, are found in its southern region. Many countries surrounding South Africa rely on it for work and trade. Racial segregation under apartheid operated from 1948 until South Africa's first multiracial elections were held in 1994. Namibia won its independence from South Africa in 1990, but neighboring Angola has been in a state of civil war since 1975.

ANGOLA

BOTSWANA

ZIMBABWE

MOZAMBIQUE

INDIAN OCEAN

NAMIBIA OCEAN

C. Fria

Etosha Pan

NAMIB DESERT

Walvis Bay

Lüderitz

WINDHOEK

Fish

Orange

Cape Columbine

Cape of Good Hope

C. Agulhas

Cape Town

NAMIBIA

NAMIBIA

SOUTH AFRICA

SOUTH AFRICA

N

| 0 | 150 | 300 | 600km |
| 0 | | 300miles | |

FLORA AND FAUNA
The unique Namibian desert
elephant, of which only 34 remain, and
the black rhino are threatened both by
illegal poaching and the disease anthrax.

KALAHARI DESERT

BOTSWANA

GABORONE

Okavango Delta

Chobe

Maun

Makgadikgadi Pans

Francistown

Limpopo

Shashe

Chitungwiza

ZIMBABWE

Bulawayo

Limpopo

MOZAMBIQUE

Beira

Save

PRETORIA

Soweto

Johannesburg

Klerksdorp

Kimberley

SOUTH AFRICA

GREAT KAROO

MAPUTO

MBABANE

SWAZILAND

Pietermaritzburg

Durban

Tugela

MASERU

LESOTHO

East London

Port Elizabeth

TRANSVAAL

SWAZILAND

SWAZILAND

LESOTHO

LESOTHO

CLIMATE
This region varies
in climate from tropical in
northern areas to temperate
in the south. Parts of some
countries are prone to drought.

INDUSTRY
Oil, diamonds, uranium, gold.
Namibia has the world's largest uranium
mine. Gold from South Africa is often
sold as special coins called Krugerrands.

Southern Africa facts

ZIMBABWE

• Most people in Zimbabwe belong to the Shona or Ndebele tribes.
• Zimbabwe was formerly known as Southern Rhodesia.

ESSENTIAL FACTS

⊙ Harare
◉ 150,800 sq miles (390,580 sq km)
♦ 10.9 million
☗ Zimbabwe dollar
♀ English

COLORFUL DECOR
Ndebele women decorate their homes with bright geometric patterns.

MOZAMBIQUE

• Over 90% of the citizens of Mozambique live in poverty.
• Polygamous marriages are common among those wealthy enough to take second wives.

ESSENTIAL FACTS

⊙ Maputo
◉ 309,493 sq miles (801,590 sq km)
♦ 15.3 million
☗ Metical
♀ Portuguese

BOTSWANA

• The people of Botswana place such value on rain as a resource that their currency, the pula, is named in its honor.

ESSENTIAL FACTS

⊙ Gaborone
◉ 224,600 sq miles (581,730 sq km)
♦ 1.4 million
☗ Pula
♀ English

SWAZILAND

⊙ Mbabane
♦ 800,000
♀ Siswati, English

ANGOLA

• Injuries caused by exploding mines have led to the nation of Angola having the highest number of amputees in the world.

ESSENTIAL FACTS

⊙ Luanda
◉ 481,351 sq miles (1,246,700 sq km)
♦ 10.3 million
☗ New kwanza
♀ Portuguese

SPRINGBOKS
These small antelopes live in the grasslands of South Africa.

Characteristic leap is known as "pronking"

MADAGASCAR

(*Indian Ocean,*
pp.362–363)

• This country is
the world's largest
producer of vanilla.
• Madagascar is a
unique environment;
80% of its plants and
animal species are
found nowhere else.

ESSENTIAL FACTS

⦿ Antananarivo

◑ 226,660 sq miles
(587,040 sq km)

♦ 13.3 million

🕸 Malagasy franc

♀ Malagasy, French

LESOTHO

⦿ Maseru

♦ 1.9 million

♀ English, Sesotho

LARGEST LEMUR
Madagascar is home to
the indri, the largest of
the world's lemurs.

COMOROS

⦿ Moroni

♦ 600,000

♀ Arabic, French

NAMIBIA

• The Namib is Earth's
oldest, and one of its
driest, deserts.

ESSENTIAL FACTS

⦿ Windhoek

◑ 318,260 sq miles
(824,290 sq km)

♦ 1.6 million

🕸 South African rand

♀ English

SOUTH AFRICA

• President Nelson
Mandela and former
president F. W.
De Klerk were awarded
the Nobel Peace Prize in
1994 for their work
dismantling apartheid.
• Tourists are
increasingly attracted to
South Africa's beaches,
stunning scenery, and
prize-winning vineyards.

ESSENTIAL FACTS

⦿ Pretoria, Cape Town,
Bloemfontein

◑ 471,443 sq miles
(1,221,040 sq km)

♦ 37.4 million

🕸 Rand

♀ Afrikaans, English,
9 African languages

▲ Multiparty republic

♦ 62 years

BURIED TREASURE
South Africa has the
world's deepest goldmine,
descending 12,392 ft
(3,777 m) underground.

NORTH AND WEST ASIA

BARENTS SEA

KARA SEA

RUSSIAN FEDERATION

(EUROPEAN RUSSIA)

KAZAKHSTAN

CASPIAN SEA

BLACK SEA

GEORGIA

UZBEKISTAN

KYRGYZSTAN

TURKEY

ARMENIA AZERBAIJAN

TURKMENISTAN

TAJIKISTAN

CYPRUS

LEBANON

ISRAEL

SYRIA

JORDAN

IRAQ

IRAN

AFGHANISTAN

KUWAIT

BAHRAIN

QATAR

UNITED ARAB EMIRATES

SAUDI ARABIA

OMAN

RED SEA

YEMEN

ARABIAN SEA

ARCTIC OCEAN

LAPTEV SEA

EAST SIBERIAN SEA

BERING SEA

SEA OF OKHOTSK

NORTH AND WEST ASIA

Asia is the largest continent in the world, occupying nearly one-third of the world's total land area. In the south, the Arabian Peninsula is mostly hot, dry desert. In the north lie cold deserts, treeless plains called steppes and the largest needleleaf forest in the world, which stretches from Siberia to northern Europe.

THE NEAR EAST

AT THE JUNCTION of Africa, Asia, and Europe, the Near East is a mosaic of deserts, mountains, and fertile valleys. After centuries of conflict, there are now hopes for peace in the region. Lebanon is beginning to emerge from a civil war that began in 1975 and the disputes over territories in Israel, such as the West Bank and the Gaza Strip, are starting to be resolved.

LEBANON

INDUSTRY
Oil, potash, cotton, fruit. Water is in short supply in this region and special irrigation techniques are used in order to avoid waste. Syria's main cash crop is cotton.

ISRAEL

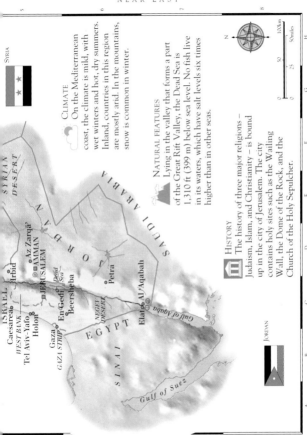

SYRIA

CLIMATE
On the Mediterranean coast, the climate is mild, with wet winters and hot, dry summers. Inland, countries in this region are mostly arid. In the mountains, snow is common in winter.

NATURAL FEATURES
Lying in the valley that forms a part of the Great Rift Valley, the Dead Sea is 1,310 ft (399 m) below sea level. No fish live in its waters, which have salt levels six times higher than in other seas.

HISTORY
The history of three major religions – Judaism, Islam, and Christianity – is bound up in the city of Jerusalem. The city contains holy sites such as the Wailing Wall, the Dome of the Rock, and the Church of the Holy Sepulcher.

JORDAN

ISRAEL
Caesarea
WEST BANK
Tel Aviv-Yafo
Holon
Gaza
GAZA STRIP
Irbid
Az Zarqá
AMMAN
JERUSALEM
En Gedi
Dead Sea
Beersheba
NEGEV DESERT
Elat
Al 'Aqabah
Gulf of 'Aqaba
EGYPT
SINAI
Gulf of Suez
SYRIAN DESERT
J O R D A N
SAUDI ARABIA
Petra

N
0   25   50miles
0   50   100km

TURKEY AND CYPRUS

BRIDGING THE CONTINENTS of Europe and Asia, Turkey was once the center of the Ottoman Empire, which at one time controlled one-quarter of Europe. Independent of the UK in 1960, Cyprus was invaded by Turkey in 1974. Southern Cyprus is Greek; Northern Cyprus is still occupied by Turkey.

TURKEY

INDUSTRY

Wheat, corn, sugar beets, nuts, fruit, cotton, tobacco, tourism. Carpet-weaving is a tradition dating back centuries. Figs and peaches are grown on the coast of the Mediterranean.

ENVIRONMENT

Turkey's dam-building projects on the Tigris and Euphrates Rivers have met with disapproval from Syria and Iraq, whose own rivers will have reduced flow as a result.

PEOPLE

The Kurds are Turkey's main minority group and one of the largest groups of stateless people in the world. Their homeland, Kurdistan, straddles three countries: Turkey, Iraq, and Iran Kurds are fighting for recognition of their rights within Turkey.

NATURAL FEATURES
Turkey lies within the pine-Himalayan mountain belt. e Arabian, African, Eurasian, gean, and Turkish plates all nverge within its borders, ulting in severe seismic activity.

CLIMATE
Coastal regions of Turkey and Cyprus have a Mediterranean climate. The Turkish interior has cold, snowy winters and hot, dry summers.

B L A C K   S E A

GEORGIA

PONTIC

ARMENIA

AZ MTS.

MOUNTAINS

Samsun

Trabzon

Kızılırmak

Yeşil

Erzurum

ANKARA

Sivas

Kızılırmak

MUNZUR MTS.

Murat

L. Van

Van

K E Y

CAPPADOCIA

Elazığ

Tigris

IRAN

Göreme

Kayseri

Seyhan

Malatya

Diyarbakir

aya

Ceyhan

Kahramanmaraş

URUS MTS.

Gaziantep

Şanlıurfa

IRAQ

Adana

Euphrates

Mersin

Antakya

S Y R I A

A CYPRUS
NICOSIA
Famagusta
Larnaca
Limassol

CYPRUS

HISTORY
Greeks colonized the Aegean coast in 700 B.C. The Temple of Artemis in the city of Ephesus is one of the seven wonders of the ancient world.

N

0   150   300km

0   100   150miles

MIDDLE EAST

ISLAM WAS FOUNDED in A.D. 570 in Mecca, Saudi Arabia, and spread throughout the Middle East, where today it is the main religion. Oil has brought wealth to the region, but in 1991 the area was financially devastated by the Gulf War.

IRAQ

INDUSTRY
Oil, natural gas, fishing, carpet-weaving, offshore banking. Saudi Arabia has the world's largest oil reserves. Over 60 percent of the world's desalination plants are used in this region to make seawater drinkable.

SAUDI ARABIA

KUWAIT

CLIMATE
Most of the countries in this region are semiarid, with low rainfall. Inland, summer temperatures can reach 119°F (48°C) with winter temperatures falling to freezing.

BAHRAIN

QATAR

HISTORY
Ancient civilizations developed about 5,500 years ago in Mesopotamia, between the Tigris and Euphrates Rivers. The Sumerian civilization had advanced methods of irrigation, sophisticated architecture, and a complex form of writing called cuneiform.

UNITED ARAB EMIRATES

YEMEN

EGYPT

JOR

Gulf of Aqaba

H
E
J

R
E
D

Mecca

⊕ ⊙●⊙
Jedda

S
E
A

Hode
Al Mu
Bab el M

IRAN

TURKEY

AZERBAIJAN

L. Urmia

CASPIAN SEA

Ardabīl

Rasht

TURKMENISTAN

Mosul

Irbil

Kirkūk

As Sulaymānīyah

Zanjān

Sanandaj

ELBURZ MTS.

Sarī

TEHRĀN

Semnān

SYRIA

IRAQ

BAGHDAD

Bakhtarān

Qom

Mashhad

DASHT-E KAVIR

AFGHANISTAN

Karbalā

Al-Hillah

Ilām

Arāk

An-Najaf

Dezfūl

Eşfahān

Euphrates

Al Amārah

Ahvāz

Yazd

An Nāşirīyah

Al-Basrah

Ābādān

ZAGROS MTS.

DASHT-E LŪT

PAKISTAN

KUWAIT CITY

Yāsūj

Kermān

Zāhedān

KUWAIT

Shīrāz

Buraydah

Persian Gulf

Jaz Mūriān Salt Lake

AD DAHNA

Ad Dammām

MANAMA BAHRAIN

Bandar-e Abbās

RIYADH

Al Hufūf

DOHA

QATAR

Strait of Hormuz

Khasab (to Oman)

SAUDI

ABU DHABI

Dubai

NEJD

UNITED ARAB EMIRATES

Gulf of Oman

ARABIA

AL FAJIRAH

MUSCAT

OMAN

RUB' AL KHALI

RAMLAT AS SAB'ATAYN

Masirah I.

Gulf of Masirah

YEMEN

HADHRAMAUT

ARABIAN SEA

N

0   300   600km

0   150   300miles

Near East facts

ISRAEL

• The average age in Israel is only 25.6 years.
• Israeli citizenship is the right of all Jews.

ESSENTIAL FACTS

⊙ Jerusalem
◖ 7,992 sq miles (20,700 sq km)
♦ 5.4 million
♨ New shekel
♡ Hebrew, Arabic
▲ Multiparty republic
♦ 76 years

WAILING WALL, JERUSALEM

CYPRUS

⊙ Nicosia
♦ 700,000
♡ Greek, Turkish

JORDAN

• King Hussein, the longest-reigning Arab ruler, has led Jordan since 1952.

ESSENTIAL FACTS

⊙ Amman
◖ 34,440 sq miles (89,210 sq km)
♦ 4.4 million
♨ Jordanian dinar
♡ Arabic

TURKEY

• Grapes, one of the world's oldest crops, were first grown in Anatolia, Turkey.

ESSENTIAL FACTS

⊙ Ankara
◖ 300,950 sq miles (779,450 sq km)
♦ 59.6 million
♨ Turkish lira
♡ Turkish
▲ Multiparty republic
♦ 67 years

LEBANON

• The press has greater freedom in Lebanon than in any other Arab country.

ESSENTIAL FACTS

⊙ Beirut
◖ 4,015 sq miles (10,400 sq km)
♦ 2.9 million
♨ Lebanese pound
♡ Arabic

SYRIA

• The world's first alphabet was found in the ancient Syrian city of Ugarit.

ESSENTIAL FACTS

⊙ Damascus
◖ 71,498 sq miles (185,180 sq km)
♦ 13.8 million
♨ Syrian pound
♡ Arabic

Middle East facts

IRAN

ESSENTIAL FACTS

- ⊙ Tehran
- ◔ 636,293 sq miles
  (1,648,000 sq km)
- ♦ 63.2 million
- 🏛 Iranian rial
- ♡ Farsi
- ▲ Islamic republic
- ♦ 67 years

SAUDI ARABIA

ESSENTIAL FACTS

- ⊙ Riyadh
- ◔ 829,995 sq miles
  (2,149,690 sq km)
- ♦ 16.5 million
- 🏛 Saudi riyal
- ♡ Arabic
- ▲ Absolute monarchy
- ♦ 69 years

QATAR	BAHRAIN
⊙ Doha	⊙ Manama
♦ 500,000	♦ 500,000
♡ Arabic	♡ Arabic

IRAQ

ESSENTIAL FACTS

- ⊙ Baghdad
- ◔ 169,235 sq miles
  (438,320 sq km)
- ♦ 19.9 million
- 🏛 Iraqi dinar
- ♡ Arabic
- ▲ Single-party republic
- ♦ 66 years

ARAB HEADDRESSES
Men and women wear
headcloths to protect
them from the sun.

UNITED ARAB EMIRATES

ESSENTIAL FACTS

- ⊙ Abu Dhabi
- ◔ 32,278 sq miles
  (83,600 sq km)
- ♦ 1.7 million
- 🏛 UAE dirham
- ♡ Arabic

KUWAIT

ESSENTIAL FACTS

- ⊙ Kuwait City
- ◔ 6,880 sq miles
  (17,820 sq km)
- ♦ 1.8 million
- 🏛 Kuwaiti dinar
- ♡ Arabic

OMAN

ESSENTIAL FACTS

- ⊙ Muscat
- ◔ 82,030 sq miles
  (212,460 sq km)
- ♦ 1.7 million
- 🏛 Omani rial
- ♡ Arabic

YEMEN

ESSENTIAL FACTS

- ⊙ Sana
- ◔ 203,849 sq miles
  (527,970 sq km)
- ♦ 13 million
- 🏛 Yemen riyal
- ♡ Arabic

CENTRAL ASIA

FOR CENTURIES, many people in central Asia lived in mountains as nomads, or in cities that sprang up along the Silk Road. When the region came under Soviet rule, industry was developed and irrigation schemes made farming possible.

Map labels: USTYURT PLATEAU · ARAL SEA · TURAN LOWLAND · CASPIAN SEA · L. Sarykamysh · Zaliv Kara-Bogaz-Gol · Nukus · UZ · Tashauz · Urgench · Krasnovodsk · Nebit Dag · TURKMENISTAN · ASHKABAD · H · A F

INDUSTRY
Cotton, gold, gas, sulfur, mercury, opium, hydroelectricity. Uzbekistan has the largest single gold mine in the world. Tajikistan has 14 percent of the world's known uranium resources.

TURKMENISTAN

HISTORY
In the early 1900s, most of this region, except for Afghanistan, came under Soviet rule, which restricted the use of local languages and Islam. Today, these newly independent countries are resuming the religions, languages, and traditions of their past.

ENVIRONMENT
Crop irrigation draws water from the Amu Darya River, reducing the amount of water flowing into the Aral Sea. By the year 2000 the Sea will have shrunk to a third of its original size.

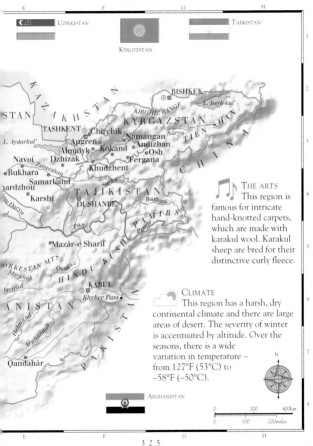

UZBEKISTAN

KYRGYZSTAN

TAJIKISTAN

E   F   G   H

1

KAZAKHSTAN

BISHKEK

KIRGHIZ RANGE

L. Issyk-kul'

KYRGYZSTAN

TIEN SHAN

TASHKENT   Chirchik

Angren   Namangan   Naryn

Almalyk   Kokand   Andizhan

Navoi   Dzhizak   Fergana   Osh

Bukhara   Khudzhent

Zeravshan

Samarkand

Gardzhou

Karshi

DUSHANBE

TAJIKISTAN

Surkhob

Vax̌š

Bartang

P A M I R S

Pamir

CHINA

STAN

L. Aydarkul'

Darya

al

TURKESTAN MTS

Morghāb

Qunduz

Jarirūd

HINDU KUSH

KABUL

Khyber Pass

ANISTAN

Helmand

Arghandāb

PAKISTAN

Qandahār

2

3

4

5

6

7

8

🎵🎵 THE ARTS
This region is famous for intricate hand-knotted carpets, which are made with karakul wool. Karakul sheep are bred for their distinctive curly fleece.

☁ CLIMATE
This region has a harsh, dry continental climate and there are large areas of desert. The severity of winter is accentuated by altitude. Over the seasons, there is a wide variation in temperature – from 127°F (53°C) to –58°F (–50°C).

N

AFGHANISTAN

0   200   400km

0   100   200miles

E   F   G   H

RUSSIAN FEDERATION AND KAZAKHSTAN

THE URAL mountains separate European and Asian Russia, which extends from the frozen arctic lands in the north to the central Asian deserts in the south. In 1991, Kazakhstan became the last Soviet republic to gain independence.

CLIMATE
Kazakhstan has a continental climate. Winter temperatures in Russia vary little from north to south, but fall sharply in the east, especially in Siberia.

PEOPLE
There are 57 nationalities, each with their own territories, within the Russian Federation. A further 95 groups are without territories of their own, although these groups make up only six percent of the total population.

Murmansk
BARENTS SE
FINLAND
ESTONIA
LATVIA   St. Petersburg
BELORUSSIA   Pskov   Arkhangel'sk
Novgorod
Smolensk
MOSCOW   Yaroslavl'
UKRAINE   Tula   Ryazan'
Voronezh   Kirov
Penza   Kazan'   Izhevsk   Perm'
Rostov-na-Donu   Simbirsk   Naberezhnyye   Chel
Saratov   Samara
Krasnodar   Tol'yatti   Ural'sk   Ufa   Yekaterinbu
GEORGIA   Volgograd   Orenburg   Chelyabins
Astrakhan   Oms
Grozny   Atyrau   Aktyubinsk   Kustanai
CASPIAN SEA   Emba   Ishim
UZBEKISTAN   KIRGHIZ STEPPE   Tselinograd
L. Tengiz
ARAL   Karaganda
SEA   KAZAKHSTAN
TURKMENISTAN   Syr Darya   Kzyl-Orda   L. Balkl
Chu
UZBEKISTAN   Shimkent   ALMA-AT

URAL MOLDA
Volga

KAZAKHSTAN

HISTORY

Kazakhstan was absorbed by Russia in e 19th century, when Russians began to tle the land used by nomadic Kazakhs. ttlement and industrial development reased after 1917.

INDUSTRY

Oil, gas, coal, gold, diamonds. Mineral-rich Kazakhstan has the world's largest chromium mine. Siberia has large gas, coal, and oil fields.

Bering St.

Wrangel I.   CHUKCHI SEA   C. Navarin

EAST SIBERIAN SEA   Anadyr'   BERING SEA

Ayon Is.

Bear Is.   Cape Olyutorskiy

Severnaya   Bolshevik I.   New Siberian Is.   Karaginskiy Is.

Zemlya   C. Chelyuskin   LAPTEV SEA   KORYAK RANGE

Belyy Is.   TAYMYR PENINSULA   Olenek   KAMCHATKA

GYDA   L. Taymyr   Bay   Korkodon   Petropavlovsk -Kamchatskiy

PENINSULA   Khatanga   CENTRAL   Magadan

Noril'sk   SIBERIAN   C. Lopatka

hodka   PUTORANA   PLATEAU   Paramushir Is.

MTS.   RUSSIAN   SEA OF OKHOTSK

FEDERATION   Yakutsk   C. Yelizavety   Kurile Islands

Lower Tunguska   SIBERIA   DZHUGDZHUR RANGE   Sakhalin

Kel'   Stony Tunguska   Angara   STANOVOY RANGE   Zeya Res.   Yuzhno-Sakhalinsk

Tomsk   Krasnoyarsk   L. Baikal   Blagoveshchensk   Khabarovsk

Novosibirsk   Abakan   Angarsk   Ulan-Ude   CHINA   SEA OF JAPAN

aul   Novokuznetsk   Bivsk   Kyzyl   Irkutsk   Vladivostok

alinsk   Zaysan   MONGOLIA   NORTH KOREA

RUSSIAN FEDERATION

N

0   600   1,200km

0   300   600miles

Central Asia facts

UZBEKISTAN

• Many young Uzbeks are sent to Turkey to study business practice.
• Arranged marriages are still the custom in rural areas.

ESSENTIAL FACTS
⊙ Tashkent
⊘ 439,733 sq miles (1,138,910 sq km)
❖ 21.1 million
❖ Som
♀ Uzbek

KYRGYZSTAN

• The nation of Kyrgyzstan is the most rural ex-Soviet republic.

ESSENTIAL FACTS
⊙ Bishkek
⊘ 76,640 sq miles (198,500 sq km)
❖ 4.6 million
❖ Som
♀ Kyrgyz

UZBEK HEADWEAR
Velvet hats like this one are commonly worn in Uzbekistan.

TURKMENISTAN

• Ashgabat is a breeding center for the Akhal-Teke, a breed of racehorse able to maintain its speed in desert conditions.
• Most Turkmen live around desert oases.

ESSENTIAL FACTS
⊙ Ashgabat
⊘ 188,455 sq miles (488,100 sq km)
❖ 4 million
❖ Manat
♀ Turkmen

TAJIKISTAN

• The traditions and language of Tajikistan are similar to those of Iran.
• Violence perpetrated by armed gangs is a major problem in all but the most remote areas.

ESSENTIAL FACTS
⊙ Dushanbe
⊘ 55,251 sq miles (143,100 sq km)
❖ 5.7 million
❖ Ruble
♀ Tajik

AFGHANISTAN

• Most Afghans live in extreme poverty.

ESSENTIAL FACTS
⊙ Kabul
⊘ 251,770 sq miles (652,090 sq km)
❖ 20.5 million
❖ Afghani
♀ Persian, Pashtu

CARROTS WERE FIRST GROWN FOR FOOD IN AFGHANISTAN

Russian Federation and Kazakhstan facts

RUSSIAN FEDERATION

• Moscow and St. Petersburg are the most popular tourist destinations in the Commonwealth of Independent States (CIS).
• Russia still maintains a military presence in most of the former USSR.
• Organized crime bosses are Russia's wealthiest group.

ESSENTIAL FACTS

⊙ Moscow

◔ 6,592,800 sq miles (17,075,400 sq km)

♦ 149.2 million

💰 Ruble

♡ Russian

▲ Multiparty republic

● 70 years

(See also **European Russia**, p.288)

EAR OF WHEAT Kazakhstan's steppes, or grasslands, were plowed up to grow grain crops in the 1950s.

KAZAKHSTAN

• Many foreign businesspeople now live in Alma-Ata.
• Kazakhstan joined the International Monetary Fund (IMF) in 1992.
• The Kazakhs remain committed to Islam and loyal to the three clan federations, or Hordes.

ESSENTIAL FACTS

⊙ Alma-Ata

◔ 1,049,150 sq miles (2,717,300 sq km)

♦ 17.2 million

💰 Tenge

♡ Kazakh

▲ Multiparty republic

● 69 years

KAZAKHSTAN SPACE CENTER
The Russian space program is based at Baykonour in Kazakhstan.

SIBERIAN HUSKIES The husky is used for pulling sleds and hunting.

The "Buran" unmanned Russian space shuttle

Буран

SOUTH AND EAST ASIA

MONGOLIA

CHINA

PAKISTAN

NEPAL

BHUTAN

BANGLADESH

INDIA

MYANMAR

LAOS

THAILAND

CAMBODIA

VIETNAM

ARABIAN SEA

Lakshadweep Islands (to India)

Andaman Islands (to India)

Nicobar Islands (to India)

MALAYS

SINGAPO

SRI LANKA

MALDIVES

INDIAN OCEAN

South and East Asia

From the Gobi desert of Mongolia to the tropical rainforests of Malaysia, the Philippines, and Indonesia, Asia is a continent of great contrasts. It is a mountainous region and contains the world's highest mountain, Mount Everest.

THE INDIAN SUBCONTINENT

SEPARATED FROM THE rest of Asia by the Himalayas, India is the second most populated country after China. It is estimated that India's population will overtake that of China by 2030. To the north, Nepal and Bhutan lie nestled in the Himalayas between China and India, and to the south lies Sri Lanka, once known as Ceylon.

INDUSTRY
Tea, jute, iron, cut diamonds, cotton, rice, sugarcane, textiles. Bangladesh exports 80 percent of the world's jute fiber. Sri Lanka is the largest tea exporter in the world. Pakistan is a major exporter of rice.

INDIA

HISTORY
In 1947, when India gained independence, religious differences led to the creation of two countries – Hindu India and Muslim Pakistan. In 1971, a short civil war broke out between East and West Pakistan and East Pakistan became Bangladesh.

NATURAL FEATURES
The Himalayas were formed as a result of a violent crumpling of the Earth's crust. Frequent earthquakes indicate that the process is continuing. The highest peaks in the world, including Mount Everest, are in this mountain system.

PAKISTAN

BHUTAN

NEPAL

awar
ISLAMABAD
•Srinagar
alpindi
•Gujranwala
hore •Amritsar
ilabad •Jalandhar
an •Ludhiana Chandigarh
Meerut
NEW
DELHI •Bareilly
Jaipur •Agra   KATHMANDU
Gwalior •Lucknow   THIMPHU
hpur •Kota Kanpur •Varanasi   BHUTAN   •Guwahati
Gandi Res. •Allahabad •Patna   Brahmaputra   •Imphal
nadabad •Bhopal •Jabalpur •Dhanbad Rajshahi   BANGLADESH
                    •Ranchi DACCA •Agartala
Todara •Indore Narmada   Khulna
rat   Tapti •Nagpur   Chittagong   MYANMAR
Nasik
•Thane   Mahanadi
mbay   Godavari
•Pune   DECCAN
Hyderabad
aji PLATEAU •Vijayawada   B a y o f B e n g a l
•Dharwad
Mangalore
•Bangalore Madras
•Coimbatore
•Cochin
•Madurai •Jaffna   SRI LANKA
ivandrum
          SRI LANKA
          COLOMBO
          •Galle

CHINA

HIMALAYAS

INDIA

EASTERN GHATS

COROMANDEL COAST

Ganges

☁ CLIMATE
Sri Lanka and southern
India are tropical, with little
seasonal variation in temperature.
The north has a cold alpine climate.
Cyclones regularly build up in the
Bay of Bengal. Bangladesh is often
flooded during the monsoon.

Indian Subcontinent facts

INDIA

- The Bombay film industry is the world's biggest producer of feature films.
- Nearly half of India's adults are illiterate.
- Cultural and religious pressures in India encourage people to have large families.

ESSENTIAL FACTS

- ⊙ New Delhi
- ◔ 1,289,338 sq miles (3,287,590 sq km)
- ♦ 896.6 million
- ♛ Rupee
- ♡ Hindi, English
- ▲ Multiparty republic
- ♦ 60 years

REGAL BEAST
The national symbol of India is the Royal Bengal tiger, which is a protected species.

THE SPICE OF LIFE
Indian cooking uses intense, zesty seasonings and subtle combinations of spices to flavor each dish.

Cilantro

Coriander

Cardamom pods

Ground turmeric

Fresh ginger

SRI LANKA

- In 1960, Sri Lanka became the first country in the world to elect a woman prime minister.
- Ethnic tension between the minority Tamils and majority Sinhalese led to civil war in 1983.

ESSENTIAL FACTS

- ⊙ Columbo
- ◔ 25,332 sq miles (65,610 sq km)
- ♦ 17.9 million
- ♛ Sri Lanka rupee
- ♡ Sinhalese, Tamil

BANGLADESH

- Most transportation in Bangladesh is via rivers and waterways.
- Destruction of crops by cyclones and flooding is a frequent problem.

ESSENTIAL FACTS

- ⊙ Dhaka
- ◔ 55,598 sq miles (143,998 sq km)
- ♦ 122.2 million
- ♛ Taka
- ♡ Bengali, Urdu

PAKISTAN

- The first woman ever to lead a Muslim country was Benazir Bhutto, elected prime minister of Pakistan in 1988.
- The Punjabi majority controls Pakistan's army and bureaucracy.

ESSENTIAL FACTS

- ⊙ Islamabad
- ◖ 307,374 sq miles (796,100 sq km)
- ♦ 128.1 million
- ▤ Pakistani rupee
- ♡ Urdu, Punjabi
- ▲ Multiparty republic
- ♦ 58 years

TOP TEAM
The nation of Pakistan has one of the world's best cricket teams.

EYES OF BUDDHA
The all-seeing eyes of Buddha adorn the walls of many temples in Nepal.

NEPAL

- Prince Siddhartha Gautama, the founder of Buddhism, was born in southern Nepal in 563 B.C.
- Nepal's divorce laws are biased in favor of the male partner.

ESSENTIAL FACTS

- ⊙ Kathmandu
- ◖ 54,363 sq miles (140,800 sq km)
- ♦ 21.1 million
- ▤ Nepalese rupee
- ♡ Nepali

NEPALESE WELCOME
A prayerlike gesture is the traditional greeting in Nepal.

SEYCHELLES
(*Indian Ocean, pp.362–363*)

- ⊙ Victoria
- ♦ 69,000
- ♡ Creole, English, French

BHUTANESE SPORT
Archery is the national sport of Bhutan.

BHUTAN

- ⊙ Thimphu
- ♦ 1.7 million
- ♡ Dzongkha

MALDIVES
(*Indian Ocean, pp.362–363*)

- ⊙ Male'
- ♦ 200,000
- ♡ Dhivehi

MAURITIUS
(*Indian Ocean, pp.362–363*)

- ⊙ Port Louis
- ♦ 1.1 million
- ♡ English

CHINA AND MONGOLIA

ISOLATED FROM THE western world for centuries, the Chinese were the first to develop the compass, paper, gunpowder, porcelain, and silk. Three autonomous regions lie within western China – Inner Mongolia, Xinjiang, and Tibet. The Gobi desert, in vast Mongolia, is the world's most northern desert.

PEOPLE
Han Chinese make up 93 percent of China's population. China has relaxed its 1979 one-child policy for minority groups, such as the Mongolians, Tibetans, and Muslim Uygurs, after some groups faced near extinction.

HISTORY
Tibet was invaded by China in 1950. The Chinese have destroyed Tibet's traditional agricultural society and Buddhist monasteries. In 1959 there were more than 6,000 monasteries – by 1980, only 179 remained.

KAZAKHSTAN
ALTAI MTS.
Har Us
XINJIANG UIGHUR
Ürümqi
AUTONOMOUS
KYRGYZSTAN
TIEN MTS.
L. Bosten
Tarim
REGION
Tarim Basin
Lop N
TAKLA MAKAN
KARAKORAM MTS.
DESERT
AFGHANISTAN
ALTUN MTS.
PAKISTAN
Aksai
Chin
(Controlled by
China, claimed
by India)
KUNLUN MTS.
BA
TIBETAN
Demchok
(Claimed by both
China and India)
AUTONOMOUS
TANGGULA M
GANGDISE RANGE
REGION
Brahmaputra (Yarlang Zangbo)
Lha
HIMALAYAS
NEPAL
BHUTAN

E   F   G   H

MONGOLIA

Amur

Argun

GREATER KHINGAN RANGE

SOUTHWESTERN
CHINA IS SHOWN
ON PP.338–339.

R U S S I A N   F E D E R A T I O N

Hovsgol

Eg

Selenga

Orhon

Uldz

Hulun
Nur

NGAYN MTS

ULAN BATOR

SEA
OF
JAPAN

M O N G O L I A

I N N E R
M O N G O L I A

NORTH
KOREA

GOBI DESERT

CHINA

BAIDAN JARAN
DESERT

Hohhot

Baotou

Great
Wall

ORDOS
DESERT

EASTERN

SOUTH
KOREA

YELLOW
SEA

Qinghai
Hu

Xining

Great
Wall

N H

MTS

CHINA

CHINA

EASTERN CHINA

INDUSTRY

Coal, tungsten, iron ore, oil.
China is the world's largest coal and
tungsten producer. Grains are grown
in Mongolia on irrigated
land or oases.

CLIMATE

In Mongolia, temperatures can
reach 106°F (41°C) and sometimes drop
to –58°F (–50°C). Northwestern China
is affected by the winter monsoon, which
brings cold, dry air from Siberia.

N

0   400   800km
0   200   400miles

E   F   G   H

CHINA AND KOREA

ONE-FIFTH OF the world's population lives in China – mostly in the eastern part of the country. Annexed to Japan in 1910, Korea was divided between the USA and Communist Russia after World War II. North and South Korea were formed in 1948.

NORTHWESTERN CHINA IS SHOWN ON PP.118–119.

RUSSIAN FEDERATION

WESTERN KHINGAN MTS.

Amur

Qiqihar

Harbin

MANCHURIA

Jilin

Changchun

Fushun

Shenyang

Anshan

Jinzhou

Dalian

Bo Hai

Tientsin

PEKING

Dông

Taiyuan

Shijiazhuang

Handan

Zhengzhou

Luoyang

Xi'an

HUANG

LING

Lanzhou

WESTERN

CHINA

NINGXIA HUI

AUTONOMOUS

REGION

Great Wall

Yellow R.

Dadu He

Datong

MONGOLIA

Great Wall

Ch'ŏngjin

NORTH KOREA

Sinŭiju

PYONGYANG

Namp'o

SEOUL

Inch'ŏn

SOUTH KOREA

Taejŏn

Taegu

Pusan

Cheju

Korea St.

JAPAN SEA

YELLOW SEA

Qingdao

Shandong Pen.

Zibo

Jinan

Zaozhuang

Huainan

Hefei

Nanjing

Wuxi

Shanghai

CHINA

338

NORTH KOREA

SOUTH KOREA

TAIWAN

TAIWAN

CHINA

PEOPLE
Korea has been inhabited by one ethnic group for 2,000 years and today those of the same surname group may not marry each other. Most Taiwanese are descendants of the Chinese supporters of the deposed Ming dynasty, who migrated in 1644.

CLIMATE
Southern South Korea and Taiwan have a tropical monsoon climate similar to that of southern China. North Korea has a continental climate.

HISTORY
On July 1, 1997, Britain returned Hong Kong to China where it is now run as a Special Administrative Region.

COMMUNICATIONS
South Korea has one of the world's best public transportation systems. Buses, trains, boats, and planes are integrated in one timetable.

INDUSTRY
Rice, electronics, wheat, finance, textiles. Hong Kong has the busiest container port in the world. Taiwan is the world's leading producer of watches, computers, televisions, and track shoes.

JAPAN

CONSISTING OF FOUR main islands and 4,000 smaller ones, Japan is the world's leading industrial nation. Since two-thirds of the land is mountainous, the majority of people live on the coast. Japan has about 1,500 minor earthquakes a year, but severe earthquakes, such as the one in Kobe in 1995, occur every few years. Underwater earthquakes sometimes cause huge surge waves, or *tsunami*, along Japan's Pacific coast.

INDUSTRY

Fishing, ship building, motor vehicles, computers, televisions, high-tech electronics. Motor vehicles are Japan's biggest export, and its stock exchange ranks second in the world. Japan excels at producing

HISTORY

Japan was once ruled by warlords called *shoguns*, who discouraged contact with the outside world. In 1639, Japan cut ties with other nations and ordered all Europeans to leave, except the Dutch who were allowed one trading ship per year.

La Pérouse Strait

SEA OF OKHOTSK

Soya Strait

Yekaterina Strait

Kunashiri Strait

Habomai Is

Kuril Islands

Hokkaidō

ISHIKARI MTS.

Ishikari R.

Ishikari Bay

Sapporo

HIDAKA MTS.

Uchiura Bay

Tsugaru Strait

OU MTS.

Mogami R.

Sendai

SEA OF JAPAN

Wakasa Bay

NATURAL FEATURES

Situated on an unstable part of the Earth's crust, Japan is prone to earthquakes and volcanic activity. There are more than 150 major volcanoes in Japan (over 60 of which are active). These form part of the "Ring of Fire" that runs along the edge of the Pacific Ocean.

COMMUNICATIONS

The Shinkansen, or bullet train, is the second fastest in the world. With an average speed of 122 mph (195 km/h), it is renowned for both its speed and reliability.

CLIMATE

The Sea of Japan has a moderating influence on Japan's climate. Winters are not as cold as on the Asian mainland, and Japan has a much higher rainfall – most of which falls in summer.

PEOPLE

The Japanese, both young and old, are avid readers of comic books, known as *manga* and newspapers. Also popular are lifestyle magazines, which encourage the Japanese to make more use of their limited leisure time.

JAPAN

N

0   150   300km
0   75   150miles

Eastern Asia facts

CHINA

• China has the world's oldest continuous civilization; recorded history began 4,000 years ago.

• Mao Tse-tung founded and dominated communist China from 1949 until his death in 1976.

ESSENTIAL FACTS

⊙ Beijing

◔ 3,628,166 sq miles (9,396,960 sq km)

♦ 1.2 billion

💰 Yuan

♀ Mandarin

▲ Single-party republic

♦ 71 years

WONDERWALL
The Great Wall of China is the longest man-made structure in the world.

BAMBOO LUNCH
Pandas living in the forests of China's Szechwan mountains feed on bamboo shoots.

MONGOLIA

• The Mongolian press is strongly outspoken, with no slander or libel laws.

• Most Mongolians are nomadic, but some now live on state-run farms.

• The poorest people in Mongolia cannot even afford to buy bread.

ESSENTIAL FACTS

⊙ Ulan Bator

◔ 604,247 sq miles (1,565,000 sq km)

♦ 2.4 million

💰 Tughrik

♀ Khalkha Mongolian

MACAO

Chinese territory under Portuguese administration until 1999.

⊙ Macao

♦ 477,850

♀ Chinese, Portuguese

MONGOLIAN YAK
Yaks provide Mongolian herders with milk, butter, meat, wool, and leather.

HONG KONG

Territory reverted to Chinese administration in 1997.

⊙ Victoria

♦ 5.8 million

♀ English, Cantonese

SOUTH KOREA

• Over 60% of South Koreans are named Kim, Lee, or Pak.
• It is not considered respectable for married women to have jobs in South Korea.

ESSENTIAL FACTS

⊙ Seoul
◔ 38,232 sq miles (99,020 sq km)
♦ 44.5 million
♒ Won
♀ Korean, Chinese
▲ Multiparty republic
♦ 70 years

NORTH KOREA

• The Korean Worker's Party is the only legal political party.
• Private telephones and cars are forbidden.

ESSENTIAL FACTS

⊙ Pyongyang
◔ 46,540 sq miles (120,540 sq km)
♦ 23.1 million
♒ Won
♀ Korean

KOREAN
GINSENG
ROOT
IS WIDELY
USED IN
TRADITIONAL
ASIAN MEDICINE

TAIWAN PRODUCES
ABOUT 10% OF
THE WORLD'S
COMPUTERS

TAIWAN

• Taiwan is the world's biggest bicycle producer.
• China regards Taiwan as a province of the Chinese mainland.

ESSENTIAL FACTS

⊙ Taipei
◔ 13,969 sq miles (36,179 sq km)
♦ 20.8 million
♒ New Taiwan dollar
♀ Mandarin

JAPAN

• People in Japan define themselves by the company they work for, not the job they do.
• Japan is Hollywood's biggest export market.
• The Japanese constitution forbids the use of troops abroad except in self-defense.

ESSENTIAL FACTS

⊙ Tokyo
◔ 149,869 sq miles (377,800 sq km)
♦ 125 million
♒ Yen
♀ Japanese
▲ Multiparty democracy
♦ 79 years

HEAVYWEIGHTS
Japanese sumo wrestlers eat a daily stew called *chanko-nabe*, made of seafood, meat, vegetables, and tofu, to maintain their bulk.

MAINLAND SOUTHEAST ASIA

FOR MOST OF its history, Thailand has been an independent kingdom. Malaysia includes 11 states on the mainland (Malaya), as well as Sabah and Sarawak in Borneo. Cambodia, Laos, and Vietnam have suffered from years of civil war. Myanmar has become more isolated from the world by its repressive government.

LAOS

MYANMAR (BURMA)

INDIA

CHINA

CHIN HILLS

ARAKAN RANGE

Chindwin

Irrawaddy

Monywa

Sagaing Amarapura

Mandalay

Minbu

Pakokku

L. Inle

Taunggyi

Pyinmana

Prome

Sittoung

Salween

Chiang Mai

Mekong

Luang
Prabang

Nam Ou

LAOS

Black R.

Red R.

L. Thac Ba

Thai Nguyen

Viet Tri

HANOI

Hong Gai

Hai Phong

Nam Dinh

Thanh
Hoa

MYANMAR

B'DESH

Saoltowan

Si

Bay of Bengal

C. Negrais

ANDAMAN SEA

Gulf of Martaban

Kyaikkami

Nakhon Sawan

Mae Nam Mun

Khon Kaen

Hue

Da Nang

Mekong

Pakxé

Qui Nhon

Ban Me Thuot

Nha Trang

Đa Lat

THAILAND

Nakhon Ratchasima

Ubon Ratchathani

Sen

San

Tonle Sap

CAMBODIA

Bien Hoa

Ho Chi Minh City

VIETNAM

Tavoy

Rat Buri

Ayutthaya

BANGKOK

Chon Buri

Bătdâmbâng

Tônlé Sap

PHNOM PENH

Kâmpóng Cham

Long Xuyên

Can Tho

Rach Gia

SOUTH CHINA SEA

CAMBODIA

Mergui Archipelago

Gulf of Thailand

ISTHMUS OF KRA

Phangan I.

Samui I.

Nakhon Si Thammarat

Songkhla

Kota Baharu

THAILAND

Kuala Terengganu

Kuantan

Phuket I.

Langkawi

Hat Yai

Pinang

Taiping

Ipoh

CAMERON HIGHLANDS

KUALA LUMPUR

Kelang

Padang

MALAYSIA

Seremban

Melaka

Johor Baharu

MALAYSIA (WEST)

SINGAPORE

Strait of Singapore

SINGAPORE

CLIMATE

Most of Southeast Asia has a tropical climate, with consistently high temperatures and one or two rainy seasons that can last up to six months.

INDUSTRY

Palm oil, lumber, tin, gems, rice, rubber, tourism. Singapore controls the shipping route between the Indian and Pacific Oceans. Thailand is a leading exporter of pineapples and shrimp.

N

0   100   200 miles

0   200   400 km

MARITIME SOUTHEAST ASIA

SCATTERED BETWEEN the Indian and Pacific Oceans are thousands of tropic[al] mountainous islands. Once called the East Indies, Indonesia was ruled by the Dutch for 350 years. More than half of its 13,677 islands are still uninhabited. The Philippines lie on the "Ring of Fire," and are subject to earthquakes and volcanic activity. Borneo is shared among Indonesia, Malaysia, and Brunei.

BRUNEI

PHI

Balaba
Sira

SOUTH CHINA SEA

Kota
Kinabalu

BANDAR SERI
BEGAWAN

BRUNEI

MALAYSIA
(EAST)

Natuna Is.

Medan

Simeulue

L.Toba

Anambas Is.

Strait of Singapore

SARAWAK

Rajang

Kuching

Borneo

Kapuas

MULLER MTS.

Samarin

Nias

Sumatra

Lingga

Pontianak

Balikpapa

Padang

Batanghari

Singkep

Bangka

Mendawai

Siberut

Jambi

BUKIT BARISAN MTS.

Palembang

Belitung

Banjarmasin

Tanjungkarang

JAVA SEA

I N

JAKARTA

Bogor Cirebon Semarang

Bandung

Yogyakarta

Kediri

Surabaya

Jember

Malang

Denpasar

Java

Lombo

N

0   300   600km
0   150   300miles

MALAYSIA (EAST)
SABAH AND SARAWAK

I N D I A N   O C E A N

PHILIPPINES

INDUSTRY
Palm oil, lumber, rice, oil, natural gas, copper, chrome, tourism. Malaysia is the largest producer of palm oil and computer disk-drives. Indonesia is a major exporter of natural gas.

ENVIRONMENT
Logging, especially in Borneo and the Philippines, is a problem in the region. Forest communities, like the Malaysian Penan, are being destroyed. Some tree species are near extinction.

CLIMATE
Countries situated around the equator are hot and humid all year. Variations in climate are related to latitude.

zon Strait

Luzon

Baguio
Dagupan
es   Cabanatuan
      MANILA
      Lucena
ngas   Naga
doro Mindoro Legaspi
rait   Calbayog
Panay Cadiz   Samar
Iloilo   Tacloban
can   Bacolod
INES   Negros   Cebu
SEA   Butuan
      Zamboanga Cagayan de Oro
                Iligan   Mindanao
Jolo   Davao
Sulu Archipelago General
                  Santos

PHILIPPINE SEA

PACIFIC OCEAN

Talaud Is.

CELEBES SEA
ssar Strait   Manado

Gulf of
Tomini   Halmahera   Supiori
Palu   Biak   Jayapura
Celebes   Sula Is.   Moluccas

          MOLUCCA SEA

          SERAM SEA   IRIAN JAYA
Kendari   Bucu   Seram   MAOKE MTS.
          Ambon   Kai Is.
Ujung Pandang BANDA SEA   ARAFURA SEA
N   E   S   I   A   Aru Is.
FLORES SEA   Dolak
mbawa   Tanimbar Is.
      Flores
ser Sunda Islands   Timor   TIMOR SEA
nba   Boti   Kupang

PAPUA NEW GUINEA

INDONESIA

F   G   H

347

Southeast Asia facts

MYANMAR

• This country is also called Burma.
• Myanmar exports the most teak in the world.

ESSENTIAL FACTS

⊙ Rangoon

◑ 261,200 sq miles (676,550 sq km)

♦ 44.6 million

♗ Kyat

♡ Myanmar (Burmese)

LAOS

• In 1994, the Mekong River's "Friendship Bridge" became the first Thai–Laos road link.

LAOS FACTS

⊙ Vientiane

◑ 91,428 sq miles (236,800 sq km)

♦ 4.6 million

♗ Kip

♡ Lao, Miao, Yao

SINGAPORE

• The nation is the world leader in new biotechnologies.
• Chewing gum is banned by law in Singapore.

SINGAPORE FACTS

⊙ Singapore City

◑ 239 sq miles (620 sq km)

♦ 2.8 million

♗ Singapore dollar

♡ Malay, Chinese, Tamil, English

THAILAND

• Criticism of the Thai king, who is head of state, is not allowed.
• Thailand, meaning "land of the free," is the only Southeast Asian nation never to be colonized.

THAILAND FACTS

⊙ Bangkok

◑ 198,116 sq miles (13,120 sq km)

♦ 56.9 million

♗ Baht

♡ Thai

▲ Multiparty democracy

♦ 69 years

MOBILE SHOP
Floating markets are a common sight on the waterways of Southeast Asia.

VIETNAM

• A new species of mammal, the Vu Quang Ox, was recently discovered in the forests of northern Vietnam.
• The Vietnam war cost two million lives.

VIETNAM FACTS

⊙ Hanoi

◑ 127,243 sq miles (329,560 sq km)

♦ 70.9 million

♗ New dong

♡ Vietnamese

KOMODO DRAGON
The "dragon" of Komodo
in Indonesia is the
world's largest lizard.

INDONESIA

• The world's biggest
island chain, Indonesia
is made up of 13,677
islands spread over
3,000 miles (4,830 km)
and three time zones.
• Indonesia was formerly
known as the Dutch
East Indies.
• Forest survival is
threatened by logging.

INDONESIA FACTS

⊙ Jakarta
◔ 735,355 sq miles
  (1,904,570 sq km)
✦ 194.6 million
💰 Rupiah
♡ Bahasa Indonesia
▲ Multiparty republic
● 62 years

BRUNEI

⊙ Bandar Seri Begawan
✦ 300,000
♡ Malay

THE PHILIPPINES

• The Filipino nation
is the only Christian
country in Asia.

PHILIPPINES FACTS

⊙ Manila
◔ 115,831 sq miles
  (300,000 sq km)
✦ 66.5 million
💰 Philippine peso
♡ Filipino, English
▲ Multiparty republic
● 65 years

CAMBODIA

• Over one million
Cambodians died
between 1975 and 1979
under Pol Pot's Marxist
Khmer Rouge regime.
• Cambodians are
descended from the
Khmers, who arrived
in Southeast Asia
around 2,000 B.C.
• Aid provides 70% of
government revenue.

CAMBODIA FACTS

⊙ Phnom Penh
◔ 69,000 sq miles
  (181,040 sq km)
✦ 9 million
💰 Riel
♡ Khmer

MALAYSIA

• The nation is the
world's leading producer
of natural rubber.

ESSENTIAL FACTS

⊙ Kuala Lumpur
◔ 127,317 sq miles
  (329,750 sq km)
✦ 19.2 million
💰 Ringgit
♡ Malay

MALAYSIAN
RUBBER
Workers extract
latex by cutting
rubber trees and
collecting the
sap that oozes
from the cut.

AUSTRALASIA AND OCEANIA

NAURU

PAPUA NEW GUINEA

SOLOMON ISLANDS

Coral Sea Islands (to Australia)

VANUATU

New Caledonia (to France)

AUSTRALIA

TASMAN SEA

SOUTHERN OCEAN

NEW ZEALA

Auckland Islands (to N.Z.)

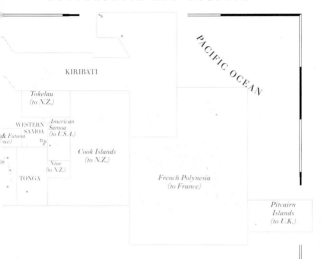

KIRIBATI

Tokelau
(to N.Z.)

WESTERN
SAMOA

*American
Samoa
(to U.S.A.)*

& Futuna
nce)

*Cook Islands
(to N.Z.)*

*Niue
(to N.Z.)*

TONGA

*French Polynesia
(to France)*

PACIFIC OCEAN

*Pitcairn
Islands
(to U.K.)*

*Chatham Island
(to N.Z.)*

AUSTRALASIA AND OCEANIA

Millions of years ago, the continent of
Australia and the islands of New Guinea
and New Zealand split away from the
other southern continents. These island
countries have many unique plants and
animals, such as Australia's marsupials,
or pouched mammals. The thousands of
islands scattered in the Pacific are either
volcanic islands or coral atolls.

PACIFIC OCEAN

THE LARGEST AND deepest
ocean, the Pacific covers a
greater area of the Earth's surface
than all the land areas together.
Its deepest point – 36,197ft
(11,033 m) – is deep enough
to cover Mount Everest.
Melanesia, Micronesia,
and Polynesia are the
main inner Pacific
island groups.

MICRONESIA

NAURU

NATURAL FEATURES
Some Pacific islands are
coral atolls – ring-shaped islands
or chains of islands surrounding
a lagoon. They are formed when
coral builds up on a sunken bank or
on a volcano crater in the open sea.

PALAU

SOLOMON ISLANDS

ENVIRONMENT
Nuclear testing by
the U.S.A. and France has
dangerously polluted areas in
the South Pacific. Countries
such as Japan, Australia, and
New Zealand want the region
made into a nuclear-free zone.

VANUATU

FIJI

N

| 0 | 1500 | 3000km |
| 0 | 750 | 1500miles |

Map labels: SEA OF OKHOTSK, ASIA, Kuril Is., Kōbe, Yokohama, Shanghai, NORTHERN MARIANAS IS., Hong Kong, Manila, GUAM, MARS ISI, MICRO, SOUTH EAST ASIA, FEDERATED STATES OF MICRO, NAURU, ARAFURA SEA, CORAL SEA, AUSTRALIA, Great Barrier Reef, Sydney, TAS

E   F   G   H

MARSHALL
ISLANDS

KIRIBATI

TONGA

OCEAN

Yukon

Bering
Strait

NORTH AMERICA

ING SEA

Aleutian Is.

Aleutian Trench

Gulf of
Alaska

Vancouver

Seattle

Mendocino
Fracture Zone

IFIC

San
Francisco

Portland

EAN

Murray Fracture Zone

Long Beach

DW'II IS.

Seamounts

HONOLULU

Hawaii

Clarion Fracture Zone

CENTRAL
AMERICA

KIRIBATI

Clipperton Fracture Zone

Albatross
Plateau

Panama
City

TOKELAU

AMERICAN
SAMOA

COOK
ISLAND

Marquesas Is.

Galapagos Is.
(to Ecuador)

SOUTH AMERICA

NIUE

Tuamotu
Archipelago

Tahiti

East Pacific Rise

Callao

Peru–Chile Trench

TONGA

*FRENCH
POLYNESIA*

PITCAIRN IS.

EALAND

Southwest
Pacific Basin

Valparaiso

Pacific

Antarctic Ridge

WESTERN
SAMOA

ington

South East Pacific Basin

C. Horn

'RN   OCEAN

TUVALU

ANTARCTICA

AUSTRALIA AND PAPUA NEW GUINEA

THE SMALLEST, flattest, and driest continent, Australia has a landscape that varies from tropical rainforest to arid desert. Lying to the north, Papua New Guinea (PNG) is so mountainous that its tribes are isolated from each other and from the outside world.

TIMOR SEA

INDIAN OCEAN

Joseph Bonaparte Gulf

DARW
ARNI
LA

KIMBERLEY PLATEAU
KING LEOPOLD RANGES
Fitzroy

NO
TE

GREAT SANDY DESERT

North West C.
HAMERSLEY RANGE
L. Macleod

L. Mackay
L. Disappointment
Alice Spr

MACDON
RANGE

Dirk Hartog I.

GIBSON DESERT

AUSTRALIA
L. Carnegie

GREAT VICTORIA DESERT

AU

L. Barlee
L. Moore

NULLARBOR PLAIN

PERTH

C. Naturaliste
C. Leeuwin

Great Australian

C. Pasley

AUSTRALIA

CLIMATE
Most people live in temperate zones that occur within 250 miles (400 km) of the coast in the east and southeast, and around Perth in the west. The interior, west, and south are arid; the north is tropical. PNG is tropical, yet snow falls on its highest mountains.

INDUSTRY
Coal, gold, uranium, cattle, tourism, wool, wine- and beer-making. Australia is a leading exporter of coal, iron ore, gold, bauxite, and copper, an has the largest known diamond deposi PNG has the largest copper mine in th world and one of the largest gold mine

FURA SEA

Torres Strait

t. Arnhem

Gulf of *Carpentaria*

CAPE YORK PENINSULA

PACIFIC OCEAN

Great Barrier Reef

Bismarck Sea

BISMARCK SEA

Bismarck Archipelago

New Ireland

New Guinea

PAPUA NEW GUINEA

New Britain

SOLOMON SEA

INDONESIA

PORT MORESBY

CORAL SEA

Mitchell

Townsville

GREAT DIVIDING RANGE

Flinders

L A K E

E Y R E

QUEENSLAND

Diamantina

SON RT

Cooper Creek

 Brisbane

Gold Coast

L I A

DERS GES

Darling

NEW SOUTH WALES

Murray

Murrumbidgee

Newcastle

SYDNEY

Wollongong

ADELAIDE

CANBERRA

AUSTRALIAN CAPITAL TERRITORY

angaroo I.

VICTORIA

Geelong

MELBOURNE

Bass Strait

Flinders I.

C. Grim

TASMAN SEA

N

TASMANIA

HOBART

South East C.

| 300 | 600km |

| 150 | 300miles |

PAPUA NEW GUINEA

PEOPLE
The first people in Australia were Aboriginals, a nomadic people who reached the continent from Southeast Asia about 50,000 years ago.

FLORA AND FAUNA
Due to its isolation, Australia has many unique animals such as koalas and kangaroos. The platypus and the echidna, which is also found in New Guinea, are the only egg-laying mammals.

NATURAL FEATURES
The Great Barrier Reef, a series of coral reefs and islands, stretches over 1,240 miles (2,000 km) just off the Queensland coast. It is the world's largest marine park and is composed entirely of living coral polyps.

New Zealand

ONE OF THE LAST
places on
Earth to be
inhabited
by people, New Zealand
lies about halfway between
the equator and the South
Pole. It is made up of the main
North and South Islands,
separated by the Cook Strait, and
numerous smaller islands. The first
settlers were Maoris, who came
from the Polynesian islands
about 1,200 years ago.

NATURAL FEATURES
New Zealand lies on the "Ring of
Fire," a band of volcanic activity that almost
encircles the Pacific Ocean. New Zealand has
about 400 earthquakes each year, although
only about 100 are strong enough to be felt.

PEOPLE
In recent years, Maoris
have protested the lack of
observance of the Treaty
of Waitangi, which
protected their rights.
About 10 percent of
the total population
are Maori.

FLORA AND FAUNA
Many of New Zealand's animals
have been introduced – two species of bat
are the only native land mammals. New

*Great
Exhibition
Bay*

*Great
Barrier I.*

*North
Island*

*Kaipara
Harbour*

Auckland

oHamilton

L. Taupo

Bay of Plenty

TASMAN SEA

*North
Island*

Hawke

356

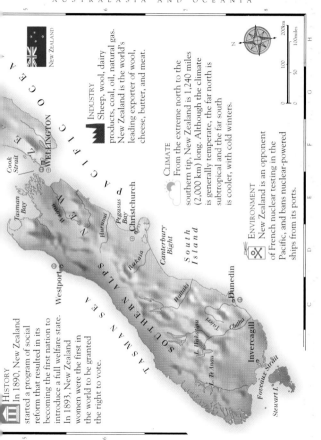

NEW ZEALAND

INDUSTRY
Sheep, wool, dairy products, coal, oil, natural gas. New Zealand is the world's leading exporter of wool, cheese, butter, and meat.

CLIMATE
From the extreme north to the southern tip, New Zealand is 1,240 miles (2,000 km) long. Although the climate is generally temperate, the far north is subtropical and the far south is cooler, with cold winters.

ENVIRONMENT
New Zealand is an opponent of French nuclear testing in the Pacific, and bans nuclear-powered ships from its ports.

HISTORY
In 1890, New Zealand started a program of social reform that resulted in its becoming the first nation to introduce a full welfare state. In 1893, New Zealand women were the first in the world to be granted the right to vote.

PACIFIC OCEAN

WELLINGTON

Cook Strait

Tasman Bay

N O R T H   I S L A N D

Westport

Hurunui

Pegasus Bay

Christchurch

Rakaia

Canterbury Bight

South Island

SOUTHERN ALPS

TASMAN SEA

Waitaki

Waiau

Taieri

Clutha

L. Hawea

L. Te Anau

Invercargill

Dunedin

Foveaux Strait

Stewart I.

Australasia and Oceania facts

AUSTRALIA

- The suburban area of the city of Sydney is the largest in the world; it is twice as large as Beijing and six times the size of Rome.
- Aboriginal land and civil rights claims are an increasingly important item on the political agenda.

ESSENTIAL FACTS

- ⊙ Canberra
- ◎ 2,967,893 sq miles (7,686,850 sq km)
- ♦ 18.5 million
- ▦ Australian dollar
- ♡ English
- ▲ Multiparty democracy
- ♦ 77 years

SURF'S UP
Surfing and water sports are popular Australian leisure activities.

NEW ZEALAND

- The landscape of New Zealand is the most varied in the world relative to its size, offering mountains, fjords, lakes, glaciers, rain forests, beaches, mud pools, and geysers.
- Many of New Zealand's top jobs in business and politics are held by women.

ESSENTIAL FACTS

- ⊙ Wellington
- ◎ 103,730 sq miles (268,680 sq km)
- ♦ 3.5 million
- ▦ New Zealand dollar
- ♡ English
- ▲ Multiparty democracy
- ♦ 75 years

PAPUA NEW GUINEA

- The feathers of certain unique bird species in Papua New Guinea produce a poison that causes painful blisters on contact with human skin.

ESSENTIAL FACTS

- ⊙ Port Moresby
- ◎ 178,700 sq miles (462,840 sq km)
- ♦ 4.1 million
- ▦ Kina
- ♡ English

KIWI BIRD
The flightless kiwi is the most famous of New Zealand's creatures.

VANUATU
⊙ Port-Vila
♦ 155,000
♡ Bislama, English, French

FIJI
⊙ Suva
♦ 700,000
♡ English, Fijian

PALAU
⊙ Koror
♦ 16,000
♡ Palauan, English

KIRIBATI
⊙ Bairiki
♦ 66,000
♡ English, Kiribati

TONGA
⊙ Nuku'alofa
♦ 101,000
♡ Tongan, English

TUVALU
⊙ Fingafale
♦ 9,000
♡ Tuvaluan, Kiribati

WESTERN SAMOA
⊙ Apia
♦ 162,000
♡ Samoan, English

NAURU
⊙ No official capital
♦ 10,000
♡ Nauruan, English

MARSHALL ISLANDS
⊙ Majuro
♦ 48,000
♡ English, Marshallese

SOLOMON ISLANDS
⊙ Honiara
♦ 400,000
♡ English

Thatched roof made of palm fronds

Simple house

Wooden outrigger boat with main hull and twin floats

Home-grown food

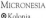

MICRONESIA
⊙ Kolonia
♦ 101,000
♡ English

ISLAND LIFE
On the more remote islands of the Pacific, people live much as their ancestors did, fishing, keeping animals, and growing fruit and vegetables.

ATLANTIC OCEAN

BENEATH THE WATERS OF the Atlantic Ocean lies the Mid-Atlantic Ridge, one of the world's longest mountain chains. Some of its peaks are so high they form islands, such as the Azores. Apart from a wide rift-valley in the center of the ridge, the ocean consists of vast featureless plains and is 5 miles (8 km) at its deepest point.

ICELAND

CAPE VERDE

ARCTIC OCEAN

GREENLAND SEA

Murmansk

Bergen

BALTIC SEA

Rotterdam

EUROPE

BLACK SEA

NORTH SEA

Aberdeen

MEDITERRANEAN SEA

GIBRALTAR

ICELAND
REYKJAVIK

Faeroe Islands
(to Denmark)

Denmark Strait

Azores
(to Portugal)

Madeira
(to Portugal)

GREENLAND

C. Farewell

Mid-Atlantic Ridge

NORTH AMERICA

Baffin Bay

Davis Strait

LABRADOR SEA

Newfoundland

Hudson Bay

St. Lawrence

New York
City

Bermuda

Mississippi

360

ENVIRONMENT
The North Atlantic was once the world's richest fishing ground, but overfishing has reduced the numbers of cod and herring to low levels.

NATURAL FEATURES
Iceland lies on the rift where the North American and European continental plates are pulling apart, and has about 200 volcanoes. Domestic heating, from geothermal sources, is almost free.

INDIAN OCEAN

THE SMALLEST OF the world's oceans, the Indian Ocean has some 5,000 islands scattered across its area. Beneath its surface, three great mountain ranges converge toward the ocean's center – an area of strong seismic and volcanic activity. The ocean's greatest depth, 24,400 ft (7,440 m), is in the Java Trench.

FLORA AND FAUNA

Owing to Madagascar's position off the African coast, many of its animals, such as tenrecs, lemurs, and fossas, are unique.

ENVIRONMENT

The Indian Ocean is at risk of pollution from tankers carrying oil from the Persian Gulf, which is already badly polluted.

CLIMATE

The monsoon winds blow over the Indian Ocean – from the southwest or from the northeast according to the season. The southwesterly monsoon brings heavy rains to southern Asia.

COMOROS

MALDIVES

SEYCHELLES

PEOPLE
Many Madagascans are descended from Indonesians who crossed the Indian Ocean. Their language, Malagasy, is Malay-Indonesian in origin.

MAURITIUS

MADAGASCAR

THE ANTARCTIC

CONTAINING 80 PERCENT of the world's freshwater, the continent of Antarctica lies buried under ice more than 1.2 miles (2 km) thick. The surrounding seas are partly frozen, and icebergs barricade over 9 percent of the coastline.

ATLANTIC OCEAN
INDIAN OCEAN
South Orkney Is. (to U.K.)
SCOTIA SEA
Elephant I. (to U.K.)
South Shetland Is. (to U.K.)
ANTARCTIC PENINSULA
QUEEN MAUD LAND
ENDERBY LAND
Lützow-Holm Bay
Drake Passage
Anvers I. (to U.S.A.)
WEDDELL SEA
PALMER LAND
C. Darr
Macker Bay
SOUTH POLAR PLATEAU
BELLINGSHAUSEN SEA
TRANSANTARCTIC MTS.
Peter the First I. (to Norway)
ELLSWORTH MTS.
South Pole
DA S
AMUNDSEN SEA
MARIE BYRD LAND
Vince Bay
PACIFIC OCEAN
C. Colbeck
ROSS SEA
C. Adare
WILKES LAND
Porpoise Ba
Balleny Is.

FLORA AND FAUNA
Not many plants and animals can survive on land, although the surrounding seas teem with life. Despite the cold, few birds and sea creatures migrate to warmer waters.

CLIMATE
Powerful winds form a narrow storm belt that creates severe blizzards. Summer temperatures barely reach over freezing, and in winter, the temperature can plummet to –112°F (–80°C).

ENVIRONMENT
Scientists estimate that the ozone hole emerged over Antarctica in 1980. Each spring, increased sunshine activates CFC leading to rapid ozone depletion.

E   F   G   H

THE ARCTIC

A FROZEN OCEAN surrounded by land, the Arctic is covered by ice up to 98 ft (30 m) thick. Most of the surrounding tundra, or vast treeless plains, are permanently frozen.

RUSSIAN FEDERATION

ALASKA
U.S.A.

CHUKCHI SEA

Pevek

Wrangel I.
(to Russian Fed.)

EAST SIBERIAN SEA

Prudhoe Bay

BEAUFORT SEA

Limit of Permanent Pack Ice

New Siberian Is.
(to Russian Fed.)

LAPTEV SEA

Banks I.
(to Canada)

Tiksi

Melville I.
(to Canada)

ARCTIC
OCEAN

Queen Elizabeth
Islands

Resolute

. North Pole

Axel Heiberg I.
(to Canada)

Severnaya Zemlya
(to Russian Fed.)

Devon I.
(to Canada)

Ellesmere I.
(to Canada)

TAIMYR PENINSULA

Baffin I.
(to Canada)

Thule

Franz Josef Land
(to Russian Fed.)

KARA SEA

Baffin Bay

KNUD RASMUSSEN
LAND

BARENTS SEA

SVALBARD
(to Norway)

Davis Strait

GREENLAND
(to Denmark)

LONGYEARBYEN

Godhavn

Spitsbergen

GODTHÅB
(NUUK)

GREENLAND SEA

Scoresbysund

Narsarsuaq

Jan Mayen
(to Norway)

PEOPLE
Inuits have lived
on the Arctic Circle
since 2500 B.C. Vikings
arrived in A.D. 986.

ATLANTIC
OCEAN

C. Farvel

Denmark Strait

ICELAND

Limit of Permanent Pack Ice

CANADA

E   G   H

WORLD TIME ZONES

IMAGINARY LINES are drawn around the globe, either parallel to the equator (latitude) or from pole to pole (longitude, or meridians). The Earth is divided into 2 time zones, one for each hour of the day. Greenwich is on 0° meridian and time advances by one hour for every 15° of longitude east of Greenwich.

TIME ZONES
The numbers on the map indicate the number of hours which must be subtracted or added to reach GMT. When it is noon at Greenwich, for example, it is 7 a.m. in New York City. Time zones are adjusted to regional administrative boundaries.

KEY TO MAP

🔴 MINUS HOURS

🔵 PLUS HOURS

⚪ GREENWICH MEAN TIME

🔵 DATE LINE

▥ TIME ZONES

GMT
Greenwich Mean
Time (GMT) is the
time in Greenwich,
England. Clocks are
set depending on
whether they are east
or west of Greenwich.

INTERNATIONAL
DATE LINE
The International
Date Line is an
imaginary line that
runs along the 180°
meridian but deviates
around countries.

PEOPLE AND SOCIETY

MYTHS AND LEGENDS

ALMOST EVERY culture has stories, or myths, to explain the world around them. Legends are tales which have some basis in real events.

MYTHICAL BEASTS

Many myths are about fantastic beasts, such as the unicorn (a single-horned horse) and the phoenix (a bird that rises from its own ashes). The dragon is a winged serpent that breathes fire. It is an important symbol in cultures as far apart as Wales and China.

DRAGON'S BREATH

KING ARTHUR

One of Britain's most famous legendary figures is the hero King Arthur, wh is thought to be based on a real 5th-century Celtic chieftain. One of the many stories about King Arthur tells how he was given the magic sword Excalibur by the Lady of the Lake, as shown in the above picture.

SACRED SITES

• Mt. Shasta in California is sacred to Native Americans.

• Uluru (Ayers Rock) in Australia is sacred to the Aboriginals.

• The Tor (mound) at Glastonbury, England, is said to be the resting place of the Holy Grail, the cup Christ drank from at the Last Supper.

This mask, made of turquoise mosaic, represents Quetzalcoatl, the chief god of the Aztecs.

AZTEC MYTHS

The mythical world of the Aztec people of Central Mexico was dominated by the figure of Quetzalcoatl. He was the chief god of the Aztecs, and took the form of a feathered serpent. According to myth, Quetzalcoatl created humans and gave them knowledge. Afterward, he sailed away on a raft of serpents.

Greek myths

Many stories are told about ancient Greece. Legendary tales, such as those surrounding the Trojan War, have a basis in historical fact, while myths about figures like Perseus and Medusa are more fantastic.

Theseus
Minotaur

PERSEUS AND MEDUSA

One Greek myth tells the story of Perseus, who beheaded a gorgon called Medusa. The gorgon's head had the power to turn people to stone.

Perseus

Gorgons have a head of snakes instead of hair

THESEUS AND THE MINOTAUR

The Minotaur was a mythical creature, half-man and half-bull, that lived in a labyrinth (maze) on the island of Crete. It was eventually slain by a Theban prince called Theseus.

Greek soldiers hid inside the huge wooden horse

MASK OF KING AGAMEMNON

TROJAN WARS

In *The Iliad*, which Homer wrote around 1200 B.C., the legend tells how Agamemnon, King of Mycenae, Greece, led an army against the Trojans to rescue his brother's captured wife, Helen.

TROJAN HORSE

According to legend, when the Greeks were fighting the Trojans, they beat them by a trick. They built a wooden horse, then hid in it, outside the gates of Troy. The Trojans dragged the wooden horse into the city to see what it was. At night, the Greek soldiers crept out and opened the city gates to let their army in.

RELIGIONS

MOST PEOPLE HAVE some kind of belief or faith that helps to explain life and death. Many worship either one or several gods. The four major world religions are Christianity, Islam, Hinduism, and Buddhism.

CHRISTIANITY

Christians believe that Jesus Christ is the Son of God, and when Jesus was crucified (nailed to a cross), he rose from the dead to join God in Heaven. Christianity has more followers than any other religion.

The cross is the symbol of Christianity.

ORIGIN
Christianity began in about A.D. 30 in Jerusalem, in present-day Israel.

THE BIBLE

This Christian holy book is made up of two parts called the Old and New Testaments. In the Old Testament are the sacred writings of the Jews. The New Testament tells the story of Christ's life and the origin of Christianity.

The first Bible was printed in 1455, by Johannes Gutenberg.

TEN COMMANDMENTS

Christians try to obey ten rules, which are adapted from the Jewish scriptures.

1 Worship one God.
2 Make no image of God.
3 Respect God's name.
4 Keep Sunday holy.
5 Honor your parents.
6 Do not kill.
7 Do not commit adultery.
8 Do not steal.
9 Do not tell lies.
10 Do not be envious.

JESUS CHRIST

Jesus lived in the Holy Land (Israel) about 2,000 years ago. From the age of 30, he began to preach and heal the sick. He was tried and put to death for openly challenging Hebrew beliefs.

ISLAM

A star and a crescent moon symbolize Islam.

The followers of Islam are Muslims, who believe in Allah. Islam means "submission," and Muslims believe they must obey Allah and live by the five pillars (rules) set out in their holy book, the *Koran*.

ORIGIN
Islam began in about A.D. 600 in Mecca, in present-day Saudi Arabia. It is now practiced all over the world.

THE KORAN

In Islam's holy book, Allah shows the prophet Muhammad how people should live. Muslims treat this book with great respect, and must wash before touching it.

KORAN (Qur'an)

MUHAMMAD

Born in Mecca, Muhammad (c. 570–632) was the last and the greatest of the 26 Islamic prophets.

Muhammad is Allah's messenger

HINDUISM

The symbol of Hinduism is the sound "Om."

Hindus worship many gods, and believe in *dharma*, the correct way to live. Like Buddhists, Hindus believe we have all lived before, as animals as well as people. By following the *dharma*, we may achieve a perfect state of *Moksha* and need never be reborn again.

ORIGIN
Hinduism began in India, around 1750 B.C. It has spread through much of Asia.

VEDAS

About 1400 B.C., Hindu beliefs were written as songs and chants in the *Vedas*.

The Rig Veda is the most important book of the Vedas.

FOUNDERS

Hinduism has no single founder. The Aryans, who invaded India nearly 4,000 years ago, brought early Hindu gods, such as Shiva.

SHIVA

373

BUDDHISM

The symbol of Buddhism is an eight-spoked wheel.

The Buddhist faith is based on the teachings of Buddha, who believed that we must rid ourselves of desire in order to free ourselves from suffering. Buddhists believe that life is a sequence of birth, death, and rebirth, and that by following the Eightfold path of Buddhism, we can reach a state of peace called *Nirvana*.

Extracts from the Pali Canon.

THE PALI
The collected teachings of Buddha are called the *Pali Canon*. The best-known is the *Dhammapada*.

ORIGINS
Buddhism began in India in around 500 B.C. It is now the religion of around 300 million people.

BUDDHA
Prince Siddhartha Gautama (Buddha) lived about 563–483 B.C. He gave up his riches to preach and meditate.

Buddha means "enlightened one."

SIKHISM

The Khanda is the symbol of Sikhism.

This faith began in northern India. It is based on the worship of one God, the eternal Guru, and on the cycle of rebirth.

GURU GRANTH SAHIB

This book is treated with great respect

GURU GRANTH
This sacred book contains hymns and poems written by the Gurus.

ORIGINS
Sikhism began in north India and Pakistan around 1500. It has spread to North America and Britain.

Sikh men wear a turban.

THE FIVE K'S
Sikhs must wear these five items: *Kesh* (uncut hair, under a turban, if a man); *Kara* (a steel bracelet); *Kangha* (a hair comb); *Kirpan* (a sword); and *Kaccha* (short pants as an undergarment).

JUDAISM

Followers of Judaism are called Jews. They believe in one God whose law is written in the *Tanach*. Judaism began about 4,000 years ago in Canaan. Today this area is mainly Israel.

The Jewish symbol is the Star of David.

ORIGINS

Judaism originated around 2000 B.C. in Canaan, "the Promised Land." Today, Judaism has spread to most parts of the world.

Tallit, or prayer shawl

Menorah, or branched candlestick

Yarmulke, or skull cap

The Tanach

TANACH

The Jewish Bible, or *Tanach*, tells the history of the Jewish people. The *Torah* is the most important part, since it contains the laws that God revealed to Moses.

SHINTOISM

In Japan, Shintoists worship gods of nature, and there are Shinto shrines in parks, gardens, and on mountains. Shintoists worship alone, and their symbol is the outline of a temple gate.

According to Shinto faith, Mount Fuji is a Shinto god. People come to pray at a shrine on its summit.

CONFUCIANISM

This faith is based on the teachings of K'ung-Fu tzu (551–479 B.C.), or Confucius, who was known for his wise sayings. In the *Analects*, Confucius taught the wisdom of living in harmony with nature. He said "Never do to others what would you would not like them to do to you."

K'UNG-FU-TZU

TAOISM

Lao-Tze founded the faith of Taoism in China 2,400 years ago. Taoists believe in many gods. Their symbol of Yin Yang represents the balance and harmony of opposites.

YIN YANG

The name Lao-Tze means "Old Master."

LAO-TZE

GODS AND GODDESSES

MANY OF THE ANCIENT civilizations, such as those in Greece, Rome, and Egypt, worshipped several gods and goddesses.

Ancient Egypt

The gods and goddesses of ancient Egypt often had the body of a human and the head of an animal, which represented that creature's power. The chief of the gods was the Sun god Re, who had different names at different times of the day.

BASTET, THE CAT GODDESS

HORUS' EYE
The symbol of the "wadjet" eye represents the vengeful eye of Horus, torn out in the struggle for Egypt.

"WADJET" EYE

BASTET
The goddess Bastet was the daughter of Re, the Sun god. She represented the power of the sun to ripen crops, and she took the form of a cat.

OSIRIS
The god of the under-world and judge of the dead was called Osiris. People believed he ruled over a world below ground that looked like Egypt. Osiris took the form of a mummified man.

OSIRIS

ANUBIS
The son of Osiris was the god Anubis, who had the head of a jackal. Anubis was said to guide the souls of the dead to Osiris for their judgment.

ANUBIS

Ancient Greece

The Greeks believed that all the gods were the descendants of Gaia (the earth) and Uranos (the sky), and that they behaved in the same way as humans.

Aphrodite

ZEUS
The King of the gods was Zeus, who is represented as a strong, middle-aged man. He was noble, but easily angered.

HEPHAESTUS
The God of fire and the husband of Aphrodite, Hephaestus was lame.

Eros

MIRROR CASE

APHRODITE
The Greek goddess of love was called Aphrodite.

Pan

APOLLO
The young god of the sun and of medicine was Apollo.

Ancient Rome

The Romans adopted many Greek gods and gave them new names. Aphrodite became Venus, Zeus became Jupiter, and Ares, the god of war, became Mars.

TEMPLES
Many emperors were made gods after their death. Temples such as this were built in their honor.

TEMPLE OF AUGUSTUS AND LIVIA

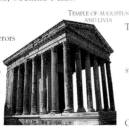

JUPITER
The king of the Roman gods, Jupiter was a sky-god whose symbols were the eagle and the thunderbolt. Jupiter was much like the Greek god Zeus.

MONEY AND TRADE

THE METAL COINS and paper banknotes that we use to buy things are called money, or currency. Money also comes in the form of credit cards, checks, and the computer records of a bank account.

Cowrie shells were used as money

EARLY MONEY
Before coins were invented, people used to exchange stones, shells, beads, and furs for food and other goods.

EARLY LYDIAN COIN

THE FIRST COINS

The earliest known coins were made in the kingdom of Lydia (now Turkey) more than 2,700 years ago. These coins were weighed lumps of electrum (a mix of silver and gold), which were stamped, or "minted," to guarantee their weight.

14TH-CENTURY CHINESE PAPER MONEY

THE FIRST PAPER MONEY

In 10th-century China, people began to leave their coins with merchants, in exchange for a handwritten paper receipt. In the 11th century, the Chinese government fixed the value of these receipts. This became the first paper money.

MAKING BANKNOTES

Banknotes have to be printed in a very elaborate and secret way to reduce the chances of forgery. The four stages of making a banknote are designing, paper-making, ink-mixing, and printing. The design is engraved on a steel plate by hand. This is called "intaglio" engraving.

Burnisher for smoothing

Sharp "burins" for engraving the design

The design for the banknote is hand engraved back-to-front on to a steel plate

PRINTING PLATE

PROOF FOR
BACKGROUND

PROOF FOR MAIN DESIGN

This design uses eight inks, printed in reds, yellows, blues, and buffs.

Every note is individually numbered

NUMBERING MACHINE

The finished specimen banknote is shown to customers all over the world.

FINISHED BANKNOTE

THE STOCK MARKET

People often raise money to start a business by selling "shares" in it. If the business make a profit, the shareholders receive a dividend (payment). The stock market is where shares, or stocks, are bought and sold by "stockbrokers."

IMPORTS AND EXPORTS

BALANCE OF TRADE

Countries measure their success at trading by their "balance of payments," which is the difference between the amount they sell abroad (exports) and the amount they buy (imports).

TOKYO STOCK EXCHANGE, JAPAN

KEY STOCK EXCHANGES		
Country	City	Index
Japan	Tokyo	Nikkei Average
United States	New York	Dow-Jones
United Kingdom	London	FTSE-100 *
Germany	Frankfurt	DAX **

* Financial Times Stock Exchange 100
** Deutsche Aktien Index

GOVERNMENT AND LAW

ALL COUNTRIES are run by a government. Some are harsh dictatorships, and others are liberal democracies. Every government implements policies that affect the everyday lives of the nation's people. The business of government is called politics.

DEMOCRACY

This system, in which a country is ruled by the people, or their elected representatives, began in Athens, Greece, 2,500 years ago. Many other countries are now governed in this way.

Pericles was leade of democratic Athens at the height of its power

POLITICAL SYSTEMS

Most countries are "capitalist," and the land and businesses are owned by individuals or small groups. In "communist" countries, all businesses are state-run. "Socialists" believe that governments should grant everyone equal rights, a fair share of money, education, health, and housing.

COMMUNIST MAGAZINE

Abrahan Lincoln wa US presider 1861–65

REPUBLIC

Most countries are republics, which have no king or queen The "head of state" is a president who is elected by the people. The government is also elected by the people. A country with a king or queen is called a monarchy. Kings were once thought to rule by God's will. Their powe is now usually limited by a set of rules called a constitution.

PARLIAMENT

In many countries, government policy is debated and the laws are agreed upon in an assembly called parliament. People elect members of parliament to act as their representatives.

HOUSE OF COMMONS, UK

BRANCHES OF GOVERNMENT

THE CAPITOL, HOME OF THE US CONGRESS, WASHINGTON, D.C.

LEGISLATURE
The legislature is an elected assembly, or "house," that amends and makes laws. In the US, it is called Congress.

EXECUTIVE
The executive puts laws into effect and administers the country. It is headed by a president or a prime minister who appoints heads of different departments.

JUDICIARY
The judiciary makes sure that laws are applied fairly. In the US, the highest legal body is the Supreme Court.

Law

Every country has rules, or laws, to help people live together and to keep them in order. Laws are decided by governments or religious leaders and they are enforced by the police and the courts.

CRIMINAL LAW
Criminal law covers crimes such as murder and theft.

CIVIL LAW
This kind of law deals with disputes, rather than crimes. Civil law also deals with day-to-day events such as buying a house and making a will.

COURT ROOM

Judge helps jury on points of law, and passes sentence if verdict is "guilty"

Lawyer

A person on trial is "the accused"

In Britain, a jury must consist of 12 men and women over 18 years old

TRIAL
People accused of crimes are usually taken to court to be "tried." Typically, trials are "adversarial" – one set of lawyers (the prosecution) tries to prove that the accused is guilty, while another (the defense) tries to prove that he or she is innocent. A judge or a jury (a group of ordinary men and women) decides who is right.

BUILDINGS

HOUSES, CHURCHES, and offices
are all buildings. The design and
construction of buildings is called
architecture.

*In Oceania, "longhouses" are built
on stilts in case of flooding.*

TRADITIONAL HOMES

People around
the world build
their homes from
the materials they
have available.
From houses of
timber or stone,
to huts of mud or
woven reeds,
every country
has its own style.

*In South Africa, the dome-
shaped kraals have grass roofs.*

*Swiss chalets are built
from wooden timbers.*

*Some Asian nomads live
in canvas or felt "yurts."*

*Algerian houses are close
together to keep out the sun.*

*Japanese houses have
sliding doors.*

*North American houses
have wooden "clapboards."*

CLASSICAL ARCHITECTURE

There are three styles, or
orders, of classical Greek
architecture: Doric,
Ionic, and Corinthian.
The columns of Greek
temples often have a
decorative head, or
capital, on the top.
Across the columns is a
broad lintel called the
entablature. This
consists of an architrave,
a frieze, and a cornice.

Entablature   Frieze

Decorative capital

CLASSICAL GREEK TEMPLE

ORDERS

These three
orders were used
in three different
periods of history.

Doric was used
from 700 B.C.

Ionic was used
from 600 B.C.

Corinthian was
used from 500 B.C.

DOMES

Curved roofs, or domes, are a feature of many religious and state buildings around the world.

HEMISPHERICAL DOME

ONION DOME

POLYHEDRAL DOME

SAUCER DOME

VAULTS

Vaults are arched roofs or ceilings. The four main types of vaults are shown here.

BARREL VAULT

GROIN VAULT

RIB VAULT

FAN VAULT

ARCHES

An arch is an opening that is curved or pointed at the top. These features are often used in large buildings to span openings and carry weight.

POINTED ARCH

HORSESHOE ARCH

LOBED ARCH

SKYSCRAPERS

The invention of reinforced concrete, plate glass, and steel in the mid 1800s enabled architects to design and build extremely tall constructions, or "skyscrapers." The first skyscrapers were built in Chicago. Giant buildings are now found in most major cities. At 452 m (1,482 ft), the Petronas Tower, in Kuala Lumpur, Malaysia, is the world's tallest building.

NEW YORK SKYSCRAPERS

Many of the skyscrapers in New York City were erected in part by Iroquois and Mohawk Indians, who showed no fear of heights.

Cathedral-like spire
WOOLWORTH BUILDING 1913

Art Deco crown
GENERAL ELECTRIC BUILDING 1930s

WORLD TRADE CENTER 1971

6500 B.C.–301 B.C.	300 B.C.–A.D. 850

c. 6500 B.C. One the first known towns, Çatal Hüyük, is built in present-day Turkey, using rectangular mud bricks.

c. 2650–2150 B.C. Pyramids are built in the lower Nile valley, in Egypt. The Step Pyramid at Saqqara is designed by a High Priest called Imhotep, who is the first known architect.

Massive stones arranged in a huge circle

STONEHENGE, ENGLAND

c. 2200 B.C. Stonehenge is built in England, using massive stones. It was probably built as a religious monument.

c. 2112–2095 B.C. The Sumerians build stepped temples called ziggurats in Mesopotamia, using mud bricks.

c. 1700–1200 B.C. Beehive tombs, or tholos, are built by the Mycenaean civilization on the Greek mainland.

c. 1500 B.C. The Minoan Palace of Knossos is rebuilt on the Greek island of Crete.

800–200 B.C. Etruscans use arches in the construction of their buildings in what is now called Italy.

700–400 B.C. The ancient Greeks build temples of such perfect proportions that their style of building becomes known as "classical." This classical style of architecture is copied many times throughout history.

THE PARTHENON, ATHENS, GREECE

c. 300 B.C. Buddhists build stupas (mounds) in India and southeastern Asia to symbolize the dome of heaven.

c. 200 B.C.–A.D. 500 Roman architecture takes over the classical Greek style and the Etruscan arch. The Romans introduce concrete, which enables them to build huge vaults and arches.

A.D. 300–1540 Pre-Columbian civilizations in the Americas build stepped pyramids crowned with temples. One of these is the pyramid known as Giant Jaguar, at Tikal in Guatemala.

330–1453 The Byzantine style of architecture develops when the Roman Empire moves its capital to Byzantium, renaming it Constantinople (now Istanbul, Turkey) The largest dome of its time, the Hagia Sophia, is built there in A.D. 537.

607–670 The oldest surviving wooden building, the Horyuji Buddhist monastery, is built at Nara, in Japan.

618–782 The earliest Chinese timber building, the Nanchan Buddhist temple, is built on a holy mountain in Shaanxi province.

690–850 Early Islamic mosques and palaces are designed around courtyards.

900–1839	1840–TODAY

900–1150 The Romanesque style of architecture spreads across western Europe, featuring round-headed arches on top of cylindrical columns.

1100–1500 The Gothic style is used in Christian churches in northern Europe. It has pointed arches and flying buttresses, allowing very tall, light structures.

1113–1150 Angkor Wat, a vast stone city, is built by the Khmers in what is now Cambodia.

c. 1420 The Renaissance begins in Italy, reviving Roman and Greek building methods. Brunelleschi (1377–1446) and Alberti (1404–72) are key figures.

The city is crowned with spires shaped like lotus buds

ANGKOR WAT, CAMBODIA

c. 1650 The Baroque style is developed. Architects are commissioned by the Catholic Church to build very grand, ornate churches and palaces.

1750–1840 Neoclassical architects return to plain, elegant Roman and Greek styles of building.

1830–1930s During a Gothic revival, architects build churches, public buildings, and even train stations, trying to recapture the style of medieval cathedrals.

1840–90 The Industrial Revolution provides new materials, such as plate glass, steel, and reinforced concrete, which transform traditional building methods.

1890 After the elevator is invented, the first skyscrapers are built in Chicago.

1900–40s American architect Frank Lloyd Wright (1867–1959) promotes "organic" architecture, designing buildings that blend in with nature.

1919–33 Walter Gropius (1883–1969) leads a design team in Weimar, Germany (the Bauhaus school), creating designs based on modern industrial technology.

1920s The Swiss architect Le Corbusier (1887–1965) leads the new style of International Modernism in building design.

1970s A "hi-tech" style, with much steel, glass, and exposed pipes, is led by Richard Rogers (b. 1933) and Norman Foster (b. 1935).

Late 1970s Postmodern design develops. New designs blend elements from the architectural styles of different eras and cultures.

1980s–1990s Architects begin to take environmental concerns into account, such as recycling and saving energy. Some new buildings feature solar power.

EMPIRE STATE BUILDING, NEW YORK CITY

ARTISTS' MATERIALS

ARTISTS paint pictures and create sculptures. The main materials that an artist needs for painting are sketching materials (for an initial drawing or a finished work), paint and paintbrushes, and a surface to paint on. This surface may be paper for watercolor painting, canvas for oils, or wood for acrylics.

SCULPTURE
A sculptor can use almost any material for sculpting, but bronze, marble, and clay are the most popular for figurative work (based on the human body).

Early sculptures, like this figurine of a woman, were made of clay.

DETAIL FROM CARAVAGGIO'S *YOUTH WITH A RAM*

A top layer of varnish protects painting

The oil paint applied i layer

Size

Priming

Ground

Drawir laye

Imprimatura

MATERIAL FACTS

• The first paintbrushes were made using hog hairs tied to sticks.

• Thousands of years ago in Australia, artists mixed natural pigments in their mouths to paint cave walls.

LAYERS OF A PAINTING
Traditionally, an oil painting has several layers By analyzing each of these layers, experts are abl to date a picture accurately, and they can also c if it is a fake. This artwork, showing a section c Caravaggio's *Youth with a Ram*, shows the layer that were used in paintings of the 17th century

Conté crayon

Charcoal

Pencil

Graphite stick

Reed pen
and ink

DRAWING TOOLS

Most drawings are sketches (quick drawings) done as a preparation for a finished work. But a drawing can also be a finished picture in itself. Artists usually draw with dry materials such as pencils, crayons, or charcoal.

PAINTS

The three main kinds of paint are oils, which were first used in the 1400s; watercolors, popular with 18th-century landscape artists; and acrylics, popular in the 1960s.

Oil paints are a mixture of dry pigment and an oil such as linseed.

Watercolor paints are pigments bound with gum arabic. They are diluted with water.

Acrylic paints are either applied with a knife or diluted and used with a paintbrush.

PAINTBRUSHES

The two main kinds of paintbrushes are soft-hair brushes for watercolors, and bristle brushes for oil paintings and acrylics. The length and shape of the hairs on a brush may be round, flat, or "filbert."

ROUND   FLAT   FILBERT

MONA LISA

The most famous painting is Leonardo da Vinci's *Mona Lisa*, painted in 1503. It is a portrait of Lisa, the wife of a nobleman named Francesco del Gioconda. That is why the painting is sometimes called *La Gioconda*.

MONA LISA, THE LOUVRE, PARIS

Malachite makes a green pigment.

Lapis lazuli makes a blue pigment.

PIGMENTS

Paint is made from powdered colors called pigments. These were originally natural colors from plants and rocks, but today most are made using chemicals.

2700 B.C.–A.D. 599

c. 27,000 B.C. Small clay statues of pregnant women, known as "Venus figurines" appear across Europe.

c. 15,000 B.C. Early artists use fingers, brushes and hollow reeds to paint animals on the walls of the Lascaux caves, France.

c. 4000–1000 B.C. Egyptian art includes wall and scroll paintings, gold jewelry, and painted statues sculpted from limestone.

VENUS FIGURINE, FRANCE c. 27,000 BC

2000–1100 B.C. Minoans on the island of Crete, Greece, decorate their palace walls with colored murals.

1600–1027 B.C. The Shang dynasty in China discovers how to cast bronze and create bowls and urns for food and wine.

c. 500 B.C. The Nok culture in Nigeria, West Africa, produces lifelike terra-cotta figurines of humans.

c. 500–323 B.C. Greek sculptors produce statues of gods and athletes made of marble, bronze, and clay.

A.D. 100–400 Gandharan sculpture develops in the Indus valley, Pakistan. It is influenced by Greek art, and shows scenes from the life of Buddha.

100–1000 Mayan carvings are created in Central America, combining ornate figures with hieroglyphs (picture writing).

400–1110 Medieval monks in Europe create illuminated manuscripts.

600–1839

600–1185 Icons (religious portraits) are painted in Eastern Europe.

618–907 Chinese artists of the T'ang dynasty paint stunning landscapes.

1000–1200 The Romanesque style develops in the church sculptures and murals of Europe.

1000–1600 Huge stone figures are made on Easter Island, Polynesia.

1368–1644 The Ming dynasty in China is famous for its blue-glazed porcelain bowls and vases.

1400–1500 The Renaissance begins in Florence, Italy. Masaccio (1401–28) uses perspective in his paintings.

Late 1400s Islamic miniature painting flourishes in Persia.

1490–1520 The High Renaissance, exemplified in works by Leonardo da Vinci

THE ANNUNCIATION, LEONARDO DA VINCI

(1452–1519), Michelangelo (1475–1564), and Raphael (1483–1520).

1600s The golden age of Dutch painting, with pictures by Rembrandt (1606–69) and Vermeer (1632–75).

Late 1700s–mid 1800s The Romantic school, notably Turner (1775–1851) and Friedrich (1774–1840) focuses on human emotions and nature.

1840–1899	1900–TODAY

1840s Realism develops in France, with painters such as Courbet (1819–77) depicting people in a more lifelike way.

THE WINNOWERS, GUSTAVE COURBET 1855

1850s–70s In England, Pre-Raphaelites such as Millais (1829–96), Burne-Jones (1833–98), and Rossetti (1828–82) are influenced by artists before Raphael, but develop their own style of painting.

1860s–90s Impressionism begins in France as painters try to capture their impressions of fleeting moments, especially Monet (1840–1926) and Manet (1832–83).

1880–1905 Postimpressionist artists such as Cézanne (1839–1906), van Gogh (1853–90), and Gauguin (1848–1903) develop their own style, using strong colors and shapes.

1880s–1890s Expressionism develops in Europe as artists such as Kirchner (1880–1938) use intense color and free brush strokes to express their feelings.

1880s–90s Symbolist artists such as Moreau (1826–98) create images based on symbolic inner meanings.

1907–1920s Cubism develops in Paris with Picasso (1881–1973) and Braque (1882–1963) using bold geometric shapes.

1910–50 Artists of the Abstract movement, led by Kandinsky (1866–1944) begin to paint and sculpt ideas instead of realistic objects.

1916 The Dada movement, originally a protest against World War I, rejects traditional forms of art.

1920s Surrealist painters such as Dali (1904–89) and Ernst (1891–1976) explore their dreams and Freud's psychoanalytic ideas in their painting.

1940s Abstract Expressionism appears in New York, where artists such as Jackson Pollock (1912–56) experiment with the physical properties of paint.

1950s–60s Pop Art develops in the US and Britain as artists such as Warhol (1928–87) begin to use consumer goods and images from the media in their art.

1960s–90s Performance artists such as Gilbert (b. 1943) & George (b. 1942) combine music, theater, film, and video in their work.

1970s–90s Video artists such as Korean-born Nam Jun-Paik (b. 1932) feature video projection and computer technology in their exhibitions.

PLANTED, GILBERT AND GEORGE, 1992

MUSICAL INSTRUMENTS

THERE ARE THOUSANDS of musical instruments, each making its own distinctive sound. They are usually grouped into percussion, strings, woodwinds, brasses, and keyboards.

Strings

All stringed instruments consist of a series of stretched strings connected to a hollow box that amplifies (makes louder) the string's vibrations. The string is set in motion by being plucked, as with a harp; by the friction of a bow, as with a violin, or by being struck, as with a piano.

HARP
Harps date back at least 6,000 years. Strings stretched over a frame are finger-plucked to give a beautiful rippling sound. This harp is for traditional Irish music.

IRISH HARP

Strands of horse hair

VIOLIN AND BOW

Tuning pins are turned to change pitch of each string

Thinnest string has highest pitch

VIOLIN
The violin family was invented in around 1550 and now consists of the violin, viola, cello and bass. The strings are usually played with a bow.

All members of the violin family have an F-shaped sound hole

Magnetic pick-ups convert string vibrations into electrical signals

Screw for tightening bow

Bridge supports strings

Machine heads for tuning strings

Frets

Neck

Steel truss rod to strengthen neck

Tremolo arm

ELECTRIC GUITAR

GUITAR
The electric guitar is a key instrument in rock and pop music. On an electric guitar, plucked strings are amplified electronically.

Crash cymbal

Tom-tom drums

Ride cymbal

DRUM KIT

Snare drum

Bass drum

PERCUSSION

Instruments that are played by striking them are called percussion. They include drums, cymbals, xylophones, gongs, and much more. Percussion underlines the rhythm of the music.

Heavy iron frame

Hammers strike strings to make sound

Tuning pins

88-note keyboard – pressing the keys swings hammers

KEYBOARD

Keyboards, including harpsichord, piano, organ, and synthesizer, are among the most versatile of all instruments. They are played by pressing levers or keys with the fingers.

WIND INSTRUMENTS

WOODWINDS

Flutes, clarinets, oboes, and bassoons all have a reed in the mouthpiece to set up the vibrations that make the sound. They are called woodwinds even though they are often made of brass.

Mouthpiece

Thumb keys

Neck

Pads change notes

SAXOPHONE
The saxophone is neither woodwind, nor brass. It is shaped like a brass instrument but has a reed.

Bell projects sound

Blow hole

FLUTE

BRASS
Brass instruments include cornet, trumpet, horn, tuba, and trombone. The sound is made by the vibration of the player's lips against the mouthpiece.

Valve

CORNET

MUSIC

ROCK, JAZZ, AND FOLK MUSIC are often played from memory by small groups of talented musicians. Some types of music, such as classical music, is written down for soloists or groups of musicians.

THE ORCHESTRA
Orchestras range from small string orchestras to huge symphony orchestras. Similar instruments are grouped together.

WOODWINDS

PERCUSSION

BRASSES

BRASSES

STRINGS

Conductor

STRINGS

A symphony orchestra usually has about 90 players.

MUSICAL GROUPS
Musical groups range from duos with two performers to symphony orchestras with up to 120.

A jazz quartet includes drums and bass; a string quartet is two violins, viola, and cello.

A quintet usually has five wind or five brass instruments.

Violin   Viola   Cello

CELLO AND PIANO DUO

STRING TRIO

JAZZ QUARTET

MIXED QUINTET

PITCH

The pitch of each note is shown by how high it sits on the staff. Musical pitch is grouped into eight notes called an octave. The notes of each octave are named from low to high using the letters A to G, plus the A that begins the next octave.

ONE OCTAVE OF THE SCALE OF C MAJOR

C Major notes on stave correspond to white keys on piano keyboard

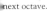

C D E F G A B C D E

PIANO KEYBOARD

NOTE VALUES

Name	Sign	Rest
Whole note (4 beats)	o	—
Half note (2 beats)		
Quarter note (1 beat)		
Eighth note (½ beat)		
Sixteenth note (¼ beat)		
Thirty-second (⅛ beat)		

Key signature shows which key music is in

More than two notes played together produces a chord

Natural sign cancels sharp or flat on next note

Rest shows length of pause in music

mf

sf

Treble clef. The bass staff has a bass clef

Time signature shows type and number of beats in a bar, or measure

Dot makes note half as long again

Eighths equal half a beat

Bar line marks end of bar, or time measure

Sforzando means accent (emphasize) the note loudly

Dynamic markings indicate how loud or soft to play music – mf means mezzo-forte, or moderately loud

MUSICAL NOTATION

Composers write down music using an international code of signs and symbols that enables musicians to interpret and play a composition. The notes are written on two bands of five lines, called staves. The lower staff (bass) is for low notes; the upper staff (treble) is for higher notes. Music is divided into measures called bars, each with the same number of beats.

15,000 B.C.–A.D. 650	770–1750

Before 15,000 B.C. Stone Age people played bone flutes.

c. 3000 B.C. Harps and lyres appear in Sumerian writing.

2600 B.C. Pa-Pab-Bi-gagir-gal of Ur in Mesopotamia is the first musician whose name is known.

c. 2500 B.C. Oldest known harp placed in Queen Puabi's tomb at Ur.

EGYPTIAN TOMB PAINTINGS

2200 B.C. Groups of musicians appear in Egyptian tomb paintings.

605 B.C. King Nebuchadnezzar of Babylon has an orchestra play at the dedication ceremony of an image of himself made in gold.

c. 550 B.C. The ancient Greek philosopher Pythagoras (580–500 B.C.) creates the first mathematical theory of musical harmony.

408 B.C. The oldest fragment of written music is a chorus for a play called *Orestes*, by ancient Greek dramatist Euripides (c. 484–406 B.C.).

A.D. 650 School for church music founded in Rome by Pope Gregory (c. A.D 540–604) develops Gregorian style of singing.

700s Orchestras play *gamelan* (gongs) in Indonesia, to accompany traditional puppet shows and dance.

750 The Court of Caliph Harun al-Rashid in Persia becomes famous for its music played by musicians, like Ishaq al-Mausili (767–850).

1100s Monks add a second or third tune to the simple "plainsong" of the Gregorian chant to create the first polyphonic music.

1300s Paris becomes focus of polyphonic music, and early French composer Guillaume de Machaut (1300–77) writes ballads (songs) in this form.

1480 First printed music in Europe.

1500s Palestrina (1525–94) and Monteverdi (1567–1643) write polyphonic vocal masses for church.

FIRST PRINTED MUSIC IN EUROPE

1500s Polyphonic music played on instruments such as viola and lutes, especially for dances such as the pavane.

1600s Opera developed by the Camerata, a group of poets and musicians in Florence, Italy.

1600–1750 Baroque-era composers write in harmony, creating melody by combining notes from the major and minor scales. Baroque pieces contrast loud and soft, fast and slow musical passages.

1650–1889

1650–1700
Composers like
J.S. Bach
(1685–1750),
Vivaldi
(1678–1741),
and Handel
(1685–1759) write
elaborate
instrumental works
called sonatas and
concerto grossos.

J.S. BACH

1750–1820 In the classical era,
instrumental pieces are clearly
structured and elegant.
Late 1700s Classical music is brought to
a peak by Mozart (1756–91) and
Beethoven (1770–1827).
Early 1800s Beethoven writes
emotional, passionate pieces on a grand
scale, ushering in the romantic era.
1820–1900 The romantic era features
composers such as Schubert
(1797–1828), Berlioz (1803–69), and
Wagner (1813–83), who write great
piano and orchestral works.
1830s–1850s Liszt (1811–86) and
Chopin (1810–49) compose dazzling,
virtuoso piano music.
1870s–1880s Verdi (1813–1901) takes
opera to new heights.
1860s–1890s Composers like Dvorák
(1841–1904), Grieg (1843–1907), and
Tchaikovsky (1840–93), are inspired by
the folk music of their countries.
1870s Wagner creates a new form
of music drama.

1890–TODAY

Late 1800s Blues played by black
Americans.
c. 1900 Jazz music appears in New
Orleans, US, combining African
rhythms and Western harmony.
Early 1900s Composers, like Stravinsky
(1882–1971) and Bartók (1881–1945),
begin to write music in which dissonance
(clashing notes) creates a thrilling sound.
1910s onward Schoenberg (1874–1951)
creates "atonal" music in which the
tonal center (key) shifts continually.
1930s Gershwin (1898–1937)
mixes jazz and classical music in
Rhapsody in Blue.
1950s Black Americans play rock and
roll, later taken up by white singers, such
as Buddy Holly and Elvis Presley.
1960s Rock and roll develops into
rock, with bands such as The Who and
The Rolling Stones, and pop, with groups
like The Beatles and The Beach Boys.
1970s Groups such as The Bee Gees and
Chic make disco music popular.
1980s Electronic
dance music emerges
from black American
neighborhoods into
mainstream music.
1990s Energetic
dance beats, such as
house, techno, and
jungle, are popular.
Emergence of guitar-
based "alternative"
rock.

SINGER
CHUCK BERRY

DANCE

OVER THOUSANDS of years, varied styles of dance have developed all over the world.

DANCE TIMELINE

15,000 B.C. Stone Age rock paintings show people dancing.

TANZANIAN ROCK PAINTING

3000–1000 B.C. Ancient Egyptians use ritual dance to worship gods such as Isis.

A.D. 400 First Kagura dances are performed at Shinto shrines in Japan.

1300–1500 Mass dances in Europe cause frenzy.

Late 1400s *Ballo*, Italian dance with a story line, is the earliest form of ballet.

c. 1600 Kathakali dance emerges in India.

1830s–1840s Romantic ballet flourishes.

c. 1900 Isadora Duncan (1877–1927) develops freer forms of modern dance.

1930s Fred Astaire popularizes tap dancing.

FRED ASTAIRE

1950s Rock-and-roll dancing.

1980s Break dancing and slam dancing are born.

1990s Companies design dances for TV and stage.

BALLET

The three main ballet styles are romantic, classical, and modern, distinguished mainly by differences in clothing and music. All ballet dancers learn five basic positions for the arms and feet.

FIVE BASIC ARM POSITIONS

FIRST

SECOND

THIRD

FOURTH

FIFTH

FIVE BASIC FEET POSITIONS

FIRST

SECOND

THIRD

FOURTH

FIFTH

Arm movements are slow

Hand movements are complex

Traditional costume

THAI CLASSICAL DANCER

TRADITIONAL DANCE

Nearly every country in the world has its own traditional form of dance. These dances have often developed from simple religious or tribal rituals into complex dance forms with set movements.

THEATER

MODERN THEATER originated in ancient Greece, where actors wearing masks were used to tell a story or demonstrate a theme.

THEATER BUILDING
The ancient Greeks saw theater in vast open-air stadiums; modern theaters are smaller and indoors, and take many forms.

Several exits for complex plays

ENGLISH 16TH-CENTURY THEATER

Rows of tiered seats gave a good view

ANCIENT GREEK AMPHITHEATER

Seats

MODERN THEATER

SHAKESPEARE
William Shakespeare (1564–1616) was born in Stratford-upon-Avon, England. In about 1590, he moved to London, where he wrote at least 37 plays, including *Hamlet* and *Romeo and Juliet*.

KABUKI THEATER
The performers of Kabuki theater are men who wear elaborate makeup to play a particular role.

WICKED MALE   CRAB   NOBLE MALE

THEATER TIMELINE

c. 3000 B.C. Religious rituals involve music and drama.

c. 1000 B.C. Chinese and Indian dance-dramas become formalized.

c. 500 B.C. Ancient Greeks see dramas by Aeschylus (525–456 B.C.), Sophocles (496–406 B.C.), and Euripides (484–406 B.C.).

A.D. 1–100 "Pantomimus" popular in Rome.

c. 1500 Commedia dell'Arte, mimed comedy, spreads from Italy.

1603 Okuni, a young Japanese woman, creates Kabuki theater.

Early 1600s Theater flourishes in

COMMEDIA DELL'ARTE

England and Spain with writers like Shakespeare and Lope de Vega (1562–1635).

c. 1800 Peking Opera begins in China.

1870s–90s New form of realistic drama created by Ibsen (1828–1906).

PEKING OPERA

3500 B.C.–A.D. 1380	1380–1840s

c. 3500 B.C. The oldest known writing, marks on clay tablets, are made at the Sumerian city of Uruk.

3300 B.C. Egyptians write in hieroglyphs (picture writing).

c. 2000 B.C. The Sumerian epic *Gilgamesh* is recorded on clay tablets.

c. 800 B.C. The Greek writer Homer writes *The Iliad*.

600 B.C. The Greek writer Aesop writes his fables, which include the story of *The Boy Who Cried Wolf* and *The Crow and Pitcher*.

AESOP'S FABLES

500 B.C. Hindu *Bhagavadgita* written.

200 B.C. Greeks invent parchment.

c. 30–19 B.C. Roman writer Virgil writes *The Aeneid*.

A.D. 105 Chinese invent paper.

868 Earliest printed book, the Chinese *Diamond Sutra*.

1007 In Japan, Murasaki Shikibu (973–1014) writes *The Tale of Genji*, the world's first novel.

1048–1123 Persian poet Omar Khayyam writes *The Rubáiyát*.

1190–1320 Icelandic saga (oral tales) written down.

1321 Dante (1265–1321) writes his *Divine Comedy* in Ravenna, Italy.

c. 1350 Boccaccio (1313–75) writes *The Decameron* in Florence.

c. 1387 Chaucer (1343–1400) writes *The Canterbury Tales* in Windsor Castle.

GUTENBERG'S BIBLE

c. 1450 Johann Gutenberg (1390–1468) invents printing by movable type in Germany.

1605 Cervantes (1547–1616) writes *Don Quixote*, a satire about an elderly Spanish knight.

1667 English poet Milton (1608–74) writes *Paradise Lost*.

1697 French author Charles Perrault (1628–1703) writes *Tales of Mother Goose*.

1719 English writer Daniel Defoe (1660–1731) writes *Robinson Crusoe*.

1808 German poet Goethe (1749–1832) writes *Faust*.

1811–1817 Jane Austen (1775–1817) writes *Pride and Prejudice*, *Emma*, and other novels.

1818 Mary Shelley (1797–1851) writes *Frankenstein*.

1830s French novelist Balzac (1799–1850) writes *Père Goriot*.

1841 American writer Edgar Allen Poe (1809–49) writes *Murders in the Rue Morgue*, the first detective story.

1840–70 Charles Dickens (1812–70) writes *Great Expectations*, *Oliver Twist*, and other novels, often in parts that were serialized in magazines of the time.

1840s–1869

1840s Charlotte Brontë (1816–55) writes *Jane Eyre*, her sister Emily (1818–48) *Wuthering Heights*.

CHARLOTTE BRONTE

1851 American writer Herman Melville (1819–91) writes *Moby Dick*.
1852 American writer Harriet Beecher Stowe (1811–96) writes *Uncle Tom's Cabin* about the injustice of slavery.
1857 French writer Gustave Flaubert (1821–80) writes *Madame Bovary*.
1862 French writer Victor Hugo (1802–85) writes *Les Misérables*.
1864 French writer Jules Verne (1828–1905) writes *Journey to the Center of the Earth*.
1865–72 Russian writer Tolstoy (1828–1910) writes *War and Peace*.
1866 Russian writer Dostoyevsky (1821–81) writes *Crime and Punishment*.
1867 French writer Émile Zola (1840–1902) writes *Thérèse Raquin*.
1873 The first typewriter is made in the US by the Remington company.
1881 American author Henry James (1843–1916) writes *Portrait of a Lady*.
1883 Robert Louis Stevenson (1850–94) writes *Treasure Island*.
1894 Rudyard Kipling (1865–1936) writes *The Jungle Book*.

1900–TODAY

1926 A.A. Milne (1882–1956) writes *Winnie-the-Pooh*.
1870–1900 Thomas Hardy (1840–1928) writes many novels and poems.
1913 Indian poet Rabindranath Tagore (1861–1941) writes *Gitanjali*.
1913 D.H. Lawrence (1885–1930) writes *Sons and Lovers*.
1917 Czech writer Franz Kafka (1883–1924) writes *The Trial*.
1922 Publication of French writer Marcel Proust's (1871–1922) *Remembrance of Things Past*; Irish writer James Joyce's (1882–1941) *Ulysses*.
1925 American writer F. Scott Fitzgerald (1896–1940) writes *The Great Gatsby*.
1929 Ernest Hemingway (1899–1961) writes *Farewell to Arms*.

EARLY PAPERBACKS

1935 The first paperback books go on sale.
1943 Dutch Jewish girl Anne Frank (1929–1945) writes her diary.
1970s Desktop publishing arrives.
1986 The first CD-ROM book.

A CD-ROM holds text, sound, and moving images, and many books can be stored on one disk.

399

PHOTOGRAPHY

MILLIONS OF TIMES a day, a camera
shutter clicks somewhere in the
world to take a photograph, making
an instant visual record of a scene,
whether it is just a family snapshot
or a dramatic news picture.

35MM
ROLL FILM

FILM FORMATS
Cameras are built to suit
particular film formats
(sizes). The most popular
format is 35mm, which is
used in most compacts and
SLRs. Studio photographe
often use a medium format
for extra quality.

INSIDE AN SLR CAMERA
The type of camera most popular with serious
amateurs and many professional photographers is
the SLR, or Single Lens Reflex. The SLR has a
prism that reflects light from the lens to the
eyepiece, allowing the photographer to see
directly through the camera lens.
It also has interchangeable lenses.

Rear viewfinder

Shutter speed dial

Frame counter

Shutter release button

Strap attachment

Film

Film take-up spool

Flash hot shoe

Aperture control ring

Light path through camera

Front lens element

Internal lens element

Lens housing

Light reflects from subject and travels in rays toward the camera

Curved glass of lens refracts (bends) light rays

Converging light rays pass through an adjustable aperture (hole)

Shutter opens at different speeds to vary time film is exposed to light

When lens is focused, light rays focus on the film to create a sharp image

LIGHT INSIDE A CAMERA

A camera is essentially a lightproof box with a hole at the front holding a glass lens. The lens projects a bright, sharp picture of the world into the camera where it is recorded on film, or, in electronic cameras such as videos), on light-sensitive cells.

PHOTOGRAPHY TIMELINE

400 B.C. Chinese scholar uses a pinhole in silk to project an image in a darkened room.

18TH-CENTURY CAMERA OBSCURA

A.D. 1020 Arab scholar Alhazen describes how a pinhole in a camera obscura (dark room) can be used to view a solar eclipse.

1558 Battista della Porta use a lens in the pinhole to sharpen the image.

1560–1860 Camera obscuras common in public buildings.

1700s Portable camera obscuras made for artists.

1727 Johann Schulze (1687–1744) shows how silver nitrate darkens when exposed to light.

c. 1800 Tom Wedgwood makes images by exposing paper coated with silver salts to the light.

1826 First photo made by Niepce (1765–1833) on a pewter plate in a camera obscura.

1839 Daguerreotype, first practical photographic process, invented by Frenchman Louis Daguerre (1789–1851).

1839 Fox Talbot (1800–77) invents Calotype process. The process produces negatives, enabling copies of photos to be made.

1851 Archer's (1813–57) Collodion allows paper prints to be made from glass negatives.

1861 Maxwell (1831–79) makes first color photo.

1888 First Kodak camera, using roll film.

1906 First practical color photo process invented by French Lumière brothers.

FIRST KODAK COLOUR FILM

1913 35mm film invented.

1924 The Leica, the first successful 35mm camera.

1935 Kodachrome color transparency (slide) film.

1947 First instant camera invented by Land (1909–91) marketed as Polaroid.

1994 First electronic still and video camera launched.

CINEMA

ARNOLD
SCHWARZENEGGER
IN TERMINATOR 2

MOVIES ARE now a multimillion-dollar business, with people all over the world going to the movies to see feature films. Many high-budget films use complex special effects as well as "movie stars" to attract audiences.

FILM

Most movies are now recorded on 35mm film. All the pictures on the film are still, but they are run through the projector so quickly – eight frames, or pictures, a second – that we see only continuous movement on the screen. One full-length feature movie uses 1.5 miles (2.5 km) of film.

9.5-mm film introduced by French Pathé company in 1922 for amateur films

Sound track

35MM FILM

FILM GENRE

Most feature films fall into one of several categories or "genres," including comedy (*Four Weddings and Funeral*), romance (*Tin Cup*), science fiction (*Terminator 2*), action (*Die Hard*), or horror (*Interview with the Vampire*).

SPECIAL EFFECTS

Computer technology has dramatically increased the scope of special effects, allowing techniques such as morphing.

The points of both the hand and the spider are plotted on the computer. When the two sets of points coincide, the transformation is complete.

Morphing is used to transform one thing into another or to create animation in a live-action film.

The outline of the spider is just visible.

The midpoint of the morphing process.

The spider is almost complete

ANIMATION

By filming drawings or models in different positions, animators can bring them to life. Computer-generated animation can produce very sophisticated animation sequences, such as those seen in *Toy Story*.

Bugs Bunny is one of the oldest cartoon characters.

Plasticine models can be moved to animate them, like this gorilla from Creature Comforts.

MOVIE TIMELINE

1879 The Zoogyroscope is developed by English photographer Eadweard Muybridge (1830–1914). It projects images of photographic sequences onto a screen in quick succession, creating an illusion of movement.

1881 Frenchman Étienne Marey (1830–1904) invents a camera that takes pictures on a revolving plate.

1894 Kinetograph (film camera) and Kinetoscope (film viewer) marketed by Americans Thomas Edison (1847–1931) and W.K. Dickson (1860–1933).

1895 French Lumière brothers show the first real movie in a movie theater in Paris.

1895 The world's first cinema opens in Atlanta, Georgia.

1913 Hollywood's first feature film, *Squaw Man*, made by Jesse Lasky (1880–1958), Cecil B. de Mille (1881–1959), and Samuel Goldwyn (1882–1974). Early films are in black and white and silent.

1920–1930s Picture palaces reach the peak of their popularity.

JAZZ SINGER POSTER

1927 *The Jazz Singer* is the first "talkie" (movie with sound).

1929 The first Oscars.

1932 Technicolor invented.

1953 Wide-screen image created by Cinemascope.

1970 Steadycam allows camera operator to move while holding camera steady.

OSCAR

1990s Computer graphics used to make movies.

THE OLYMPIC GAMES

HELD EVERY FOUR YEARS, the modern Games began in 1896 as the brainchild of French scholar Pierre de Coubertin, who was inspired by stories of the ancient Greek games. Separate Winter Olympics have been staged since 1924, and Special Oympics for the disabled since 1960.

OLYMPIC FLAME
Following ancient Greek tradition, the Olympics are still started by a torch, which is lit on Mount Olympus in Greece and carried by runners in relays to the Olympic stadium.

OLYMPIC SYMBOL
The five Olympic rings represent the five continents of the world. Some 200 nations send more than 10,000 entrants to compete in nearly 30 different sports

OLIVE WREATH
In the ancient Greek games, 2,000 years ago, winners were crowned with a sacred olive wreath.

PARALYMPICS
Like the Olympics, the Special Olympics for disabled people are held every four years.

OLYMPIC MEDALS
In the modern Olympics, individuals and teams compete for gold (first), silver (second), and bronze (third) medals.

GOLD MEDAL FROM
THE 1984 GAMES

WINTER OLYMPICS
The Winter Games, held two years after the Summer Olympics include skiing, figure and speed skating, and ice hockey.

CLASSIFICATION OF SPORTS
The many different types of sports can be classified into three basic groups, which can then be subdivided further.

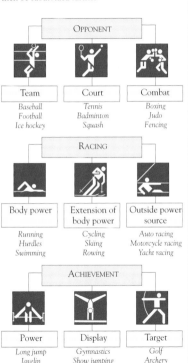

OPPONENT		
Team	**Court**	**Combat**
Baseball	*Tennis*	*Boxing*
Football	*Badminton*	*Judo*
Ice hockey	*Squash*	*Fencing*

RACING		
Body power	**Extension of body power**	**Outside power source**
Running	*Cycling*	*Auto racing*
Hurdles	*Skiing*	*Motorcycle racing*
Swimming	*Rowing*	*Yacht racing*

ACHIEVEMENT		
Power	**Display**	**Target**
Long jump	*Gymnastics*	*Golf*
Javelin	*Show jumping*	*Archery*
Weight lifting	*Figure skating*	*Darts*

BALL GAMES

MANY TEAM GAMES are played with a large, inflated ball. Soccer, volleyball, and basketball are played with a round ball, American football and rugby with an oval ball.

FOOTBALL

Leather ball
Helmet
Shoulder pad
Arm pad
Rib pad
Leg pad
Boots
THE EQUIPMENT

THE GAME
American football is a tough game of running, passing, and body-tackling. The field is divided into strips. When a team has the ball, it tries to advance the ball strip by strip in a series of "downs."

THE SNAP
Each down starts with a snap, as the center passes the ball back to the quarterback, who sets up a play by throwing a pass or slipping the ball to a running back.

SOCCER

Team colors on shirt

SOCCER PLAYER

THE GAME
Soccer is the world's most widely played game, and attracts more spectators than any other sport.
A match is played between two teams of 11 players each, and the aim is to score by kicking or heading the ball into the opponent's goal.

Round leather ball

45–90 m wide
Penalty area
90–120 m long
Center circle
Halfway line
Penalty spot
Goal area

THE FIELD
Soccer fields are almost always of grass and vary in size, but penalty areas are always the same.

VOLLEYBALL

Two teams of six players use their hands and arms to knock a ball over a net. A point is won if the ball lands in the opposition's court or if they fail to return it. The high net means players must jump high.

OVERHAND SERVE

Forearms or fingers are used to knock the ball up, ready for the spike.

UNDERHAND SERVE

PREPARING TO SPIKE (SMASH)

A team may touch the ball up to three times before returning it.

FOREARM PASS (DIG)

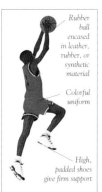

Rubber ball encased in leather, rubber, or synthetic material

Colorful uniform

High, padded shoes give firm support

BASKETBALL

In this fast, popular game, teams of five dribble the ball with their hands or pass and compete to throw the ball into the opponents' net.

RUGBY

Rugby Union has teams of 15 players; Rugby League has 13. Both games involve running, passing, and body-tackling. In Union, play often restarts with a scrum in which forwards interlock and try to push each other over the ball.

Scrum breaks when ball is cleared.

RUGBY UNION SCRUM

AUSTRALIAN RULES

This 18-a-side game, developed in Melbourne c. 1858, is played on an oval field in four quarters of 25 minutes each. Players kick, handpass, and run with the oval ball.

Goalposts

AUSTRALIAN RULES FIELD

STICK AND BALL GAMES

MANY OF THE WORLD'S most popular games involve hitting a small ball with a stick, a bat, or a racket.

BASEBALL

PITCH AND STRIKE
Two teams of nine take it in turns batting and fielding. The batter has three attempts to hit the ball thrown by the pitcher, then run around all the bases before the ball is fielded.

THE FIELD
The batter can only run if the ball lands within "fair territory," which consists f the infield (inside the ases) and the outfield.

Bats may be up to 42 in (107 cm) long

BASEBALL BAT

Outfield

2nd base

Infield

3rd base

Pitcher's mound

1st base

Home plate

CRICKET

BATTING
Cricket is an 11-a-side game. Two batsmen are in at any one time. The batsman stands at the crease and defends the wicket with the bat as the ball is bowled. He must try to hit the ball to score runs.

DISMISSING THE BATSMAN

BOWLED
The ball hits the wicket. If the batsman blocks a ball with his body he is "leg before wicket."

Crease

Wicket

RUN OUT
The fielders team hit a wicket before the batsmen return.

Batsman tries to hit ball

STUMPED
The batsman leaves the crease, and the fielders hit the wicket.

HOCKEY AND LACROSSE

HOCKEY

Two teams of 11 use a stick to drive the ball into their opponent's goal. Goalkeepers have to be protected from the ball, which can travel at 100 mph (160 km/h).

GOALKEEPER

HOCKEY OUTDOOR STICK

Helmet

Goal-keeper's glove

Kicker enables keeper to use his or her feet

Side shooting

Men's lacrosse teams have 10 players, women's teams have 12.

Cradling the ball

Throwing the ball

LACROSSE

Players use the net to carry and pass the ball and drive it into their opponent's goal.

RACKET GAMES

TENNIS

Players use a racket to hit a ball over a net so that the ball lands in the opposite court and cannot be returned. Matches are played in sets of games, with a maximum of five sets for men and three for women. The court may be grass or clay. A doubles court is bigger than a singles court.

TENNIS RACKET

Singles sideline

Net

Doubles sideline

TENNIS COURT

SQUASH

A squash game is played in an enclosed court. Players aim to hit the ball onto one or more walls so their opponent cannot hit it before it bounces twice on the floor. Games are played to nine points, matches to the best of three or five games.

SQUASH

COMPETITION SPORTS

ATHLETICS AND OTHER sports like gymnastics and weight lifting are based on individual prowess.

TRACK EVENTS
Most running events take place on the track.

3,000 m, 5,000 m

Back straight

3,000 m steeplechase

200 m

RUNNING TRACK

1,500 m

Synthetic surface, usually plastic

110 m hurdles

Finishing straight

Finish line for all events

Relays, 400 m, 400 m hurdles

100 m, 100 m hurdles

10,000 m

800 m

FIELD EVENTS

These include jumping events, such as long jump, triple jump, high jump, and pole vault, and throwing events, such as the shot, discus, hammer, and javelin. Women do not take part in the pole vault or hammer in the Olympics.

THE SHOT
The athlete puts (throws) from the shoulder and must not step out of the circle.

THE JAVELIN
The throw is measured to where the point first touches the ground.

THE DISCUS
Usually thrown after a couple of wind-up swings and a full turn.

THE HAMMER
This metal ball on a wire is hurled after 3 or 4 full turns.

TRIPLE JUMP
This consists of a hop, step, and jump, starting with a run-up and ending in a sandpit.

HOP

COMBINED EVENTS

First day	Second day
Decathlon (men)	
100 m race	110 m hurdle
Long jump	Discus
Shot put	Pole vault
High jump	Javelin
400 m race	1500 m race

Heptathlon (women)	
100 m hurdle	Long jump
High jump	Javelin
Shot put	800 m race
200 m race	

WEIGHT LIFTING

There are two categories: snatch, and clean and jerk.

SNATCH

Bar is lifted first to the shoulders, then to full arm's length overhead as the lifter stands up.

Bar is lifted to full arm's length overhead in a single movement. The lifter then stands up.

CLEAN AND JERK

GYMNASTICS

Gymnast must change hand-holds and direction constantly

Points are given for good continuity and rhythm

Gymnastics consists of exercises on the floor, beam, rings, uneven, parallel, and horizontal bars, vaulting horse, and pommel horse. Judges award marks out of ten for the gymnast's performance at the exercise. Rhythmic gymnastics for women is performed to music with ribbons, balls, ropes, clubs, or hoops.

UNEVEN BARS

Beam is 4 ins (10 cm) wide and 16.4 ft (5 m) long

Female gymnasts walk, run, leap, and somersault along a beam for 70–90 seconds

THE BEAM

STEP

JUMP

Athlete throws arms forward, ready for landing

WINTER SPORTS

THE SLIPPERINESS of snow and ice has inspired a range of winter sports, from the grace of figure skating to the thrill of downhill skiing.

ICE HOCKEY PLAYER

SPEED SKATING
In long-track racing, two skaters race against the clock on an outdoor 400 m track. In short-track racing, four or six skaters race each other round a 111.12 m indoor track.

SPEED SKATER

ICE HOCKEY
Ice hockey is a fast and furious six-a-side game in three 20-minute periods. The aim is to shoot the hard rubber puck into the opposition's goal.

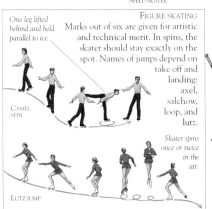

FIGURE SKATING
Marks out of six are given for artistic and technical merit. In spins, the skater should stay exactly on the spot. Names of jumps depend on take off and landing: axel, salchow, loop, and lutz.

One leg lifted behind and held parallel to ice

CAMEL SPIN

Skater spins once or twice in the air.

LUTZ JUMP

Blocking pad

Catch glove

Leg pad

THE GOALKEEPER
Goalkeepers need a lot of extra protection from the puck, which travels at high speed.

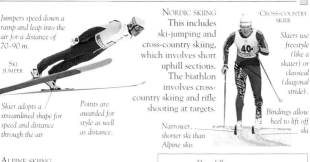

Jumpers speed down a
ramp and leap into the
air for a distance of
70–90 m.

SKI
JUMPER

NORDIC SKIING
This includes
ski-jumping and
cross-country skiing,
which involves short
uphill sections.
The biathlon
involves cross-
country skiing and rifle
shooting at targets.

CROSS-COUNTRY
SKIER

Skiers use
freestyle
(like a
skater) or
classical
(diagonal
stride).

Bindings allow
heel to lift off
ski

Skier adopts a
streamlined shape for
speed and distance
through the air

Points are
awarded for
style as well
as distance.

Narrower,
shorter ski than
Alpine skis

ALPINE SKIING
This type of skiing involves slalom and
downhill races, which are all run against
the clock, and freestyle, which is judged
on style and technique. In downhill
racing, each skier races once; slalom
and giant slalom are decided on the
combined time for two runs.

Downhill
course

Super giant slalom, vertical
drop: 500–600 m (men);
350–500 m (women)

Giant
slalom,
vertical
drop:
250–400 m
(men);
250–350 m
(women)

Slalom:
55–75 gates
(men);
40–60
gates
(women)

In downhill, skiers
hurtle down a set
route at speeds of
up to 86 mph
(140 km/h).

In slalom, skiers zigzag
between red and blue
flags without knocking
them down.

Freestyle skiers perform
acrobatics by jumping off
"moguls" (snow bumps)
and ramps.

COURSES
AND GATES
Flags marking the course are set on
single poles for slalom gates, double
poles for giant, and super giant slalom.

WATER SPORTS

THE POPULARITY of water sports, both indoors in pools and outdoors on rivers, lakes, and the sea, has increased greatly in recent years.

WINDSURFING
Also called board-sailing, windsurfing uses a sailboard with a swiveling sail that propels and steers the board. The windsurfer holds the boom which surrounds and supports the sail.

Mast

Sail

Window

Boom

Board

Universal joint swivels in all directions

Wet suits protect against cold

Boards are usually made of fiberglass

SURFING
Surfing is a spectacular sport in which surfers paddle out to sea on boards and ride big breakers back to shore. In competition, surfers are judged for style, grace, and timing.

YACHT TYPES

ONE-PERSON DINGHY
Simple one-person dinghys, such as the Topper class, are designed as training boats but are also raced.

TWO-PERSON BOAT WITH TRAPEZE
A two-person boat, such as the 470 class, is used in Olympic racing.

CATAMARAN
Twin-hulled, two-person catamarans , such as the Tornado class, also sail in Olympic races.

TWO-PERSON DINGHY
A two-person dinghy, such as the Flying Dutchman class, is used for training and racing.

OCEAN-GOING YACHT
An ocean-going yacht, such as the 12 m class, sail heavy seas in offshore racing.

SWIMMING STROKES

FRONT CRAWL
This is the fastest stroke and is used in freestyle races.

Legs move up and down from the hips

Arms and legs move alternately

Body kept straight and flat

BREASTSTROKE
This is the slowest stroke. Arms and legs stay underwater.

Arms move together, circling from outstretched position

Legs kick out like a frog

BACKSTROKE
This is the only stroke that swimmers start in the water.

Legs paddle

Arms pull alternately in windmill motion

Body kept straight and flat

BUTTERFLY
Like the breaststroke, this is a symmetrical stroke, but it is very energetic.

Strong double-arm pull

Dolphinlike double leg kick.

DIVING TYPES
In diving, marks are awarded for springboard (3 m above the water) and highboard (10 m). There are over 80 standard dives. Shown here are three of the best known dives.

Twisting in midair

Arms spread wide

Body straight for entry

TWIST DIVE

Pike position

Hands touch toes

Feet lift up for straight entry

INWARD DIVE PIKED

Pike position

Shoulders fall back for vertical entry

REVERSE DIVE PIKED

COMBAT SPORTS

BOXING AND WRESTLING are combat sports, as are fencing, archery, and shooting, and the martial arts of East Asia.

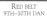

RED BELT 9TH–10TH DAN	
BLACK BELT 1ST–5TH DAN	
BROWN BELT 1ST KYU	
BLUE BELT 2ND KYU	
GREEN BELT 3RD KYU	
ORANGE BELT 4TH KYU	
YELLOW BELT 5TH KYU	

MARTIAL ARTS

KARATE
Strikes and kicks are used in karate, which means "empty hands."

AIKIDO
Meaning "the way of all harmony," aikido uses only defensive techniques.

JU JITSU
This is the ancient Japanese fighting art from which judo and aikido developed.

KENDO
Japanese sword-fighting, or kendo, is practised in armour.

JUDO
Competitors in the martial art of Judo, which means "the gentle way", use throws and holds to defeat their opponent. Grades or "belts" range from "kyu" (student) to "dan" (advanced).

BOXING
Governed by strict protective rules, competitors wear gloves. Professional fights are up to 12 three-minute rounds. Amateurs go three rounds.

BOXING WEIGHTS	PROFESSIONAL	AMATEUR
Flyweight	108–112 lb	106–112 lb
Featherweight	122–126 lb	119–126 lb
Lightweight	130–135 lb	126–132 lb
Middleweight	154–160 lb	157–165 lb
Heavyweight	Over 190 lb	179–201 lb

ARCHERY

Archers fire "rounds" of arrows at a target. The number varies with the event. The aim is to hit the center of the target, worth ten points.

TARGET

Magnesium handle

Finger tab

Sight

Fletch

QUIVER

Glove

Shaft

Bracer protects bow arm from string

Stabilizer to keep bow steady

BOW

The quiver worn on the archer's belt contains arrows with metal tips and carbon or aluminum points.

Modern bows have bowsights to help the archer adjust for wind and height.

FENCING

In fencing, two opponents compete in a bout using one of three weapons: saber, foil, or épée. A bout lasts until the agreed number of hits have been made, or until a preset time limit has been reached, e.g. five hits within a time limit of six minutes.

Weight: less than 500 g
Blade length: 88 cm

Weight: less than 500 g
Blade length: 90 cm

Weight: less than 770 g
Blade length: 90 cm

SABER

FOIL

EPEE

EQUESTRIAN EVENTS

COMPETITIONS ON HORSEBACK are known as equestrian events. They include racing, show-jumping, and eventing. In eventing, the riders' skill is tested as they take their horses through three disciplines over three days: show jumping, speed and endurance, and dressage.

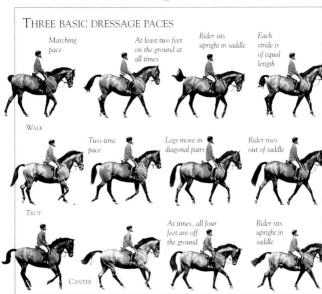

THREE BASIC DRESSAGE PACES

Marching pace

At least two feet on the ground at all times

Rider sits upright in saddle

Each stride is of equal length

WALK

Two-time pace

Legs move in diagonal pairs

Rider rises out of saddle

TROT

At times, all four feet are off the ground

Rider sits upright in saddle

CANTER

SHOW JUMPING

If the horse clips an obstacle, the rider incurs a fault. Riders with fewest faults compete against each other against the clock.

Landing *Flight* *Take-off*

Rider bends forwards from the hip and straightens on landing.

SHOW JUMPING COURSE

Start *Gate* *Triple bars* *Wall*

Finish

OBSTACLES

Obstacles must be jumped in a set order between start and finish.

SHOW JUMPING FAULTS

ERROR	FAULT
Fence (or part of) down	4
Foot in water	4
Refusal	3
2nd refusal	6
3rd refusal	Elimination
Fall (horse or rider)	8
Exceeding time allowance	¼ per sec
Jumps taken out of sequence	Elimination

HORSE RACING

There are two kinds of horse racing: steeplechase, which includes jumps over fences, ditches, and water jumps, and hurdles, which are 2–3.5 mile races for three-year-olds and older. The horses are almost always Thoroughbreds.

JOCKEY'S HELMET

A jockey wears a crash helmet under his or her cap, and carries a whip.

Shirt and cap in owner's colors

THOROUGHBRED

Jockeys are light; some weigh under 97 lb (44.5 kg).

Thoroughbred horses are all descended from three original Arab stallions.

Whip

Pocket for lead weights to handicap horses with the best race records

Helmet covered in silk

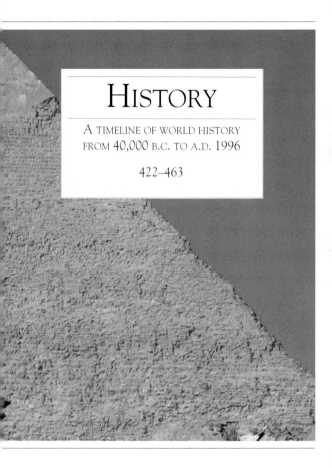

HISTORY

A TIMELINE OF WORLD HISTORY
FROM 40,000 B.C. TO A.D. 1996

422–463

	40,000–32,501 B.C.	32,500–25,001 B.C.
AFRICA	**c. 34,000** Hunter-gatherers occupy areas of present-day Lesotho and Zambia.	**30,000** Disappearance of Neanderthals. **Ostrich** *Wild ostriches formed part of the ancient African diet.*
ASIA	**40,000** Cro-Magnon humans live in Palestine at Skhūl and Kafzel.	**27,000–19,000** Female statuettes called "Venus" figurines, thought to have been used in worship, are made at various sites in Russia, France, and Italy.
EUROPE	**40,000** Neanderthals active in France, at La Chapelle-Aux-Saints, La Ferassie, and La Quina. Cro-Magnons start to spread to Europe. **35,000** Start of Upper Paleolithic Period. Use of flaked stone tools, and bone and horn implements.	**"Venus" figurines** *These rounded statuettes of female figures may have been symbols of fertility.*
AMERICAS	**35,000** First humans arrive in North America from Asia.	**27,000–19,000** Probable date of earliest figurative art in Dordogne, France.
OCEANIA	**40,000** Probable arrival of Aboriginals in Australia.	

Early flint tool

25,000–17,501 B.C.	17,500–10,001 B.C.

15,000 Last rainy period in northern Africa.

20,000 The Ice Age causes the world's average temperature to drop and sea levels to lower. Humans have to adapt and work together to survive.

Mammoth hunt
Ice Age people hunted in groups and shared the kill.

16,000 Coldest point in glaciation.
14,000–11,000 El-Kebarch culture in Israel builds freestanding round huts.
11,000 Natufian culture in Palestine becomes one of the first groups to form permanent settlements.
10,500 Earliest-known pottery produced, Fukui cave, Japan.

Natufian huts
The mud, reed, and timber huts of the Natufians were often used to store grain.

15,000 Wall paintings made in caves at Lascaux, France.
15,000–10,000 High point of art produced by Magdalenian culture.
12,500 Magdalenian toolmakers make the first bone and antler harpoons and fishing spears.
11,000 Cave paintings created at Altamira, Spain.
The origins of art
Early artists painted images of animals and humans on the walls of caves.

25,000 Cave dwellers present in Brazil.	**15,000** First Brazilian cave art.
24,000 Earliest-known cremation at Lake Mungo, New South Wales, Australia.	**16,000** Cave art, north coast of Australia.

	10,000–8501 B.C.	8500–7001 B.C.
AFRICA	**10,000** Hunting camps established in Sahara region after Ice Age ends.	**8500** Earliest Saharan rock paintings. **8000** Pottery made in Sahara region.
ASIA	**9000–8000** Wheat and barley grown in Jordan and Syria. Pottery produced at Mureybet, Syria. Goats and sheep domesticated in Iran and Jordan.	**8000** Jericho, the first town, appears. Ice Age ends in Far East. **7500** Pigs domesticated in Crimea.
EUROPE	**10,000** Ice cap retreats.	**8300** Retreat of glaciers.
AMERICAS	**10,000** First people reach southern tip of South America. **9000** Clovis hunter-gatherers in the Great Plains of North America begin to hunt bison.	**8500** Wild grasses and beans cultivated in Peru. **8000** Semipermanent settlements established in North America.
OCEANIA		

Early farming
Grain crops were first cultivated in the Middle East in 8000 B.C.

Domesticated pig
The modern pig evolved from the wild boar, domesticated by early farmers.

Jericho Tower
The ancient town of Jericho was strongly built to last, with a stone wall, tower, and defensive ditch.

North American bison

7000–5501 B.C.	5500–4001 B.C.

6500 Cattle domesticated.
7000–6000 Discovery that heating certain rocks (ores) releases pure metal that can then be shaped or molded occurs.

Early metal-workers

7000–6500 Oxen domesticated in eastern Mediterranean.
6500–5700 Important early town forms at Çatal Hüyük, Turkey. Its houses are built of mud brick and share walls.
6200 Copper smelted in Turkey.

Çatal Hüyük

5000 Irrigation in Mesopotamia. Rice farming in China. Ubaid culture in Mesopotamia.
4500 Farming around Ganges River in India.
4400 Horses domesticated in Russia.

5000 Farming begins in western Europe. Gold and copper used in Balkans.
4500 First megalithic chamber tombs built in Portugal and in Brittany, France. Their remains (dolmens) show a great knowledge of engineering.

Dolmens at Carnac
Upright stones placed in a row and roofed to form a covered walk can be seen at Carnac, Brittany.

6500 Britain separated from mainland as ice melts.
6500 First farming communities established in southeastern Europe.

6500 Potatoes cultivated in Peru.

c. 4000–5000 First settlements form at Anáhuac, Mexico. Corn grown in Mexico. Pyramid temples built in Peru.

5000 New Guinea and Tasmania separated from Australia as sea level rises.

	4000–3376 B.C.	3375–2751 B.C.
AFRICA	**3750** Earliest known production of bronze alloy. The process is also developed in Sumer, southern Babylonia. **3500** First sailing vessels built in Egypt.	**3100** Pharaoh Menes the Fighter unites Upper and Lower Egypt. **3000** Hieroglyphic writing develops in Egypt.

Egyptian mummy
Preserving the bodies of important people was an ancient Egyptian custom.

	4000–3376 B.C.	3375–2751 B.C.
ASIA	**4000** Beginning of bronze casting in the Middle East. **3500** Earliest Chinese city at Liang-ch'eng chen. Sumerians invent the wheel and plow.	**3500** Ancient Egyptians establish one of the world's longest-lasting civilizations.

Mesopotamian wheel

EUROPE		**3250** Earliest picture-writing by Sumerians in Mesopotamia. **3000** Development of Sumerian cities. First use of the plow in China. **2850** Legendary reign of the Chinese Xia dynasty.

	4000–3376 B.C.	3375–2751 B.C.
AMERICAS	**c. 4000** Domestication of llama and alpaca in Andes, South America.	**3200** Beginnings of early Cycladic civilization in Aegean islands. **3000** Spread of copper use. **2900** Danubian culture in central Europe.

Inca llama figurine
The Incas of South America used llamas as pack animals and also for meat.

3200 Corn farmed in South America. **3000** First pottery in Americas.

Corn

OCEANIA		**3000** Probable introduction of dogs in Australia.

2750–2126 B.C.

2686 Beginning of ancient Egyptian Old Kingdom.
2646 Pyramid of Zoser built at Saqqara.
2590 Building of Great Pyramid of Khufu at Giza begins.
2500 Sahara region begins to dry out.
2150 Decline of ancient Egyptian Old Kingdom.
2133 Rise of ancient Egyptian Middle Kingdom.

2750 The legendary King Gilgamesh reigns in Uruk, Mesopotamia.
2500 Birth of Indus Valley civilization in Pakistan. Horse domesticated in Central Asia.
2371 Semite people establish Mesopotamia's greatest empire.

Indus Valley sculpture
This sculpture of a priest or divine king was made by people in the Indus Valley city of Mohenjo-Daro.

2500 Earliest barrow burials in Britain. Beginnings of Dolmen period of Scandinavian Neolithic age.
2200 The first Stonehenge is built in England.

2500 First large settlements and building of temple mounds in Andes area.

2125–1501 B.C.

1786 Egyptian Middle Kingdom ends.
1652 War between Egypt and Asian Hyksos people.
1550 Rise of Egyptian New Kingdom.

2000 Hittites begin invasions of Anatolia.
1900 Fall of Indus civilization.
1800 Beginnings of Assyrian Empire.
1792 Birth of Hammurabi, founder of Babylonian Empire.

Lotus-design tile
This tile dates from the reign of King Akhenaten in the Egyptian New Kingdom.

2000 Rise of the prosperous Minoan sea-trading civilization in Crete.
1600 Origins of Mycenean civilization.
1500 Linear B script in use on Crete.

Minoan wall painting
The wealthy Minoan people decorated the walls of their palaces with colorful murals.

2000 Earliest Peruvian metalworking. Inuits reach northern Greenland.

2000 Beginnings of settlement of Melanesia in the South Pacific.

	1500–1276 BC	1275–1051 B.C.

AFRICA	**1300** Temple of Abu Simbel built in Nubia for Rameses II.
	
	Hittite soldier
		1218 Egypt invaded by Sea Peoples from the Aegean.
		    1182 Second invasion of Egypt by
		        Aegean Sea Peoples.

ASIA	**1500** Phrygia established by people moving from Thrace in the Balkans to Asia Minor. Composition of hymns of Rig Veda. **1400** Chinese capital moved to Anyang, in present-day South Korea.	**c. 1375** First alphabet script devised by Phoenicians. **1294** Egyptians fight Hittites at Qadesh for control of Palestine. **1200** Collapse of Hittite Empire. Jews settle in Palestine. **1100** Phoenician traders begin to spread out from eastern Mediterranean.
EUROPE	**1500** Beginning of Bronze Age in Scandinavia. **1450** Decline of Minoan civilization in Crete.	**1200** Decline of Mycenean culture in Greece. **c. 1120** City of Mycenae destroyed.
AMERICAS	**1300** Rise of Olmec civilization in Mexico. **Olmec stone carving** *This colossal stone head of an Olmec king was carved from basalt.*	**Mycenean bull's head** *This clay bull's head has small holes in its mouth and was used as a ritual sprinkler at religious ceremonies.*
OCEANIA	**1300** Settlers reach Western Polynesia (Fiji).	

1050–826 B.C.	825–601 B.C.
900 Foundation of kingdom of Kushin Nubia.	**814** Phoenicians found the city-state of Carthage in northern Africa.

1027 Zhou warriors overthrow the Shang dynasty in China.
1000 Kingdom of Israel under King David.

Shang Fang Ding
This four-legged food vessel was made in China during the Shang dynasty (c. 1600–1027 BC).

800 Aryans from present-day Iran spread into southern India.
771 Zhou dynasty collapses in China.
721–05 Assyrian Empire at height of its powers.
660 Reign of Jimmu, legendary first Japanese emperor.
650 Chinese begin to use iron.
612 Decline of Assyrian power.
c. 604–562 Nebuchadnezzar II rules Neo-Babylonian (Chaldean) Empire. Hanging Gardens built in city of Babylon, Mesopotamia.

Sentry at the Ishtar Gate, Babylon

1000 Etruscans arrive in Italy and begin building a loosely connected alliance of city-states.

Etruscan warrior figurine
The Etruscans produced unique, high-quality sculpture and bronze work.

776 First recorded Olympic Games in Greece.
753 Foundation of Rome.
750 Greek city-states establish settlements around Mediterranean.
700 Iron Age culture of Hallstatt, Austria, spreads through central and western Europe.
650 Earliest surviving Latin inscriptions.
621 The Laws of Dracon become the first written laws of Athens, Greece.

900 Height of Chavin farming civilization in Andes, South America.
800 Zapotec civilization of Central America produces first writing in Americas.

1000 Most of Polynesian Islands settled.

	600–451 B.C.	450–301 B.C.
AFRICA	600 Phoenicians sail around Africa. 600 Building of Temple of the Sun at Meroë, Sudan. 500 Ironworking Nok culture begins in Nigeria.	304 Egypt independent under Ptolemy I.
ASIA	560 Lao–Tze writes his philosophical work, Tao Te Ching, in China. 550 King Cyrus II of Persia founds Persian Empire. 486 Death of Siddhartha Gautama, founder of Buddhist religion.	403 Start of "Warring States" period in China. 334–26 Alexander the Great conquers Asia Minor, Persia, and parts of India. 323 Death of Alexander the Great and division of his empire. 322 Chandragupta founds Mauryan Empire in India. **Alexander the Great** *The Macedonian warrior-king Alexander the Great built an empire that helped spread Greek culture over western Asia.*
EUROPE	510 Origins of Roman Republic. 505 Establishment of democracy in Athens. 500 Celtic people flourish in central Europe. 490 Greeks defeat Persians at Battle of Marathon.	**Buddhist stupa at Sanchi, India** *Mauryan emperor Asoka became a Buddhist and set up thousands of monuments (stupas) around the empire. Each is said to contain a part of the Buddha's body.*
AMERICAS		450 Iron Age culture firmly established in central and western Europe. 431–04 Sparta defeats Athens in Peloponnesian Wars. 338 Macedonians gain control of Greece at Battle of Chaeronea.
OCEANIA	500 Trading contacts established in South Pacific islands.	400 Decline of Olmec civilization.

Decorative Celtic horned helmet

300–151 B.C.	150–1 B.C.

300–151 B.C.

290 Foundation of library at Alexandria, Egypt.

262 Mauryan Emperor Asoka converts to Buddhism.
240 Beginning of Parthian dynasty in northern Persia.
221 Chinese unity brought about by the first emperor, Qin Shi Huangdi.
207 Disintegration of unity in China.
202 China reunited under Han dynasty.

290 Rome gains control of central Italy.
264–41 Rome victorious against Carthage in First Punic War and wins control of Sicily.
218–01 Carthaginians, led by Hannibal, defeated in Second Punic War by Roman general Scipio.

Roman sword

300 Mound-building cultures flourish in North America. Beginning of early Mayan civilization in Central America.
200 Rise of Nazca civilization in Peru, South America.

150–1 B.C.

149–6 Rome destroys Carthage in Third Punic War and founds province of Africa.
100 Camels introduced into Sahara region.
30 Egypt becomes Roman province on death of Mark Antony and Cleopatra.

112 Opening up of "Silk Road" trade route gives the West some access to China.
64 Roman general Pompey conquers Syria.
53 Parthia halts eastward expansion of Rome.

49 Rome under Julius Caesar invades Gaul.
45 Julius Caesar becomes sole ruler of Rome after civil war.
31 Battle of Actium gives Octavian power over Rome.
27 Roman Empire replaces Republic. Octavian becomes Augustus, the first emperor.

100 Emergence of Anasazi, Hohokam, and Mogollon peoples as they begin farming in southwestern North America. Okvik hunters settle in northern Alaska.

Nazca pottery
The Nazca produced decorative textiles, metalworks, and pottery.

	A.D. 1–149	A.D. 150–299
AFRICA	c. 17–24 Tacfarinas leads Numidian people in revolt against Roman government in northern Africa. 50 Kingdom of Axum begins to expand in Ethiopia. 61–63 Roman forces move into Sudan.	150 Berber and Mandingo barbarians start to dominate Sudan area. 250 Axum (Ethiopia) controls trade in Red Sea.
ASIA	9 Overthrow of Han dynasty in China. 25 Han dynasty restored. c. 33 Jesus Christ crucified in Jerusalem. 60 Beginning of Kushan Empire in India. 70 Romans seize control of Jerusalem in Israel and destroy Jewish temple. 105 Paper first used in China. 132 Jewish revolt against Roman rule.	**Circular Sassanian city at Firuzbad, Persia (Iraq)**
EUROPE	43 Romans invade Britain. 79 Mount Vesuvius erupts and destroys the town of Pompeii in southern Italy. 117 Height of Roman Empire.	200 Mishnah, the book of Jewish law, completed. Indian epics of Ramayana and Mahabharata composed. Creation of the Hindu scripture, Bhagavad Gita.
AMERICAS	1 Beginning of Moche civilization in northern Peru. 50 Nazca people create vast lines and patterns in the desert.	**The four tetrarchs** In A.D. 293, Emperor Diocletian divided the Roman Empire in two, appointing an emperor and deputy to rule each half. This sculpture represents the Empire's four leaders (tetrarchs).
OCEANIA	1–100 Hindu-Buddhists from Southeast Asia colonize Sumatra and Java in Indonesia.	**Bust of Augustus, the first Roman emperor**

A.D. 300–449

325 Axum destroys kingdom of Meroë.
400 Adoption of Christianity in Axum.
439 Vandals establish kingdom in northern Africa.

304 Invasion of Huns creates further division of China.
320 Chandragupta I founds Gupta Empire in northern India.

The symbol of Christianity
The teachings of the Jewish preacher Jesus Christ, who was crucified c. A.D. 33, spread around the world after his death. The faith gained widespread acceptance after the Roman emperor Constantine converted to Christianity in A.D. 313. Christ's death on the cross led to its use as a symbol of the faith.

313 Edict of Milan leads to toleration of Christianity throughout Roman Empire.
330 Emperor Constantine moves capital of Roman Empire to Constantinople, at site of present-day Istanbul, Turkey.
410 Invading Visigoths sack Rome.

300 Rise of great Monte Alban and Teotihuacán civilizations in Mexico.

300 Eastern Polynesia settled.

A.D. 450–599

533 Emperor Justinian wins back northern Africa for Rome.

480 End of Indian Gupta Empire.
520 Rise of mathematics in India with invention of decimal number system.
531 Height of Sassanian Empire in Persia.
550 Buddhism introduced into Japan.
589 Reunification of China under Sui dynasty.

Japanese carving of a sleeping Buddha

450 Angles, Jutes, and Saxons settle in Britain.
476 Overthrow of Romulus Augustulus, the last western Roman emperor.
486 Clovis people establish Frankish kingdom in present-day northern France, Belgium, and parts of western Germany.
493 Ostrogoths gain power in Italy.
552 Emperor Justinian restores Italy to Roman control.
568 Lombards take over northern Italy.

c. 450–600 Population of city of Tiahuanaco in Bolivia reaches 50,000.

	A.D. 600–724	A.D. 725–849
AFRICA	**c.700** Trans-Saharan trade brings prosperity to Kingdom of Ghana. Bantu Africans cross Limpopo River and take ironworking technology to the south.	**751** Muslims defeat Mongols at Samarkand in central Asia. **794** Kyoto, ancient capital of Japan, established. **802** Khmers found empire in Cambodia and Laos.
ASIA	**618** Reunification of China under T'ang dynasty. **622** Year One of the Islamic calendar. **637** Followers of Islam (Muslims) seize Jerusalem.	
EUROPE	**c. 675** Nomadic Bulgar people settle in lands south of the Danube. **711** Islamic Moors invade Spain.	**732** Defeat of Moors by Frankish leader Charles Martel halts advance of Muslims through Europe. **768** Charlemagne crowned King of the Franks. **844** Defeat of Picts unites Scotland.
AMERICAS	**600** Mayan civilization in Central America flourishes. Mayans build great pyramidal temples and develop writing and advanced mathematics.	
OCEANIA		

Muslim at prayer
The Arab merchant Muhammad founded the Islamic religion in A.D. 610. His teachings inspired the Arab peoples, and by A.D. 750 Muslims had gained control of land stretching from Spain to Afghanistan.

King Charlemagne
The Holy Roman Empire was founded by King Charlemagne of the Franks in A.D. 800 after he conquered most of the Christian lands of western Europe.

Temple at Palenque
This Mayan temple contained the funeral chamber of the lord Pacol, who died in A.D. 683 after ruling for 68 years.

A.D. 850–974	A.D. 975–1099

900 Hausa kingdom of Daura founded in northern Nigeria.
920 The Kingdom of Ghana in western Africa begins a prosperous golden age.

980 Arab traders settle on eastern coast of Africa.
1054 Ghana conquered by Muslim Almoravid dynasty.

888 Chola dynasty of Tamil kings replaces the Pallavas in southern India and Sri Lanka.
935–41 Civil war in Japan.
960 Sung dynasty begins rule in China.
1007 Japanese noblewoman Murasaki Shikubu writes the first novel.

Japanese literature
More than 600,000 words long, The Tale of Genji, *a prince in search of love and wisdom, was the first novel.*

1044 Gunpowder invented in China.

911 The Viking leader Rollo is granted land in Normandy by the King of France.
930 Córdoba becomes the seat of Arab learning in Spain.
966 Conversion of Poles to Christianity.

Viking longship
Late in the eighth century the Viking people of present-day Scandinavia went in search of treasure to plunder and new lands to settle. Their golden age of trade, exploration, and colonization lasted until A.D. 1100.

982 The Viking warrior Erik the Red settles in Greenland.
1000 Leif Eriksson, son of Erik the Red, sails down North American coast and names it "Vinland."
1066 William of Normandy defeats King Harold of England at Battle of Hastings.
1096 First Crusades begin.

980 Toltec people build their capital city at Tula in Mexico.
1000 Foundation of Chima civilization in Peru.

900 Beginnings of Mixtec civilization in Mexico.

950 Polynesian navigator Kupe discovers New Zealand, and Maori settlers arrive.

Maori hek tiki
This hek tiki, or neck pendant, was worn by the first Maori settlers to bring good luck or ward off evil spirits.

1100–1149	1150–1199

AFRICA

c. 1100 First Iron Age settlement in Zimbabwe, Southern Africa.

1169 Saladin, a Muslim warrior and commander in the Egyptian army, becomes ruler of Egypt.
1190 Lalibela rules as Emperor of Ethiopia.

ASIA

1104 Acre in Israel captured by Crusaders. Their name comes from the Latin *crux*, or cross, the symbol of Christ.

Knights of Christ
European Christians sent armed expeditions called Crusades to recapture the holy lands from Saracen Muslims.

1156 Civil war between rival clans in Japan leads to domination of the country by its Samurai warlords.
1187 Saladin captures Jerusalem from Crusaders.
1191 Zen Buddhism introduced to Japan.

EUROPE

1115 French philosopher Peter Abelard begins teaching in Paris, France. St. Bernard establishes important monastery at Clairvaux, France.
1119 Foundation of Bologna University in Italy.
1142 Alfonso Henriques becomes first King of Portugal.

Zen Buddhist monks in meditation
The practice of Zen Buddhism is unlike other faiths in its belief that the path to self-knowledge lies in personal instruction by a master rather than the study of scriptures.

AMERICAS

c. 1100 Chimu civilization flourishes in Peru on northwest coast.

1170 Murder of Thomas à Becket, Archbishop of Canterbury, England.
1174 Building of Old London Bridge in England and the "Leaning Tower" in Pisa, Italy.

"Leaning Tower" of Pisa

OCEANIA

1100s Giant statues built on Easter Island, South Pacific.

Chimu ear ornament

1170s Chichimec nomads overthrow Toltec capital city of Tula in Mexico, leading to fall of Toltec Empire.

1200–1249

1234 Sun Diata founds
the Mali Empire in
West Africa.

1206 Genghis Khan
establishes the
Mongol Empire.
The Islamic faith
takes root in new
Kingdom of Delhi,
India.
1229 Sixth
Crusaders
recapture Jerusalem.
1232 Explosive rockets used in war
between Chinese and Mongols.
1237 Mongol army begins
conquest of Russia.
1244 Egyptians retake Jerusalem.

Genghis Khan
*The Mongol chieftain
Temujin was proclaimed
Genghis Khan, or
"Universal Ruler."*

1250–1299

1250 Mamluk rebel slave-soldiers
become the rulers of Egypt.

1250 The Japanese monk Nicherin
proclaims *Lotus Sutra* the supreme
Buddhist scripture.
   1260 Mamluks halt Mongol advance
   at Battle of Ain Jalut in Palestine.
   1291 Saracens capture Acre,
ending the Crusades.
1281 Mongol invaders' fleet driven from
Japan by the Kamikaze, or "Divine Wind."
c.1294 Persians convert to Islam.

1204 Constantinople sacked and
looted by Fourth Crusaders.
1209 Franciscan order founded by
St. Francis of Assisi, Italy.
1215 St. Dominic establishes
Dominican Order in Spain. King John
of England grants political rights to
barons by signing the Magna Carta.
1240s Foundations laid in Germany for
commercial and defensive Hanseatic
League of northern European trade towns.

**Marco Polo and
fellow travelers in the Far East**

1271 Aged only !6, Marco Polo
begins his journeys around the
Far East, traveling from Venice,
Italy, to China.
1273 Rudolf Hapsburg becomes ruler
of Germany and founds the powerful
Hapsburg dynasty.

c.1200 Incas in Peru centered around
settlement at Cuzco. First corn farmers by
Mississippi River in North America.

1200 First settlers from Indonesia and
Philippines arrive in Fiji and spread
throughout Polynesia.

c. 1250 Restoration of Mayan Empire
and building of a new capital at Mayapan
in Mexico. Incas expand their capital
at Chan-chan in northern Peru.

c. 1250 Stone platforms later used to
erect religious statues built in Polynesia.

1300–1339

1340–1379

AFRICA

1300 Origins of Benin kingdom in Nigeria.
1324 Mansa Musa makes pilgrimage to Mecca.

1348 Population of Egypt devastated by the Black Death plague.
1352 Moroccan scholar Ibn Battuta makes his great journey across the Sahara to Mali.

Mansa Musa, Emperor of Mali
The West African Mali Empire under Mansa Musa was famed for its size and wealth.

ASIA

c. 1300 Osman I establishes Ottoman dynasty in Turkey.
1321 Tughluq dynasty founded in Delhi, India.

1340 Indian Hindu empire of Vijayanagar becomes center of resistance to Islam.
1350 Majapahit Empire founded in Java.
1368 Mongols driven from China by Tai Tsu, founder of the Ming dynasty.

1346 The 100 Years War between England and France begins with the Battle of Crécy.
1347 The Black Death reaches Europe.
1358 Peasant revolt near Paris, France.

EUROPE

1309 The Pope moves from Rome, Italy, to Avignon, France, creating a rift in the Western Church.

Plague carriers
Fleas on rats carried and transmitted the Black Death, a combination of bubonic and pneumonic plague, which killed a quarter of the European population.

AMERICAS

c.1300 Major expansion of Incas through Andes.
1325 Aztecs found capital at Tenochtitlán.

1350 Acamapitchli becomes Aztec ruler and begins expansion of the empire.

Human sacrifice
Aztec and Inca civilizations believed their angry gods could only be soothed by blood sacrifice.

OCEANIA

1350 Maoris create rock art in New Zealand.

1380–1419

c.1400 Kingdom of Zimbabwe thrives on gold trade.

1398 Mongol leader Tamerlane sacks Indian city of Delhi.
1404–33 Chinese navigator Chang Ho explores India and East Africa.
1405 Death of Tamerlane leads to fall of Mongol Empire.
1411 Ahmad Shah founds Ahmadabad, an important commercial city in India.

The murder of Wat Tyler
Peasant revolts in the years following the Plague were ruthlessly put down.

1381 Wat Tyler and John Ball lead Peasants' Revolt in England against high taxes and low pay. The uprising is crushed and the leaders killed.
1389 Ottoman Turks crush Christian Serbs at Kossovo, Serbia.
1415 French defeated by the English at the Battle of Agincourt in France.

c. 1400 Viracocha becomes first Inca empire builder, establishing permanent rule over conquered neighboring lands.

1420–1459

1432 Portuguese explorers reach the Azores Islands.

1448 Major reforms begin in Thailand under King Traillok.

Thai bronze Buddha
The dominant religion in 15th-century Thailand was Buddhism.

1429 Joan of Arc leads French forces and lifts the Siege of Orléans.
1450 Italian cities of Florence, Milan, and Naples form an alliance.
1450s German craftsman Johannes Gutenberg produces the first printed books in Europe.
1453 Constantinople falls to Ottoman sultan Muhammad II, ending the centuries-old Byzantine Empire.

Muhammad II
Ottoman leader Muhammad II dragged 70 ships overland to avoid a huge iron chain protecting the waterway into Byzantium when he invaded the city.

1438 Inca overlord Pachacuti greatly enlarges the Inca Empire.

	1460–1479	1480–1499
AFRICA	**1464** Sonni Ali becomes ruler of Songhai people in West Africa.	**1482** First Portuguese settlements established on Gold Coast of West Africa. **1488** Sea route from Europe to Asia opened by Portuguese navigator Bartolomeu Diaz, sailing around the Cape of Good Hope, South Africa.
ASIA	**1467** Beginning of the Onin War in Japan, which continues for more than 10 years. It leads to the end of the feudal system and the rise of large territories. **Battling warriors in the Onin civil war**	**1497–98** Portuguese explorer Vasco da Gama sails to India via Africa. **Portuguese caravel** *The caravel ships used by Portuguese explorers were longer, narrower, and easier to manuever than earlier craft.*
EUROPE	**1463–79** Ottoman Turks and Venetians from Italy fight for control of the Mediterranean. The Turks are the eventual victors. **1479** Kingdoms of Aragon and Castille in Spain united by the marriage of King Ferdinand and Queen Isabella.	**1492** Christian conquest of Granada ends Islamic regional control in Spain and results in expulsion of Jews. **1494** Treaty of Tordesillas leads Spain and Portugal to agree to divide the unexplored world between their two nations. **The Renaissance** *The rediscovery or "renaissance" of Greek and Roman ideas on art, literature, and science spreads through Europe from Italy during the 14-1500s.*
AMERICAS	**1470s** Collapse of Chimu culture in Northern Peru. **1473** Aztec capital Tenochtitlán absorbs neighboring city of Tlatelolco.	
OCEANIA	**1450–1500** Widespread cultivation of wet taro, a starchy root vegetable, in the Hawaiian islands.	**1492** Italian explorer Christopher Columbus reaches the Caribbean islands of the Americas. **1497** John Cabot of Italy discovers Newfoundland, present-day Canada.

1500–1519

1500s Southern African Bantus trade with Europeans. Hausa states develop in West Africa.
1517 Ottomans conquer Eygpt.

1502 Safavid dynasty begins in Persia.

c. 1503 Italian artist Leonardo da Vinci begins painting the Mona Lisa.
1512 Michelangelo paints ceiling of the Sistine Chapel, Italy.
1517 European Reformation begins.

The Reformation
Protestant (protesting) churches were formed after Martin Luther called for reform of the corrupt Catholic Church in a list he nailed to his church door in 1517.

1501–02 Amerigo Vespucci of Italy explores the coast of Brazil. First African slaves taken to the West Indies.
1519 Portuguese explorer Ferdinand Magellan sails across the Pacific Ocean.
1520 Spaniard Hernando Cortés brings down the Aztec Empire.

Moctezuma's headdress
This is a replica of a headdress said to have belonged to the last Aztec ruler Moctezuma, who was murdered by Cortés of Spain in 1520.

1520–1539

1520–21 Portuguese traders reach China.
1526 Babur I becomes first Moghul Emperor of India.

Babur I of India
A descendant of Genghis Khan, Babur I was a brilliant military leader who also took an interest in art and poetry.

1529 Ottoman Turks besiege Vienna.
1533 Ivan the Terrible comes to the throne in Russia.

1532 Francisco Pizarro of Spain overthrows Incas in South America by kidnapping and murdering their Emperor, Atahualpa. The leaderless Inca Empire then crumbles.
1534 French explorer Jacques Cartier sails along the St. Lawrence River in Canada.

Inca knife

1526 Portuguese begin landings in Polynesia.

	1540–1564	1565–1589
AFRICA	**c. 1540s** Portuguese begin organization of the transatlantic slave trade.	**1566** Sulayman I, ruler of the Ottoman Empire, dies as his empire reaches its peak. **1577** Akbar the Great completes unification of northern India, providing a structured system of government.
ASIA	**1542** Traders from Portugal reach Japan. **1546** King Tabinshweti unites Burma. **1556** Akbar the Great becomes Moghul emperor of India.	**Akbar the Great in religious discussion** *The Islamic Moghul emperor Akbar was renowned for his tolerance of other religions.*
EUROPE	**1541** French Protestant reformer John Calvin sets up Puritan state in Geneva, Switzerland. **1545** Meeting of Catholic leaders at Council of Trent in northern Italy begins Catholic Counter-Reformation. **1564** Birth of English playwright William Shakespeare.	**1571** European alliance defeats Ottoman Turkish fleet at Battle of Lepanto, Greece. **1572** St. Bartholomew's Day Massacre of Protestants (Huguenots) in France. **1588** English navy defeats the Armada, Spain's huge invasion fleet.
AMERICAS	**1540s** Spanish arrive in California on the west coast of North America.	**St. Bartholomew's Day Massacre** **1567** Portuguese establish Rio de Janeiro in Brazil. **1579** Francis Drake claims the west coast of North America for England.
OCEANIA	**1550** Maoris sail from North Island, New Zealand, to settle on South Island.	**1567** Spanish explorer Mendaña becomes first European to reach Solomon Islands.

Maori migration

1590–1614	1615–1639

1591 Moroccans and European mercenaries destroy Songhai Empire.
1600s Trading posts set up on African coast by all major European powers.

1620s Queen Nzinga of Ndongo defeats the Portuguese in Angola.

1590 Shah Abbas of Persia makes peace with Ottoman Turkey.
1592 Japan invades Korea under commander Hideyoshi.
1603 Ieyasu of Tokugawa clan becomes ruler of Japan. English East India Company established.
1602 Dutch East India Company founded.

Gatehouse of Edo Castle, Japan
The Tokugawa shogun (ruler) Ieyasu built a heavily fortified castle at the capital city of Edo, now modern Tokyo.

1620s Formation of Japanese national policy restricting contact with the outside world.

1598 Edict of Nantes ends civil war in France, giving Catholics and Huguenots equal rights.
1604 Russians settle in Siberia.
1605 Failure of Gunpowder Plot in London, England, and arrest of ringleader Guy Fawkes.
1610 French King Henry IV assassinated.
1613 Michael Romanov becomes first Russian Romanov Tsar (king).

1618 Beginning of Thirty Years' War in Europe between Catholic and Protestant powers.

1620 Mayflower pilgrims set sail from England for North America.
1625 French begin to settle West Indies.
1626 Dutch found New Amsterdam on site of present-day New York.
1630 Dutch East India Company seizes part of Brazil for its sugar and silver.

1607 John Smith establishes a colony in Virginia at Jamestown.
1608 Foundation of Quebec in Canada.
1609 Henry Hudson sails up the Hudson River on the east coast of North America.

1595 Mendaña lands on Marquesas Islands in the central South Pacific.
1606 Spanish explorer Luis Vaez de Torres sails between Australia and New Guinea. Portuguese arrive at Tahiti.

Building Manhattan
The first brick house on the site of present-day Manhattan, New York, was built on The Strand in New Amsterdam, now Whitehall Street.

1640–1669

1670–1699

AFRICA

1652 Dutch found colony at Cape Town in southern Africa.
1663 Death of Queen Nzinga of Ndongo in Angola.

Manchu lord with Chinese subjects, pigtailed to show inferiority

1670s French colonists settle in Senegal.
1690s Ashanti kingdom established on Gold Coast of West Africa.

ASIA

1644 Manchus invade China, replacing Ming dynasty.
1657 City of Edo on site of present-day Tokyo, Japan, is destroyed by fire.

1683 K'ang Hsi of China conquers Formosa, now modern Taiwan.
1690 Job Caharnock of the English East India Company founds city of Calcutta.

1672 Third Anglo-Dutch trade war begins.
1677 Ottoman Empire at war with Russia.
1682 Peter the Great of Russia starts reign.
1685 Louis XIV of France abolishes Edict of Nantes' protection of the rights of Huguenot protestants. Many flee to England as a result.

EUROPE

1642 Civil War in England.
1643 Louis XIV of France begins reign.
1648 End of the Thirty Years' War in Europe.
1649 Oliver Cromwell executes Charles I of England and sets up Commonwealth.

1688 Protestant William of Orange defeats Catholic James II at the Battle of the Boyne and becomes king of England.

Louis XIV of France in classical costume

AMERICAS

1642 French explorer De Maisonneuve founds Ville-Marie (Montreal) in Canada.
1664 English forces seize New Amsterdam from Dutch and rename it New York.

1670 Colony founded in South Carolina. English Hudson's Bay Company established.
1675 War between colonists and Native Americans devastates New England.
1680 French explorer Robert Cavalier de la Salle claims Mississippi valley for France.
1692 Salem witch trials begin in New England.

OCEANIA

1642 Dutch explorer Abel Tasman becomes first European to reach Van Dieman's Land, Tasmania.

1680 The dodo becomes extinct.

Dodo

1700–1729

1702 French win "Asiento," or monopoly on shipping of African slaves to Spanish colonies.
1712 Rise of Futa Jalon kingdom in West Africa.

1707 Death of Moghul leader Aurangzeb leads to breakup of the empire and new opportunities for European traders.
1727 Border fixed between China and Russia.

1700 Death of Charles II of Spain, leaving a French heir, leads to War of Spanish Succession.
1703 Russian Czar Peter the Great founds St. Petersburg.
1707 Act of Union joins England and Scotland.
1709 Abraham Darby's use of coke instead of charcoal to extract metal from iron ore (smelting) starts English Industrial Revolution.

Peter the Great forced nobles to shave

1709 Mass emigration of Germans to America begins.
1710 South Sea Company increases British trade with South America.
1720–22 Spanish occupation of Texas. Collapse of English South Sea and French Mississippi Companies.

1722 Dutch navigator Roggeveen reaches Samoa and Easter Island.

1730–1759

1739 Nadir Shah of Persia defeats the Moghuls and captures city of Delhi, India.
1740s Anglo/French rivalry in India.
1750 China conquers Tibet.
1757 Bengali army defeated by the British at the Battle of Plassey.

1746 Victory of English at Battle of Culloden, Scotland, ends Scottish revolt.
1748 Marie Theresa becomes Empress of Austria.
1755 Earthquake at Lisbon in Portugal.
1756–1763 Seven Years War between Britain and France.

Captured slaves assembled for sale
Slaves transported from Africa to the Americas were often worked to death on plantations owned by European settlers.

1733 England passes the Molasses Act, forbidding trade between American and West Indian colonies. Colony of Georgia founded.
1739 Slave uprising in South Carolina.
1759 English forces defeat French on Plains of Abraham in Quebec, Canada.

	1760–1779	1780–1799
AFRICA	**1764** Osei Kwadwo becomes Ashanti ruler in western Africa. **1768** Independent Eygpt under Ali Bey.	Ashanti gold weight **1794** Beginning of Qaja dynasty's rule in Persia.
ASIA	**1761** Marathas defeated by Afghans at Battle of Panipat. **1763** Treaty of Paris makes Britain dominant power in India.	**1789** French Revolution begins in Paris. **1795** Formation of France's Directoire government. **1796** Edward Jenner introduces smallpox vaccine in England. French general Napoleon Bonaparte begins Italian campaigns.
EUROPE	**1762** Catherine the Great begins reign over Russia. **1751–1786** Ideas of Enlightenment thinkers published in L'Encyclopedie.	

Inspirational reading
L'Encyclopedie expressed the ideals of justice, equality, and rational thought proposed by followers of the Enlightenment movement.

Storming the Bastille
The Bastille prison in Paris was a symbol of aristocratic tyranny. Its overthrow by the people in 1789 launched the French Revolution.

	1760–1779	1780–1799
AMERICAS	**1773** Rebel colonists throw English tea into the harbor at the Boston Tea Party. **1775–83** American colonists fight against British rule in Revolutionary War. **1776** Signing of US Declaration of Independence.	**1780** Tupac Amara leads Incas of Peru in revolt against Spain. **1787–9** US Constitution and Bill of Rights written and ratified. **1791** Revolution in Haiti led by former slave Toussaint L' Ouverture. **1793** City of York founded on site of present-day Toronto in Canada.
OCEANIA	**1770** Captain James Cook reaches Australia.	**Captain Cook trades with Islanders** *English navigator James Cook explored the South Pacific and was renowned for taking great care of his crews.* **1788** Foundation of British colony of New South Wales in Australia.

1800–1819

1804 British win control of Cape of Good Hope.
1816 Shaka becomes leader of the Zulu warriors.

1815 Java restored to Dutch by the British.
1819 Singapore founded by Stamford Raffles.

Zulu warrior

1805 English admiral Horatio Nelson dies victorious against the French at the Battle of Trafalgar.
1812 French rule under Emperor Napoleon Bonaparte in almost all of Europe.
1815 Napoleon finally defeated at Battle of Waterloo.

Napoleon Bonaparte

1811 Paraguay and Venezuela gain independence from Spain.
1812–1815 British Canada resists invasion from the US.

1806 First white women arrive in New Zealand.
1817 First European emigrants settle Australian grasslands.

1820–1839

1822 Liberian republic for freed slaves founded in west Africa.
1830 French invade Algeria. British and Dutch South Africans (Boers) clash in South Africa.
1836 Start of Great Trek of the Boer farmers to establish independent republics in Transvaal and the Orange Free State.

1824 Britain and Burma at war.
1839–42 China seizes opium imports from India, starting First Opium War.

1821–9 Greek War of Independence from Ottoman Turkey.
1825 First passenger railroad opens in England.
1830 French King Charles X overthrown in July Revolution.
1832 First Reform Act extends voting rights in Britain.
1837 Queen Victoria begins reign in England.

The Rocket
English engineer George Stephenson built this early steam-powered locomotive in 1829.

1821 Mexico wins independence from Spain. Mexicans rule Texas until 1836.
1822 Brazil gains independence from Portuguese.
1832 Samuel Morse invents electric telegraph in US.

•••••–––•••
S. O. S.

Morse code

1825 Charles Darwin begins a five-year voyage to the Pacific for scientific research.

	1840–1844	1845–1849
AFRICA	**1840** Iman Sayid Said, ruler of Oman, makes the island of Zanzibar off the east African coast his capital. **1843** British take over Boer colony in northeastern province of Natal.	**1847** Bantus defeated by British in southern Africa.
ASIA	**1842** Treaty of Nanking gives Hong Kong to Britain and opens trading links with China.	**1845–9** Anglo/Sikh war ends in defeat for Sikhs and the beginning of British rule over their homeland, the Punjab. **1848** Nasir ud-Din begins reign as Shah (ruler) of Persia.
EUROPE	**1840** The introduction of the Penny postage stamp leads to a low-cost, universally priced postal service.	**1845–46** Failure of potato crop in Ireland leads to severe famine. **1848** Year of Revolution in Europe. **1849** Collapse of revolutionary movements.
AMERICAS	**1840** First general anesthetic used in America by C.W. Long. Upper and Lower Canada form self-governing union.	**1845** Texas and Florida become US states. **1846** US and Mexico at war over Texas. **1848** California Gold Rush leads to rapid population growth in western United States. First US women's rights convention in New York State.
OCEANIA	**1840** Treaty of Waitangi signed in New Zealand. Last convict-settlers arrive in Australia.	

Penny Black stamp

Native Americans defend their land
Increased numbers of European settlers threatened Native American territories.

British and Maoris at Waitangi
The Treaty of Waitangi gave Britain possession of New Zealand in return for recognizing ancient Maori land rights.

1850–1854

1854 Independent Orange Free State set up in South Africa.

1850–64 Taiping revolt in China.
1852–53 Second war between England and Burma.
1853–54 US Navy forces Japan to open up to Western trade.

1851 Great Exhibition celebrating the industrial age held at the Crystal Palace in London.
1853–56 Crimean War between Russia, Britain, and France.

Crystal Palace

1850 California becomes a US state.
1851 First pedal-powered sewing machine made by I.S. Singer.
1853 Completion of railroad from New York to Chicago.

1850 Australian Colonies Act enables New South Wales, Tasmania, and South Australia to have virtual self-government.
1851 Australian Gold Rush begins.

Gold miners

1855–1859

1855 Discovery of Victoria Falls by English explorer Livingstone leads to European exploration of African interior.

1856–57 Persia's seizure of Herat, Afghanistan, leads to war with Britain.

Uprising in India
The refusal of Hindu and Muslim soldiers to comply with an order on religious grounds led to a major protest against British rule in 1857.

1857 Britain governs India directly after "Indian Mutiny."
1858 Treaty of Tientsin forces China to trade with the West.

1856 Henry Bessemer invents industrial steelmaking process in England.
1859–61 Giuseppe Garibaldi leads the "red shirts" in the War of Italian Unification, capturing Sicily and southern Italy to form a new Italian state.

Garibaldi

1858 Reformer Benito Juarez becomes president of Mexico.
1856 Formation of anti-slavery Republican party in US.

1856 Major Australian colonies achieve self-government.

1860–1869

1870–1879

AFRICA

1860s Britain, France, Belgium, Germany, and Portugal begin to explore and colonize inner Africa. **1869** Opening of the Suez Canal in Egypt links the Mediterranean Sea with the Indian Ocean.

1879 British defeat Zulu uprising led by King Cetshwayo at Ulundi, South Africa. **1881** Boers rebel against British rule in South Africa, leading to First Boer War.

Zulu shield
The South African Zulu people fought the British and Boer settlers to protect their land.

ASIA

1861 Empress Tze Hsi begins her 47-year rule of China. **1862** French occupation of Indo-China in Southeast Asia.

1870s Japan begins industrialization. **1872** Feudal control of Japan ends. Compulsory education is introduced.

EUROPE

1864–66 Prussian forces defeat Denmark and Austria. **1866** Swedish chemist Alfred Nobel invents dynamite.

Empire builder
Chief minister of the Prussian state in Germany, Otto von Bismarck united the country and founded the German Empire in 1871 with Prussian King William I as emperor.

1870s Most Western European countries start industrialization. **1871** Otto von Bismarck invades and defeats France. Britain legalizes trade unions. **1876** French build refrigerated cargo ships.

Key innovations
The late 19th century saw dramatic advances in technology with the development of new inventions like electric light and telephones.

AMERICAS

1861 US Civil War begins. **1865** Union victory in Civil War. President Abraham Lincoln assassinated. **1867** British North America Act creates Dominion of Canada.

North v. South
The split of 11 Southern states from the Union in 1861 led to civil war in the US.

1876 Sioux and Cheyenne tribes defeat Custer at the Battle of Little Bighorn. **1876–1911** Porfirio Diaz begins rule as President of Mexico. **1879–84** Chile defeats Peru and Bolivia in the War of the Pacific. **1883** Thomas Edison invents the lightbulb.

OCEANIA

1860–70 War between Maoris and white settlers in New Zealand.

1876 Tahiti becomes a French colony.

1880–1889

1882 British rule of Egypt begins.
1886 Gold discovered in South Africa.

1880s Britain and France move into Burma and Vietnam.
1885 Indian National Congress Party formed.

Chinese revolt against Western power

1884 Berlin Conference decides colonial divisions in Africa. First deep underground railroad built in London.
1885 Karl Benz builds first car driven by internal combustion engine in Germany.
1888 Scottish surgeon John Dunlop patents pneumatic (air-filled) tire.
Kaiser (Emperor) William II starts German reign.

Benz Motorwagen

1882 Thomas Edison designs the first hydroelectric power station.
1884 First skyscraper built in Chicago.
1889 King Pedro II deposed by army revolt and Brazil declared a republic.

1884 Volcano erupts on island of Krakatoa in Indonesia.
1885-86 Opening up of gold fields in New Guinea.

1890–1899

1896 Ethiopians defeat Italian army.
1899 Second Boer War begins in South Africa.

1899-1901 Chinese government supports peasant revolt by the Society of Harmonious Fists to rid China of all foreigners. This so-called "Boxer Rebellion" is crushed by Western forces.

1896 Modern Olympic Games introduced in Greece.
1897 Greece and Turkey at war.

1890 Last massacre of Native Americans in US at Battle of Wounded Knee in Dakota. First moving picture (film) shows appear in New York.
1895 Cuban revolt against Spanish rule.
1896 Gold struck in Klondike, Canada.
1898 US wins Spanish-American War and takes over the Philippines. Cuban independence from Spain.

Sioux warrior
About 300 members of the Sioux tribe were slaughtered at the Battle of Wounded Knee.

1893 New Zealand Prime Minister Richard Seddon introduces advanced social reforms, including granting women the vote.

	1900–1904	1905–1909
AFRICA	**1902** Ovimbundu people of Angola revolt against Portuguese rule. **1904** Federation of French West Africa created.	**1905** Independent Union of former Boer republics founded in South Africa.
ASIA	**1904-5** Russo-Japanese war in Manchuria, ending in defeat for Russia and the total destruction of its fleet. **Russians fight the Japanese at the Battle of Liaio-Yang**	**1907** Discovery of oil in Persia, now modern Iran. **1909** Conflict between China and Tibet.
EUROPE	**1900** Expansion of German navy begins arms race with Britain. **1903** Votes for Women Movement formed in Britain by suffragette Emmeline Pankhurst. First Tour de France bicycle race. **1904** French and British empires agree to Entente Cordiale (friendly understanding).	**1905** Czar of Russia forced to grant democratic rights in October Manifesto. Physicist Albert Einstein formulates his Special Theory of Relativity. **1908** The AEG turbine factory in Berlin, Germany is built. It is the world's first steel and glass building.
AMERICAS	**1900** Coca-Cola first produced in US. **1901** Theodore Roosevelt becomes youngest-ever US president after assassination of President McKinley. **1902** Plastic invented in US. **1903** Orville and Wilbur Wright build the first airplane and make a successful powered flight.	**1906** US forces occupy Cuba. Major earthquake damage in San Francisco. **1907** First comic strips appear in US. **1908** Henry Ford manufactures first Model T motor car.
OCEANIA	**1900** Australia becomes a Commonwealth. New Zealand takes over the Cook Islands. **Wright Flyer**	**1907** New Zealand becomes a dominion. Minimum basic wage law set in Australia.

1910–1914

1911 Lamogi people of Uganda rebel against British rule.
1912 African National Congress formed to fight for black people's rights.

1910 Japan takes over Korea.
1911 Chinese revolution overthrows Manchu dynasty.

The sinking of the _Titanic_

1910 Halley's Comet appears.
1911 Norwegian explorer Roald Amundsen reaches South Pole.
1912 The _Titanic_, the world's largest ocean liner, strikes an iceberg on her maiden voyage, sinking with the loss of 1,513 lives.
1912–13 Greece, Serbia, Bulgaria, and Montenegro unite to defeat Ottoman Turkey in the Balkan War.
1914 European alliances break down with the assassination of Archduke Ferdinand, heir to the Austro-Hungarian Empire. World War I begins.

German soldiers, World War I

1911 Mexican dictator Diaz overthrown in revolution.
1912–33 US troops occupy Nicaragua.
1914 Opening of Panama Canal.

1914 Australia and New Zealand join the Allies in World War I.

1915–1919

1917 Ras (Prince) Tafari takes power in Ethiopia.

1915 Mohandas Gandhi becomes leader of the Indian National Congress Party.
1919 British troops fire on peaceful Indian protest in Amritsar Massacre, killing 379 people.

1915 Bulgaria aligns with Central Powers (Germany, Austro-Hungary) and Italy joins Allies (Britain, France, Russia, Serbia) in World War I.
1916 Irish revolt against British rule in Easter Rising.
1917 Communists take over from Czar in Russian Revolution, leading to civil war. Greece joins the Allies.
1918 World War I ends with Allied victory.

Comrades in arms
Russian workers inspired by Vladimir Lenin of the Communist Bolshevik Party overthrew the tyrannical Czar Nicholas II in 1917.

1915–16 Unrest in Haiti and Dominican Republic put down by US troops.
1917 US enters World War I.

1919 Australia acquires former German colonies in the Pacific.

	1920–1924	1925–1929
AFRICA	**1922** Egypt under King Faud wins conditional independence from Britain. **1923** Ethiopia joins League of Nations.	**1926** End of Berber and Arab revolt against Europeans in North Africa. **1927** Communists, led by Mao Tse-tung, attempt to overthrow Chinese government. **1929** Arabs attack Jews in Jerusalem, Palestine in a conflict over the Wailing Wall.
ASIA	**1923** Major earthquake in Tokyo, Japan. End of Ottoman Empire as Mustafa Kemal becomes president of new Republic of Turkey.	**Dictator of Italy** *Fascist leader Benito Mussolini led Italy into World War II on Germany's side in 1940. He was captured and executed in 1945.* **1925** Mussolini, Fascist leader of Italy, rules the country as a dictator. **1926** Police and army defeat general strike in Britain.
EUROPE	**1920** Communist Red Army under Leon Trotsky wins Russian Civil War. **1922** Benito Mussolini becomes prime minister of Italian government. **1923** Partial Irish independence from Britain with creation of Irish Free State. **1924** Russian leader Vladimir Lenin dies and is succeeded by Josef Stalin.	**1927** *The Jazz Singer*, starring Al Jolson, is released in the US. It is the first "talkie," or film including a synchronized speech and music soundtrack. **1929** Prices of shares on American stock exchange fall rapidly in Wall Street Crash.
AMERICAS	**1920** Prohibition (banning) of the manufacture and sale of alcohol begins in USA. **1924** US military planes make first airborne trip around the world.	**The Great Depression** *In October 1929, panicking share dealers on Wall Street, sold 13 million shares in one day. This contributed to the worldwide economic crisis called the Great Depression, in which millions of people lost their jobs, businesses, savings, and homes.*
OCEANIA	**1923** Ross area of Antarctica becomes New Zealand dependency.	**1927** Canberra becomes capital of Australia.

1930–1934

1930 Ras Tafari crowned as Haile Selassie I in Ethiopia.
1934 Lagos Youth Movement formed, demanding self-government of Nigeria.

1930s Indian leader Gandhi leads nonviolent opposition to British rule in India.
1934–35 Long March of Communists across China to find sanctuary in the Shaanxi province. Troops supporting the Nationalist leader Chiang Kai-shek pursue them daily.

Chinese Communist troops on the Long March

1933 Adolf Hitler, Führer (leader) of the Nazi Party, becomes German Chancellor.

Führer of the Nazis
Hitler's dreams of German world domination contributed to the outbreak of World War II. The war resulted in the mass murder, or holocaust, of 6 million Jews in Nazi concentration camps.

1931 British Parliament grants Canada full independence.
1933 Franklin D. Roosevelt becomes US President, ending prohibition of alcohol.

1931 First solo trans-Tasmanian flight.
1934 Airmail service from Australia to Britain introduced.

1935–1939

1935 Italian forces invade Ethiopia.

1936 Signing of alliance between Japan and Germany.
1937 Japan occupies much of Chinese coast, leading to war between the nations.

The rise of Japan
Military rule of Japan in the late 1930s led to displays of the nation's strength in warfare and empire building.

1936 Olympic Games in Berlin, Germany.
1936–39 Spanish Civil War ends in victory for Fascists and defeat for Communists.
1937 Frank Whittle invents the jet engine in Britain.
1938 Czechoslovakia taken over by German forces.
1939 Britain and France declare war on Germany after Hitler invades Poland. Beginning of World War II.

1935 US National Labor Relations Act comes into force.

1937 Formation of Royal New Zealand Air Force.
1939 Australia and New Zealand join Allied forces against Germany.

	1940–1941	1942–1943
AFRICA	**1940** British Navy sinks French fleet at Oran to prevent its capture by Germany. **1941** Allied troops overrun Italy's African colonies. German forces led by Erwin Rommel arrive in Libya to help Italy.	**1942** Allied troops land in Morocco and force Rommel's troops to retreat from El Alamein.
ASIA	**1941** French colonies in Southeast Asia taken over by Japanese. **1941–42** Japan captures the Philippines, Malaya, Hong Kong, Singapore, Burma, and Indonesia.	**1942** US Navy defeats Japan in Coral Sea of New Guinea and at Midway Island. **1943–44** Series of victories by US in Pacific islands pushes back Japanese forces.\
\
Winston Churchill\
The many rousing speeches given on the radio by Britain's wartime leader Winston Churchill helped inspire the Allies to victory.
EUROPE	**1940** Germany occupies Denmark, Norway, France, Belgium, and the Netherlands. Winston Churchill becomes Prime Minister of Britain. British air force prevents German invasion in the Battle of Britain. **1941** Hungary, Bulgaria, Greece, and parts of Yugoslavia and Russia under Germans.	**1943** Allied troops take over Sicily, then invade Italian mainland. **1943** German forces driven out of Russia.
AMERICAS	**1940** Xerox photocopying machine invented. Development of penicillin and other early antibiotics. **1941** US joins Allies in World War II after Japanese attack on US Navy at Pearl Harbor in Hawaii.	**1942** Enrico Fermi builds first US nuclear reactor. Mexico and Brazil join Allies. Nylon used for hosiery and parachutes first produced in US. \
\
Nylon stockings\
\
Attack on Pearl Harbor\
The surprise assault by Japanese forces on the US Navy fleet at Pearl Harbor, Hawaii, in 1941 sank or damaged 18 ships and destroyed 200 aircraft.
OCEANIA	**1940s** Australia prepares for the eventuality of a Japanese invasion.	**1942** Japanese bomb Darwin, Australia, and invade New Guinea and part of Papua.

1944–1945

1944 Japan attacks India but is defeated at Kohima.
1945 US drops first atomic bombs on Japanese cities of Hiroshima and Nagasaki. Emperor Hirohito authorizes Japanese surrender.

Emperor Hirohito of Japan
Japanese pilots thought of Emperor Hirohito as a god and considered it an honor to die for him on "kamikaze" missions, which involved crash-diving explosive-packed planes into Allied ships.

1944 Allies invade France and drive back Germans.
1945 German forces surrender.

1945 US tests first atomic bomb in New Mexico.

Dawn of the Nuclear Age
The first atomic bomb was dropped on Hiroshima, Japan, in 1945, instantly killing about 80,000 people. A second bomb was dropped on the city of Nagasaki three days later, leading to the surrender of Japan and the end of World War II.

1944 Mass breakout of Japanese prisoners of war in Australia.
1945 Australia recovers New Guinea and Papua territory from Japan.

1946–1947

Gandhi and followers

1947 India gains independence from Great Britain amid riots that kill 500,000 people. Indian leader Gandhi begins a protest fast against the continuing violence.

1947 Marshall Plan offers US aid to help European countries rebuild their economies after World War II.

United Nations flag
The United Nations (UN) was established in 1945 to foster friendly relations between nations and to try to solve international disputes without war.

1947 US government promises to aid any country resisting communism.

1947 South Pacific Commission formed to discuss economic and health issues of South Pacific islands.

	1948–1950	1951–1953
AFRICA	**1950** Group Areas Act enforcing racial segregation (apartheid) passed in South Africa.	**1951** Libyan independence from Italy sanctioned by US. **1953** Military coup in Egypt ends anarchy and establishes a republic.
ASIA	**1948** Gandhi assassinated in India. State of Israel created in Palestine. **1949** Founding of Mao Tse-tung's new Communist Republic in China.	**1950-53** War between communist North Korea and US-occupied South Korea. **1953** Edmund Hillary and Sherpa Tenzing Norgay are first people to reach summit of Mount Everest.
EUROPE	**1948** Berlin Airlift of supplies defeats USSR's blockade of West Berlin. **1949** Germany divided in two, with US, France, and Britain running the West, and USSR controlling the East. Western Europe and US form defensive NATO alliance against attack by USSR.	**1952** Greece and Turkey join NATO. **1950s** Black Americans intensify their campaign for civil rights. **1953** Link between smoking and lung cancer first established in US.
AMERICAS	**1948** Harry Truman wins Presidential election in US. **1950** Senator Joseph McCarthy begins anti-communist "witch-hunts" in US.	
OCEANIA		**1951** Australia, New Zealand, and US sign ANZUS Pact defense alliance.

Jewish nation
In 1948, the United Nations established the state of Israel in the ancient Jewish homeland of Palestine. The resulting conflict over territory between Israelis and Arab Palestinians has continued ever since.

Hillary and Tensing

Post-war Europe
After World War II, Europe was divided into the USSR-controlled East and the US-backed West. The uneasy peace between each side, known as the Cold War, led to an arms race between the US and USSR in which both superpowers began to stockpile nuclear weapons.

1954–1956

1954 National Liberation Front formed in Algeria to fight French rule.
1955 African National Congress (ANC) pressure group in South Africa adopts antiracist Freedom Charter.
1956 Eygptian leader Nasser captures the Suez Canal.

1954 French defeated by communist forces at Dien Bien Phu, North Vietnam. Vietnam divided into communist North and US-backed South.
1956 Israel captures Sinai peninsula from Arab forces in eight days.

Symbol of Soviet Communism

1955 Warsaw Pact defense treaty signed by communist nations, allowing Soviet (USSR) troops to be stationed in any communist Eastern European country. West Germany joins NATO and East Germany becomes part of Warsaw Pact.
1957 USSR launches Sputnik I, the world's first artificial satellite.

1955 Military coup in Argentina overthrows President Juan Perón.

1957–1959

1957 Ghana becomes first country in sub-Saharan Africa to gain independence.

1958 King Faisal II of Iraq is removed by a military revolt and a new republic founded.
1959 Tibetan uprising against Chinese occupation crushed. The Dalai Lama, Tibet's spiritual leader, is forced to flee the country.

The Dalai Lama

1958 Charles de Gaulle begins strong presidential rule in France.

1958 US's first atomic-powered submarine, *USS Nautilus*, makes undersea crossing of North Pole.

Sputnik I satellite

1959 Revolution in Cuba brings communist Fidel Castro to power, strengthening Cuban ties with the Soviets.

1959 Olympics held in Melbourne, Australia. Antarctic Treaty preserves the area for research.

	1960–1963	1964–1967
AFRICA	**1960** Independence gained by 17 African colonies. A peaceful demonstration in Sharpeville against white rule in South Africa ends in the death of 69 protestors and banning of the ANC.	**1964** ANC leader Nelson Mandela jailed in South Africa. **1965** White-ruled Rhodesia declares independence from Britain. **1967** Dr. Christiaan Barnard completes first heart transplant in South Africa.
ASIA	**1963** Diem, leader of South Vietnam, is assassinated in a military coup.	**Cultural revolution in China** *Mao Tse-tung's "cultural revolution" brought Chinese industry and agriculture under state control and closed schools and colleges, forcing teachers and students to work on the land. Any opposition was brutally put down by the Red Guards, the Communist Party police.*
EUROPE	**1961** Berlin Wall built. Russian cosmonaut Yuri Gagarin is first man in space. **1962** British pop group The Beatles release *Love Me Do*, their first hit record.	**1965** US troops start arriving in South Vietnam to help in the fight against communist North Vietnam. **1966** Chinese Cultural Revolution begins. **1964** Fighting between Greeks and Turks in Cyprus. **1967** Military coup in Greece.
AMERICAS	**1960** Election of John F. Kennedy, the youngest US president. **1962** Cuban Missile Crisis. **1963** President Kennedy assassinated.	**Fidel Castro** *In 1962, Cuban dictator Fidel Castro allowed the USSR to build missile bases on Cuban soil. The US Navy blockaded Cuba and the Russians withdrew.* **1965** Malcolm X, campaigner for black civil rights, assassinated. Riots break out in Chicago and Los Angeles. **Martin Luther King Jr.** *During the 1960s, civil rights leaders such as Martin Luther King and Malcolm X campaigned for the rights of black Americans.*
OCEANIA	**1960** Aboriginals recognized as Australian citizens, gaining full voting rights two years later.	**1965** Ferdinand E. Marcos elected President of the Philippines.

1954–1956

1954 National Liberation Front formed in Algeria to fight French rule.
1955 African National Congress (ANC) pressure group in South Africa adopts antiracist Freedom Charter.
1956 Eygptian leader Nasser captures the Suez Canal.

1954 French defeated by communist forces at Dien Bien Phu, North Vietnam. Vietnam divided into communist North and US-backed South.
1956 Israel captures Sinai peninsula from Arab forces in eight days.

Symbol of Soviet Communism

1955 Warsaw Pact defense treaty signed by communist nations, allowing Soviet (USSR) troops to be stationed in any communist Eastern European country. West Germany joins NATO and East Germany becomes part of Warsaw Pact.
1957 USSR launches Sputnik I, the world's first artificial satellite.

1955 Military coup in Argentina overthrows President Juan Perón.

1957–1959

1957 Ghana becomes first country in sub-Saharan Africa to gain independence.

1958 King Faisal II of Iraq is removed by a military revolt and a new republic founded.
1959 Tibetan uprising against Chinese occupation crushed. The Dalai Lama, Tibet's spiritual leader, is forced to flee the country.

The Dalai Lama

1958 Charles de Gaulle begins strong presidential rule in France.

1958 US's first atomic-powered submarine, *USS Nautilus*, makes undersea crossing of North Pole.
1959 Revolution in Cuba brings communist Fidel Castro to power, strengthening Cuban ties with the Soviets.

Sputnik I satellite

1959 Olympics held in Melbourne, Australia. Antarctic Treaty preserves the area for research.

	1960–1963	**1964–1967**
AFRICA	**1960** Independence gained by 17 African colonies. A peaceful demonstration in Sharpeville against white rule in South Africa ends in the death of 69 protestors and banning of the ANC.	**1964** ANC leader Nelson Mandela jailed in South Africa. **1965** White-ruled Rhodesia declares independence from Britain. **1967** Dr. Christiaan Barnard completes first heart transplant in South Africa.
ASIA	**1963** Diem, leader of South Vietnam, is assassinated in a military coup.	**Cultural revolution in China** *Mao Tse-tung's "cultural revolution" brought Chinese industry and agriculture under state control and closed schools and colleges, forcing teachers and students to work on the land. Any opposition was brutally put down by the Red Guards, the Communist Party police.*
EUROPE	**1961** Berlin Wall built. Russian cosmonaut Yuri Gagarin is first man in space. **1962** British pop group The Beatles release *Love Me Do*, their first hit record.	**1965** US troops start arriving in South Vietnam to help in the fight against communist North Vietnam. **1966** Chinese Cultural Revolution begins. **1964** Fighting between Greeks and Turks in Cyprus. **1967** Military coup in Greece.
AMERICAS	**1960** Election of John F. Kennedy, the youngest US president. **1962** Cuban Missile Crisis. **1963** President Kennedy assassinated.	**1965** Malcolm X, campaigner for black civil rights, assassinated. Riots break out in Chicago and Los Angeles.
OCEANIA	**1960** Aboriginals recognized as Australian citizens, gaining full voting rights two years later.	**1965** Ferdinand E. Marcos elected President of the Philippines.

Fidel Castro
In 1962, Cuban dictator Fidel Castro allowed the USSR to build missile bases on Cuban soil. The US Navy blockaded Cuba and the Russians withdrew.

Martin Luther King Jr.
During the 1960s, civil rights leaders such as Martin Luther King and Malcolm X campaigned for the rights of black Americans.

1968–1971	1972–1975
1970 Biafra region defeated by Federal Nigerian government in civil war.	**1975** Portuguese colonies in Africa win independence.

1968 US soldiers kill hundreds of unarmed civilians in Vietnamese village of My Lai.
1971 East Pakistan gains independence from India, becoming Bangladesh.

Allied troops in Vietnam

1972 Ceylon becomes Republic of Sri Lanka.
1973 US, Australian, and New Zealand allied troops withdraw from Vietnam. Arab states attack Israel in October War and raise oil prices, leading to a world economic crisis.

Arabian oil
Many countries dependent on Arabian oil faced economic disaster when the Arab states raised their oil prices in 1973.

1968 Riots in Paris as students call for educational and social reform and workers demand a new minimum wage. Anti-communist uprising in Prague, former Czechoslavkia.
1969 Britain sends troops to Northern Ireland.

1972 "Bloody Sunday" in Londonderry, Northern Ireland, as British troops fire on civil rights marchers.

1968 Assassination of Martin Luther King in Memphis.
1969 US astronauts Neil Armstrong and Edwin "Buzz" Aldrin walk on the moon.

Men on the Moon
The live television broadcast of Neil Armstrong taking humankind's first steps on the lunar surface was seen by about 600 million people.

1973 Elected Chilean president Allende killed in military coup led by General Pinochet.
1974 US President Richard Nixon resigns in disgrace after Watergate scandal.

1973 Sydney Opera House opens in Australia.

1975 Australia grants Papua New Guinea independence.

	1976–1980	1981–1985
AFRICA	**1976** Riots in black townships across South Africa. **1979** Ugandan leader Idi Amin ousted by Tanzanian-backed rebels. **1980** Independent Zimbabwe formed under leadership of Robert Mugabe.	**1983** War and drought lead to famine in Ethiopia. **Ethiopian Famine**
ASIA	**1976** North and South Vietnam reunited as a communist country after 22 years of separation. **1979** Camp David peace treaty between Egypt and Israel. Islamic revolution in Iran.	**1982** Israeli troops invade southern Lebanon. Palestinians massacred in Beirut refugee camp. **1984** Siege at Amritsar, India, ends with Sikh extremists being forced out of Golden Temple. Indian Prime Minister Indira Gandhi assassinated by her Sikh bodyguards. **Iranian Revolution** *Ayatollah Khomeini, a fundamentalist (strict) Muslim hostile to the West, led the Islamic revolution that overthrew the Shah (King) of Iran in 1979. The exiled Shah's entry into the USA led to Iranian students taking 53 Americans hostage in the US embassy in Tehran.*
EUROPE	**1976** Adoption of Helsinki Convention on human rights. **1978** Margaret Thatcher becomes Britain's first woman Prime Minister. **1980** President Tito of Yugoslavia dies. Lech Walesa leads Solidarity trade union in Poland.	
AMERICAS	**1977** Jimmy Carter elected US President. **1979** Sandinista guerillas defeat government forces and take power in Nicaragua.	**1981** Death of 11 Irish republican prisoners on hunger 6strike. **1984** French and US scientists independently identify the AIDS virus. **1980s** First personal computers developed in US. **1980** Victory for Ronald Reagan in US Presidential elections. **1982** Britain defeats Argentine forces occupying British-held Falkland islands in Falklands War. Creation of Canadian constitution independent from UK.
OCEANIA	**1978** The Solomon islands of Tuvalu and Dominica become independent nations. **Personal computing** *The first personal desktop computer (PC) was developed by the American company IBM in 1981.*	**1984** New Zealand declares itself a nuclear-free zone.

1986–1990	1991–1997
1990 Dismantling of apartheid begins in South Africa as Nelson Mandela is freed after 27 years in prison. Namibia gains independence from South Africa. **1990** Civil war begins in Liberia.	**1991** Collapse of government rule in Somalia. **1992** US leads UN troops into Somalia. **1993** Eritrea gains independence from Ethiopia. **1994** ANC wins South Africa's first free elections. Civil war in Rwanda.
1988 Ceasefire in Iran-Iraq war ends eight years of conflict. **1989** Chinese security forces kill pro-democracy protestors in Beijing's Tiananmen Square. **1990** Iraq invades Kuwait. Protester at Tiananmen Square	**1994** Palestinian self-rule over the Gaza Strip under 1993 peace treaty between Israel and the Palestinian Liberation Organization (PLO). **Yasser Arafat, leader of the PLO** **1991** Gulf War ends with Iraq being driven from Kuwait by UN forces. **1995** Israeli Prime Minister, Yitzhak Rabin, is assassinated.
1986 New Soviet leader Mikhail Gorbachev introduces the policies of *glasnost* (openess) and *perestroika* (remodeling), eventually resulting in the breakup of the Soviet Union. **1989** Communist governments overthrown in Romania, Hungary, East Germany, and Czechoslovakia.	**1991** Dissolution of Soviet Union into Commonwealth of Independent States. **Fall of USSR** **1992–95** Civil war between countries in former Yugoslavia. **1997** Tony Blair becomes Britain's new Labour Prime Minister.
1986 "Irangate" revelations as US President Reagan questioned on secret arms deals with Iran. **1989** George Bush becomes US President.	**1993** Canada creates Nunavut, its largest Native territory at 850,000 sq miles (2.2 million sq km). Bill Clinton elected as US President.
1986 Treaty of Rarotonga sets up South Pacific Nuclear-Free Zone.	**1991** John Howard becomes Australian Prime Minister.

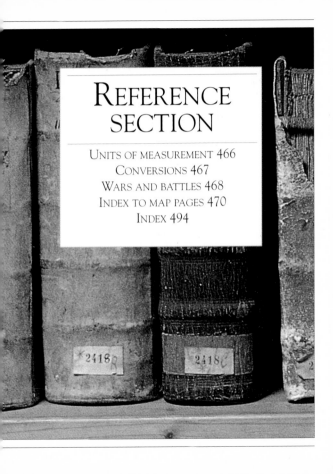

Major wars

3100 B.C. First recorded war. Pharaoh Narmer unites Upper and Lower Egypt.

c.1200 B.C. Trojan War War between Greeks and Trojans, as in Homer's *Iliad*.

264–146 B.C. Punic Wars Three wars between Rome and Hannibal's Carthage, which is destroyed.

c. A.D. 1096–1291 Crusades Series of religious wars in which European Christians try to recapture Holy Land from Muslims.

1337–1453 Hundred Years War English and French battle for control of France. The French win.

1455–1485 Wars of the Roses English war between Houses of York and Lancaster for control of English throne.

1618–1648 Thirty Years War Initially between German Catholics and Protestants but later involves all Europe.

1756–1763 Seven Years War Prussia and England fight against Austria and France for control of Germany.

1775–1783 American Revolution American colonists fight for independence from British rule. After they win, they form the USA.

1792–1815 Napoleonic Wars Fought between Napoleon's France and Austria, Britain, Russia, Prussia, and Sweden

1821–1829 Greek War of Independence Greeks fight Turkish rule.

1825–1830 Java War Revolt of Indonesians against Dutch.

1839–1842 Opium War Trade war between Britain and China.

1846–1848 Mexican-American War Mexico and USA battle over Texas.

1853–1856 Crimean War Turkey, allied with Britain, France, and Sardinia, fights Russia in the Black Sea.

1861–1865 American Civil War Civil war between Unionists of north and Confederates of south.

1870–1871 Franco-Prussian War Prussian war against France ends with establishment of German Empire.

1894–1895 Chinese-Japanese War Japanese defeat Chinese.

1899–1902 Boer War Britain and the Commonwealth fight Boers for control of South Africa.

1914–1918 World War I Britain, France, Russia, USA and others in global war against Germany, Austria-Hungary, and Turkey.

1939–1945 World War II Global war between Axis powers of Germany, Italy, and Japan and Allied powers of Britain, USA, and USSR.

1950–1953 Korean War Communist North Korea fights against South Korea and US allies.

1965–1975 Vietnam War Communist North Vietnam fights against South Vietnam and US allies.

1967 Six Day War Egypt against Israel.

1980–88 Iran-Iraq War

1991 Gulf War Saddam Hussein's Iraq defeated by United Nations forces.

1991–1996 Bosnian war Civil war in former Yugoslavia

Famous battles

490 B.C. Marathon (Greece) Athenians defeat Persians and save Greece.

331 B.C. Gaugamela (Persia) Alexander the Great's greatest victory, defeating the Persian King Darius II.

31 B.C. Actium (Greece) Octavian defeats Mark Antony and Cleopatra of Egypt and becomes Emperor Augustus, ending the Roman civil wars.

A.D. 378 Adrianople (Turkey) Goths (Germanic tribes) defeat Romans.

636 Yarmuk (Israel) Arabs under Khalid ibn–al Walid defeat Byzantines in desert sandstorm.

732 Tours (France) Charles Martel leads Franks to victory over Moors to halt their advance in Europe.

1066 Hastings (Britain) Normans under William the Conqueror invade England and beat the Saxons.

1429 Orléans (France) French heroine Joan of Arc lifts English siege of Orléans.

1453 Constantinople (Turkey) Turks besiege and capture Constintinople (Istanbul), ending Byzantine Empire.

1526 Panipat (India) Babur conquers Delhi and establishes Mughal empire

1571 Lepanto (Greece) End of Turkish seapower in the Mediterranean.

1588 Spanish Armada (Britain) English ships and storms defeat great Spanish invasion fleet of 130 ships.

1704 Blenheim (Germany) British-Austrian army led by Duke of Marlborough beats French, limiting French power in Europe.

1709 Poltava (Ukraine) Peter the Great of Russia defeats Swedes under Charles XII to control the Baltic Sea.

1759 Quebec (Canada) Britain gains control of Canada.

1777 Saratoga (USA) Decisive battle in American Revolution. British, led by Gen. Burgoyne, surrender to Americans.

1781 Yorktown (USA) George Washington leads Americans to final victory over British, ending American Revolution.

1805 Trafalgar (South of Spain) Nelson's British fleet destroys French and Spanish fleet.

1815 Waterloo End of Napoleonic wars. Allies under Wellington crush Napoleon.

1863 Gettysburg (USA) Decisive battle of American Civil War. Unionists defeat Confederates.

1914 Marne (France) Allies halt German advance on Paris.

1916 Somme (France) The deadliest battle of World War I. 1,265,000 men are killed in a few days.

1940 Battle of Britain Aircraft of British Royal Air Force (RAF) drive off German bombing raids.

1942 Midway (Pacific) Japanese aircraft fail to capture Midway Island from the USA.

1944 D–day (Normandy, France) Allies invade German-occupied France.

1991 Operation Desert Storm (Iraq) Airborne attack on Iraq by United Nations forces turns Gulf War.

Units of measurement

The metric system, based on the number ten, is the most common system of measurement and is used by scientists worldwide. Certain countries, such as the USA, use the older imperial system.

TEMPERATURE CONVERSIONS

To convert Fahrenheit (°F) into centigrade (°C), use the formula:
°C = (°F – 32) ÷ 1.8

To convert centigrade (°C) into Fahrenheit (°F), use the formula:
°F = (°C x 1.8) + 32

VOLUME

1 cubic in (in³)	
1 cubic ft (ft³)	144 in³
1 cubic yd (yd³)	9 ft³
1 fluid oz (fl oz)	4,840 yd³
1 pint (pt)	20 fl oz
1 gallon (gal)	
1 cubic mm (mm³)	
1 cubic cm (cm³)	100 mm³
1 cubic meter (m³)	1,000,000 cm³
1 liter (l)	1,000 cm³

LENGTH

1 inch (in)	
1 foot (ft)	12 in
1 yard (yd)	3 ft
1 mile	1,760 yd
1 millimeter (mm)	
1 centimeter (cm)	10 mm
1 meter (m)	100 cm
1 kilometer (km)	1,000 m

AREA

1 square inch (in²)	
1 sq foot (ft²)	144 in²
1 sq yard (yd²)	9 ft²
1 acre	4,840 yd²
1 sq mile	640 acres
1 sq millimeter (mm²)	
1 sq centimeter (cm²)	100 mm²
1 sq meter (m²)	10,000 cm²
1 hectare	10,000 m²
1 sq kilometer (km²)	1,000,000 m²

MASS AND WEIGHT

1 ounce (oz)	
1 pound (lb)	16 oz
1 stone	14 lb
1 hundredweight (cwt)	8 stones
1 ton	20 cwt
1 gram (g)	
1 kilogram (kg)	1,000 g
1 tonne (t)	1,000 kg

Conversions

You can convert between the metric and imperial systems of measurement by using the following conversion tables.

LENGTH

To convert	Into	X by
in	cm	2.54
ft	m	0.3048
yd	m	0.9144
miles	km	1.6093
cm	in	0.3937
m	f	3.2808
m	yd	1.0936
km	miles	0.6214

AREA

To convert	Into	X by
sq in	sq cm	6.4516
sq ft	sq m	0.0929
sq yd	sq m	0.8361
acres	hectares	0.4047
sq miles	sq km	2.59
sq cm	sq in	0.155
sq m	sq ft	10.7639
sq m	sq yd	1.1960
hectares	acres	2.4711
sq km	sq miles	0.3861

MASS AND WEIGHT

To convert	Into	X by
oz	g	28.3495
lb	kg	0.4536
stones	kg	6.3503
cwt	kg	50.802
tons	tonnes	1.0161
g	oz	0.0352
kg	lb	2.2046
kg	stones	0.1575
kg	cwt	0.0197
tonnes	tons	0.9842

VOLUME

To convert	Into	X by
in^3	cm^3 (milliliters)	16.3871
ft^3	liters	28.3169
yd^3	m^3	0.7646
fl oz	cm^3	28.4131
pints	liters	0.5683
gallons	liters	4.5461
cm^3	in^3	0.0610
cm^3	fl oz	0.0352
liters	ft^3	0.0353
m^3	yd^3	1.3080
litres	pints	1.7598
litres	gallons	0.2200

PREFIXES

kilo	=	1000	centi	=	$\frac{1}{100}$
hecto	=	100	milli	=	$\frac{1}{1,000}$
deci	=	$\frac{1}{2}$	micro	=	$\frac{1}{1,000,000}$

Index to map pages

Grid references in the Index help find features on the map. If you look up Nairobi in the Index, you will see 302 F4. The first number, 302, is the page number on which the map of Nairobi appears. Next, find the letters and numbers which border the page and trace a line across from the letter and down from the number. This will direct you to the exact grid square in which the city of Nairobi is located.

Amundsen Sea Antarctica 364 B6

Amur (R.) China/Rus. Fed. 327 G6/337 G1/338 G1

An Nāşīryah Iraq 321 F3

An-Najaf Iraq 321 E3

Anadyr' Rus. Fed. 327 H2

Anchorage Alaska USA 206 C5

Andalusia Spain 259 E7

Andaman Is. India 362 F4

Andaman Sea Indian Ocean 318 F4/345 C5

Andes (Mts.) 237–240/242–243

Andizhan Uzbekistan 325 F3

Andorra (Country) 261 E8

Andorra la Vella Andorra 261 E8

Andros (I.) Greece 279 F5

Angarsk Rus. Fed. 327 F6

Angeles Philippines 347 E2

Anglesey (I.) UK 253 E6

Angola (Country) 310

Angren Uzbekistan 325 F3

Anguilla UK 231 H5

Ankara Turkey 319 E4

Ann Arbor USA 215 G5

Annaba Algeria 295 F2

Annapolis USA 213 H2

Anshan China 338 G3

Antakya Turkey 318 D6/ 319 F6

Antananarivo Madagascar 363 C5

Antarctica (Continent) 364/353 F8

Antigua & Barbuda (Country) 231 H5

Antwerp Netherlands 255 D5

Apeldoorn Netherlands 254 F3

Apennines (Mts.) Italy 262 D4

Appalachian Mts. USA 210 D7/213 F3

Aqaba, Gulf of S.W. Asia 300 D3/317 C7/320 D3

Arabia (Country) 362 C4

Arabian Sea 362 D4/ 321 G8/352 C4

Arad Romania 276 C3

Arafura Sea Australia 347 G7/352 C5/355 E1

Araguaia (R.) Brazil 241 E5

Arāk Iran 321 F3

Aral Sea Kazakhstan/ Uzbekistan 324 D1/ 326 C6

Arctic Ocean 206 C3/365/ 248 F2/353 E1

Ardabil Iran 321 F1

Ardennes (Mts.) Belgium 255 E6

Arequipa Peru 237 C7

Argentina (Country) 242–243

Århus Denmark 249 B7

Arica Chile 242 A2

Arizona (State) USA 218 D4

Arkansas (State) USA 212 C3

Arkhangel'sk Rus. Fed. 284 D4/326 C3

Arlon Belgium 255 F7

Armenia (Country) 287

Arnhem Netherlands 254 F4

Arno (R.) Italy 262 C4

Aruba Netherlands 231 F7

As Sulaymānīyah Iraq 321 F2

Ascension I. UK 361 E6

Ashkhabad Turkmenistan 324 D4

Asmara Eritrea 301 E5

Assen Netherlands 254 F2

Astrakhan Rus. Fed. 285 C7/326 C6

Asunción Paraguay 242 E3

Aswân Egypt 300 D4

Asyût Egypt 300 C3

Atacama Desert Chile 242 B3

Athens Greece 279 E5

Atlanta USA 213 E4

Atlantic Ocean 240 F3/ 242–243/365 F8/ 360–361/260/294/ 296 C7/305 B6/310–311

Atlas Mts. Morocco 294 D3

Attawapiskat Canada 208 D4

Auckland NZ 356 F3

Augsburg Germany 269 F7

Augusta USA 211 G3

Austin USA 219 G6

Australia (Country) 354–355

Australian Capital Territory Australia 355 F6

Austria (Country) 271

Axel Heiberg I. Canada 207 F2/365 F5

Ayutthaya Thailand 345 D5

Az Zarqā Jordan 317 D5

Azerbaijan (Country) 287

Azores (Is.) Portugal 360 E4

Azov, Sea of Rus. Fed./ Ukraine 285 A6/287 E5

B

Babruysk Belarus 283 F6

Bacău Romania 276 F3

Bacolod Philippines 347 E3

Badlands USA 217 E2

Baffin Bay Canada/ Greenland 207 F3/ 365 F6/360 C3

Bafoussam Cameroon 305 C5
Baghdad Iraq 321 E3
Baguio Philippines 347 E2
Bahamas (Country) 231 E2
Bahrain (Country) 321 F5
Baia Mare Romania 276 D3
Baikal, Lake Rus. Fed. 327 F6
Baja California Mexico 222 C3
Baker City USA 220 D4
Bakhtarān Iran 321 F2
Baku Azerbaijan 287 H7
Balaton, Lake Hungary 275 E3
Balearic Is. Spain 259 H5
Bali (I.) Indonesia 346 D8
Balikesir Turkey 318 C4
Balikpapan Indonesia 346 D6
Balkan Mts. S.E. Europe 277 D5
Balkhash, Lake Kazakhstan 326 D7
Balsas (R.) Mexico 225 F6
Baltic Sea N. Europe 360 G3/249/266 D2/ 282 B4
Baltimore USA 213 H2
Bamako Mali 296 D5
Ban Me Thuot Vietnam 345 G6
Banda Sea Indonesia 347 F7
Bandar Seri Begawan Brunei 346 D5
Bandar-e Abbās Iran 321 G5
Bandundu Congo (Zaire) 305 D6
Bandung Indonesia 346 C8
Bangalore India 333 E7
Bangkok Thailand 345 D5

Bangladesh (Country) 333 G4
Bangui Central African Republic 305 E5
Banja Luka Bosnia & Herzegovina 275 E6
Banjarmasin Indonesia 346 D7
Banjul Gambia 296 B5
Banská Bystrica Slovakia 267 E6
Baotou China 337 F4
Baranavichy Belarus 283 D6
Barbados (Country) 231 H7
Barcelona Spain 259 G3
Bareilly India 325 F3
Barents Sea Arctic Ocean 365 H6/284 E3/ 326 D3
Bari Italy 263 G5
Barinas Venezuela 236 C3
Barnaul Rus. Fed. 327 E6
Barquisimeto Venezuela 236 D3
Barranquilla Colombia 236 B3
Barysaw Belarus 283 F6
Basle Switzerland 270 B4
Basque Provinces Spain 259 E2
Bassein Myanmar 345 B5
Bata Equatorial Guinea 305 B5
Batangas Philippines 347 E2
Bătdâmbâng Cambodia 345 E6
Baton Rouge USA 212 D5
Bavaria Germany 269 F6
Bavarian Alps (Mts.) Germany 269 F7
Bayan Har Mts. China 336 D6

Beaufort Sea 206 D3/ 365 F3
Beaumont USA 219 H6
Béchar Algeria 294 D3
Beersheba Israel 317 C6
Beira Mozambique 311 G5/363 B6
Beirut Lebanon 316 C4
Beja Portugal 258 C6
Belém Brazil 240 F4
Belfast Northern Ireland UK 253 D5
Belgium (Country) 255
Belgrade Yugoslavia 276 B4
Belize (Country) 230 B4
Bellevue USA 220 B3
Bellingshausen Sea Antarctica 364 B4
Belmopan Belize 230 B4
Belo Horizonte Brazil 241 F6
Belarus (Country) 283
Bengal, Bay of India/ South Asia 362 F4/ 333 G5/344 A4
Benghazi Libya 295 G3
Benin (Country) 297 F6
Berbera Somalia 301 G6
Berbérati Central African Republic 305 D5
Bergen Norway 360 F3/ 249 A5
Bergen op Zoom Netherlands 254 C4
Bering Sea Pacific Ocean 206 B4/327 H2/353 E2
Bering Strait Arctic Ocean/Pacific Ocean 206 B3/327 H1/353 E1
Berlin Germany 268 G4
Bermuda (I.) UK 360 C4
Bern Switzerland 270 B4
Bernese Alps (Mts.) Switzerland 270 B6

Beskid Mts. Poland 267 F5

Bhopal India 333 E4

Bhutan (Country) 333 G3

Bielefeld Germany 268 D4

Bien Hoa Vietnam 345 G6

Bila Tserkva Ukraine 286 D3

Birmingham UK 253 F6

Birmingham USA 213 E4

Biscay, Bay of Spain 259 E1

Bishkek Kyrgyzstan 325 G2

Bissau Guinea-Bissau 296 C4

Bitola Macedonia 277 C6

Biysk Rus. Fed. 327 E6

Black (R.) China/Vietnam 344 E4

Black Forest Germany 269 D6

Black Sea 277 H6/285 A7/ 287 G6/318– 319

Blagoveshchensk Rus. Fed. 327 G6

Blanco, Cape USA 220 A4

Blantyre Malawi 303 F7

Bob-Dioulasso Burkina Faso 297 E6

Bogor Indonesia 346 C7

Bogotà Colombia 236 B4

Bohemia Czech Republic 266 C6

Boise USA 216 C3

Bolivia (Country) 237 E7

Bologna Italy 262 D4

Bombay India 362 E4/ 333 E5

Bomu (R.) Central African Republic/Zaire 305 F5

Bonifacio, Strait of Sardinia 263 B5

Bonn Germany 269 C5

Borås Sweden 249 C7

Bordeaux France 260 D6

Borneo (I.) Indonesia 363 G5/346 D5

Bosnia & Herzegovina (Country) 274– 275

Bosporus Turkey 318 D3

Boston USA 211 G5

Bothnia, Gulf of Sweden/ Finland 249 E5

Botswana (Country) 311

Bouvet I. Norway 361 F7

Bradford UK 253 G5

Brahmaputra (var. Yarlung Zangbo) (R.) 333 H3/336 C7

Brăila Romania 276 G4

Brasília Brazil 241 F5

Braşov Romania 276 E4

Bratislava Slovakia 266 D7

Brazil (Country) 240– 241

Brazilian Highlands (Mts.) Brazil 241 G5

Brazzaville Congo 305 D6

Brecon Beacons (Mts.) UK 253 E7

Breda Netherlands 254 D4

Bregenz Austria 270 D4

Bremen Germany 268 D3

Brest Belarus 283 C7

Brest France 260 C3

Bridgeport USA 211 F6

Brisbane Australia 355 G4

Bristol UK 253 F7

Bristol Bay Alaska USA 206 B5

British Columbia (Province) Canada 206 D7

British Indian Ocean Territory UK 363 E5

British Virgin Is. UK 231 H5

Brittany France 260 C3

Brno Czech Republic 266 D6

Bruges Belgium 255 B5

Brunei (Country) 346 D4

Brunswick Germany 268 E4

Brussels Belgium 255 D5

Bucharest Romania 276 E4

Budapest Hungary 275 E2

Buenaventura Colombia 236 B4

Buenos Aires Argentina 243 E5/361 C6

Buenos Aires, Lake Argentina 243 C7

Buffalo USA 210 D4

Bug (R.) Poland/Ukraine 267 F3

Bujumbura Burundi 302 D4

Bukavu Congo(Zaire) 305 G6

Bukhara Uzbekistan 325 E4

Bulawayo Zimbabwe 311 E5

Bulgaria (Country) 277

Buraydah Saudi Arabia 321 E4

Burgas Bulgaria 277 F3

Burgundy France 261 F3

Burkina Faso (Country) 297 E5

Bursa Turkey 318 D4

Burundi (Country) 302 D4

Butuan Philippines 347 F3

Buzău Romania 276 F4

Bydgoszcz Poland 267 E3

C

Cabanatuan Philippines 347 E2

Cabinda Angola 310 A3

Cabora Bassa, Lake Mozambique 310 F4

Cadiz Philippines 347 E3

Caen France 260 D2

Caesarea Israel 317 C5

Churchill (R.) Canada 207 F7

Cincinnati USA 215 G7

Cirebon Indonesia 346 C8

Ciudad Bolívar Venezuela 236 E3

Ciudad del Este Argentina 242 F3

Ciudad Guayana Venezuela 236 E3

Ciudad Juárez Mexico 223 E2

Ciudad Madero Mexico 223 F5

Clermont-Ferrand France 261 E5

Cleveland USA 215 H5

Cluj-Napoca Romania 276 C3

Coatzacoalcos Mexico 223 G7

Cochabamba Bolivia 237 D7

Cochin India 362 E4/ 333 E7

Cod, Cape USA 211 G5

Coeur d'Alene USA 216 C2

Coihaique Chile 243 C7

Coimbatore India 333 E7

Coimbra Portugal 258 C4

Cologne Germany 269 C5

Colombia (Country) 236 C4

Colombo Sri Lanka 333 F8

Colorado (R.) USA 218 D4/ 353 G3

Colorado (State) USA 219 F3

Colorado Springs USA 219 F3

Columbia (R.) USA 220 C3

Columbia (South Carolina) USA 213 F4

Columbus (Georgia) USA 213 E4

Como, Lake Italy 262 C3

Comodoro Rivadavia Argentina 243 C7

Comoros (Country) 363 C5

Conakry Guinea 296 C6

Concepción Chile 243 B6

Concord USA 211 F4/ 221 B6

Congo (Country) 305 D6

Congo (R.) Zaire 305 E5

Connecticut (R.) USA 211 F4

Connecticut (State) USA 211 F5

Constance, Lake Switzerland 269 D7/ 270 C4

Constanţa Romania 276 G4

Constantine Algeria 295 F2

Cook Is. New Zealand 353 E5

Copenhagen Denmark 249 B7

Copiapó Chile 242 B4

Coquimbo Chile 242 B4

Coral Sea Pacific Ocean 352 D5/355 H2

Córdoba Argentina 242 C4

Corfu Greece 278 C3

Corinth, Gulf of Greece 279 E5

Cork Ireland 253 B6

Corpus Christi USA 219 G7

Corrientes Argentina 242 E4

Costa Rica (Country) 230 C7

Côte d'Azur France 261 G7

Côte d'Ivoire (Country) 296 D7

Craiova Romania 276 D4

Crete Greece 279 F8

Crete, Sea of Greece 279 F7

Crimea Rus. Fed./Ukraine 287 E5

Croatia (Country) 274

Cubango (R.) Southern Africa 310 B4

Culiacán Mexico 223 D4

Cumaná Venezuela 236 E3

Curitiba Brazil 241 E7

Cyclades (Is.) 279 F6

Cyprus (Country) 319

Czech Republic (Country) 266

D

Da Lat Vietnam 345 G6

Da Nang Vietnam 345 G5

Dacca Bangladesh 333 G4

Dagupan Philippines 347 E2

Dakar Senegal 296 B5

Dakhla Western Sahara 294 B5

Dalian China 338 F3

Dallas USA 219 G5

Damascus Syria 316 D4

Danube (R.) C. Europe 269 E7/271 G2/267 E8/ 274 E5/277 C5

Dar es Salaam Tanzania 303 G5/363 C5

Darling (R.) Australia 355 F5

Darwin Australia 354 D1

Datong China 338 E3

Daugavpils Latvia 283 E5

Davao Philippines 347 F4

Davis Sea Antarctica 364 D5

Davis Strait Greenland/ Canada 207 G3/ 365 E7

Dawson Canada 206 D5

Dayton USA 215 G7

Dead Sea Israel 317 C5

Death Valley USA 221 E7

Debrecen Hungary 275 G2

Hejaz Saudi Arabia 320 D4
Helena USA 216 D2
Helsinki Finland 249 F6
Helwân Egypt 300 C3
Henzada Myanmar 344 B4
Herāt Afghanistan 324 D6
Hermosillo Mexico 222 D2
Hidaka Mts. Japan 340 F2
Highlands (Mts.) UK
    252 E3
Himalayas (Mts.) S. Asia
    333 F2/336 C7
Ḥimş Syria 316 D4
Hindu Kush (Mts.)
    Afghanistan 325 F5
Hiroshima Japan 341 B5
Ho Chi Minh City Vietnam
    345 F6
Hobart Australia 355 F8
Hodeida Yemen 320 D8
Hohe Tauern (Mts.)
    Austria 271 F4
Hohhot China 337 F4
Hokkaidō (I.) Japan 340 F2
Hollywood (Florida) USA
    213 F8
Holon Israel 317 C5
Homyel' Belarus 283 G7
Honduras (Country) 230 B4
Hong Gai Vietnam 344 G4
Hong Kong 339 E6/ 352 C3
Hongshui He (R.) China
    359 C5
Honolulu USA 353 E3
Honshū (I.) Japan 340 E4
Horlivka Ukraine 287 F4
Hormuz, Strait of Iran/
    Oman 321 G3
Horn of Africa Somalia
    301 H6
Horn, Cape Chile 243 D8/
    361 C7/353 H7
Houston USA 219 H6
Hrodna Belarus 283 C6

Huainan China 338 E4
Huambo Angola 310 B4
Huancayo Peru 237 B6
Hudson Bay Canada
    208 D3/207 G5
Hudson Strait Canada
    207 G4/209 E1
Hue Vietnam 345 G5
Hulun Nur (Lake) China
    337 G2
Hungary (Country) 274–275
Huntsville USA 213 E3
Huron, Lake Canada/USA
    208 C7/215 G3
Hyderabad India 335 E6
Hyderabad Pakistan
    352 D3

I
Iaşi Romania 276 F3
Ibadan Nigeria 297 F7
Ibiza Balearic Is. Spain
    259 G5
Ica Peru 237 B7
Iceland (Country) 360 E3
Idaho (State) USA 216 C3
Ilām Iran 321 F3
Ilebo Zaire 305 E6
Iligan Philippines 347 F4
Illinois (R.) USA 215 E7
Illinois (State) USA 215 E6
Iloilo Philippines 347 E3
Ilorin Nigeria 297 F6
Imphal India 333 H4
Inch'ŏn South Korea 338 G3
India (Country) 332–333
Indian Ocean 301 H7/
    311–363/346 C8
Indiana (State) USA F6
Indianapolis USA 215 F7
Indigirka (R.) Rus. Fed.
    327 G3
Indonesia (Country)
    346–347

Indore India 333 E4
Indus (R.) Pakistan
    332 D3
Inn (R.) Austria 271 E4
Inner Mongolia China
    337 G3
Innsbruck Austria
    271 E5
Insein Burma 345 C5
Invercargill NZ 357 B8
Ionian Is. Greece 278 C4
Ionian Sea Greece 263 H7/
    278 C4
Iowa (State) USA 217 G4
Ipoh Malaysia 345 D8
Iquitos Peru 237 C5
Iraklion Greece 279 F8
Iran (Country) 321 G3
Iraq (Country) 321 E2
Irbid Jordan 317 D5
Irbil Iraq 321 F2
Ireland (Country)
    252–253
Irian Jaya Indonesia
    347 H6
Irish Sea 253
Irkutsk Rus. Fed. 327 F6
Irrawaddy (R.) Myanmar
    208 C3/362 F3
Ishikari Mts. Japan 340 F2
Islamabad Pakistan
    333 E1
Ismâ'iliya Egypt 300 D3
Isparta Turkey 318 D5
Israel (Country) 317
Istanbul Turkey 318 C4
Italy (Country) 262– 263
Izhevsk Rus. Fed. 285 E5/
    326 C3
Izmir Turkey 318 C5
Izmit Turkey 318 D3

J
Jabalpur India 333 F4

Jackson USA 212 D4
Jacksonville USA 213 F6
Jaffna Sri Lanka 333 F7
Jaipur India 333 E3
Jakarta Indonesia 346 C7
Jalandhar India 333 E2
Jamaica (Country) 231 E4
Jambi Indonesia 346 B6
James Bay Canada 208 D4
Jan Mayen I. Norway
    365 G8
Japan (Country) 340–341
Japan, Sea of E. Asia 327
    H6/340 D4/352 D2
Java (I.) Indonesia 363 G5/
    346 C8
Java Sea Indonesia 346 C7
Jayapura Indonesia 347 H6
Jedda Saudi Arabia 320 D5
Jefferson City USA 217 H5
Jember Indonesia 346 D8
Jersey (I.) UK 253 F8
Jerusalem Israel 317 C5
Jilin China 338 G2
Jinan China 338 E3
Jingdezhen China 338 F5
Jodhpur India 333 E3
Johannesburg South
    Africa 311 E6
Johor Baharu Malaysia
    345 E8
Jönköping Sweden 249 C7
Jordan (Country) 317
Juan de Fuca, Strait of
    USA/Canada 220 A2
Juneau Alaska 206 D6
Jutland Denmark 249 A7

K
Kabul Afghanistan 325 F6
Kabwe Kenya 305 D7
Kagoshima Japan 341 B6
Kahramanmaraş Turkey
    319 F5

Kalahari Desert Botswana
    311 D6
Kalemie Congo (Zaire)
    305 G7
Kaliningrad Rus. Fed.
    283 B5
Kamchatka Rus. Fed.
    327 H3
Kampala Uganda 302 E3
Kâmpóng Cham
    Cambodia 345 E6
Kano Nigeria 297 G5
Kanpur India 333 F3
Kansas (State) USA
    217 G5
Kansas City USA 217 G5
Kao-hsiung Taiwan 339 F5
Kara Sea Rus. Fed. 365 H5/
    284 G3/326 D3
Karachi Pakistan 362 E3/
    332 D3
Karaganda Kazakhstan
    326 D6
Karakorum Mts. China
    336 B5
Karakum Canal
    Turkmenistan 324 C4
Karbala Iraq 321 E3
Kariba, Lake Zambia/
    Congo (Zaire)
    305 C7/311 E5
Karlsruhe Germany 269 D6
Karpathos (I.) Greece
    279 G7
Karshi Uzbekistan 325 E4
Kasai (R.) Zaire 305 E6
Kathmandu Nepal 333 F3
Katowice Poland 267 E3
Kattegat Denmark 249 B7
Kaunas Lithuania 283 C5
Kawasaki Japan 341 F5
Kayseri Turkey 319 E5
Kazakhstan (Country) 326
Kazan' Rus. Fed. 285 D6/

326 C5
Kediri Indonesia 346 D8
Kelang Malaysia 345 D8
Kendari Indonesia 347 E6
Kentucky (State) USA
    213 E2
Kenya (Country) 302
Kermān Iran 321 G4
Khabarovsk Rus. Fed.
    327 H6
Khadzhent Tajikistan
    325 F3
Kharkiv Ukraine 287 E3
Khartoum Sudan 301 D5
Khasab Oman 321 G5
Kherson Ukraine 287 E4
Khmel'nyts'kyy Ukraine
    286 D3
Khon Kaen Thailand
    345 E5
Khulna Bangladesh 333 G4
Khyber Pass Afghanistan/
    Pakistan 325 F6
Kiel Germany 268 C2
Kiev Ukraine 286 D3
Kigali Rwanda 302 D4
Kimberley South Africa
    311 D7
King Leopold Range
    (Mts.) Australia 354 C3
Kingston Jamaica 231 E4
Kinshasa Congo (Zaire)
    305 D6
Kirghiz Range (Mts.)
    Kyrgyzstan 325 G2
Kiribati (Country) 353 E4
Kirkūk Iraq 321 F2
Kirov Rus. Fed. 326 C4
Kisangani Congo (Zaire)
    305 F6
Kismaayo Somalia 301 F8
Kitakyūshū Japan 341 B6
Kithira (I.) Greece 279 E7
Kitwe Zambia 305 C6

Kivu, Lake Congo
(Zaire)305 G6
Kizilirmak (R.) Turkey
319 E4
Kjølen (Mts.) Norway
248 D4
Klagenfurt Austria 271 G5
Klaipéda Lithuania 283 B5
Klamath Falls USA 221 C5
Klerksdorp South Africa
311 E6
Knud Rasmussen Land
Greenland 365 F6
Kōbe Japan 341 D5/
352 D3
Kokand Uzbekistan 325 F3
Kola Peninsula Rus. Fed.
284 D3
Kolyma (R.) Rus. Fed.
327 G3
Konya Turkey 319 E5
Korea Strait Korea/Japan
338 H3/341 A5
Kos (I.) Greece 279 G6
Košice Slovakia 267 F6
Kosovska Mitrovica
Yugoslavia 275 G5
Kota Baharu Malaysia
345 E7
Kota India 333 E3
Kota Kinabalu Malaysia
346 D4
Kowloon Hong Kong 339 E6
Kraków Poland 267 E5
Kraljevo Yugoslavia
276 B4
Kramators'k Ukraine
287 E4
Krasnodar Rus. Fed.
285 A7/326 B5
Krasnovodsk
Turkmenistan 324 B3
Krasnoyarsk Rus. Fed.
327 E6

Kruševac Yugoslavia 276 C4
Kryvyy Rih Ukraine 287 E4
Kuşadasi Turkey 318 C5
Kuala Lumpur Malaysia
345 E8
Kuantan Malaysia 345 E8
Kuching Malaysia 346 C5
Kumamoto Japan 341 B6
Kumanovo Macedonia
277 C5
Kumasi Ghana 297 E7
Kunlun Mts. China 336 C6
Kunming China 339 B5
Kupa (R.) Croatia 274 D5
Kupang Indonesia 347 F8
Kurile Is. E. Asia/Rus. Fed.
327 H5/340 G1/ 352 D2
Kustanai Kazakhstan
326 D6
Kütahya Turkey 318 D4
K'ut'aisi Georgia 287 G6
Kuujjuaq Canada 209 E2
Kuwait (Country) 321 F4
Kuwait City Kuwait 321 F4
Kwilu (R.) Angola/Congo
(Zaire) 305 E7
Kyaikkami Myanmar
345 C5
Kyōto Japan 341 D5
Kyrgyzstan (Country) 325
Kyūshū (I.) Japan 341 B6
Kyzyl Rus. Fed. 327 E6
Kzyl-Orda Kazakhstan
326 D7

L
La Guaira Venezuela
361 C5
La Paz Bolivia 237 D7
La Paz Mexico 222 D4
La Pérouse Strait Japan
340 E1
La Serena Chile 242 B4
Labrador (Province)

Canada 209 F4
Labrador Sea 209 F2/
360 C3
Ladoga, Lake Rus. Fed.
284 C4
Lagos Nigeria 360 F5/297 F7
Lagos Portugal 258 C7
Lahore Pakistan 333 E2
Lake District UK 253 F5
Lakshadweep Is. India
363 E4
Lansing USA 215 G5
Lanzhou China 338 C3
Laos (Country) 344–345
Laptev Sea Rus. Fed.
365 H4/327 F3
Laredo USA 219 G7
Larisa Greece 279 E3
Larnaca Cyprus 319 E7
Las Vegas USA 218 D3
Latvia (Country) 282 D4
Lausanne Switzerland
270 B6
Laval Canada 209 E7
Le Havre France 260 D2
Le Mans France 260 D3
Le Port Réunion 365 D6
Lebanon (Country) 316
Leeds UK 253 G5
Leeuwarden Netherlands
254 F2
Leeward Is. 231 H5
Leicester UK 253 G6
Leipzig Germany 269 G5
Lena (R.) Rus. Fed. 327 F4
León Mexico 223 G4
Leskovac Yugoslavia 277 C5
Lesotho (Country) 311 E7
Lesser Antilles (Is.) 231 G7
Lesser Sunda Is. Indonesia
347 E8
Lesvos (I.) Greece 279 G3
Lewis (I.) UK 252 D2
Lhasa China 336 D7

Liberia (Country) 296 D7
Libreville Gabon 305 B6
Libya (Country) 295
Libyan Desert Egypt 300 B4
Liechtenstein (Country) 270 D5
Liège Belgium 255 E6
Liepāja Latvia 282 B4
Ligurian Sea Italy 262 B4
Likasi Congo (Zaire) 305 G8
Lille France 261 E1
Lilongwe Malawi 305 E7
Lima Peru 237 B6
Limassol Cyprus 319 E7
Limnos (I.) Greece 279 F3
Limoges France 261 E5
Limpopo (R.) Mozambique/Southern Africa 311 E6/363 B6
Lincoln USA 217 G4
Linköping Sweden 249 D6
Linz Austria 271 F3
Lipari Is. Italy 263 F7
Lisbon Portugal 258 C5
Lithuania (Country) 283 C5
Little Rock USA 212 D3
Liverpool UK 253 F6
Ljubljana Slovenia 274 C4
Lobito Angola 310 A4
Loch Ness UK 252 E3
Łódź Poland 267 E4
Lofoten Vesterålen (Is.) Norway 248 D3
Logrono Spain 259 F2
Loire (R.) France 260 D4
Lombardy Italy 262 C3
Lombok (I.) Indonesia 346 D8
Lomé Togo 297 E7
London Canada 208 D8
London UK 253 G7
Londonderry Northern

Ireland UK 252 C4
Long Beach USA 221 D8/355 F3
Long I. USA 211 F6
Long Xuyen Vietnam 345 F6
Longyearbyen Svalbard Arctic Ocean 365 G7
Lopatka, Cape Rus. Fed. 327 H4
Los Àngeles Chile 245 B6
Los Angeles USA 221 D8
Louang Phrabang Laos 344 E4
Louisiana (State) USA 212 C5
Louisville USA 213 E2
Lower Tunguska Rus. Fed. 327 E5
Lualaba (R.) Congo (Zaire) 305 G6
Luanda Angola 310 A3
Luanshya Zambia 305 C6
Lubbock USA 219 F5
Lübeck Germany 268 E3
Lublin Poland 267 F4
Lubumbashi Congo (Zaire) 305 G8
Lucena Philippines 347 E2
Lucerne, Lake Switzerland 270 C5
Lucknow India 333 F3
Ludhiana India 333 E2
Luhans'k Ukraine 287 F4
Luoyang China 338 E4
Lusaka Zambia 303 C7
Luts'k Ukraine 286 C3
Luxembourg (Country) 255 F7
Luxor Egypt 300 D4
Luzon (I.) Philippines 347 E1
L'viv Ukraine 286 C3

Lyon France 261 F5

M

Maas (R.) W. Europe 254 F4
Maastricht Netherlands 255 E5
Macao Portugal 339 E6
Macdonnell Ranges (Mts.) Australia 354 D4
Macedonia (Country) 277
Maceió Brazil 241 H5
Mackenzie (R.) Canada 207 E5
Madagascar (Country) 363 C6
Madeira (Is.) Portugal 360 E4
Madeira (R.) Bolivia/ Brazil 240 C4
Madison USA 215 E5
Madras India 362 E4/ 333 E7
Madrid Spain 259 E4
Madurai India 333 E7
Magadan Rus. Fed. 327 H4
Magdalena (R.) Colombia 236 B3
Magdeburg Germany 268 F4
Magellan, Strait of Chile 243 D8
Maggiore, Lake Italy 270 C6/262 B3
Mahilyow Belarus 285 G6
Mai-Ndombe, Lake Zaire 305 E6
Maine (State) USA 211 G2
Mainz Germany 269 D5
Majorca Balearic Is. Spain 259 H5
Makassar Strait Indonesia 347 E6
Malabo Equatorial Guinea 305 B5

Málaga Spain 259 E7

Malang Indonesia 346 D8

Malatya Turkey 319 F5

Malawi (Country) 303

Malaysia (Country) 345

Malaysia (East) Borneo/
S.E. Asia 346 D5

Maldives (Country) 362 D4

Male Maldives 362 E4

Mali (Country) 297 E4

Malmo Sweden 249 C7

Malta (I.) 263 F8

Mamry, Lake Poland 267 F2

Man, Isle of UK 253 E5

Manado Indonesia 347 F5

Managua Nicaragua 230 B6

Manama Bahrain 321 F5

Manaus Brazil 240 D4

Manchester UK 253 F5

Manchuria China 338 G2

Mandalay Myanmar 344 C3

Mangalore India 333 E6

Manila Philippines 347 E2

Manisa Turkey 318 C5

Manitoba (Province)
Canada 207 F7

Mannheim Germany
269 D6

Maputo (Mozambique)
311 F6

Mar del Plata Argentina
243 E5

Maracaibo Venezuela
236 C3

Marañón (R.) Peru 237 B5

Maribor Slovenia 274 D4

Mariupol' Ukraine 287 E4

Marmara, Sea of Turkey
318 C3

Maroua Cameroon 304 D4

Marquesas Is. France
353 F5

Marquette USA 215 F3

Marrakesh Morocco 294 D3

Marseilles France 261 F7

Marshall Is. (Country)
352 D4

Martinique France 231 H7

Maryland (State) USA
213 H2

Masai Steppe Tanzania
302 F4

Maseru Lesotho 311 E7

Mashhad Iran 321 H3

Massachusetts (State) USA
211 F5

Massif Central (Mts.)
France 261 E6

Matadi Congo (Zaire)
305 D7

Maturín Venezuela 236 E3

Mauritania (Country)
296 C4

Mauritius (Country)
363 D6

Mayotte (I.) France 363 C5

Mazâr-e Sharîf Afghanistan
325 E3

Mazyr Belarus 285 F7

Mbabane Swaziland 311 F6

Mbandaka Zaire 305 E6

Mbeya Tanzania 305 E5

Mbuji-Mayi Congo (Zaire)
305 F7

Mead, Lake USA 218 D4

Mecca Saudi Arabia 320 D5

Medan Indonesia 346 A5

Medellín Colombia 236 B3

Mediterranean Sea 360 G4/
259 F7/261/263/294/300
C2/ 318 /316 C4

Meerut India 333 E3

Mekong (R.) Asia 362 G3/
337 E7/339 B5/344 D4/
345 F6

Melaka Malaysia 345 E8

Melbourne Australia
355 F7

Melville I. Canada 207 E3/
365 F4

Memphis USA 212 D3

Mendoza Argentina 243 B5

Mérida Mexico 223 H6

Mérida Venezuela 236 C3

Mersin Turkey 319 E6

Mesa USA 218 D5

Messina Sicily 263 F7

Messina, Strait of Italy
263 G7

Mestre Italy 262 D3

Meta (R.) Colombia/
Venezuela 236 C4

Meuse (R.) Western
Europe 255 D6

Mexicali Mexico 222 D1

Mexico (Country)
222–223

Mexico, Gulf of USA 213 E6

Mexico City Mexico 223 F6

Michigan (State) USA
215 F3

Michigan, Lake USA
215 F4

Micronesia, Federated
States of (Country)
352 D4

Middleburg Netherlands
254 C4

Midway Is. USA 353 E3

Milan Italy 262 C3

Milos (I.) Greece 279 F6

Milwaukee USA 215 F5

Minbu Myanmar 344 B4

Mindano (I.) Philippines
347 F4

Mindoro (I.) Philippines
347 E2

Minho (R.) Portugal 258 C2

Minneapolis USA 214 D4

Minnesota (State) USA
214 D2

Minorca Balearic Is. Spain
259 H4

Minsk Belarus 283 E6
Miskolc Hungary 275 F2
Mississippi (R.) USA
212 D3/214 D3
Mississippi (State) USA
212 D4
Missouri (R.) USA 217 E2
Missouri (State) USA 217 H5
Mitumba Mts. Congo
(Zaire) 305 G7
Mobile USA 212 D5
Mogadishu Somalia 301 G7
Mojave Desert USA 221 E7
Moldova (Country) 286
Molucca Sea Indonesia
347 F5
Moluccas (Is.) Indonesia
347 F6
Mombasa Kenya 302 G4/
363 C5
Monaco (Country) 261 G7
Mongolia (Country)
336–337
Monrovia Liberia 296 C7
Mons Belgium 255 C6
Montana (State) USA
216 D2
Monte Carlo Monaco
261 G7
Montenegro (Republic)
Yugoslavia 277
Monterrey Mexico 223 F4
Montevideo Uruguay
243 E5
Montgomery USA 213 E4
Montpelier USA 211 F4
Montpellier France
261 F7
Montréal Canada 209 E7
Montserrat UK 231 H6
Monywa Myanmar 344 B3
Morava (R.) Czech
Republic/Slovakia 266 D6
Moravia Czech Republic

267 D5
Morocco (Country) 294
Moroni Comoros 363 C5
Moscow Rus. Fed. 285 C5/
326 C4
Mosel (R.) Germany 269 C6
Moselle (R.) France 261 G3
Mostar Bosnia &
Herzegovina 275 E7
Mosul Iraq 321 E2
Moulmein Myanmar
345 C5
Moundou Chad 304 D4
Mozambique (Country)
310–311
Muang Phitsanulok
Thailand 345 D5
Mufulira Zambia 303 C6
Mull (I.) UK 252 D3
Multan Pakistan 333 E2
Munich Germany 269 F7
Münster Germany 268 C4
Murcia Spain 259 F6
Murmansk Rus. Fed.
360 G3/284 D3/326 D3
Murray (R.) Australia
355 E6
Murrumbidgee (R.)
Australia 355 F6
Muscat Oman 321 G6
Mwanza Tanzania 302 E4
Mweru, Lake Zambia/
Zaire 303 C5
Myanmar (Country)344
Mykolayiv Ukraine 286 D4

N
Naberezhnyye Chelny
Rus. Fed. 285 E6/326 C5
Nacala Mozambique 310 H4
Naga Philippines 347 E2
Nagoya Japan 341 D5
Nagpur India 333 E4
Nain Canada 209 F3

Nairobi Kenya 302 F4
Nakhodka Rus. Fed.
327 E4
Nakhon Ratchasima
Thailand 345 E5
Nakhon Sawan Thailand
345 E5
Nakhon Si Thammarat
Thailand 345 D7
Nam Dinh Vietnam 344 F4
Namangan Uzbekistan
325 F3
Namibe Angola 310 A4
Namibia (Country) 311
Namp'o North Korea
338 G3
Nampula Mozambique
310 H4
Namur Belgium 255 D6
Nanchang China 339 E5
Nancy France 261 F2
Nanjing China 338 F4
Nanning China 339 D6
Nantes France 260 D4
Napier NZ 356 G4
Naples Italy 263 F6
Narsarsuaq Greenland
365 E8
Nashville USA 213 E3
Nasik India 333 E5
Nassau Bahamas 231 E2
Natal Brazil 240 H4
Nauru (Country) 352 D4
Navarin, Cape Rus. Fed.
327 H2
Navoi Uzbekistan 325 E3
Naxos (I.) Greece 279 F6
N'djamena Chad 304 D4
Ndola Zambia 303 C6
Nebit Dag Turkmenistan
324 C3
Nebraska (State) USA
217 F4
Negro (R.) Brazil 240 C4

Ohio (R.) USA 215 G7
Ohio (State) USA 215 G6
Ohrid, Lake Albania/
  Macedonia 277 C7
Ohře (R.) Czech Republic/
  Germany 266 C5
Okayama Japan 341 C5
Okhotsk, Sea of Japan
  327 H4/340 F1/352 D2
Okinawa (I.) Japan 341 A8
Oklahoma (State) USA
  217 G7
Oklahoma City USA 217 G7
Oleněk Bay Rus. Fed.
  327 F3
Olympia USA 220 B3
Omaha USA 217 G4
Oman (Country) 321 G7
Oman, Gulf of 321 G6
Omdurman Sudan 301 D5
Omsk Rus. Fed. 326 D6
Onega (R.) Rus. Fed. 284 D4
Onega, Lake Rus. Fed.
  284 C4
Onitsha Nigeria 297 F7
Ontario (Province) Canada
  208 C5
Ontario, Lake Canada/
  USA 208 D8/ 211 E4
Oran Algeria 295 E2
Orange (R.) Southern
  Africa 311 C7
Ordos Desert China 337 F5
Örebro Sweden 249 D6
Oregon (State) USA
  220 C4
Orenburg Rus. Fed.
  285 E6/326 C5
Orinoco (R.) Venezuela
  236 E3
Orkney Is. UK 252 F2
Orlando USA 213 F6
Orléans France 261 E3
Orsha Belarus 283 G5

Oruro Bolivia 237 D7
Ōsaka Japan 341 D5
Osh Kyrgyzstan 325 G3
Oshogbo Nigeria 297 F7
Osijek Croatia 275 E3
Oslo Norway 249 D6
Osorno Chile 243 B6
Ostrava Czech Republic
  267 E6
Otranto, Strait of 275 E7
Ottawa Canada 209 E7
Ou Mts. Japan 340 F3
Ouagadougou Burkina
  Faso 297 E5
Ouargla Algeria 295 E3
Oujda Morocco 295 E2
Oulu Finland 248 F4
Outer Hebrides UK 252 D2
Oviedo Spain 258 D2
Oxnard USA 221 D8
Ozark Plateau USA 217 H6

P
Pacific Ocean 206/
  340-341/347/352-353
Padang Indonesia 346 B6
Padua Italy 262 D3
Painted Desert USA
  219 E4
Pakistan (Country)
  332-333
Pakokku Myanmar 344 B4
Pakxé Laos 345 F5
Palau (I.) USA 352 D4
Palawan (I.) Philippines
  347 E3
Palembang Indonesia
  346 B7
Palermo Sicily Italy 263 E7
Palma de Mallorca
  Majorca 259 H5
Palmer Land Antarctica
  364 B4
Palu Indonesia 347 E6

Pamirs (Mts.) Tajikistan
  325 G4
Pamplona Spain 259 F2
Pamukkale Turkey 318 D5
Pančevo Yugoslavia 276 C4
Panaji India 333 E6
Panama (Country) 230 D7
Panama Canal Panama
  230 D7
Panama City Panama
  230 D7/361 B5/353 H4
Panay (I.) Philippines
  347 E3
Panevėžys Lithuania
  283 D5
Papua New Guinea
  (Country) 355 G2
Paraguay (Country) 242 D3
Paraguay (R.) Paraguay
  242 E3
Paramaribo Surinam
  236 G4
Paraná (R.) S. America 241
  E6/243 D5
Paraná Argentina 242 D4
Paris France 261 E3
Paros (I.) Greece 279 F6
Pasadena USA 219 H6/
  221 D8
Patagonia Argentina
  243 C7
Paterson USA 211 F6
Patna India 333 F4
Patrai, Gulf of Greece
  278 D5
Peč Yugoslavia 277 B5
Pécs Hungary 275 E4
Pegu Myanmar 345 C5
Peipus, Lake Estonia
  282 E3
Peking China 338 E3
Pelagie Is. Italy 263 D8
Peloponne Greece 278 D5
Pennines UK 253 F5

Pennsylvania (State) USA
210 D6

Penza Rus. Fed. 285 C6/
326 C5

Peoria USA 215 E6

Perm' Rus. Fed. 285 E5/
326 D5

Persian Gulf 362 D5/
321 F4

Perth Australia 354 B6

Peru (Country) 237 B6

Peshawar Pakistan 333 E1

Petra Jordan 317 C6

Petropavlovsk-
Kamchatskiy Rus. Fed.
327 H4

Philadelphia USA 211 E7

Philae Egypt 300 D4

Philippines (Country) 347

Phnom Penh Cambodia
345 F6

Phoenix USA 218 D5

Phuket (I.) Thailand
345 C7

Piatra-Neamţ Romania
276 F3

Pierre USA 217 F3

Pietermaritzburg South
Africa 311 F7

Pilcomayo (R.) Bolivia/
Paraguay 242 D3

Pinang Malaysia 345 D7

Pindus Mts. Greece
278 D3

Pinsk Belarus 283 D7

Piraeus Greece 279 E5

Pitcairn Is. UK 353 F5

Piteşti Romania 276 E4

Pittsburgh USA 210 D6

Piura Peru 237 A5

Plate (R.) Argentina/
Uruguay 243 E5

Pleven Bulgaria 277 E5

Ploieşti Romania 276 F4

Plovdiv Bulgaria 277 E5

Plymouth UK 253 E7

Plzeň Czech Republic
267 B5

Po (R.) Italy 262 D3

Podgorica Yugoslavia
275 E6

Podlasie Poland 266 G3

Pointe-Noire Congo 305 C7

Poitiers France 260 D5

Poland (Country) 266– 267

Polynesia Pacific Ocean
353 F5

Pontianak Indonesia
346 C6

Port Elizabeth South
Africa 311 D7

Port Harcourt Nigeria
297 F7

Port Louis Mauritius
363 D6

Port Moresby Papua New
Guinea 355 G2

Port of Spain Trinidad
231 H8

Port Said Egypt 360 H4/
300 D5/362 B3

Port Sudan Sudan 301 E5

Port-au-Prince Haiti 231 F5

Port-Gentil Gabon
305 B6

Portland USA 220 B3

Pôrto Alegre Brazil 241 E7

Porto Portugal 258 C3

Porto-Novo Benin 297 F7

Portugal (Country) 258

Posadas Argentina 242 E4

Potsdam Germany
268 G4

Powell, Lake USA 219 E3

Poza Rica Mexico 225 F4

Poznań Poland 266 D4

Prague Czech Republic
267 B5

Prespa, Lake S.E. Europe
275 G7

Pretoria South Africa 311 E6

Priština Yugoslavia 277 B5

Prince Edward I.
(Province) Canada
209 F6

Prince of Wales I. Canada
207 F3

Prome Myanmar 344 B4

Provence France 261 G7

Providence USA 211 F5

Prudhoe Bay Alaska USA
206 D3

Pskov Rus. Fed. 326 C3

Puebla Mexico 225 F6

Puerto Montt Chile
243 B6

Puerto Rico USA
231 G5

Puerto Santa Cruz
Argentina 243 D8

Pune India 333 E5

Punta Arenas Chile
243 C8

Purus (R.) Brazil/Peru
240 C4

Pusan South Korea 338 H3

Putorana Mts. Rus. Fed.
327 E4

Pyinmana Myanmar
344 C4

Pyongyang North Korea
338 G3

Pyrénées (Mts.) S.W.
Europe 259 G2/260 D8

Q

Qandahār Afghanistan
325 E7

Qatar (Country) 321 F5

Qena Egypt 300 D4

Qinghai China 337 E6

Qiqihar China 338 F2

Qondūz (R.) Afghanistan 325 F5

Québec (Province) Canada 209 E5

Queensland (State) Australia 355 F4

Qui Nhon Vietnam 345 G5

Quito Ecuador 237 A5

R

Rabat Morocco 294 D2

Rach Gia Vietnam 345 F6

Rajkot India 332 D4

Rajshahi Bangladesh 333 G4

Raleigh USA 213 G3

Ranchi India 333 F4

Rangoon Myanmar 362 F4/345 C5

Rasht Iran 321 F2

Rat Buri Thailand 345 D5

Rawalpindi Pakistan 333 E1

Recife Brazil 241 H5

Red (R.) China/Vietnam 344 E3

Red Sea 300 E4/362 C3/ 320 D5

Redding USA 221 B5

Regina Canada 207 F8

Reno USA 218 C2

Resistencia Argentina 242 E4

Reşiţa Romania 276 B4

Reykavik Iceland 360 E3

Rheims France 261 F2

Rhine (R.) W. Europe 254 F4/268 C7/270 C4

Rhode I. (State) USA 211 G5

Rhodes (I.) Greece 279 H7

Rhône (R.) W. Europe

261 F6/270 B6

Richmond USA 213 G2

Riga Latvia 282 D4

Riga, Gulf of Estonia/ Latvia 282 D4

Rîmnicu Vîlcea Romania 276 D4

Río Cuarto Argentina 243 C5

Rio de Janeiro Brazil 241 G6/360 D5

Río Grande (R.) Mexico 223 F3

Rio Grande USA 219 F6

Riverside USA 221 D8

Rivne Ukraine 286 C3

Riyadh Saudi Arabia 321 E5

Roanoke USA 213 G2

Rochester USA 211 E4

Rockford USA 215 E5

Rocky Mts. N. America 206 D6/219 E4

Romania (Country) 276

Rome Italy 263 D5

Rosario Argentina 243 D5

Rostock (Germany) 268 F3

Rostov-na-Donu Rus. Fed. 285 B6/326 B5

Rotterdam Netherlands 360 F4/254 D4

Rouen France 261 E2

Rovuma (R.) C. Africa 310 H4

Rub' al Khali Saudi Arabia 321 E7

Ruse Bulgaria 277 E5

Russian Federation (Country) 283 B5/ 284– 285/ 326– 327

Rwanda (Country) 302 D4

Ryazan' Rus. Fed. 285 C5/ 326 C4

S

Saarbrücken Germany 269 C6

Sabah Malaysia 346 D5

Sabhā Libya 295 G4

Sacramento USA 221 B6

Sagaing Myanmar 344 C3

Sahara (Desert) N. Africa 294–295/296–297

Sahel West Africa 297 E5

Sakhalin (I.) Rus. Fed. 326 H5

Salem USA 220 B4

Salt Lake City USA 218 D2

Salta Paraguay 242 C3

Salton Sea USA 221 E8

Salvador Brazil 241 H5

Salween (R.) Myanmar/ China 337 E7/339 B5/ 344 C4

Salzburg Austria 271 F3

Samar (I.) Philippines 347 F3

Samara Rus. Fed. 285 D6/ 326 C5

Samarinda Indonesia 346 D6

Samarkand Uzbekistan 325 E4

Sambre (R.) Belgium/ France 255 D6

Samos (I.) Greece 279 G5

Samsun Turkey 319 F3

San'a Yemen 321 E8

San Antonio USA 219 G7

San Bernardo Chile 243 B5

San Diego USA 221 D8

San Francisco USA 221 B6

San José Costa Rica 230 C7

San Jose USA 221 B7

San Juan Puerto Rico 231 G5

San Luis Potosí Mexico 225 F5
San Marino (Country) 262 D4
San Miguel de Tucumán Argentina 242 C4
San Salvador El Salvador 230 B5
San Salvador de Jujuy Paraguay 242 C3
Sanandaj Iran 321 F2
Sandoway Myanmar 344 B4
Santa Ana USA 221 D8
Santa Barbara USA 221 C8
Santa Cruz Bolivia 237 E7
Santa Fe Argentina 242 D4
Santa Fe USA 219 F4
Santa Marta Colombia 236 B3
Santander Spain 259 E2
Santarém Brazil 240 E4
Santiago Chile 243 B5
Santiago de Compostela Spain 258 C2
Santo Domingo Dominican Rep. 231 F5
São Francisco (R.) Brazil 241 G5
São Luís Brazil 240 G4
São Paulo Brazil 241 F6
São Tomé & Prîncipe (Country) 361 G5/305 B6
Sapporo Japan 340 F2
Sarajevo Bosnia & Herzegovina 275 E7
Saratov Rus. Fed. 285 C6/326 C5
Sarawak Malaysia 346 D5
Sardinia (I.) Italy 263 B6
Sargasso Sea 360
Sarh Chad 304 E4
Sarī Iran 321 G2
Saskatchewan (Province) Canada 207 F7

Saskatoon Canada 207 F7
Satu Mare Romania 276 D2
Saudi Arabia (Country) 321 E6
Sault Ste Marie Canada 208 C6/215 G3
Savannah USA 213 F5
Savannakhét Laos 345 F5
Saxony Germany 268 E3
Schwerin Germany 268 F3
Scilly, Isles of UK 253 C8
Scoresbysund Greenland 365 F8
Scotia Sea 364 B3/361 D7
Scotland UK 252
Seattle USA 220 B3/353 F2
Seine (R.) France 261 E2
Semarang Indonesia 346 C8
Semipalatinsk Kazakhstan 327 E6
Semnān Iran 321 G2
Sendai Japan 340 F4
Senegal (Country) 296 C4
Seoul South Korea 338 G3
Seram (I.) Indonesia 347 F6
Serbia (Republic) 276 C4
Seremban Malaysia 345 E8
Sétif Algeria 295 E2
Setúbal Portugal 258 C6
Sevastopol' Ukraine 287 E5
Severn (R.) UK 253 F7
Severnaya Zemlya (Is.) Rus. Fed. 327 E2
Seville Spain 258 D7
Seychelles (Country) 365 D5
Sfax Tunisia 295 F3
Shanghai China 338 F4/352 C3
Shannon (R.) Ireland 253 B5
Shaoxing China 338 F4
Sheffield UK 253 G6
Shenyang China 338 G3

's-Hertogenbosch Netherlands 254 E4
Shetland Is. UK 252 G1
Shijiazhuang China 338 E3
Shikoku (I.) Japan 341 C6
Shîrâz Iran 321 F4
Sholapur India 333 E5
Shreveport USA 212 C4
Shumen Bulgaria 277 F5
Shymkent Kazakhstan 326 D7
Šiauliai Lithuania 283 C5
Siberia Rus. Fed. 327 E5
Sibiu Romania 276 D4
Sicily (I.) Italy 265 E7
Sidi Bel Abbès Algeria 295 E2
Sierra Leone (Country) 296 C6
Sierra Madre (Mts.) Mexico 222 D3/223
Sierra Nevada (Mts.) Spain 259 E7
Sierra Nevada USA 221 C6
Silesia Czech Republic/Poland 266 D3
Simbirsk Rus. Fed. 285 D6/326 C5
Simferopol' Ukraine 287 E5
Simpson Desert Australia 355 E4
Sinai (Peninsula) Egypt 300 D3
Singapore (Country) 345 E8
Sinŭiju North Korea 338 G3
Sirte, Gulf of Libya 295 G3
Sivas Turkey 319 F4
Skiros (I.) Greece 279 F4
Skopje Macedonia 277 C5
Skye (I.) UK 252 D3
Sliven Bulgaria 277 F5

Taipei Taiwan 339 G5
Taiping Malaysia 345 D8
Taiwan (Country) 339 G5
Taiwan Strait 339 F5
Taiyuan China 338 E3
Talcahuano Chile 243 B6
Tallahassee USA 213 E5
Tallinn Estonia 282 D3
Tamanrasset Algeria
    295 E6
Tampa USA 213 F7
Tampere Finland 249 F5
Tanganyika, Lake C.
    Africa 305 H7/305 D5
Tanggula Mts. China
    336 D6
Tangier Morocco 294 D2
Tangshan China 338 F3
Tanjungkarang Indonesia
    346 C7
Tanzania (Country)
    302– 303
Tapachula Mexico 225 G8
Tapajós (R.) Brazil 240 D4
Taranto Italy 263 G6
Tartu Estonia 282 E3
Tashauz Turkmenistan
    324 D3
Tashkent Uzbekistan
    325 F3
Tasman Sea 352 D6/
    355 F7/353 E4
Tasmania (State) Australia
    355 E7
Taunggyi Myanmar 344 C4
Taupo, Lake NZ 356 F4
Taurus Mts. Turkey 319 E6
Tavoy Myanmar 345 C5
Tbilisi Georgia 287 G7
Tegucigalpa Honduras
    230 B5
Tehran Iran 321 G2
Tel Aviv-Yafo Israel
    317 C5

Temuco Chile 243 B6
Tennessee (R.) USA 213 E2
Tennessee (State) USA
    213 E3
Teresina Brazil 240 G4
Ternopil' Ukraine 286 C3
Tetovo Macedonia 277 B5
Texas (State) USA 219 G6
Thai Nguyen Vietnam
    344 F4
Thailand (Country)
    344– 345
Thames (R.) UK 253 F7
Thane India 333 E4
Thanh Hoa Vietnam
    344 F4
Thaton Myanmar 345 C5
Thessaloniki Greece
    279 E2
Thimphu Bhutan 333 G3
Thule Greenland 365 F6
Thunder Bay Canada
    208 C6
Tibetan Autonomous
    Region China 336 C6
Tientsin China 338 E3
Tierra del Fuego (I.)
    Argentina/Chile 243 D8
Tigris (R.) S.W. Asia 319
    G5/316 H2/321 E2
Tijuana Mexico 222 C1
Timbuktu Mali 297 E4
Timmins Canada 208 D6
Timor (I.) Indonesia
    347 F8
Tirana Albania 275 F6
Tîrgoviște Romania
    276 E4
Tîrgu Mureș Romania 276 D3
Tobago (I.) 231 H8
Togo (Country) 297 F4
Tokelau (Is.) NZ 353 E5
Tokyo Japan 341 F5
Toledo Spain 259 E5

Toledo USA 215 G5
Tol'yatti Rus. Fed. 285 D6/
    326 C5
Tomsk Rus. Fed. 327 E6
Tonga (Country) 353 E5
Tongking, Gulf of China/
    Vietnam 339 D6/
    344 G4
Topeka USA 217 G5
Toronto Canada 208 D7
Toulouse France 261 E7
Trabzon Turkey 319 G3
Transantarctic Mts.
    Antarctica 364 C5
Trenton USA 211 E6
Trieste Italy 262 E3
Trinidad and Tobago
    (Country) 231 H8
Tripoli Lebanon 316 D4
Tripoli Libya 295 F3
Tristan da Cunha (I.) UK
    361 F7
Trondheim Norway 249 C5
Trujillo Peru 237 A6
Tselinograd Kazakhstan
    326 D6
Tuamotu Archipelago
    (Is.) France 353 F5
Tucson USA 218 D5
Tulsa USA 217 G6
Tunis Tunisia 295 F2
Tunisia (Country) 295 F3
Turin Italy 262 B3
Turk and Caicos Is. UK
    231 F4
Turkana, Lake Ethiopia/
    Kenya 301 E7/302 F3
Turkey (Country) 318–319
Turkmenistan (Country)
    324– 325
Turku Finland 249 F6
Tuvalu (Country) 353 E5
Tuzla Bosnia &
    Herzegovina 275 E6

Index

Acknowledgments

PAGEOne and Dorling Kindersley would like to thank:
Christiane Gunzi for editorial assistance; Sarah Watson for general assistance; Thomas Keenes for design assistance; Hilary Bird for the index; Gordon Models, Peter Griffiths, and John Holmes for model making; Ashmolean Museum; Beaulieu Motor Museum; The British Library; Capotine Museum; Ermine Street Guard Museum; Louisiana State Museum; Musée du Louvre; Museum of London; Museum of Mankind; Museum of the Moving Image; Museum of Natural History; National Railway Museum; Pitt Rivers Museum; Royal Academy of Arts; The Science Museum, London; Uffizi, Florence; University Museum of Archaeology and Anthropology, Cambridge.

Photographs by:
Geoff Brightling, Jane Burton, P. Chadwell, Peter Chadwick, Andy Crawford, Geoff Dann, Philip Dowell, Mike Dunning, Neil Fletcher, Philip Gatward, Steve Gorton, Frank Greenaway, Colin Keates, Gary Kevin, Dave King, Nick Nicholls, Andrew McRobb, Ray Moller, Stephen Oliver, Roger Phillips, Tim Ridley, Karl Shone, James Stevenson, Clive Streeter, Kim Taylor, Andreas Von Einsiedel, Matthew Ward, Jerry Young, Christian Zuber.

Illustrations by:
Evi Antoniou, Rick Blakely, Peter Bull, Mike Courtney, John Crawford Fraser, Bill Donohoe, Simone End, Eugene Fleury, Giuliano Fornari, Ann George-Marsh, Jeremy Gower, Elizabeth Gray, Andrew Green, Ray Grinaway, Nick Hewetson, Dave Hopkins, Aziz Khan, Jason Lewis, Stuart Mackay, Judith Maguire, Janos Marffy, Kevin Marks, Angus Mcbride, Sean Milne, Sergio, Colin Salmon, Michael Saunders, Rodney Shackell, Rob Shone, Clive Spong, Roger Stewart, John Temperton, Pete Visscher, Richard Ward, John Woodcock, Dan Wright.

Picture credits:
a = above, b = below, l = left, t = top
The publisher would like to thank the following for their kind permission to reproduce the photographs:

Aardman Animations 403bl; Action Plus/Glyn Kirk 412ac; AKG, London, 349acl; AKG, Berlin, 442bcr; Ancient Art and Architecture 437tc; Directed and produced by Animation City/A.C. Live 402cl; Audi 185br; Austin Brown and The Aviation Picture Library 197br; Biology Media 142cl; Bettmann Archive 443br; Bridgeman Art Library/Glraudon 389acl; Museum of Mankind 370bc; Museum of Natural History, London, 99br; The British Museum 371tr, 371ac, 376ar, 376bl, 376br, 377acl, 377acr,

377br, 378al, 378acl, 378br, 379ac, 427ar, 428br, 430tc, 439cl; Camera Press/Ian Stone 460ac; Carolco 1991, courtesy of Kobal collection 402tr; J. Allan Cash 430cr; Christie's Colour Library 313br; Bruce Coleman Ltd/Jeff Foott Productions 224cl; Christian Zuber 307tr; Colorsport © Duono; David Madlen 404bl; Comstock 432ar; James Davis 375bl; et archive 427acl, 434tr, 436al, 437cr, 439br, 452ac; Mary Evans Picture Library 69ac, 370tr, 375bc, 375br, 380tr, 397bcl; The British Library 372cl, 446acl, 446acr, 449br, 454bc; Exeter Maritime Museum 190acr, 190bcl; Fiat 185bcl, Gilbert and George, courtesy of Anthony d'Offay Gallery, London, 389br; Ronald Grant Archive 396bl, 403cr; Sonia Halliday 371br; Robert Harding Picture Library 181tr, 423bcl, 436bl, 439tr, 444bc; Michael Holford 377ar, 429acl, 432br, 434bc; Hulton-Getty Picture Collection 380cr; Robert Hunt Library 454acl; Hutchison Library, 373br, 374bl; J.G. Fuller 235bl; Image Bank/Kaz Mori 66-67; Image Select 395tcl, 399tcl, 444tcl; Ann Ronan 394cr; Simon James 377bl; David King 380cl; Kobal Collection 403bc; Magnum/ Cagnoni 460cl; Mander & Mitcheson 397cr; Museum of the Moving Image/ © Academy of Motion Picture Arts and Sciences R 3br, 403br; Nasa 5al, 32bcl, 32bcr, 36acr, 36br, 37cl, 37tcr, 37br, 461bc; National Maritime Museum, 190bcr, 190b, 193br, 440acr; Peter Newark Pictures 435c, 451cr; Oxford Scientific Films/Root; Okapia 111cl; Ann and Bury Peerless, 372bc, 374acr; Photostage/Donald Cooper 397br; Popperfoto 456ac, 457bc, 459acr; Press Association 380bcl; Redferns 395br;

Renault 185bl; Rex features 381tl; 461tc, 462ar; Cheryl Hatch, Sipa Press, 463acr; Coll. Privé, Sipa 457tl; Setbon, Sipa Press 462c; Royal Geographical Society/Paul Harris 288ac, jacket spine bcr; The Royal Ballet School 396bcl, 396acr; Scala 371bcl, 377tl; Biblioteca Nazionale Centrale, Florence 438bc; Science Photo Library/George Bernard 144-5; Biology Media 142cl; Chris Bjornberg 12-13; Jeremy Burgess 84tr; Cern 149tl; CNRI 79bcl; Tony Hallas 16tr; Adam Jones 38-39; James King-Holmes 171br; Thomas Ligon 198-99; Lawrence Migdale 171cr; Prof. P. Motta, Dept. of Anatomy, University Lasapienza, Rome 114-115; Professors P.M. Motta, K.R Porter & P.M Andrews 123tr; NOAO 32bc; Novostl 36cl, 329bl; Omikron 128tr; David Parker 171tr; John Sanford 32ar; David Sharfe 133cr; Simon Terrey 146tr; Sporting Pictures (UK) Ltd 156tr, 187tc, 189tc, 404bcr, 413tl, 413tr; Tony Stone Images/Tony Craddock 257tr; Sepp Dietrich 273br, Ian Murphy 396br; Hugh Sitton 306cl; Suzuki/Farquhar PR 185bcr; Warner Brothers/courtesy Kobal Collection 403cl; Werner Forman Archives 370acl, 396tl, 420-421, 428cl; Jerry Young 103br, Michael Zabé 441bc; Zefa Pictures 379bl, 464-465; Ian Bradshaw 368-369; Stockmarket 322c; Krebs 176-177; Joe Cornish 281.

Every effort has been made to trace the copyright holders and we apologise in advance for any unintentional omissions. We would be pleased to insert the appropriate acknowledgment in any subsequent edition of this publication.